Out Of Our League

Published by:

The Junior League of Greensboro, Inc.
Greensboro, North Carolina

First Printing, October 1978   7,000 Copies
Second Printing, January 1979 10,000 Copies
Third Printing, February 1980 20,000 Copies
Fourth Printing, May 1981   30,000 Copies

ISBN 09605788-0-3

Kingsport Press, Inc.
Kingsport, Tn.

FOREWORD

In attempting to establish a long-term fund raiser for our community projects, The Junior League of Greensboro has developed a truly unique cookbook.

From *Out Of Our League* we present to you a collection of both traditional and innovative recipes, developed and perfected by our leading Carolina hostesses.

Each selection has been tested and carefully edited in an effort to clarify both instructions and ingredients. We share them with you, knowing some will become your new favorites, as they have ours. This book includes more than just outstanding recipes — its style and content are a new, fresh approach which will be entertaining as well as useful. It can serve as the basic cookbook for the new bride, as well as an interesting guide of festive menus for the most sophisticated gourmet.

Out Of Our League is published by The Junior League of Greensboro and proceeds from its sale will go to support the many worthwhile projects sponsored by The Junior League. From *Out Of Our League* to you, your family and guests, our sincere thanks for your support.

For additional copies, use the order blanks in the back of the book or write directly to:

OUT OF OUR LEAGUE
The Junior League of Greensboro, Inc.
113 South Elm Street
Greensboro, North Carolina 27401

Checks should be made payable to Out Of Our League for the amount of $7.95 plus $1.50 postage and handling. North Carolina residents please add 32¢ sales tax per book.

OUT OF OUR LEAGUE

CHAIRMEN
Marilyn Burris   Dale Caldwell

COVER DESIGN AND ART
Carol Long

COMMITTEE MEMBERS
Mary James Lawrence   Peggy Brame
Margie P. Allen   Judy Bell
Mary Skewes Fisher   Pam Hitchcock
Ruth Stickley   Ann Dixon

A Note From the Cookbook Committee —

We wish to express our warmest thanks to those of you who shared your ideas and "all-time favorites" for *Out Of Our League*. Due to similarities and lack of space, all could not be included in this book. After three years of collecting and testing recipes, we have attempted to present the best, and yet be diversified enough to make every cook happy.

We are especially grateful to Ralph Porter and Greensboro Printing Company for being patient and generous with their professional advice, and to all of the testers and typists who helped organize the material for publication. A special thanks to our families who have been so patient and supportive during the past three years.

RECIPE AND IDEA CONTRIBUTORS

Abel, Clare
Abernathy, Mrs. James K.
Adams, Mrs. James B.
Aderhold, Mrs. H. H.
Alexander, Mrs. J. Cantey, Jr.
Allen, Mrs. William R. III
Andresen, Mrs. Fred H.
Anthony, Mrs. James B.
Aplington, Mrs. James P.
Aycock, Mrs. William P. II
Banner, Mrs. Charles W. Jr.
Banner, Mrs. Jack L. Jr.
Barber, Mrs. James B.
Barney, Mrs. John E.
Baynes, Emma Garvin
Beard, Mrs. Thomas R.
Beaver, Mrs. David
Bell, Mrs. Homer C. III
Bell, Mrs. Steven D.
Betts, Mrs. John M. Jr.
Black, Mrs. John W.
Bledsoe, Miss Jeanette B.
Boone, Mrs. Frances Taylor
Borden, Mrs. Robert H.
Brabham, Mrs. Vance W. III
Brame, Mrs. Margaret Weant
Brown, Mrs. Jack H.
Brown, Mrs. P. David
Bryan, Mrs. A. Clayton, Jr.
Burke, Ann
Burnett, Mrs. Timothy B.
Burris, Mrs. Marilyn Stadler
Burwell, Mrs. Robert P.
Butler, Mrs. Ronald M.
Bullock, Mrs. Frank W. Jr.
Bynum, Mrs. Mary Jane Crowell
Caldwell, Miss Margaret
Caldwell, Mrs. Robert H.
Carter, Mrs. Wilbert J.
Causey, Mrs. Charles W. Jr.
Chamblee, Mrs. H. Milton III
Cloninger, Mrs. C. William, Jr.
Cloninger, Mrs. Kenneth L. Jr.
Clifford, Mrs. Locke T.
Coltrane, Mrs. Patti J.
Cooper, Mrs. N. Carter
Covington, Mrs. J. Phillip
Crawford, Mrs. Branch M.
Cunningham, Mrs. Decatur
Denby, Mrs. Warren W.
Detgen, Mrs. John R.
Dillard, Mrs. Stark S.
Dingeldein, Mrs. George P.
Dixon, Mrs. Anna Wolff
Dixon, Mrs. Sewell H. Jr.

Doolan, Mrs. Edward E.
Dowtin, Mrs. James M. Jr.
Doyle, Mrs. Owen
Dusenbury, Mrs. A. Blair
Edwards, Mrs. Kay Bryan
Elrod, Mrs. T. Clyde
English, Mrs. Edward R.
Eskridge, Mrs. James L. Jr.
Evans, Mrs. David
Faison, Mrs. Walter C.
Fisher, Mrs. Edgar B. Jr.
Fisher, Mrs. Otis N., Jr.
Flebotte, Mrs. Paul R.
Foster, Mrs. C. Allen
Foxworth, Mrs. Robert P.
Frazier, Mrs. Herbert
Frazier, Mrs. Robert H.
Friday, Mrs. Julian B.
Fuller, Mrs. W. Erwin, Jr.
Gallagher, Mrs. Avis
Gavin, Mrs. C. Edward, Jr.
Gee, Mrs. Ellen Finley
Gilliam, Elizabeth V.
Glenn, Mrs. Robert W.
Golden, Mrs. Ralph J.
Goodson, Mrs. William A.
Grant, Mrs. James N.
Gregory, Mrs. John T.
Gresham, Mrs. Lawton D.
Griffin, Mrs. James
Hageseth, Mrs. Gaylord T.
Haley, Mrs. Daniel W.
Hamilton, Mrs. Susan Kirk
Harmon, Mrs. Susan Petty
Harrington, Mrs. E. Jackson
Henson, Mrs. Harriet Hall
Hines, Mrs. Carolyn R.
Hitchcock, Mrs. Fred C., Jr.
Hodges, Mrs. Sam, Jr.
Holderness, Mrs. Janet Samonds
Holt, Mrs. Edward L., Jr.
Hummel, Mrs. Sam D.
Humphrey, Mrs. Hubert B.
Hunt, Mrs. Clyde L.
Hunt, Mrs. Joseph M.
Irick, Mrs. Robert
James, Frances Rae Stephens
Jennings, Mrs. Dorothy Culp
Jensen, Mrs. Jack H.
Jones, Mrs. Charles R.
Jones, Mrs. C. H. Eckess, Jr.
Jordan, Mr. Harold
Jordan, Mrs. William W.
Joyce, Mrs. G. Donald
Keith, Mrs. Marian Yates

Keith, Mrs. R. B.
Lambert, Mrs. Jerry C.
Lambert, Mrs. Pat W.
Landry, Mrs. Patrick G., Jr.
Lane, Mrs. McKibben, Jr.
Lawrence, Mrs. Robert L.
Lawson, Mrs. Jan Robinson
Leach, Mrs. Katherine
Lee, Mrs. J. Gary
Legette, Mrs. James F.
Lilly, Mrs. Eric V.
Lindley, Sheila Johnson
Lineweaver, Mrs. F. B.
Long, Mrs. James A., Jr.
Long, Mrs. Martha
Lucas, Mrs. Edwin F., Jr.
Lyon, Laura L.
MacRae, Mrs. John
Marshall, Mrs. Ruth Shuping
Matteson, Mrs. Milo H.
Maxwell, Mrs. Richard
McCormick, Mrs. Kay Lindley
McCoy, Mrs. E. C.
McLendon, Mrs. Charles A.
McMillion, Mrs. Donald C.
McNairy, Mrs. Darst Murphy
McPhail, Mrs. S. Dean
Melvin, Mrs. E. S.
Miller, Mrs. Richard, IV
Milligan, Mrs. Jay A.
Mills, Mrs. Annette Barham
Milton, Mrs. Jack
Mims, Mrs. V. G., Jr.
Morris, Mrs. Lewis S.
Murphy, Mrs. E. Louise Fluharty
Murray, Mrs. William G.
Noland, Mrs. E. William
Osteen, Mrs. William L.
Palmer, Miss Gale
Pannill, Mrs. Robert S.
Parham, Mrs. William M.
Peebles, Mrs. E. B.
Peterson, Gail Schoolfield
Pethel, Mrs. Frank
Phipps, Mrs. Roy M., Jr.
Pierce, Mrs. Daniel G.
Poole, Mrs. James W.
Pope, Mrs. A. Harrell
Prichard, Mrs. Theodore T.
Purcell, Mrs. David A., Jr.
Ravenel, Mrs. Thomas P.
Reams, Mrs. George
Reinecke, Mrs. Fred C.
Rice, Mrs. Susan Swart
Ridenhour, Patricia Parker

Rietze, Mr. Ed
Rightsell, Mrs. Helen C.
Roe, Mrs. Phillip D.
Reid, Mrs. Richard
Rule, Mrs. Kay Hartzoge
Sachs, Mrs. E. J.
Sallez, Mrs. Alain
Schmoker, Mrs. Richard
Scott, Mrs. William J., Jr.
Sellars, Mrs. Rainey
Sherrill, Mrs. Frank O., Jr.
Sherrill, Mrs. John R.
Sherrill, Mrs. John R., Jr.
Shuler, Mrs. Conrad
Shuping, Mrs. Hampton
Sitton, Mrs. Larry B.
Skewes, Mrs. William
Smith, Mrs. G. Gregory
Smith, Mrs. Julius C. III
Smith, Mrs. Marcus W.
Smothers, Thelma Wagg
Sprock, Mrs. Howard M., Jr.
Stadler, Mrs. LeRoy A.
Stern, Mrs. Sidney J., Jr.
Stevens, Mrs. Elliott, Jr.
Stickley, Mrs. Robert H.
Stocks, Mrs. Beverly S.
Stone, Mrs. Alma
Stout, Mrs. M. D. III
Sturm, Mrs. Ted A.
Sullivan, Mrs. John
Sutherland, Mrs. Marvin
Suttle, Mrs. William A.
Swart, Mrs. Donna Watkins
Taft, Mrs. Gary F.
Tisdale, Mrs. Wright, Jr.
Tyndall, Mrs. Vernon L.
Upton, Mrs. Jack
Vaughan, Mrs. L. C., Jr.
Wagg, Mrs. Anne Pritchett
Walke, Mrs. Bill D.
Walton, Mrs. John T.
Watson, Mrs. John C., Jr.
Weigel, Mrs. John T., Jr.
Wilcox, Mrs. Bert F.
Wilkerson, Mrs. William H.
Williams, Mrs. E. Monroe
Williams, Mrs. James T.
Williamson, Mrs. Glenn I.
Willis, Mrs. Richard W., Jr.
Willson, Mrs. William W.
Woltz, Mrs. John M., Jr.
Wood, Mrs. Bennett
Wright, Mrs. Sally Hough
Williams, Mrs. James T.

4

TABLE OF CONTENTS

   submitted by the wives of golfers
   attending the Greater Greensboro Open
   Golf Tournament

   unique ideas and unusual favors to make
   at Christmas or anytime for your friends;
   miscellaneous tips

   fun things from mom to keep the children
   occupied; party ideas and suggestions

UNDERSTANDING THE METRIC SYSTEM

Most of the common ingredients used in cooking will be measured in **milliliters** and **liters**. This includes such things as: milk or any liquid, flour, sugar, butter, grated cheese, salt and pepper, spices, chopped vegetables, — almost anything, dry or liquid, that you would normally measure by the teaspoon, tablespoon or cup.

Teaspoons and Tablespoons

⅛ tsp = .6 ml	1 tsp = 5 ml	½ Tb = 7.5 ml	3 Tb = 45 ml
¼ tsp = 1.25 ml	1¼ tsp = 6.25 ml	1 Tb = 15 ml	4 Tb = 60 ml
⅓ tsp = 1.6 ml	1½ tsp = 7.5 ml	1½ Tb = 22.5 ml	5 Tb = 75 ml
½ tsp = 2.5 ml	2 tsp = 10 ml	2 Tb = 30 ml	6 Tb = 90 ml
¾ tsp = 3.7 ml	3 tsp = 15 ml	2½ Tb = 37.5 ml	

Measuring in Cups

¼ cup = 59 ml	1¼ cups = 296 ml	2½ cups = 592 ml	5 cups = 1.18 l
⅓ cup = 79 ml	1⅓ cups = 316 ml	3 cups = 710 ml	5½ cups = 1.30 l
½ cup = 118 ml	1½ cups = 355 ml	3½ cups = 828 ml	6 cups = 1.42 l
⅔ cup = 158 ml	1¾ cups = 414 ml	4 cups = 946 ml	6½ cups = 1.54 l
¾ cup = 177 ml	2 cups = 474 ml	4½ cups = 1.06 l	8 cups = 1.89 l
1 cup = 237 ml	2¼ cups = 533 ml		

Volume Measurements

½ pt = 237 ml	3 qts = 2.84 l	3 oz = 90 ml	8 oz = 240 ml
1 pt = 474 ml	3½ qts = 3.31 l	4 oz = 118 ml	10 oz = 295 ml
1 qt = 946 ml	1 gal = 3.79 l	5 oz = 148 ml	13 oz = 385 ml
1½ qt = 1.42 l	1 oz = 30 ml	6 oz = 177 ml	28 oz = 829 ml
½ gal = 1.89 l	1½ oz = 45 ml	7 oz = 210 ml	46 oz = 1.36 l
2½ qts = 2.35 l	2 oz = 59 ml		

Temperatures

200°F = 93°C	275°F = 135°C	375°F = 191°C	450°F = 232°C
225°F = 107°C	300°F = 149°C	400°F = 204°C	475°F = 246°C
240°F = 115°C	325°F = 163°C	425°F = 218°C	500°F = 260°C
250°F = 121°C	350°F = 177°C		

Measuring in Inches

⅛″ = .32 cm	⅜″ = .96 cm	1″ = 2.54 cm	2″ = 5.08 cm
¼″ = .64 cm	½″ = 1.27 cm	1½″ = 3.81 cm	2½″ = 6.35 cm

... YOUR MOST COMMON INGREDIENTS AND MEASUREMENTS

Solid ingredients such as: ground beef or meat, cream cheese, jello, Cool Whip, pineapple, coconut, canned soups, etc. will be measured in **grams** and **kilograms**. This includes most packaged and canned items and jars — anything pertaining to the weight of the package or container. A few examples...

1 cup of cherries = 237 ml   1 cup of soup = 237 ml
1 8 oz jar of cherries = 227 g   1 10¾ oz can of soup = 305 g

1 lb of cheese = 454 g
1 cup of grated or cubed cheese = 237 ml

Measuring In Ounces And Pounds

1 oz = 28 g	9 oz = 255 g	14 oz = 397 g	1¼ lb = 567 g
2 oz = 57 g	10 oz = 284 g	15 oz = 425 g	1½ lb = 680 g
2½ oz = 71 g	10½ oz = 298 g	20 oz = 567 g	2 lbs = 908 g
3 oz = 85 g	10¾ oz = 305 g	28 oz = 784 g	2½ lbs = 1.1 kg
4 oz = 113 g	11 oz = 312 g	¼ lb = 113 g	3 lbs = 1.4 kg
5 oz = 140 g	12 oz = 340 g	½ lb = 227 g	4 lbs = 1.8 kg
6 oz = 170 g	13 oz = 369 g	¾ lb = 340 g	5 lbs = 2.3 kg
7 oz = 198 g	13½ oz = 383 g	1 lb = 454 g	6 lbs = 2.7 g
8 oz = 227 g			

Baking Dishes

1 qt = 946 ml   2 qt = 1.89 l   3 qt = 2.8 l
1½ qt = 1.42 l   2½ qt = 2.4 l   3½ qt = 3.2 l

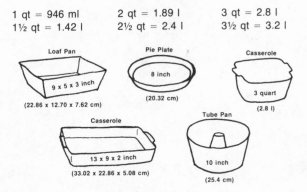

Loaf Pan
9 x 5 x 3 inch
(22.86 x 12.70 x 7.62 cm)

Pie Plate
8 inch
(20.32 cm)

Casserole
3 quart
(2.8 l)

Casserole
13 x 9 x 2 inch
(33.02 x 22.86 x 5.08 cm)

Tube Pan
10 inch
(25.4 cm)

Dish and Pan Sizes

Loaf Pans:
9 x 5 x 3 inch = 22.86 x 12.70 x 7.62 cm
8½ x 4½ x 3 inch = 21.59 x 11.43 x 7.62 cm
10" Tube Pan = 25.4 cm

8" Pie Plate = 20.32 cm
9" Pie Plate = 22.86 cm

Menu Section

...On Menu Planning

There are several thoughts to keep in mind when planning your menu — you want your guests to enjoy the meal you have prepared and you want to enjoy preparing the menu.

To insure a successful meal, the experienced hostess will pay attention to both balance and contrast. For example, when you plan a rich main course, serve a light appetizer or soup. Try to achieve taste contrasts between courses so that a creamy soup is not followed by a main course with a rich sauce and a creamy dessert.

Also, there are certain natural marriages of meat and vegetables such as: lamb and tomatoes, veal and mushrooms, beef and onions — try to use them.

Your menus should be planned so that you can also participate in the evening. Until you have mastered the art of preparing things in advance, do not be over-ambitious. As a host or hostess, your job is to be relaxed and gracious, providing an atmosphere for pleasurable dining.

The following menus are merely suggestions to facilitate and enhance your own ideas in menu planning. From a "Christmas Open House" to a "Debutante Tea," you should find these selections delightful. Also included are menu suggestions from January to December, for each month of the year, all recipes selected of course from "Out Of Our League" to you!

JANUARY

New Year's Day Bowl Buffet

Bloody Marys (p. 30)
Herbed Boursin/Carr Wafers (p. 56)
Egg Brunch (p. 142)
Fresh Strawberry and Pineapple
Bowl
Garlic Grits (p. 152)
Lemon Squares (p. 363)
Dark Secrets (p. 370)
Coffee

Super Bowl Sunday Buffet

Red Wine
Bleu Cheese Dip (p. 48)
with Fresh Vegetables
Pasta Griffiana (p. 169)
Orange-Avocado Toss (p. 283)
Easy French Bread (p. 114)
German Chocolate Pie (p. 336)
Jamaican Pound Cake (p. 340)

FEBRUARY

Valentine Dinner Party

Mushroom or Shrimp
Turnovers (p. 66)
Filet of Boeuf with
Perigueux Sauce (p.160)
Wild Rice with Consommé (p. 256)
Avocado and Hearts of
Palm Salad (p. 285)
Rum Rolls (p. 122)
Rainbow Sherbets
Red Wine/Coffee

MARCH

St. Patrick's Day Brunch

Sausage and Egg
Casserole (p. 147)
Apples in Sauterne (p. 273)
Hot Rolls
Creme de Menthe Mousse (p. 308)
Irish Coffee

APRIL

Easter Dinner

Cocktail Rounds (p. 60)
Tomato-Orange Soup (p. 84)
French Ham (p. 176)
with Frosted White Grapes (p. 273)
Sweet Potato Balls (p. 254)
Asparagus with Herb
Butter (p. 409)
Tossed Salad
Quick Caesar Dressing (p. 270)
Buttermilk Rolls (p. 122)
Chocolate Cheese Cake (p. 301)

MAY

Mother's Day Brunch

Curried Shrimp (p. 215)
with Green Grapes
Plain or Saffron Rice
Heavenly Orange Fluff (p. 278)
Condiments
(raisins, peanuts, coconut,
chutney, toasted almonds)
French Breakfast Muffins (p. 127)
Cheese and Date Tarts (p. 300)
Individual Cheese Cakes (p. 300)

JUNE

Father's Day Buffet

Crab and Almond Crepes (p. 219)
Zucchini-Tomato Summer
Casserole (p. 260)
Asparagus Salad (p. 286)
Cottage Cheese Bread (p. 119)
Strawberries à La
Chantilly (p. 310)

JULY

Fourth of July Cookout

Fresh Vegetables (p. 47)
(kept cold in a wheel barrow
filled with ice)
Your Favorite Dip
Teriyaki Steak (p. 164)
Hamburgers
Mother's Potato Salad (p. 286)
French Bread and Buns
Apricot-Brandy Pound Cake (p. 340)
Fresh Peach Ice Cream Cones
Aunt Susan's Lemonade (p. 40)

AUGUST

End of Summer Cocktail Party

Open Bar
Welcome Wafers (p. 61)
Barbequed Chicken Wings (p. 74)
Cucumber Dip/Raw
Vegetables (p. 49)
Salmon Supreme (p. 59)
Dried Beef Roll-Ups (p. 63)
Stuffed Edam Ball (p. 56)
Mints (p. 379)

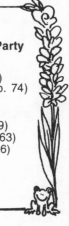

SEPTEMBER

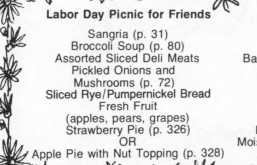

Labor Day Picnic for Friends

Sangria (p. 31)
Broccoli Soup (p. 80)
Assorted Sliced Deli Meats
Pickled Onions and
Mushrooms (p. 72)
Sliced Rye/Pumpernickel Bread
Fresh Fruit
(apples, pears, grapes)
Strawberry Pie (p. 326)
OR
Apple Pie with Nut Topping (p. 328)

Labor Day Barbecue

Gazpacho (p. 82)
Barbequed Beef Brisket (p. 161)
Tomatoes Stuffed with
Mushrooms (p. 262)
Delicious Squash
Casserole (p. 260)
Dill Buns (p. 123)
Lemon Chess Pie (p. 334)
Moist Fudge Sheet Cake (p. 343)

OCTOBER

Children's Halloween Party

Chilled Cider
Apples Cored and Filled with
Peanut Butter
Pizza Burgers (p. 98)
Cheese Biscuits (p. 128)
Tiger Cookies (p. 359)
Sharon's Butterscotch
Oaties (p. 361)

NOVEMBER

**Traditional Thanksgiving
Dinner**

Roast Turkey with
Oyster Dressing
OR
Fresh Baked Pork Ham
Buttered Mashed Potatoes
Giblet Gravy
Onion Casserole (p. 251)
Buttered Sesame Spinach (p. 259)
Cranberry Salad (p. 280)
Corn Bread (p. 129)
Coffee Pumpkin Flan (p. 297)
OR
Chiffon Pumpkin Pie (p. 333)
Coffee

DECEMBER

**Christmas Day Lunch for
Family and Friends**

Orange Duck (p. 195)
OR
Cornish Hens with Cumberland
Sauce (p. 183)
Scalloped Oysters Deluxe (p. 223)
Sweet Potatoes with
Orange Sauce (p. 255)
Waldorf-Cranberry Salad (p. 277)
Cheese Spoon Bread (p. 130)
Neiman Marcus Cherry
Nut Cake (p. 349)
Coffee

**New Year's Eve Seated
Dinner**

Beef Tender (p. 157)
OR
Pork Tenderloin a La
Asparagus (p. 172)
Armenian Rice Pilaf (p. 256)
Cauliflower au Gratin
Congealed Vegetable
Salad (p. 279)
Easy French Bread
Frozen Delight Mousse (p. 296)
OR
Rum Cheese Cake (p. 302)

From morning til night...

MORNING COFFEE

Pitchers of Orange, Pineapple
& Tomato Juice
Claverton Manor Cheese Biscuits (p. 67)
Marshmallow Crescent Puffs (p. 118)
Asparagus Roll-Ups (p. 65)
Hermit Cake (p. 351)
Ice Box Cookies (p. 366)
Coffee

GREATER GREENSBORO OPEN BRUNCH

Eggs Royal Casserole (p. 142)
and
Chicken Chasseur Casserole (p. 188)
Coconut Fruit Bowl (p. 272)
Fabulous Aspic (p. 281)
Buttermilk Rolls/Preserves (p. 122)
Individual Cheese Cakes (p. 300)
Coffee

AUXILIARY BOARD LUNCHEON

Chicken Divan (p. 192)
Fruit Salad/Minted Dressing
(p. 267)
Bran Muffins (p. 127)
Bread Pudding with Brandy
Sauce (p. 296)
Lemon Iced Tea (p. 41)

DEBUTANTE TEA

Strawberry Punch (p. 39)
Spinach Balls (p. 65)
Finger Tip Sandwiches (p. 103-106)
Zippy Beef Olive Spread (p. 56)
Assorted Crackers
Strawberries and Grapes
(accompaniment of sour cream,
sugar & cinnamon
combined to your taste)
Chocolate Pound Cake (p. 344)
Apricot Chews (p. 369)
Tea

SWEET SIXTEEN LUNCHEON

Hot Chicken Salad (p. 193)
Blueberry Salad (p. 278)
Assorted Relishes, Olives
Pickles, Carrot Sticks
Banana Bread (p. 113)
Birthday Cake
Ice Cream Custard (p. 313)
Apricot Iced Tea (p. 41)

GARDEN WALK TEA

Cheese and Strawberries (p. 57)
Cream Puffs with Fillings (p. 62)
Party Sandwiches (p. 103-106)
Toastettes (p. 61)
Kefflings (Norwegian Cookies)
(p. 365)
Peanut Butter Bars (p. 360)
Lemon Punch (p. 39)
Tea

TEENAGE PARTY

Iced Cheese Squares (p. 67)
Easy Lasagna (p. 170)
Salad Bar
Vinaigrette Dressing (p. 270)
French Bread with Garlic Spread
(p. 110)
Fudge Brownies (p. 371)

CHRISTENING PARTY

Champagne Punch (p. 35)
Egg-Seafood Roll (p. 141)
Garlic Grits (p. 152)
Exotic Fruit (p. 275)
Lemon Muffins (p. 126)
Fresh Grape Dessert (p. 309)
OR
Orange Ice (p. 310)
Coffee

HOLIDAY BUFFET

Open House Punch (p. 33)
Hot Crabmeat Spread (p. 51)
Sauerkraut Balls (p. 64)
Roquefort Mousse (p. 57)
/Melba Rounds
Steak Tartare (p. 59)
Vegetables for Dipping
Curry OR Vegetable Dip (p. 48)
Orange Blossoms (p. 125)
Peppermint Rounds (p. 368)

CHRISTMAS OPEN HOUSE

Holiday Eggnog (p. 38)
Artichoke Spread (p. 58)/Sesame
Crackers
Quiche Lorraine Hors d'Oeuvre (p. 75)
Hot Mushrooms in Sour Cream (p. 50)
Cookie Press Cheese Straws (p. 61)
Cheese and Date Tarts (p. 300)
Peppermint Candy Canes (p. 367)
Ginger Ale Punch for a Crowd (p. 40)

ATLANTIC COAST CONFERENCE
COCKTAIL PARTY

Open Bar OR Open House Punch
(p. 33)
Dipsidoodle Crab Dip (p. 50)
Bugles OR Crackers
Olive Quiche (p. 75)
Hot Buttered Brie with Almonds (p. 54)
Crusty French Bread
Cream Puffs/Deviled Ham Filling
(p. 62)
Chocolate Date Bars (p. 370)
Coffee Thins (p. 367)

POST SYMPHONY DINNER

Shrimp and Artichoke Casserole
(p. 400)
Apples in Sauterne (p. 273)
Hot Rolls
Frozen Grand Marnier Soufflé (p. 307)
White Wine/Coffee

DINNER FOR THE BOSS

Baked Stuffed Flank Steak
(p. 395)
Buttered Noodles
Broccoli Cheese Dish (p. 401)
Tossed Salad
Crusty Hard Rolls
Million Dollar Pie (p. 404)
Coffee

6 P.M. BEFORE THE OPERA DINNER

Pecan Dip (p. 52)
Assorted Crackers
Shrimp and Crab Casserole (p. 228)
Stafford's Broccoli Supreme (p. 243)
Oranges in Red Wine (p. 274)
Cheese Poppy Seed Bread (p. 114)
Orange Walnuts (p. 373)
Welsh Cookies (p. 360)
Coffee

COLD BUFFET DINNER

Vichyssoise (p. 86)
(passed in mugs or cups
on a tray)
Salmon Mousse with
Cucumber Dill Sauce (p. 221)
Sliced Virginia Ham
Hot Buttered Croissants
Moist Coconut Cake (p. 403)
White Wine

SEAFOOD BUFFET

Shrimp and Vegetable Creole (p. 214)
with Rice
OR
Coquilles St. Jacques (p. 226)
Scalloped Potatoes & Carrots (p. 400)
Fresh Mushroom Salad (p. 289)
Refrigerator Rolls (p. 123)
Sherbet
Crescent Cookies (p. 363)
White Wine/Coffee

SUMMER ICE CREAM SOCIAL

Vanilla, Chocolate, Strawberry,
Peach and Butter Pecan
Ice Cream
Ice Cream Cones
Your Favorite Pound Cake
Hot Fudge Sauce (p. 316)
Nesselrode Sauce (p. 317)
Pineapple Sauce (p. 318)
Sweetened Whipped Cream

DESSERT SPECTACULAR

Java Angel Cake (p. 345)
Jamaican Pound Cake (p. 340)
Pumpkin Ice Cream (p. 401)
Blitz Torte (p. 304)
Coffee

A Progressive Dinner Party

A progressive dinner — where each course is served at a different home — is a great way to entertain a large group of people with a minimum of effort for those involved.

Sixteen people is an ideal number for this kind of party — four courses at four homes with an extra couple assigned to each to help prepare the food.

Schedule a preliminary get-together for menu planning to make sure each course will complement the others. Otherwise, you may end up with spinach appetizers and spinach salad accompanying the entree — a combination that would not be appealing to anyone.

Don't forget to include the travel time in your schedule. Obviously, it's ideal if four houses are within walking distance, but if you must use a car, double up so there are no more than four cars. It's best to assemble around 6:00 or 6:30 P.M. especially if your group likes to be home at a reasonable hour.

The third home, where the main course is served, should borrow card tables to supplement dining table space. Before moving on to each home, help your hostess by getting all the dishes into the kitchen. Also make sure ovens and burners are off and candles extinguished before leaving.

House 1

Cocktails
Spinach Dip (p. 48)   Assorted Crackers
Beer Batter Shrimp with Sauce (p. 73)

House 2

Cream of Cauliflower Soup (p. 83)
Make Your Own Salad

House 3

Tenderloin Tips with Mushrooms (p. 161)
Almond-Poppy Seed Noodles (p. 152)
Spinach Madeline (p. 258)
Home Made Rolls
Red Wine

House 4

Peach Bavarian with Raspberry Sauce (p. 295)
OR
English Trifle (p. 348)
Butter Cookie Crispies (p. 366)
Coffee OR Tea
Cordials (optional)

A QUICK CHECK LIST:

One Month Before
    Invite Guests
    Assign menu and houses accordingly

One Week Before
    Check liquor and wine and purchase where needed
    Purchase non-perishable ingredients
    Select serving dishes

The Day of the Party
    Set up bar, set out napkins, glasses and small plates
    For each house, prepare as much of the food as possible the
    day before the party, or the day of the party, preferably early in
    the morning.

Good planning and organization chart the best route to a successful
progressive dinner party. Most of the food can be prepared in advance
and held until ready to be served. Have a wonderful moveable feast!

Tailgate Picnic

Tailgating is picnicking for adults only, in the Fête Champêtre tradition. It requires wicker hampers, plates, cutlery and napery. It brings to mind the spirits of Sangria or red and white wines properly chilled, thin slices of melon or other fresh fruit, boned breasts of chicken stuffed with something out of the ordinary, or patés with crusty French bread as an example.

Of course, tailgating fare need not be this elaborate. The picnic as in other outings should have prescribed menus to suit the occasion.

Soup is tailgating food. Fish chowder goes with football games in cold weather. Hot consommé with a dash of sherry is a perfect soup before an evening basketball game.

If you plan a tailgate picnic, make it simple, or elaborate, but be sure to plan your logistics as carefully as though you were in charge of a large party. Make your lists of things you need to do or purchase. Review all of your equipment at the last minute to be sure that you haven't forgotten the salt grinder or pepper mill or whatever is required to lift the occasion above the mundane. Remember:

1. Use the right menu for the occasion.

2. Don't try to exceed your capabilities.

3. Be sure that you have all the necessary items for serving and eating in the style you wish.

4. Be sure when you serve something hot, it is hot! Also, the same goes for anything that is served cold. Have plenty of ice on hand.

Take along packaged throw-away wash cloths for sticky fingers. And, last but not least, when the picnic is over, be sure to dispose of paper plates or any other disposable items in their appropriate place.

Whether your facilities include a luxurious motor home or a tailgate and some folding chairs; the fans in your party will have something to cheer about with winning menus like these:

Tailgate Menu

Sangria (p. 31)
Washington Dip (p. 48) OR Kentucky Derby
Cheese Dip (p. 49)
Assorted Crackers
Cucumber-Spinach Soup (p. 81)
Corned Beef Sandwiches (p. 98)

OR

Chilled Reuben Sandwiches (p. 100)
Pickled Mushrooms and Onions (p. 72)
Fudge Pudding Cake (p. 345)
Molasses Cookies (p. 362)
Coffee

Luxurious Motor Home Pre-Game Party

Chicken Tetrazzini (p. 187)
Pineapple Carrots (p. 244)
Lettuce Salad with Sesame Seeds (p. 283)
Onion Cheese Corn Bread (p. 129)
Italian Cream Cake (p. 351)
Orange Rum Punch (p. 33)
Coffee

Cocktail Parties

Rapidly becoming one of our most popular fashions in informal entertaining, the cocktail party is also one of the simplest to give. From the intimate little "come over for cocktails" gathering to the elaborate, full-scaled cocktail party, success depends almost entirely on good planning, well in advance. Once the guests begin to arrive, your only remaining responsibilities are passing the canapes, nudging your spouse when the shy guest's glass is empty, and enjoying yourself and your guests.

The "little" cocktail party is practically effortless — a few friends are invited in, most often in the late afternoon, pre-dinner hours. Cocktails can be served from a tray around the living room coffee table or on the patio. A nearby side-board or table holds all the appurtenances for a self-service bar: cocktail napkins, 6 to 8 ounce glasses, filled ice bucket, bar spoon, jigger, mixers of soda, ginger ale and water, a bowl of lemon twists, a bottle each of Bourbon and Scotch, at least one non-alcoholic drink, plus the tray of cocktail glasses and shaker or pitcher of Martinis (or Manhattans). Guests are requested to be their own bartenders, unless you have a bartender or the man of the house takes over the job.

The hostess passes the canape trays or has help to provide this service, along with tiny cocktail napkins, and places the trays where guests may conveniently serve themselves.

At a large cocktail party, the self-service bar may be used or a few friends of the host might take turns pinch-hitting as bartenders, so the host is left free to circulate among his guests. A buffet table is set with candles and flowers, serving forks and spoons, small napkins, small plates and constantly replenished trays and platters of canapes and dips. And, most of all, the cocktail party can make it possible for the host and hostess to enjoy their party with the guests. Most of the food can be prepared ahead, and you can also feature foods that can be cooked at the last minute. Plain or fancy, big or small, cocktail parties are among the easiest parties to give.

Cocktail Party Menus

Open Bar
Shrimp and Horseradish Dip (p. 50)
Caviar Surprise (p. 60)
Cocktail Rye Bread
Cocktail Meatballs with Madiera Sauce (p. 54)
Strawberries with Powdered Sugar
Marinated Mushrooms (p. 71)
Coconut Balls (p. 364)
Apricot Chews (p. 369)

Frozen Daiquiris (p. 31)
Whiskey Sours (p. 30)
Hot Pepper Jelly
Cream Cheese and Crackers
Hot Cheese Dip with Apple Slices (p. 51)
Spinach Balls (p. 65)
Stuffed Mushrooms (p. 67)
Asparagus Roll-Ups (p. 65)
Lemon Squares (p. 363)

Open Bar
Cheese and Strawberries/Triscuits (p. 57)
Cocktail Rounds (p. 60)
Marinated Spinach (p. 70)
Pecan Dip (p. 52)
Hot Mushrooms in Sour Cream (p. 50)
Almond Delight (p. 378)
Dark Secrets (p. 370)

The Buffet

You will like to serve buffet meals. They create a friendly, informal atmosphere. Your guests will enjoy moving around to visit with each other, and serving themselves at your attractive table. Best of all, your meal will be easier to prepare and to serve than the usual type of "company" dinner.

While this seems to suggest that buffet service is just for informal occasions, you can make it more if you wish, for weddings, anniversaries and receptions.

Plan a buffet breakfast, brunch, luncheon, or carry over this idea for your bridge and club meetings in the late afternoon and for early or late evening suppers.

It's the logical service, too, for the covered dish or pot-luck luncheons and Sunday night suppers we all enjoy. Also, church suppers, when the number of people to be served is indefinite, run smoothly when served buffet style.

Whatever the setting, your table is the center of interest. Originally the term "buffet" was applied to service from the buffet or sideboard. Now we use the table but the idea is the same and often the sideboard is used in addition to the table arrangement.

Place your table to give the best use of space or the effect you desire. It may be in the center of the room, at one end, or at the side, or you may choose to push the table against the wall. This limits the amount of table edge space, but you can create interesting and unusual decorations at the back of the table against the wall.

Buffet Dessert Course

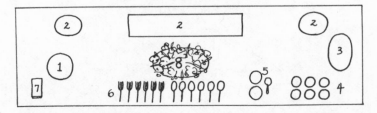

1. dessert plates
2. choice of desserts
3. beverage service
4. cups

5. cream and sugar
6. silver
7. napkins
8. centerpiece

Table Arrangement For a Main Course

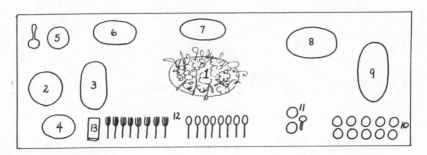

1. centerpiece	6. vegetable	11. cream, sugar
2. plates	7. rolls	and spoon
3. main dish	8. relish plate	12. Silver
4. vegetable	9. coffee service	13. napkins
5. gravy	10. cups	

Arrangement of a Pot Luck Table

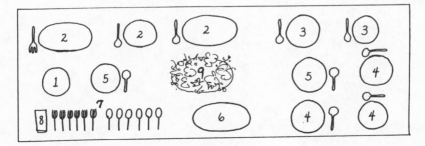

1. dinner plates	4. salads	7. silver
2. main dishes	5. assorted	8. napkins
3. vegetables	relishes	9. centerpiece
	6. sandwiches	
	or rolls	

Beverages

Beverages

For The Bar...

If you're planning to serve liquor at a party in your home, use the following information as a "check-list" of items to have on hand for the occasion. A bartender is usually necessary for large open house parties, however, if you prefer, your guests can mix their own drinks if you're willing to have them do the mixing and have adequate room.

THE BASICS

ice bucket and tongs
corkscrew
bottle and can opener
long-handled mixing spoon

measuring glass
cutting board and knife
water pitcher
cocktail napkins

AVERAGE SUPPLIES

scotch	**beer**	**club soda**	**lemons**
bourbon	**sherry**	**ginger ale**	**limes**
vodka	**brandy**	**cola drinks**	
gin	**rum**	**quinine water**	

Planning A Party...

Liquor can be quite expensive for entertaining a large group of people. Two common ways to cut costs are to: serve set-ups and have the guests bring their own liquor or, serve set-ups plus one kind of liquor or wine, with guests bringing any extras they might want.

No. of Guests	No. of 1½ oz. drinks to allow	No. of fifths needed
4	8-12	1
6-8	12-24	2
12	24-36	3
20	40-60	4
50	100-150	9

29

Bloody Mary

Can do ahead   Yield: 1 gal (3.79 l)

2 cans, 46 oz *(1.36 l)* tomato juice   1 tsp *(5 ml)* salt
¼ cup *(59 ml)* lemon juice   ½ tsp *(2.5 ml)* pepper
2 oz *(59 ml)* Worcestershire sauce   1 fifth *(768 ml)* vodka
½ tsp *(2.5 ml)* Tabasco

Blend together in a large container. If making ahead, mix all ingredients except vodka and add when serving. Garnish with a slice of lemon, lime or a stalk of celery.

Whiskey Sour

Yield: 1 drink

1 oz *(30 ml)* frozen lemonade   2 oz *(60 ml)* bourbon
  concentrate, thawed   cracked ice

Mix lemonade and bourbon in old fashioned glass. Add cracked ice to top.

Sherry Sours

Serves: 8-10

1 can, 6 oz *(177 ml)* frozen   1 fifth dry sherry
  lemonade   2 Tb *(30 ml)* lemon juice

Mix in blender and chill for 3 or 4 days. Garnish with cherries when serving.

Variation: Blend sherry and lemonade in blender; add ice until you reach the consistency you prefer. Freeze in milk cartons or plastic jugs. Keep frozen until ready to serve.

Strawberry Daiquiri

Serves: 8

6 oz *(177 ml)* vodka or gin   1 can, 6 oz *(177 ml)* pink lemonade
1 pkg, 10 oz *(284 g)* frozen   ¼ cup *(59 ml)* sugar
  strawberries

Put all of the above ingredients into a blender and add ice. Blend until ice is crushed very fine. Add more ice until blender is almost full.

Variation: For frozen strawberries, substitute 2 peaches and skin using limeade or lemonade.

Frozen Daiquiri

Serves: 6

1 can, 6 oz *(177 ml)* frozen
concentrated limeade
6 oz *(177 ml)* light rum

1 can, 6 oz *(177 ml)* frozen
pineapple juice concentrate

Combine ingredients with ice in blender. Blend until smooth.

Banana Daiquiri

Serves: 2-4

1 large banana, peeled and sliced
½ cup *(118 ml)* rum

juice of a fresh lime
4-6 ice cubes

Mix in blender until smooth.

Piña Colada

Serves: 1

⅔ cup *(158 ml)* pineapple juice
4 ice cubes, crushed

⅓ cup *(79 ml)* cream of coconut
5 Tb *(75 ml)* dark rum

Combine all ingredients in blender and mix until smooth. Serve in 12 inch (30.48 cm) chilled glasses. Garnish with pineapple spear and maraschino cherry.

Sangria

Serves: 4

1 bottle Spanish red wine or a
cheap red wine
1 bottle, 7 oz *(207 ml)* club soda
juice of a whole lemon

2 Tb *(30 ml)* sugar
1 lemon, sliced thin
½ orange, sliced thin
1 peach, sliced

Mix ingredients, add ice and serve.

Variation: Use 2 bottles wine and add 2 cans, 6 oz (177 ml) pink lemonade and 3 more oz (90 ml) club soda.

Brandy Alexander

Serves: 2-3

3 oz *(90 ml)* brandy
3 oz *(90 ml)* white cream de cacao

3-4 scoops vanilla ice cream
nutmeg

Blend first 3 ingredients in blender. Pour into champagne glasses and sprinkle with nutmeg.

Bossa Nova

Yield: 1 drink

1 oz *(30 ml)* galliano
1 oz *(30 ml)* light rum
¼ oz *(7.5 ml)* apricot brandy

2 oz *(60 ml)* pineapple juice
½ oz *(15 ml)* egg white
¼ oz *(7.5 ml)* lemon juice

Combine in cocktail shaker and shake vigorously. Pour into tall glass with ice cubes.

Strawberry Cooler

Serves: 4-6

2½ cups *(592 ml)* strawberries
1½ cups *(355 ml)* water
½ cup *(118 ml)* sugar

2 Tb *(30 ml)* lemon juice
1 tsp *(5 ml)* lemon rind, grated
½ cup *(118 ml)* white wine

In blender, purée 2 cups (474 ml) strawberries, reserving the half cup (118 ml) for garnishing. Add remaining ingredients to blender and blend well. Chill.

Eric Punch

Can do ahead

Serves: 32   4 oz (118 ml) servings

¼ lb *(113 g)* sugar
1 qt *(946 ml)* strong tea, made with
  7 tsp *(35 ml)* tea
1 pt *(474 ml)* lemon juice
1 qt *(946 ml)* gin

1 pt *(474 ml)* Jamaican rum
1 tsp *(5 ml)* Angostura bitters
1 qt *(946 ml)* ginger ale
orange slices

Combine tea with sugar. Add remaining ingredients except ginger ale which is to be added just before serving. Float orange slices on top.

Red Christmas Punch

Serves: 12

1 pt *(474 ml)* **vodka**
1 pt *(474 ml)* **bourbon**
2 pts *(946 ml)* **cranberry OR cranapple juice**
2 qts *(1.89 l)* **ginger ale**

16 oz *(474 ml)* **frozen lemonade, undiluted**
16 oz *(474 ml)* **frozen orange juice, undiluted**

Mix everything together except ginger ale, and add it just before serving.

Orange Rum Punch

Serves: 2

1½ oz *(45 ml)* **Bacardi dark rum**
1 oz *(30 ml)* **apricot brandy**
1½ oz *(45 ml)* **pineapple juice, unsweetened**
3 oz *(90 ml)* **light rum**

5-6 oz *(150-180 ml)* **fresh orange juice**
1½ oz *(45 ml)* **fresh lime juice**
1 tsp *(5 ml)* **sugar**

Combine all ingredients and pour over coarsely chopped ice. Serve in large tall glasses with straws.

Open House Punch

Yield: 18 cups (4.26 l)

MIX

1 can, 6 oz *(177 ml)* **frozen orange juice**
2 cans, 6 oz *(177 ml)* **frozen lemonade**

¾ cup *(177 ml)* **fresh lemon juice OR reconstituted lemon juice**

PLAIN PUNCH

3¼ cups *(769 ml)* **mix**

3¼ qts *(3.07 l)* **7-Up**

SPIKED PUNCH

3¼ cups *(769 ml)* **mix**
2¼ qts *(2.13 l)* **7-Up**

2½ cups *(592 ml)* **Southern Comfort**

Planter's Punch

Serves: 2

1½ oz *(45 ml)* Myers rum
1 oz *(30 ml)* apricot brandy
6 oz *(180 ml)* pineapple juice,
  unsweetened

3 oz *(90 ml)* light rum
juice of ½ lime OR lemon
1 tsp *(5 ml)* sugar
cherries, orange slice

Combine all ingredients and pour over very coarsely chopped ice. Garnish with cherries and orange. Chopped ice is a must.

Luncheon Punch

Must do ahead

Serves: 14-16
Preparing: 10 min
Chilling: 3-4 hrs

4 fresh peaches, sliced
⅔ cup *(158 ml)* sugar
1 cup *(237 ml)* lemon juice
1 cup *(237 ml)* peach brandy

2 qts *(1.89 l)* ginger ale
1 bottle sauterne
1 bottle rosé wine
1 cup *(237 ml)* orange juice

Combine first 4 ingredients in blender; purée and strain. Chill several hours. When ready to serve, add remaining ingredients and serve over ice.

Rosy Wassail Warm Wine
Delightful for holiday gatherings

Serves: 12-14

1 pt *(474 ml)* cranberry juice
  cocktail
1 can, 6 oz *(177 ml)* frozen orange
  juice, thawed
2 cups *(474 ml)* warm water
1 Tb *(15 ml)* sugar

¼ tsp *(1.25 ml)* allspice
3¼ cups *(769 ml)* dry sauterne
1 orange
cloves
red food coloring

In large kettle, combine cranberry juice, orange juice concentrate, water, sugar and allspice; bring **almost** to simmering. Add sauterne and heat through; do not boil. If desired, stir in a few drops of red food coloring. Stud thick orange slices with whole cloves. Pour punch into preheated punch bowl; float orange slices atop.

Rosé Glow Punch

Serves: 18-20

1 can, 6 oz *(177 ml)* frozen daiquiri
  mix concentrate
2 fifths *(768 ml)* rosé wine
½ cup *(118 ml)* brandy

1 quart *(946 ml)* ice cubes
1 bottle, 12 oz *(355 ml)* carbonated
  water

Combine thawed daiquiri mix concentrate, wine and brandy in a large pitcher or bowl. Add ice cubes. Gently stir in carbonated water. Add granulated sugar if desired to sweeten.

B
E
V
E
R
A
G
E
S

Champagne Rosé Punch

Yield: 27 half-cup (118 ml) servings

2½ cups *(592 ml)* OR 2 pkgs, 10 oz
  (284 g) strawberries
6½ cups *(1.54 l)* rosé, chilled

1 can, 6 oz *(177 ml)* frozen
  lemonade, thawed
1 fifth *(768 ml)* champagne

Cover and let strawberries and half of the rosé stand for 1 hour. Strain into a 3 quart (2.84 l) container. Add lemonade and remainder of rosé. Add champagne. For each additional 12 cups (2.84 l) desired, increase by one recipe.

Champagne Punch

Yield: 2 gal (7.58 l)

2 fifths champagne
1 fifth sauterne

1 large bottle soda water

Mix and serve over ice.

Children's Champagne

Can do ahead

Serves: 12-14

1 can frozen lemon juice, thawed
¾ cup *(177 ml)* **Karo**

1 qt *(946 ml)* ginger ale, chilled

Mix lemon juice and Karo. Add ginger ale when ready to serve.

35

Hot Mulled Apple Juice

Serves: 12

juice of 1 lemon
juice of 2 oranges
4 whole cloves
2 sticks cinnamon
3 whole allspice

2 cups *(474 ml)* water
¼ cup *(59 ml)* brown sugar
1 qt *(946 ml)* apple juice
pinch of salt

Squeeze lemon and oranges, reserving juices. Place rinds in saucepan with spices and water. Bring to a boil, and simmer for 5 minutes. Strain, add sugar, salt and juices and heat.

Hot Spiced Percolator Punch

Serves: 8-10

2½ cups *(592 ml)* pineapple juice
1¾ cups *(414 ml)* water
2 cups *(474 ml)* cranberry juice
1 Tb *(15 ml)* whole cloves

½ Tb *(2.5 ml)* whole allspice
3 sticks cinnamon, broken
¼ tsp *(1.25 ml)* salt
½ cup *(118 ml)* brown sugar

Put pineapple juice, water and cranberry juice in bottom part of an 8 cup (1.89 l) percolator and the remaining ingredients in the basket on top. Perk for 10 minutes or until spices permeate. Serve hot.

Frosty Fruit Cooler

Serves: 6-8

3 cups *(710 ml)* apricot nectar, chilled
3 cups *(710 ml)* pineapple OR orange juice, chilled

1 qt *(946 ml)* ginger ale, chilled
2 cups *(474 ml)* pineapple OR orange sherbet

In a punch bowl or large 2 quart (1.8 l) container combine first two ingredients. Just before serving, add ginger ale. Float scoops of sherbet on top. Serve immediately.

For individual servings, place a scoop of sherbet in each glass. Fill glasses ¾ full with equal amounts of chilled apricot nectar and juice. Add ginger ale to fill glasses.

Kentucky Mint Julep

fresh mint leaves, no stems
granulated sugar

finely crushed ice
100 Proof Kentucky
Bourbon Whiskey

Crush or bruise the mint leaves in a bowl containing sugar and water. This is best done by using what is known as a muddler (mortar & pestle will do) whereby the leaves are crushed into the sugar syrup giving the syrup a good mint flavor. Strain out the little parts of the mint leaves so they do not clog the straw later. Usually 1½ teaspoons (7.5 ml) of syrup is sufficient per julep. The procedure is to first half fill your julep cup with crushed ice over which you pour the syrup then add additional ice and pour approximately an ounce and a half of bourbon into the cup. After this fill the cup entirely with crushed ice and vigorously stir holding your hand on the top of the cup rather than on the side of the cup. This is done to permit the silver cup to frost in the process of stirring. After this add a couple sprigs of mint in the cup and take a short straw and place it in the cup so it is about the same height as the sprigs of mint coming out of the cup. The purpose of this straw in this height is to permit the drinker to smell the mint as he tastes the julep.

After Dinner Coffee

Serves: 1

¾ oz *(22.5 ml)* **brandy**
¾ oz *(22.5 ml)* **Kahlua**

black coffee
sweetened whipped cream

Put brandy and Kahlua in cup and fill with coffee. Top with whipped cream.

Easy Eggnog

Serves: 8

12 large eggs, separated
1 pt *(474 ml)* **whipping cream,**
  whipped

¾ cup *(177 ml)* **bourbon**
1¾ cups *(414 ml)* **sugar**

Beat egg whites until slightly stiff, adding sugar gradually. In small bowl, whip cream. In a large bowl, beat egg yolks until light in color; add bourbon gradually. Fold cream into yolk mixture; then egg whites.

Holiday Eggnog

Can partially do ahead

Serves: 30-40
Preparing: 20-30 min
Chilling: 1 hr

24 egg yolks
2 cups *(474 ml)* **sugar**
1 qt *(946 ml)* **bourbon**
1 pt *(474 ml)* **brandy**

1 qt *(946 ml)* **heavy cream**
2 qts *(1.89 l)* **milk**
1 qt *(946 ml)* **vanilla ice cream**
24 egg whites, stiffly beaten

Beat egg yolks and sugar until thick and lemon-colored. Add bourbon and brandy and stir thoroughly. Blend in cream and milk and continue stirring. Add ice cream and mix well. Fold in stiffly beaten egg whites last.

Place in refrigerator to cool at least 1 hour before serving. Can all be done ahead except for adding egg whites. Add them one hour before serving.

Coffee Punch

Serves: 35-40

30 cups *(7.1 l)* **coffee, chilled**
½ gal *(1.89 l)* **vanilla ice cream**
1 ctn, 9 oz *(255 g)* **Cool Whip**

½ cup *(118 ml)* **sugar**
1 bottle, 16 oz *(480 ml)* **Coke**
  OR Pepsi

Thirty minutes before serving, take half of the ice cream, cut in fourths, rub in punch bowl and allow to melt. When ready to serve, add the other half of the ice cream along with remaining ingredients.

Ice Cream Favorites

ONE

1½ oz *(45 ml)* **creme de menthe**
1½ oz *(45 ml)* **brandy**

¾ cup *(177 ml)* **vanilla ice cream**

Blend in blender. Serves 1.

TWO

1 jigger **Cointreau**
1 jigger **white creme de menthe**

2 jiggers **brandy**
1 pt *(474 ml)* **vanilla ice cream**

Blend in blender. Serves 4-5.

THREE

1½ oz *(45 ml)* **Grand Marnier**
¼ cup *(59 ml)* **cream**

¾ cup *(177 ml)* **vanilla ice cream**

Blend in blender. Sprinkle with nutmeg if desired. Serves 1.

Lemon Punch

Serves: 20-25 people

2-3 bottles, 28 oz *(829 ml)* **Collins Mixer**
1 qt *(946 ml)* **lemon ice milk**
2 cups *(474 ml)* **vanilla ice milk**

2 cups *(474 ml)* **orange, lime OR pineapple sherbet**
1 **ice ring with cherries and mint at different intervals**

Put ice milk and sherbet in punch bowl, then add the Collins Mixer pouring over the top of ice ring and ice milk. Do all this about 20 minutes before your guests arrive.

Strawberry Punch

Can do ahead

Serves: 50

2 cups *(474 ml)* **cold water**
1 pkg, 6 oz *(170 g)* **strawberry jello**
1 can, 6 oz *(177 ml)* **frozen orange juice**
1 can, 6 oz *(177 ml)* **frozen lemonade**

2 cups *(474 ml)* **boiling water**
1 can, 46 oz *(1.36 l)* **pineapple juice**
1 cup *(237 ml)* **sugar**
1 qt *(946 ml)* **ginger ale**
1 pkg, 10 oz *(284 g)* **frozen strawberries**

Add boiling water to jello and dissolve. Add cold water, fruit juices, and sugar. Add the ginger ale and berries when ready to serve.

Variation: The flavor and color of this tasty punch can be changed by using different flavors of jello.

Wanda's Orange Julius

Cannot do ahead   Yield: 3 cups (710 ml)

½ can, 6 oz *(177 ml)* orange juice
  concentrate
½ cup *(118 ml)* milk
½ cup *(118 ml)* water

¼ cup *(59 ml)* sugar
½ tsp *(2.5 ml)* vanilla
5-6 ice cubes

Put the above ingredients in a blender and blend until smooth — about 30 seconds. Serve immediately. Double recipe to get 6 cups (1.42 l).

Ginger Ale Punch For A Crowd

Serves: 90 four oz
(118 ml) servings

1 qt *(946 ml)* orange juice
1 qt *(946 ml)* grapefruit juice
1 qt *(946 ml)* pineapple juice
1 cup *(237 ml)* lemon juice

1 cup *(237 ml)* lime juice
sugar to taste
8 qts *(7.58 l)* ginger ale, room
  temperature

Blend all fruit juices and sugar. Freeze into ice cubes or a fruit ring garnished with strawberries or cherries and sprigs of mint. Pour ginger ale over to serve.

Creamy Instant Hot Chocolate

1 box, 8 qt *(7.58 l)* nonfat dry milk
  powder
1 box, 2 lb *(908 g)* chocolate
  flavored drink mix

1 jar, 6 oz *(170 g)* powdered
  creamer
½ cup *(118 ml)* powdered sugar

Mix all ingredients thoroughly and store in an airtight container. Use ½ cup (118 ml) of mixture in a cup and finish filling with boiling water. Stir well. Keeps indefinitely.

Aunt Susan's Lemonade

Yield: 1½ qts (1.42 l)

2 cups *(474 ml)* sugar
2½ cups *(592 ml)* water
juice of 6 lemons

juice of 2 oranges
rind of 1 orange, grated

Boil sugar and water 5 minutes. Cool; add remaining ingredients.

Lemon Iced Tea

Yield: 1 gal (3.79 l)

½ gal *(1.89 l)* water
2 cups *(474 ml)* sugar

2 family size tea bags
1 can, 6 oz *(177 ml)* lemonade

Bring water to a boil. Add sugar and tea bags. Allow to cool. Add lemonade and enough water to add up to one gallon (3.79 l).

Apricot Iced Tea

Serves: 6

4 cups *(946 ml)* water
6 tea bags, small
¾ - 1 cup *(177 ml - 237 ml)* sugar
1 can, 12 oz *(354 ml)* apricot nectar

juice of 4 lemons
2 oz *(59 ml)* rum OR 4 oz *(118 ml)* apricot liqueur, optional

Boil water in covered pot. Put in tea bags and turn heat off. Leave bags in 4-5 minutes. Add sugar, apricot nectar, and lemon juice. Pour over ice while still warm.

Add rum or apricot liqueur just prior to serving, if desired.

Russian Tea

Can do ahead

Yield: 3½ qts (3.31 l)

1 qt *(946 ml)* water
4 regular tea bags
1 stick cinnamon
1 Tb *(15 ml)* whole cloves
2 qts *(1.89 l)* water

1 can, 6 oz *(177 ml)* frozen lemonade
1 can, 6 oz *(177 ml)* frozen orange juice
1 can, 6 oz *(177 ml)* pineapple juice
1½ cups *(355 ml)* sugar

Boil 1 quart water, tea bags, stick cinnamon, and whole cloves for 4 minutes. Strain into the 2 quarts water and add the lemonade, orange juice, pineapple juice and sugar. Stir all together and strain again. Serve hot.

Know Your Wines

APPETIZER WINES

light and highly flavored; served with hors d'oeuvres and cheese; alcoholic content rather high; usually served **chilled.**

Dubonnet
Madeira (dry)
Sherry (dry)
Vermouth

RED TABLE WINES

dry, slightly tart; served at **room temperature;** served with heavy entrées such as meat, game, starchy foods and cheese dishes.

DESSERT WINES

sweeter and heavier than table wines; served **chilled** or at cool room temperature; serve with desserts, fruits, nuts, cakes, cookies or alone after the meal.

Bordeaux (sweet)
Madeira (sweet or medium)
Muscatel
Angelica
Port

Sherry (sweet or medium)
Sauterne (sweet)
Tokay
Cream (sweet) Sherry

WHITE TABLE WINES

delicate flavors; usually served **chilled**; served with light entrées such as fish, fowl (especially white meat) and eggs.

Sauterne (dry)
Rhine wine
Chablis (White Burgundy)
Graves (White Bordeaux)
Moselle

SPARKLING WINES

bubbling; served anytime; appetizer, main course, desserts or alone. Serve **chilled**.

Champagne
Sparkling Burgundy

HOW MUCH YOU WILL NEED

Size of Bottle	Approximate Servings Per Bottle	
	Dinner and Sparkling (4 oz. servings)	Dessert Wines (3 oz. servings)
Fifth	6	8
Quart	8	11
Half Gallon	16	21
Gallon	32	42

Hors d'Oeuvres

Hors d'Oeuvres

Easy Hors d'Oeuvres

Mix bought deviled ham with chopped salted pecans. Two parts ham to one part nuts. Serve with thin rye bread.

Mix 1 cup *(237 ml)* sour cream with 3½ cups *(828 ml)* chopped canned French fried onion rings, to make a crunchy dip. Serve with Fritos.

Blend 3 oz *(85 g)* Roquefort cheese with 3 Tb *(45 ml)* red wine or sherry and 3 Tb *(45 ml)* melted butter. Chill.

Soak cheddar cheese cubes in port or sherry wine. Refrigerate at least a week. Drain to serve on toothpicks.

Cream 3 oz *(85 g)* Roquefort cheese and blend with 2 stiffly beaten egg whites. Spread on crackers or toast.

Simmer link sausages in dry white wine for 10 minutes. Drain and serve on toothpicks.

Blend 1 can condensed cream of mushroom soup with 1 roll of garlic cheese. Serve warm in chafing dish with toast.

Brush any cracker *(even saltines)* with melted butter. Sprinkle with any combination of celery, onion, or garlic salt, caraway, dill, poppy or sesame seeds. Heat on cookie sheet at 350° *(177° C)* for 5 minutes.

Sprinkle bite-size pieces of raw chicken with salt and pepper. Coat chicken with beaten egg and milk mixture. Dredge with self-rising flour; fry. Serve on toothpicks.

Spread butter on Triscuits and sprinkle with lemon pepper marinade mix. Bake at 350° *(177° C)* until hot.

Fill raw mushroom caps with cream cheese and horseradish blended together with a little cream or milk.

Fill mushroom caps with sausage. Bake at 350° *(177° C)* for 20 minutes. Top with Parmesan cheese and broil 2 minutes.

Serve shrimp with dressing made of half mayonnaise, half chutney, and onion juice.

Mix 4 cups *(946 ml)* small shrimp, 1 pkg Good Seasons Italian dressing and 1 pt *(473 ml)* sour cream. Chill 1 hour. Serve with Melba toast.

Cut 4 slices of toast into 16 slices. Dip top of slice in Durkees dressing — about ½ cup *(118 ml)* — then in 1 can of crumbled onion rings. Bake at 350° (177° C) for 15 minutes.

Spread 1 can of deviled ham on bread. Then spread with softened cream cheese. Bake at 375° (191° C) until brown.

Mash 1 very ripe avocado. Blend in 1 grated hard cooked egg and 4 oz *(113 g)* cream cheese with the juice of 1 lemon, salt and pepper. Serve on crackers.

Peel and cube avocado into ¾" *(1.91 cm)* cubes. Roll in lemon juice, then in French dressing, then in crushed potato chips. Serve on toothpicks.

Spread slices of bread with cream cheese. Cut off crusts. Roll slice up and wrap in a strip of bacon. Fasten with a toothpick. Broil 10 minutes. Serve hot.

Split doughnuts through the center. Spread each half with butter and sprinkle with brown sugar. Toast in the oven until the butter and sugar have melted. Can cut each half in bite-size pieces.

Mix cream cheese and apricot preserves and spread on date nut bread.

Roll asparagus tips in boiled ham and serve with toothpicks.

Remove crusts from bread. Spread to edges with pimento cheese and a little butter creamed together. Roll up and chill. When ready to serve, toast slowly. Serve hot.

Cut large green olives in half lengthwise and remove pits. Mix cream cheese to a paste with mayonnaise. Roll into small balls and then into chopped nuts. Place between olive halves and press together.

Cut a slice from one end of a dill pickle. Remove center with an apple corer. Drain out as much liquid as possible. Fill center with tinted cream cheese or cheese-relish spread. Chill for 1 hour, then cut crosswise into ½ inch slices. May be decorated with caviar.

Tiny red or green peppers may be stuffed with cream cheese, chilled, and then cut in slices or sections.

Make an assorted cheese tray and garnish with apples and small bunches of grapes.

Cook chopped oysters and mushrooms together in a cream sauce. Serve hot in patty shells.

Fresh strawberries with stems are good to dip in a bowl of powdered sugar.

Combine 1 can, 15 oz (426 g) chili without beans, 1 cup (237 ml) cheddar cheese, shredded, and ½ tsp (2.5 ml) cayenne pepper. Heat until melted. Serve with corn chips. Yield: 2 cups (474 ml) .

Mix 8 oz (227 g) plain yogurt, 3 Tb (45 ml) strawberry jam, ¼ tsp (1.25 ml) cinnamon and 1 tsp (5 ml) grated lemon rind. Serve chilled with fruit dippers such as apple wedges, fresh pineapple wedges, or melon balls.

Wrap cocktail wieners in ready-to-bake refrigerator biscuits. Bake according to package directions. Serve with catsup or mustard.

Mix a block of cream cheese with desired amount of chopped pecans and chopped olives. Moisten with mayonnaise. Spread on thin slices of toast. Ripe olives may also be used.

Spread thin crackers with pimento cheese flavored with A-1 sauce and a dash of onion salt or grated onion.

Variety Sandwiches — on tiny biscuits spread either chicken salad, tuna, crab, or chopped ham.

Heat asparagus tips in butter until heated. Place on strips of buttered toast. Sprinkle with American cheese and put under broiler until the cheese melts.

Mix cream cheese with dates cut fine and chopped nuts. Add enough mayonnaise so it will spread. Put between buttered slices of wheat bread and cut into desired shapes.

Chop the leaves and stems of watercress very fine. Blend with mayonnaise and season with dry mustard. Spread on buttered rounds of toast or bread.

Cold Dips
Vegetables For Dipping

Use very fresh vegetables and serve cold and crisp. Arrange in varying colors on plate around dip.

Cauliflower — divided into small flowerets

Radishes — quartered lengthwise

Celery — sliced lengthwise

Carrots — sliced lengthwise or curled

Cucumbers — sliced lengthwise, peeled

Green Pepper Strips

Small Green Onions with stalks — cut part of ends off

Chinese Cabbage — roll up leaves

Mushrooms — sliced or small whole ones

Zucchini Squash — sliced lengthwise or across

Summer Squash — sliced

Raw Turnips — sliced

Cocktail Tomatoes — whole or halved

Broccoli — divided into small flowerets

All of the following cold dips will be easy and can be done ahead. The preparation time will be approximately 5-15 minutes.

GINGER DIP
Yield: 3 cups (710 ml)

1 cup *(237 ml)* **mayonnaise**
1 cup *(237 ml)* **sour cream**
¼ cup *(59 ml)* **onion, grated**
¼ cup *(59 ml)* **parsley, minced**
1 **can**, 5 oz *(140 g)* **water chestnuts, chopped**
3 Tb *(45 ml)* **or more chopped candied ginger**
1 **clove garlic, minced**
1 Tb *(15 ml)* **soy sauce**
dash Tabasco
salt and Accent

Combine and chill several hours. Serve as a dip or spread.

Variation: Omit ginger and soy sauce. Add ½ cup (118 ml) minced dill pickle and 1 tsp. (5 ml) dried dill weed.

MAYONNAISE DIP
Yield: 1½ cups (355 ml)

⅔ cup *(158 ml)* **mayonnaise**
⅔ cup *(158 ml)* **sour cream**
1 Tb *(15 ml)* **fresh dill**
1 Tb *(15 ml)* **fresh parsley**
1 Tb *(15 ml)* **onion, chopped**
½ tsp *(2.5 ml)* **salt**

Mix and chill the day before using. Serve with raw vegetables.

ASPARAGUS DIP
Yield: 1 cup (237 ml)

1 **can**, 14-16 oz *(397-454 g)* **asparagus spears, cut and drained**
½ cup *(118 ml)* **sour cream**
¼ tsp *(1.25 ml)* **Tabasco**
¼ tsp *(1.25 ml)* **dill weed**

Mix in blender. Serve with raw vegetables.

WASHINGTON DIP
Yield: 2 cups (474 ml)

¾ cup *(177 ml)* **sour cream**
¾ cup *(177 ml)* **mayonnaise**
1 Tb *(15 ml)* **fresh or dried parsley**
1 Tb *(15 ml)* **fresh, frozen, or dried chives**
1 Tb *(15 ml)* **Beau Monde or Bon Appetit seasoning**
1 tsp *(5 ml)* **dill weed**

Mix all ingredients. Store in refrigerator in sealed container. Will keep a long time. Use with fresh vegetables or on baked potatoes.

CURRY DIP
Yield: 2 cups (474 ml)

2 cups *(474 ml)* **mayonnaise**
1 Tb *(15 ml)* **curry powder**
1 tsp *(5 ml)* **lemon juice**
1 tsp *(5 ml)* **Worcestershire sauce**
1 tsp *(5 ml)* **A-1 sauce**
1 tsp *(5 ml)* **black pepper**
½ tsp *(2.5 ml)* **celery salt**
dash of Tabasco

Mix in order given and serve with raw vegetables.

BLEU CHEESE DIP
Yield: 2 cups (474 ml)

¼ lb *(114 g)* **bleu cheese**
4 oz *(113 g)* **cream cheese**
3 Tb *(45 ml)* **vermouth**
1 small garlic clove, minced
sour cream

Combine first 4 ingredients; add enough sour cream to thin. Serve with raw vegetables.

VEGETABLE DIP
Yield: 1½ cups (355 ml)

1 cup *(237 ml)* **mayonnaise**
1½ cups *(355 ml)* **chili sauce**
1 small onion, grated
2 heaping Tb *(30+ml)* **horseradish**
2 tsp *(10 ml)* **mustard seed**
Tabasco sauce to taste

Blend together and chill at least 1 hour before serving. Serve with shrimp or raw vegetables. Keeps for weeks!

Spinach Dip

Can do ahead

Yield: 4 cups (946 ml)
Preparing: 15 min

1 pkg, 10 oz *(284 g)* **frozen, chopped spinach**
1 cup *(237 ml)* **sour cream**
1 cup *(237 ml)* **mayonnaise**
½ cup *(118 ml)* **fresh parsley, chopped**

½ cup *(118 ml)* **green onion, chopped**
1 tsp *(5 ml)* **salt**
1 tsp *(5 ml)* **Beau Monde**
½ tsp *(2.5 ml)* **dill weed**
juice of 1 lemon

Thaw, drain and blot spinach dry. Mix well with other ingredients. Serve with potato chips.

Cucumber Dip

Can do ahead

Yield: 2½ cups (592 ml)
Preparing: 20 min

1 pkg, 8 oz *(227 g)* **cream cheese**
1 cup *(237 ml)* **mayonnaise**
1 medium **cucumber, grated;**
   reserve juice and add last
½ **onion, grated**
⅓ tsp *(1.6 ml)* **celery salt**

⅓ tsp *(1.6 ml)* **salt**
¼ tsp *(1.25 ml)* **garlic salt**
½ cup *(118 ml)* **sour cream**
2 or 3 drops **green food**
   coloring

Combine in order given. Cream with mixer.

Kentucky Derby Cheese Dip

A different flavor for cheese

Can do ahead
Can freeze

Yield: 5 cups (1.18 l)
Preparing: 20 min

2 lb *(908 g)* **sharp cheese, grated**
½ medium **onion, chopped fine**
2 **garlic cloves, chopped fine**

1 tsp *(5 ml)* **Worcestershire**
   sauce
¼ tsp *(1.25 ml)* **cayenne pepper**
1 can, 12 oz *(340 g)* **stale beer**

Heat beer to simmer. Blend remaining ingredients with an electric mixer. Chill. Will keep for months.

Clam Dip

Must do ahead
Can freeze

Yield: 1½ cups (355 ml)
Preparing: 10 min.

1 can, 7½ oz *(212 g)* **clams,**
   minced
2 tsp *(10 ml)* **parsley, chopped**
1 pkg, 8 oz *(227 g)* **cream cheese**
2 Tb *(30 ml)* **mayonnaise**

2 tsp *(10 ml)* **onion, chopped**
1 tsp *(5 ml)* **Worcestershire**
   sauce
Dash of hot pepper sauce

Drain clams and combine with remaining ingredients. Mix well. Chill for several hours to blend flavors. Serve with crackers.

Dipsidoodle Crab Dip

Can do ahead

Serves: 8-10
Preparing: 10 min

1 cup *(227 g)* **sour cream**
¼ cup *(59 ml)* **mayonnaise**
½ lb *(227 g)* **crabmeat,**
  fresh or frozen
1 Tb *(15 ml)* **onion, grated**

1 Tb *(15 ml)* **lemon juice**
½ tsp *(2.5 ml)* **Worcestershire**
  sauce
salt and pepper to taste

Combine all ingredients and chill thoroughly. Delicious using "Bugles" for dipping.

Shrimp And Horseradish Dip

Can do ahead
Can freeze

Yield: 1 pint (474 ml)

2 pkgs, 3 oz *(85 g)* **cream cheese**
⅛ tsp *(.6 ml)* **red pepper**
⅓ cup *(79 ml)* **catsup**
1 tsp *(5 ml)* **onion juice**

½ tsp *(2.5 ml)* **Worcestershire**
  sauce
1 tsp *(5 ml)* **horseradish**
½ lb *(227 g)* **cooked shrimp,**
  chopped
salt to taste

Blend all ingredients together. Serve with Triscuits or cracker of your choice.

CHAFING DISHES

Hot Mushrooms In Sour Cream

Can do ahead

Serves: 8-10
Preparing: 10 min
Cooking: 10 min

6 Tb *(90 ml)* **butter**
1 clove **garlic, minced**
1 lb *(454 g)* **fresh mushrooms,**
  sliced
2 Tb *(30 ml)* **parsley flakes**

½ tsp *(2.5 ml)* **salt**
¼ tsp *(1.25 ml)* **pepper**
1 Tb *(15 ml)* **flour or more**
  to thicken
1 cup *(237 ml)* **sour cream**

Melt butter, add garlic, mushrooms, parsley flakes, salt and pepper. Sauté, stirring frequently until mushrooms are tender. Stir in flour and sour cream. Blend well. Serve hot from chafing dish with Melba Toast. Can be made ahead and heated slowly before serving.

Hot Crabmeat Spread

Serve warm or cold

Can do ahead

Serves: 6
Preparing: 15 min
Baking: 15 min

1 can, 7¾ oz *(230 g)* crabmeat
OR 1 pkg, 6 oz *(170 g)* frozen
Wakefield crabmeat
1 pkg, 8 oz *(227 g)* cream cheese
3 Tb *(45 ml)* sherry or white wine

½ tsp *(2.5 ml)* horseradish
2 Tb *(30 ml)* onion, minced
dash of Tabasco and
Worcestershire sauce

Soften cream cheese and mix all ingredients. Place in shallow 9 x 9 inch (22.86 x 22.86 cm) pan or 1 quart (946 ml) casserole. Sprinkle with paprika and bake in 350° (177° C) oven until bubbly and light brown — about 15 minutes. Serve with crackers or toast.

Hot Cheese Dip With Apple Slices

Can do ahead

Yield: 4 cups (946 ml)
Preparing: 15 min
Cooking: 10 min

6 slices of bacon
1 pkg, 8 oz *(227 g)* cream cheese
2 cups *(474 ml)* or ½ lb *(227 g)*
cheddar cheese, shredded
6 Tb *(90 ml)* half and half cream
1 tsp *(5 ml)* Worcestershire
sauce

¼ tsp *(1.25 ml)* dry mustard
¼ tsp *(1.25 ml)* onion salt
3 drops Tabasco sauce
unpared apples, cut in wedges
lemon juice

Cut bacon into ¼ inch (.64 cm) slices; sauté until crisp; drain on absorbent paper. Meanwhile, in top of double boiler or in heavy sauce pan, combine the next seven ingredients. Heat over hot water or over low heat, stirring occasionally, until cheese melts and mixture is hot. Add bacon pieces. Use this as a dip for apple wedges which have been dipped in lemon juice. The dip may be served in a chafing dish and will hold well for several hours if stirred occasionally. If mixture becomes too thick, more half and half can be added. Red Delicious apples are good with this dip.

Pecan Dip

Serve hot or room temperature

Can do ahead

Serves: 15-20
Preparing: 20 min
Cooking: 20 min

1 pkg, 8 oz *(227 g)* **cream cheese**
2 Tb *(30 ml)* **milk**
½ cup *(118 ml)* **sour cream**
¼ cup *(59 ml)* **green pepper,
chopped**
1 Tb *(15 ml)* **onion, minced**

½ tsp *(2.5 ml)* **garlic salt**
1 jar, 2½ oz *(71 g)* **dried beef**
2 Tb *(30 ml)* **butter**
½ cup *(118 ml)* **pecans,
coarsely chopped**
½ tsp *(2.5 ml)* **salt**

Blend cream cheese, milk and sour cream. Add green pepper, onion and garlic salt. Shred dried beef into small pieces. Fold beef into cream cheese mixture and turn into an 8 inch (20.32 cm) pie plate or ovenproof dish. In small skillet melt butter. Add salt and pecans. Sauté until crisp. Sprinkle on top of cheese mixture. Bake at 350° (177° C) for 20 minutes. Serve hot with crackers.

Variation: Add 1 can, 4 oz (113 g) mushrooms, drained.

Sausage Balls

Can do ahead
Can freeze

Serves: 8-10
Preparing: 20 min
Cooking: 30 min

1 lb *(454 g)* **hot OR mild bulk
pork sausage**
1 egg, slightly beaten
⅓ cup *(79 ml)* **seasoned bread
crumbs OR herb stuffing mix**
¼ tsp *(1.25 ml)* **ground sage**

¼ cup *(59 ml)* **catsup**
¼ cup *(59 ml)* **chili sauce**
1 Tb *(15 ml)* **soy sauce**
2 Tb *(30 ml)* **brown sugar**
1 Tb *(15 ml)* **vinegar**
½ cup *(118 ml)* **water**

Combine first four ingredients and mix thoroughly. Shape into balls the size of a quarter. Brown on all sides in dry skillet. Drain on paper towels. Drain fat from skillet; then add catsup, chili sauce, soy sauce, brown sugar, vinegar and water. Stir well. Return meatballs to skillet; cover and simmer for 30 minutes.

This can be refrigerated or frozen. When ready to serve, reheat, place in chafing dish, and serve with cocktail picks.

Sweet And Sour Meatballs

Can do ahead
Can freeze

Yield: 48 meatballs
Preparing: 45 min
Cooking: 45 min

MEATBALLS:

¾ lb *(340 g)* ground beef
1 Tb *(15 ml)* Worcestershire sauce
¼ lb *(113 g)* ground pork OR
  pure pork sausage
¾ cup *(177 ml)* rolled oats
½ cup *(118 ml)* milk

¼ cup *(59 ml)* water chestnuts,
  finely chopped
½ tsp *(2.5 ml)* onion salt
½ tsp *(2.5 ml)* garlic salt
few drops hot pepper sauce
2 Tb *(30 ml)* butter

Combine all ingredients except butter. Shape into balls and brown in butter. Drain on paper towels and add to sweet and sour sauce. Simmer 30 minutes in sauce. Serve in chafing dish with toothpicks. If frozen, thaw meatballs the day of serving. Make sauce the day of serving.

SWEET and SOUR SAUCE:

1 cup *(237 ml)* sugar
¾ cup *(177 ml)* vinegar
¾ cup *(177 ml)* water
1 tsp *(5 ml)* paprika

½ tsp *(2.5 ml)* salt
2 Tb *(30 ml)* cornstarch
1 Tb *(15 ml)* cold water

Combine first 5 ingredients. Cook 5 minutes. Blend cornstarch with water and add to hot mixture. Cook until thick.

Appetizer Cheese Meatballs

Can do ahead
Can freeze

Yield: 6 dozen
Preparing: 20 min
Cooking: 3 to 5 min

1½ lbs *(680 g)* ground beef
1 pkg, 3 oz *(85 g)* Roquefort cheese,
  crumbled
¾ tsp *(3.7 ml)* salt

⅛ tsp *(.6 ml)* pepper
½ cup *(118 ml)* Burgundy wine
  OR beef bouillon

Combine first 4 ingredients. Shape into balls using one heaping teaspoonful of meat mixture for each. Brown meatballs in butter. Add wine or bouillon and cover. Cook slowly 3 to 5 minutes. Serve in a chafing dish.

Cocktail Meatballs With Madeira Sauce

Can do ahead

Can freeze

Serves 25-30

Chilling: 2 hours

Preparing: 1 hour

MEATBALLS:

6 Tbs *(90 ml)* onions, finely chopped

4 Tbs *(60 ml)* butter

⅔ cup *(158 ml)* fine bread crumbs

2 cups *(474 ml)* half and half

2 lbs *(908 g)* ground round

2 eggs

3 tsp *(15 ml)* salt

½ tsp *(2.5 ml)* pepper

¼ tsp *(1.25 ml)* nutmeg

Sauté onion in butter until brown. Soak crumbs in half and half. Combine all ingredients until smooth. Chill 2 hours. Shape into balls about 1 teaspoon *(5 ml)* each. Fry in butter until evenly browned. Place all meatballs in glass chafing dish container. Pour the following sauce over meatballs and warm before serving. Garnish with snipped parsley.

SAUCE:

1 chicken bouillon cube

1 cup *(237 ml)* water

¼ cup *(59 ml)* Madeira wine

Heat the three sauce ingredients and dissolve bouillon cube completely.

May be frozen, sauce and all. If so, bake at 350° *(177° C)* until bubbly.

Hot Buttered Brie With Almonds

A delectable delight

Serve immediately

Serves: 4-6

Preparing: 5 min

Baking: 15 min

1 medium wheel of well-ripened Brie

½ to ¾ *(59 to 90 ml)* stick of butter, softened

1 cup *(237 ml)* slivered almonds, mildly toasted

Place cheese in a large oven-proof serving dish. Spread top of cheese with softened butter. Add slivered almonds on top of Brie. Cover and bake at 325° (163° C) for 15 minutes or until cheese is soft and creamy. Serve on round platter with assorted crackers.

Barbequed Corned Beef

Can do ahead

Serves: 24
Preparing: 25 min
Cooking: 15 min

6-8 slices bacon
1 medium green pepper, chopped
1 large onion, chopped
1 can, 12 oz *(340 g)* corned beef
1 cup *(237 ml)* oily French
  dressing
1 can, 3 oz *(85 g)* chopped
  mushrooms, drained

1 Tb *(15 ml)* Worcestershire
  sauce
1 tsp *(5 ml)* chili powder
1 cup *(237 ml)* cheddar cheese,
  grated
¼ cup *(59 ml)* catsup
1 Tb *(15 ml)* mustard
rye crackers

Cook bacon until crisp. Brown onion and green pepper in 1 Tb *(15 ml)* bacon grease. Add corned beef. Continue cooking until beef is stringy. Add mushrooms, Worcestershire sauce, and chili powder. Add cheese, stirring constantly until melted. Add dressing and continue cooking for 15 minutes, stirring occasionally. Add catsup and mustard and stir well. Serve hot with rye crackers. Taste improves if made one day ahead and reheated.

SPREADS

Easy Cream Cheese Spreads
Serve with crackers

almonds, blanched and slivered
butter

Major Grey's chutney
cream cheese

Toast almonds in a slow oven using a small amount of butter until they are golden brown. Stick them porcupine fashion into the sides of the cream cheese blocks. Ladle chutney that has been diced into manageable pieces over the top. Serve with sesame seed wafers.

VARIATION:
Top a block of cream cheese with Worcestershire or Pickapeppa Sauce, hot pepper jelly or a small jar of caviar.

Zippy Beef-Olive Spread

Can do ahead

Serves: 8-10
Preparing: 15 min

1 tsp *(5 ml)* **instant minced onion**
1 Tb *(15 ml)* **dry sherry**
1 pkg, 8 oz *(227 g)* **cream cheese**
2 Tb *(30 ml)* **mayonnaise**

1 pkg, 3 oz *(85 g)* **smoked sliced
beef, finely chopped**
¼ cup *(59 ml)* **stuffed green
olives, chopped**

Soften minced onion in sherry. Blend in cream cheese with mayonnaise into onion mixture. Stir in beef and olives. Serve with Triscuits or Wheat Thins. This is better if prepared the night before using.

Herbed Boursin

Must do ahead

Serves: 4-6
Preparing: 10 min

1 pkg, 8 oz *(227 g)* **cream cheese**
1 clove **garlic, crushed**
1 tsp *(5 ml)* **caraway seed**
1 tsp *(5 ml)* **basil**

1 tsp *(5 ml)* **dill weed**
1 tsp *(5 ml)* **chives, chopped**
lemon pepper

Blend cream cheese with garlic, caraway, basil, dill weed and chives. Pat into a round flat shape. Roll on all sides (lightly) in lemon pepper. Make a few days ahead. Serve with assorted crackers.

Stuffed Edam Ball

Can do ahead
Can freeze

Yield: 1 ball
Preparing: 20 min

1 ball **Edam cheese, room
temperature**
1 cup *(237 ml)* **beer**
¼ cup *(59 ml)* **butter**

1 tsp *(5 ml)* **caraway seed**
1 tsp *(5 ml)* **dry mustard**
½ tsp *(2.5 ml)* **celery salt**

Slice one inch (2.54 cm) off top of Edam. Scoop out and reserve cheese. Return shell to refrigerator. Mash cheese and add remaining ingredients, re-stuffing shell. Serve with rye or pumpernickel bread.

Roquefort Mousse

Must do ahead

Yield: 6 cup (1.42) mold
Preparing: 30 min

1 envelope unflavored gelatin
¼ cup *(59 ml)* lemon juice
1 cup *(237 ml)* boiling water
¼ lb *(113 g)* Roquefort cheese
1 cup *(237 ml)* cucumber, grated
4 Tbs *(60 ml)* parsley, minced
2 Tbs *(30 ml)* pimento, minced

1 Tbs *(15 ml)* capers, minced
1 tsp *(5 ml)* onion, grated
dash salt
dash pepper
1 cup *(237 ml)* heavy cream,
 whipped

Soften gelatin in lemon juice and dissolve in boiling water. Mash Roquefort cheese and combine with cucumber, parsley, pimento, capers, and onion. Add salt and pepper to taste. Stir in the dissolved gelatin. Cool and chill the mixture just until it begins to gel. Fold in whipped cream. Spread the mousse in a 6 cup (1.42 l) ring and chill for 4 hours or until completely firm. Unmold on chilled serving platter.

SERVING SUGGESTIONS: Fill center with a seafood salad and garnish with parsley dusted with paprika. Complete your menu with asparagus in vinaigrette dressing. This can also be done in a different shape mold and served with crackers or melba toast.

Cheese And Strawberries

Can do ahead

Serves: 24
Preparing: 20 min

1 lb *(454 g)* sharp cheese, grated
1 cup *(237 ml)* nuts, chopped
1 cup *(237 ml)* mayonnaise
1 small onion, grated

dash of salt, pepper,
 and cayenne pepper
1 jar, 12 oz *(340 g)* strawberry
 preserves

Combine all ingredients except preserves. Refrigerate. One hour before serving, form into a ring mold and put strawberry preserves in the middle. Serve with crackers.

Artichoke Spread

Can do ahead

Yield: 3 cups (710 ml)
Preparing: 5 min
Baking: 20-30 min

1 cup *(237 ml)* mayonnaise
1 can, 14 oz *(397 g)* artichokes,
drained OR Seabrook frozen

1 cup *(237 ml)* Parmesan cheese

Mix with mixer in order given. Heat in moderate oven for 20-30 minutes. Dip or spread on toast rounds.

Molded Egg Salad

Must do ahead

Serves: 12
Preparing: 45 min

18 hard-boiled eggs, shelled
½ cup *(118 ml)* green pepper,
chopped
¼ cup *(59 ml)* pimento, diced
⅓ cup *(79 ml)* celery, finely cut
3 Tb *(45 ml)* chili sauce

2 Tb *(30 ml)* parsley, chopped
1 medium onion, minced fine
2 pkgs, 8 oz *(227 g)* cream cheese
½ cup *(118 ml)* mayonnaise
salt and pepper to taste

Mash eggs and add green pepper, pimento, celery, parsley and onion. Mash cream cheese, stir in mayonnaise and chili sauce. Combine with egg mixture and season with salt and pepper. Shape into a ring mold and chill 4 or 5 hours.

Shrimp Mold

Must do ahead

Yield: 5 cup (1.18 l) mold
Preparing: 30 min

1 pkg, 8 oz *(227 g)* cream cheese
1 cup *(237 ml)* celery, chopped
¾ cup *(177 ml)* onion, chopped
1 cup *(237 ml)* mayonnaise

2 cans, 4½ oz *(128 g)* tiny
shrimp, drained
salt and pepper
1 can tomato soup, warmed
1½ Tb *(22.5 ml)* gelatin, dissolved

Combine cream cheese, celery, onion, mayonnaise, salt and pepper to taste. Mix well and add shrimp. Dissolve gelatin in small amount of cold water and mix with warm soup. Add to other ingredients and pour into a 5 cup (1.18 l) mold. Chill for several hours.

Salmon Supreme

Wow your guests with a beautifully decorated salmon

Can do ahead

Serves: 16 to 20
Preparing: 45 min

2 cans, 16 oz *(454 g)* **pink salmon**
1½ pkgs, 8 oz *(227 g)* **cream
cheese**
5 Tb *(75 ml)* **lemon juice**
4 Tb *(60 ml)* **onion, diced**
2 Tb *(30 ml)* **prepared horseradish**

½ tsp *(2.5 ml)* **salt**
parsley, chopped
pecans, chopped
chives, chopped
hard-boiled egg slices

Mix first six ingredients and shape into ball. Roll in parsley, pecans and chives and place on platter. Serve with crackers.

GARNISHING IDEAS — see drawing:
Mold mixture into shape of a fish. Cover head with pecans, separating head from body with thin strip of pimento. Cover body with parsley. Place egg white slices so as to resemble fins. Use sliced olive for eye and pimento for mouth.

Steak Tartare

Can do ahead

Serves: 4
Preparing: 10 min

1 lb *(454 g)* **ground round steak**
1 onion, chopped
1½ tsp *(7.5 ml)* **mustard**
¼ jar, 3½ oz *(99 g)* **capers,
drained**

2 Tb *(30 ml)* **Real Lemon**
2 raw egg yolks
salt
pepper
parsley, chopped

Combine all ingredients except parsley. Mold into desired shape and cover with parsley. Serve with crackers. Keeps for several days in the refrigerator.

Caviar Surprise

Delicious and unusual

Can do ahead

Serves: 12-16
Preparing: 20 min

2 jars, 3½ oz *(99 g)* caviar
1 pt *(474 ml)* sour cream
1 can, 8½ oz *(241 g)* artichoke
  hearts

½ onion, diced
½ tsp *(2.5 ml)* parsley
1½ tsp *(7.5 ml)* chives
3 hard-boiled eggs, diced

Combine all ingredients except caviar. Add 1½ jars of caviar, then taste before adding more. Stir very gently so caviar eggs don't pop. If not too salty, add more caviar saving some for garnishing. Garnish with parsley and serve with cocktail rye bread.

Mock Caviar

Must do ahead

Yield: 2 cups (474 ml)
Preparing: 45 min

1 large eggplant
2 Tb *(30 ml)* oil
1 small onion, chopped fine
1 garlic clove, minced
1 tsp *(5 ml)* coarse ground pepper

¼ cup *(59 ml)* green pepper,
  chopped fine
1½ Tb *(22.5 ml)* lemon juice
1 tsp *(5 ml)* salt

Slice eggplant in half and oil the flat surface. Place halves flat side down on a baking pan. Broil 3″ from heat 20-25 minutes or until soft. Remove skin and mash pulp. Sauté onion and garlic and remaining ingredients in oil. Chill 3 hours. Serve with crackers.

FINGER FOODS

Cocktail Rounds

Can do ahead

Yield: 1½ cups (355 ml)
Preparing: 5 min

1 cup *(237 ml)* mayonnaise
1 medium onion, grated
½ cup *(118 ml)* Parmesan cheese

paprika
bread

Mix the first three ingredients. Spread on a slice of bread and then cut bread into quarters. Place on cookie sheet and sprinkle with paprika. Bake at 400° (204° C) for 8 to 10 minutes.

Toastettes

Can do ahead

Yield: 60-75
Preparing: ½ hr
Baking: 30 min

1 cup *(237 ml)* margarine, softened
2 Tb *(30 ml)* sesame seeds, toasted
2 Tb *(30 ml)* dried parsley
1 Tb *(15 ml)* freeze-dried chives

1 tsp *(5 ml)* dried tarragon
1 tsp *(5 ml)* sweet marjoram
1 loaf Arnold or Pepperidge
    Farm sandwich bread

Mix first six ingredients; spread on bread slices. Cut bread into thirds or smaller. Bake at 200° (93° C) 30 minutes on cookie sheets. Turn off oven and leave 1 hour. Cool on paper towels. Store in tins for several weeks.

Welcome Wafers

Can do ahead
Can freeze

Yield: 48
Chilling: 60 min
Baking: 8-10 min

¾ cup *(177 ml)* butter, softened
½ cup *(118 ml)* cheddar cheese,
    shredded
½ cup *(118 ml)* bleu cheese,
    crumbled

⅛ tsp *(.6 ml)* garlic, minced
1 tsp *(5 ml)* minced parsley
1 tsp *(5 ml)* chopped chives
2 cups *(474 ml)* flour, sifted

Cream butter with cheeses. Add dry ingredients; mix and shape in 1½ inch roll and chill. Slice thinly and bake 375° (191° C) on ungreased cookie sheet 8-10 minutes. Keeps for weeks if stored in tin cans. The dough as well as the baked wafers can be frozen.

Cookie Press Cheese Straws

Can do ahead
Can freeze

Yield: 150
Preparing: 1 hr
Baking: 10 min

1 lb *(454 g)* sharp cheddar
    cheese, grated
2¾ sticks *(326 ml)* margarine,
    softened
1 tsp *(5 ml)* Tabasco sauce

4 scant cups *(946 ml)* flour, sifted
1 tsp *(5 ml)* paprika
2 tsp *(10 ml)* salt
cayenne pepper to taste

Blend cheese, margarine and Tabasco; set aside. Sift flour, paprika, salt and cayenne pepper. Sift flour mixture gradually over cheese mixture; work like pastry. Knead until soft and well blended. Use the "star" pattern of cookie press or Play Dough Fun Factory; turn out in 3 inch lengths on ungreased cookie sheet. Bake 10 minutes or until golden brown in 400° (204° C) oven. Remove immediately to cake rack; cool completely before storing. Dough ball may be stored in refrigerator for later use.

Cream Puffs For Hors d'Oeuvres

An easy way to make cream puffs that are light and airy

Can do ahead
Can freeze

Yield: approx 100
Preparing: 15 min
Baking: 20 min

½ cup *(118 ml)* butter
1 cup *(237 ml)* water, boiling
1 cup *(237 ml)* plain flour

½ tsp *(2.5 ml)* salt
4 eggs

Put butter in boiling water till melted. Add flour, salt and stir vigorously over low heat until dough forms a ball in middle of pan. Cool for a minute. Add one egg at a time — beating till all trace of egg disappears (done by hand with a table fork). Drop from teaspoon on greased cookie sheet in small-size balls (size of moth ball). Cook in 375° (191° C) oven 15 to 25 minutes depending on oven heat. Check at end of 15 minutes. This recipe makes 150 bite size or 80-100 small-sized puffs that can be frozen for months. Reheat when thawing them. At serving time they can be filled with your choice from chocolate to lobster salad. Heat at 375° (191° C) for 4 minutes. This recipe will fill 5 cookie sheets. Takes time, but can all be done in advance.

Cream Puff Fillings

CREAM CHEESE AND
ROQUEFORT:
1 pkg, 3 oz *(85 g)* cream cheese
Roquefort cheese to taste
dry Sherry to moisten

Blend well.

DEVILED HAM:
2 pkg, 3 oz *(85 g)* cream
cheese, softened
1 can, 2¼ oz *(64 g)* deviled ham
catsup to moisten

Blend well.

OTHER SUGGESTED FILLINGS:
Chicken, tuna, lobster, or egg salad may be used.

Stuffed Celery Appetizers

Can do ahead

Yield: 25-30 pieces
Preparing: 10 min

1 pkg, 8 oz *(227 g)* cream cheese,
softened
⅓ cup *(79 ml)* pecans, minced
¼ cup *(59 ml)* catsup

2 Tb *(30 ml)* stuffed green olives,
minced
1 tsp *(5 ml)* onion, grated
10 celery stalks cut into 2½"
(6.35 cm) pieces

Mix cream cheese, pecans, catsup, olives, and onion until well blended. Fill celery stalks. Garnish with chopped celery if desired.

Sharp Cheddar Cheese Canape

Can partially do ahead
Can freeze

Yield: 20
Preparing: 20 min

2 oz *(59 g)* **sharp cheddar cheese, shredded**
1 oz *(28 g)* **bleu cheese, crumbled**
2 oz *(59 g)* **butter, softened**
2 oz *(59 g)* **cream cheese, softened**
1 Tb *(15 ml)* **sherry wine**

¼ tsp *(1.25 ml)* **Worcestershire sauce**
3 drops **Tabasco**
5 slices **whole grain bread**
mandarin orange slices

Cream all ingredients together. You can make this part ahead and refrigerate, but take it out of the refrigerator ½ hour before using. Quarter and crust 5 slices of Wild's Whole Grain bread. (You can find it in the gourmet section of the grocery store.) Use a decorating bag to pipe the cheese onto the bread. Garnish with mandarin orange slices.

Dried Beef Roll-Ups

Can do ahead

Serves: 16-20
Preparing: 30 min

¼ lb *(113 g)* **sliced dried beef**
2 pkgs, 3 oz *(85 g)* **cream cheese**
3 tsp *(15 ml)* **onions, grated**

2 tsp *(10 ml)* **prepared horseradish**
dash of Worcestershire sauce
2 Tb *(30 ml)* **white wine**

Rinse the dried beef in cold water. Dry. Combine the remaining ingredients. Beat until creamy. Add an extra teaspoon or two (5-10 ml) of wine if needed. Place small amount of mixture on each slice of dried beef. If the slices are large, cut them in half. Roll up; fasten with toothpick. Chill thoroughly, covered with foil. Cut in 1 inch (2.54 cm) pieces, spear with toothpicks.

BOLOGNA WEDGIES:

½ lb *(227 g)* **bologna, thinly sliced**
1 pkg, 3 oz *(85 g)* **cream cheese, softened**
2 Tb *(30 ml)* **cream**
1 Tb *(15 ml)* **fresh horseradish, grated**

Blend all four ingredients well. Spread bologna slices and stack like a layer cake. Chill, then cut into wedges. Spear with a toothpick.

PASTRAMI ROLLS:

1 pkg, 8 oz *(227 g)* **cream cheese, softened**
2 tsp *(10 ml)* **Pickapeppa Sauce OR Worcestershire sauce**
Crazy salt, as desired
4 pkgs **Pastrami (that comes in thin squares)**

Mix first 3 ingredients. Spread on each slice of pastrami and roll each piece up like a jelly roll. Cut each roll in thirds. Serve with toothpicks.

Gougère

Serve immediately

1 cup *(237 ml)* **water**
6 Tb *(90 ml)* **butter**
1 tsp *5 ml)* **salt**
⅛ tsp *(.6 ml)* **pepper**

1 cup *(237 ml)* **flour**
4 **eggs**
1 cup minus 2 Tb *(207 ml)* **Gruyère cheese, finely diced**

Preheat oven to 425° (218° C). Place water, butter, salt and pepper in a saucepan and heat until butter melts and the mixture begins to boil rapidly. Add flour to mixture all at once and continue stirring until it forms a ball and leaves side of pan clean — this takes only a minute or so. Remove pan from heat and beat in eggs, one at a time, being sure to blend each in completely before adding the next. Stir in Gruyère cheese. Now, on a lightly greased cookie sheet, place rounded tablespoons of the dough, touching each other in the shape of a ring about 8 or 9 inches (20.32 or 22.86 cm) in diameter. Sprinkle dough with rest of Gruyère and bake 40-45 minutes or until puffed and golden brown. Serve fresh from oven sliced in wedges.

Sauerkraut Balls

Can partially do ahead
Can freeze

½ lb *(227 g)* **lean boneless ham**
½ lb *(227 g)* **lean boneless pork**
½ lb *(227 g)* **corned beef**
1 medium **onion, chopped fine**
1 tsp *(5 ml)* **parsley, minced**
3 Tb *(45 ml)* **shortening**
2 cups *(474 ml)* **flour**
1 tsp *(5 ml)* **dry mustard**

1 tsp *(5 ml)* **salt**
2 cups *(474 ml)* **milk**
2 lbs *(908 g)* **sauerkraut, chopped**
4 **eggs**
bread crumbs
shortening

Grind meats together or process in food processor. Add onion and parsley. Blend well. Brown in shortening. Gradually add flour, mustard, salt and milk. Continue to cook, stirring constantly, until thick. Drain sauerkraut well. Add to meat mixture and cook stirring constantly until very thick. Refrigerate. Form into balls the size of a walnut. Slightly beat the eggs. Dip balls in egg then roll in dry bread crumbs. Fry in hot, deep fat until brown. These freeze well — reheat in oven to serve — no need to thaw. Do not double recipe — too bulky.

Asparagus Roll-Ups

Can do ahead
Can freeze

Yield: 72
Preparing: 30-40 min
Baking: 15 min

18 slices of thin-sliced bread
8 oz *(227 g)* **Roquefort cheese**
8 oz *(227 g)* **cream cheese**
1 egg

1 Tb *(15 ml)* **mayonnaise**
1 can, 14½ oz *(411 g)* **asparagus**
spears
½ cup *(118 ml)* **butter, melted**

Make mixture of cheese, egg and mayonnaise. Cut crust from bread and roll flat. Spread with cheese mixture. Roll 1 stalk of asparagus in each slice of bread and cut into 3 pieces. Dip each piece into melted butter. Seams may need to be secured with a toothpick. Bake at 350° (177° C) 15 minutes or until browned.

Spinach Balls

Can do ahead
Must freeze

Yield: 30 balls
Preparing: 25 min
Cooking: 25 min

1 pkg, 10 oz *(284 g)* **frozen spinach**
1 cup *(237 ml)* **herb-seasoned**
stuffing mix
½ cup *(118 ml)* **Parmesan cheese,**
grated

3 eggs, beaten
6 Tb *(90 ml)* **butter, softened**

Cook spinach and drain very well. Combine all ingredients, mixing well. Roll into balls. Freeze. To serve, place on cookie sheet still frozen and bake for 25 minutes at 350° (177° C).

Artichoke Appetizers

Can partially do ahead

Serves: 12
Preparing: 10 min
Baking: 10 min

1 pkg, 8 oz *(227 g)* **cream cheese**
1 egg
chives
2 dashes Worcestershire sauce

1 dash Tabasco
2 Tb *(30 ml)* **butter**
1 can, 14 oz *(397 g)* **artichokes**
pie shells

Cream ingredients together. Put into individual small pie shells. Bake at 350° (177° C) for 30 minutes. These can also be made bite-sized and baked for 10 minutes. NOTE: The artichokes can be placed in the middle of each mixture or they can be cut up and creamed with mixture.

Mushroom Or Shrimp Turnovers

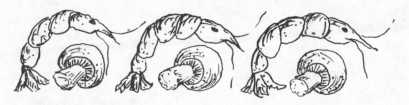

Can partially do ahead
Can freeze

Yield: 40
Preparing: 2 hr
Baking: 20 min

CREAM CHEESE PASTRY:

1 pkg, 8 oz *(227 g)* **cream cheese, softened**
½ lb *(227 g)* **butter OR margarine, softened**

dash of salt
2 cups *(474 ml)* **presifted flour**
1 egg yolk
2 tsp *(10 ml)* **cream OR milk**

Combine cheese, butter, and salt. Work in the flour with a fork or your fingers until a smooth dough is formed. Refrigerate for several hours or overnight before using. Roll dough on a floured surface to about ⅛ inch (.32 cm) thickness and cut into 3 inch (7.62 cm) round circles. Place a teaspoon of filling just off center on each circle. Fold dough over filling and crimp edges with a floured fork. Freeze turnovers uncovered on a tray. Place them in a plastic bag for freezer storage. When ready to serve, brush tops with beaten egg yolk and cream. Bake frozen turnovers in 375° (191° C) oven for 15-20 minutes.

SUGGESTED FILLINGS

MUSHROOM:

½ lb *(227 g)* **fresh mushrooms**
3 Tb *(45 ml)* **butter**
1 onion, minced
2 tsp *(10 ml)* **flour**

½ tsp *(2.5 ml)* **salt**
pepper to taste
1 tsp *(5 ml)* **dried dill**
½ cup *(118 ml)* **sour cream**

Wash mushrooms, trim off toughest stems and chop finely. Sauté onions and mushrooms in butter until tender. Add flour, salt and pepper. Cook for 1-2 minutes. Remove from heat and stir in sour cream and dill. Cool.

SHRIMP:

2 cans, 4½ oz *(128 g)* **shrimp**
3 green onions, chopped
2 tsp *(10 ml)* **spicy prepared mustard**

salt to taste
½ tsp *(2.5 ml)* **tarragon**
6 Tb *(90 ml)* **sour cream**

Drain and finely chop the shrimp. Thoroughly combine all ingredients.

Claverton Manor Cheese Biscuits

A favorite at Claverton Manor in England

Yield: 60
Preparing: 30 min
Chilling: 45 min
Baking: 25 min

2 cups *(474 ml)* self-rising flour
½ lb *(227 g)* butter
8 oz *(227 g)* cheddar cheese, finely grated
1 tsp *(5 ml)* salt

1 tsp *(5 ml)* pepper
1 tsp *(5 ml)* curry powder
2 egg yolks
almonds, finely chopped

Rub butter and flour into seasonings; add cheese and use egg yolks to bind. Chill well. Roll out thinly and cut into rounds. Brush with milk and press finely chopped almonds on tops. Bake at 325° (163° C) about 25 minutes or until brown and crisp.

Iced Cheese Squares

Can partially do ahead
Can freeze

Yield: 48
Preparing: 30 min
Baking: 10 min

2 jars Olde English cheese
1 egg
1 cup *(237 ml)* margarine, softened

1 large loaf thin sliced sandwich bread

Whip cheese, egg, and margarine in electric mixer until creamy. Trim bread (optional) and cut each slice into 4 squares. Use 2 squares, each time, and fill with mixture, also ice the sides and top of sandwich. Bake at 400° (204° C) for 10 minutes. Serve warm. Can bake these for 8 minutes and freeze to rebake for 2-3 minutes before serving.

Stuffed Mushrooms

Can do ahead

Yield: approx 30
Preparing: 20 min
Baking: 6-8 min

12 oz-1 lb *(340-454 g)* fresh mushrooms
1 Tb *(15 ml)* onion, chopped
1 tsp *(5 ml)* oil
¼ cup *(59 ml)* salami, finely chopped

¼ cup *(59 ml)* smoked cheese spread
1 Tb *(15 ml)* catsup
bread crumbs

Chop mushroom stems and sauté. Sauté onion in oil. Add salami, cheese spread, and catsup. Stuff crowns. Sprinkle crumbs on top. Bake at 425° (218° C).

Toasted Clam Rounds

Must do ahead

Yield: 24
Preparing: 5 min
Chilling: 2 hr
Broiling: 1 min

1 pkg, 8 oz *(227 g)* **cream cheese**
¼ tsp *(1.25 ml)* **garlic powder**
1 tsp *(5 ml)* **Worcestershire
   sauce**
pinch of salt

1 can, 7½ oz *(212 g)* **minced
   clams, drained**
24 Melba Toast rounds

Mash cream cheese; blend with garlic powder, Worcestershire and salt, beat until soft and creamy. Add clams. Chill two hours. Spoon mixture on Melba toast rounds, mounding high so that it will not run off (center should be about one inch high). Place on foil-lined cookie sheets, broil quickly until golden. Serve immediately.

Bacon Bites

Wrap a half slice of bacon around any of the following, securing with a toothpick. Broil until the bacon is crisp, or bake at 350° (177°C) until crisp.

pineapple chunks
canned peach chunks
cooked chicken livers
Brazil nuts
raw scallops
raw or canned oysters
luncheon meat cubes
Vienna sausages
artichoke hearts

hot dog chunks
stuffed olives
pitted prunes or dates
pickle chunks
pickled onions
cooked shrimp
watermelon rind
canned mushrooms

CHEESE ROLL-UPS

Trim crusts from thin sliced bread and spread lightly with Olde English cheese spread. Cut each slice in half. Roll bread up and wrap with ½ slice bacon. Secure with toothpick. Bake on broiler pan at 400° (204° C) until crisp. Turn once.

PITTED PRUNES

Prunes may be soaked for several days in Sherry and then stuffed with: pineapple chunks, split water chestnuts, or cheddar cheese cubes. Wrap with bacon piece and cook until bacon is done.

DATES

1 pkg, 8 oz *(227 g)* **pitted dates**
bacon, cut in thirds

Wrap dates with bacon and secure with toothpicks. Bake at 350° (177° C) about 15 minutes. Yields: approximately 3 dozen. Dried dates may be soaked in Sherry for 36 hours then split and filled with chopped nuts, cream cheese or both, or cheddar cheese. Wrap with bacon and bake.

CLUB CRACKERS

Wrap ½ slice of thin bacon around cracker. Place on broiler pan and bake about 10 minutes at 350° (177° C).

Marinated Water Chestnuts

1 can, 5 oz *(142 g)* **water chestnuts,**
  drained
¼ cup *(59 ml)* **soy sauce**

¼ cup *(59 ml)* **sugar**
bacon slices, cut in thirds
brown sugar

Marinate chestnuts in soy sauce 30 minutes. Cut larger chestnuts in half. Roll each chestnut in sugar, then wrap in bacon and secure with toothpick. Put on broiler rack, sprinkle with brown sugar. Bake at 400° (204° C) for 20 minutes. Drain on paper towel. Best when made in the morning and reheated that night at 350° (177° C) for 6-7 minutes.

Anchovy/Oysters

1 lb *(454 g)* **bacon**
1 tube, 2 oz *(57 g)* **anchovy paste**

2 jars, 12 oz *(340 g)* **oysters**

Cut bacon in half. Spread sparingly with paste and wrap around oysters. Secure with toothpicks and broil.

Mushroom-Bacon Wrap-Ups

1 can, 10¾ oz *(305 g)* **cream of**
  mushroom soup
10-15 slices of white bread

15-20 slices of bacon
35 wooden toothpicks

Trim crust off bread and cut each slice in 3 strips. Spread each strip with undiluted mushroom soup. Cut bacon in half and place each piece under bread strip and wrap tightly securing with a toothpick. Place on cookie sheet with sides and bake at 300° (149° C) for 1 hour. Can be made a day ahead. Yield: 35-45.

Marinated Broccoli

Must do ahead

Serves: 25
Preparing: 10 min
Chilling: 24 hr

3 bunches fresh broccoli, cut in
  small flowerettes
1 cup *(237 ml)* cider vinegar
1 Tb *(15 ml)* sugar
1 Tb *(15 ml)* dill weed
1 Tb *(15 ml)* Accent

1 tsp *(5 ml)* salt
1 tsp *(5 ml)* pepper
1 tsp *(5 ml)* garlic salt
1½ cups *(355 ml)* vegetable oil
1 head cauliflower florets
  (optional)

Mix all ingredients and pour over broccoli. Cover and refrigerate for 24 hours. Baste from time to time. Drain and serve. Will keep 5 days or more.

Marinated Cucumbers

Must do ahead

Serves: 8
Preparing: 20 min
Marinating: 2 hr

½ tsp *(2.5 ml)* salt
½ tsp *(2.5 ml)* sugar
½ tsp *(2.5 ml)* red pepper, cayenne
  if wanted hot
½ cup *(118 ml)* garlic wine
  vinegar
1 ctn whipping cream

2 tsp *(10 ml)* chives, chopped
OR 1 tsp *(5 ml)* onion, grated
1 tsp *(5 ml)* celery seeds
2-3 medium-size cucumbers,
  sliced and edges scored
  with fork tines, drained
1 Tb *(15 ml)* dill (optional)

Dissolve salt, sugar and pepper in wine vinegar. Whip cream until smooth and stiff. Add chives and celery seeds. Combine cucumbers with dressing and chill at least 2 hours. Serve in bowl with toothpicks on side.

Marinated Spinach

Must do ahead

Serves: 36-40
Preparing: 15 min

3 pkgs, 10 oz *(284 g)* frozen
  chopped spinach, thawed,
  drained and squeezed dry

2 bottles, 8 oz *(236 ml)*
  A & P Italian dressing

Marinate spinach in dressing overnight. Squeeze most of the liquid out when ready to serve. Put in a dish with small fork and serve with Triscuits only. (Other crackers will get soggy.)

Marinated Shrimp

Must do ahead

Serves: about 25
Preparing: 60 min
Marinating: overnight

5 lbs *(2.3 kg)* **shrimp**
1 Tb *(15 ml)* **salt**
1 pkg, 3 oz *(85 g)* **crab-boil**
1 jar, 14 oz *(396 ml)* **olive salad mix**

1 large onion, cut in rings
1 bottle, 8 oz *(227 g)* **Kraft**
  herb and garlic dressing
cherry tomatoes

Boil shrimp in crab-boil and salt for 15 minutes. Peel shrimp. Add all other ingredients except tomatoes and marinate overnight. Add tomatoes before serving.

Marinated Mushrooms

Must do ahead

Serves: 16-20
Preparing: 25 min
Cooking: 1 min
Chilling: 24 hr

2 lbs *(908 g)* **fresh button**
  mushrooms (OR canned)
¼ cup *(59 ml)* **lemon juice**
1 Tb *(15 ml)* **fresh OR dried parsley**
2 Tb *(30 ml)* **onion, finely chopped**
2 Tb *(30 ml)* **garlic, minced**
½ tsp *(2.5 ml)* **salt**

2 Tb *(30 ml)* **pimento, chopped**
⅛ tsp *(.6 ml)* **oregano**
⅛ tsp *(.6 ml)* **pepper**
½ tsp *(2.5 ml)* **sugar**
¼ cup *(59 ml)* **water**
¼ cup *(59 ml)* **oil**
½ cup *(118 ml)* **cider vinegar**

Clean the mushrooms. If they are large, slice so the pieces are bite-size and can be speared with a toothpick. Place the mushrooms in a pot. Cover with water and add the lemon juice. Bring to a boil and simmer for 1 minute. Drain. Mix the remaining ingredients and toss the mushrooms in the mixture. Store the mushrooms and the dressing in a covered container in the refrigerator. The mushrooms should marinate for 24 hours prior to serving. Drain the liquid off prior to serving and serve with toothpicks. Will keep 2 weeks in refrigerator.

Pickled Mushrooms And Onions

Must do ahead

Yield: 2 cups (474 ml)
Preparing: 5 min
Cooking: 5 min

⅓ cup *(79 ml)* **red wine vinegar**
⅓ cup *(79 ml)* **salad oil**
**1 small onion, thinly sliced and
separated into rings**
1 tsp *(5 ml)* **salt**

2 tsp *(10 ml)* **dried parsley flakes**
1 tsp *(5 ml)* **prepared mustard**
1 Tb *(15 ml)* **brown sugar**
2 cans, 6 oz *(170 g)* **mushroom
crowns, drained**

In small saucepan, combine all ingredients except mushrooms; bring to a boil. Add mushrooms; simmer 5 to 6 minutes. Pour into a bowl; cover; chill several hours or overnight, stirring occasionally. Drain; serve with cocktail picks.

Sea Shell Ice Ring

Can do ahead

Serves: 10-12
Preparing: 30 min

Fill a large mold (12 to 15 inches in diameter) about ⅓ full of water. Arrange sea shells in water with showy top sides down. Be sure the shells are completely covered with water so they will stay in place. Freeze. Fill remainder of mold with water and again freeze firm. Before serving time, remove ice ring from mold pretty side up. It is a good idea to use a rack on your serving tray so food will not be in water as ice melts. Cover rack with parsley or watercress. Place sauce in glass bowl in center of ice ring, and place shrimp surrounding ring.

PICKWICK SEAFOOD SAUCE

2 Tb *(30 ml)* **tarragon vinegar**
½ pint *(237 ml)* **mayonnaise**
½ tsp *(2.5 ml)* **Tabasco sauce**

1 tsp *(5 ml)* **anchovy paste**
½ pint *(237 ml)* **chili sauce**

Add anchovy paste to vinegar and blend till smooth. Add Tabasco and mix with mayonnaise; add remaining ingredients and more anchovy paste if not salty enough. Whip in blender if not smooth and thoroughly blended.

Beer Batter Shrimp

Can partially do ahead

PUNGENT FRUIT SAUCE:

¾ cup *(177 ml)* orange, lemon or lime marmalade

4 Tb *(60 ml)* lemon OR orange juice

2 tsp *(10 ml)* prepared horseradish

½ tsp *(2.5 ml)* powdered ginger

Pinch of dry mustard (optional)

Combine ingredients in blender and purée until smooth. Can do ahead and set aside.

BEER BATTER:

1 can, 12 oz *(340 g)* light beer

1 cup *(237 ml)* all-purpose flour, sifted

1 Tb *(15 ml)* salt

1 Tb *(15 ml)* paprika

Pour beer into bowl. Sift flour, salt and paprika into beer stirring with a wire whisk until the beer is light and frothy. This can be done several hours ahead. Keep mixed when using.

SHRIMP:

Large shrimp, 10-12 per person

oil for deep frying

flour

beer batter

Remove shells from shrimp, leaving the tails, and devein. Heat oil in pan or deep fryer. Dredge shrimp in flour coating entirely. Then dip in beer batter, coating well. Drop into hot oil and fry until golden brown. Drain on paper towel. Serve with Pungent Sauce.

Spareribs

Can partially do ahead

3 lbs *(1.4 kg)* spareribs cracked in 3" pieces

1 tsp *(45 ml)* Accent

3 Tb *(45 ml)* soy sauce

½ cup *(118 ml)* prepared mustard

1 cup *(237 ml)* brown sugar

Bake ribs at 325° (163° C) for 1½ hours. Drain on paper towels. Make a sauce from Accent, soy sauce, mustard and brown sugar and brush ribs. Return ribs to 300° (149° C) oven and bake 45 minutes, basting often.

Beef Tenderloin
A wonderful buffet fare.

Must do ahead

Serves: 12-16
Preparing: 10 min
Chilling: Overnight
Baking: approx 30 min

1 5-7 lb *(2.3-3.2 kg)* **whole beef**
tenderloin, trimmed

salt and pepper

Sprinkle beef with salt and pepper. Bake at 425° (218° C) until meat thermometer registers 140° (42.22° C) for rare; or 160° (53.34° C) for medium rare. DO NOT OVERCOOK. Cool; refrigerate overnight. Slice tenderloin into quarter inch slices. May be served cold or warm. Serve on party rye with Horseradish Whip (see index) or any other desired spread.

Chicken Wings

Can do ahead
Can freeze

Yield: 2½ doz
Preparing: 15 min
Baking: 30-35 min

1 envelope, 4¾ oz *(134 g)*
  seasoned dry coating mix for
  chicken
2 tsp *(10 ml)* **curry powder**

¼ cup *(59 ml)* **almonds, ground**
2½ dozen chicken wings
¼ cup *(59 ml)* **milk or water**

Empty dry ingredients into a bag. Cut off drumstick end of wing at joint. Moisten with milk or water and shake in bag. Arrange drumsticks in shallow pan 12 x 15 inch (30.48 x 38.10 cm) and bake at 400° (232° C).

Barbequed Chicken Wings

Must do ahead

Serves: 12
Preparing: 10 min
Marinating: 16 hrs
Baking: 1½-2 hrs

2-3 lbs *(908 g-1.4 kg)* **chicken wings**
1 cup *(237 ml)* **soy sauce**
3 tsp *(15 ml)* **sugar or** ¼ cup *(59 ml)*
  pineapple syrup
¼ cup *(59 ml)* **white wine**

2 cloves garlic mashed OR
  sprinkle wings with garlic
  powder
¼ cup *(59 ml)* **Mazola oil**
1 tsp *(5 ml)* **Accent**
1 tsp *(5 ml)* **ground ginger**

Combine and marinate for 16 hours. Bake at 325° (163° C) for 1½ to 2 hours. Sauce may be saved in refrigerator or frozen and used again.

Olive Quiche

Can do ahead
Can freeze

Yield: 40 small bars
Preparing: 45 min
Baking: 45 min

6 eggs
1 jar, 5 oz *(142 g)* **stuffed green
olives, thinly sliced**
1 carton, 16 oz *(454 g)* **sour cream**
1½ cups *(355 ml)* **Swiss cheese,
shredded**

1 tsp *(5 ml)* **oregano**
2 Tbs *(30 ml)* **chives**
¾ tsp *(3.7 ml)* **salt**
dash cayenne pepper
piecrust mix for two-crust
pie or homemade

Beat the eggs in a large bowl. Add all other ingredients (except pie crust mix) and mix well. Prepare pastry according to package directions. Roll out and line the bottom and sides of a 12 x 15 inch (30.48 x 38.10 cm) jellyroll pan. Pour olive mixture over pastry and bake at 425° (218° C) for 15 minutes. Reduce temperature to 375° (191° C) and continue baking for about 30 minutes or until filling is set. Cool slightly and cut into bars 1½ x 2½ inch (3.81 x 6.35 cm).

Quiche Lorraine Hors d'Oeuvres

Can do ahead
Can freeze

Serves: 16 or 24
Preparing: 30 min
Chilling: 1 hour
Baking: 30 min

PASTRY:
1 pkg, 3 oz *(85 g)* **cream cheese,
room temperature**
½ cup *(118 ml)* **margarine,
room temperature**

1 cup *(237 ml)* **sifted flour**

Blend cream cheese, margarine, and flour; chill 1 hour. Line 24 tart-size pastry or 16 muffin-size tins.

FILLING:
¼ lb *(113 g)* **bacon, fried
and crumbled**
1 cup *(237 ml)* **domestic Swiss
cheese, grated**

2 eggs
1 cup *(237 ml)* **light cream**
¼ tsp *(1.25 ml)* **salt**
dash of cayenne pepper

Sprinkle bacon over bottom of unbaked pastries. Sprinkle grated cheese over bacon. Blend eggs and cream, but do not beat. Add seasonings and pour into pastries. Bake at 375° (191° C) for 30 minutes or until filling is firm. Serve warm.

Basic Deviled Eggs

Can do ahead

Serves: 6
Preparing: 30 min

6 eggs
¼ cup *(59 ml)* **mayonnaise**
1 tsp *(5 ml)* **vinegar**

1 tsp *(5 ml)* **prepared mustard**
½ tsp *(2.5 ml)* **salt**
dash of pepper

Pierce end of eggs with a pin or needle to prevent cracking. Boil eggs. Shell and slice lengthwise. Put yolks in a bowl and mash. Add remaining ingredients and then re-stuff eggs, topping with paprika.

Dogs 'n Things

SAUSAGES:
⅓ cup *(79 ml)* **prepared mustard**
½ cup *(118 ml)* **currant jelly**

2 pkg, 8 oz *(227 g)* **cocktail brown and serve sausages**

Heat mustard and jelly in double boiler until dissolved and heated. Cut sausages in bite-size pieces and serve in chafing dish. Serves 10-12.

HOT DOGS:
1 lb *(454 g)* **all-beef hot dogs**
1½ cups *(355 ml)* **catsup**
¾ cup *(177 ml)* **bourbon**

½ cup *(118 ml)* **brown sugar**
1 Tb *(15 ml)* **onion, grated**

Cut hot dogs into ½" slices and put into skillet with remaining ingredients. Simmer on very low about 45-60 minutes. Serve in a chafing dish. Serves 24.

HOT SAUSAGES:
Penrose hot sausages
1 bottle catsup

1 can beer
2 Tb *(30 ml)* **brown sugar**

Drain sausages and cut into bite-size pieces. Add to sauce made from the above ingredients and simmer slowly 2 to 3 hours. Serve in chafing dish.

VARIATION:
2 lbs (908 g) of hot dogs cut in bite size pieces can be served in a chafing dish with 1 jar of apricot preserves and 1 jar of horseradish mustard.

76

Soup and Sandwiches

Soups and Sandwiches

Introduction To Soups

TYPES OF SOUPS

Cream Soups contain both milk and butter in addition to the vegetable which usually gives them their flavor.

Chowders are a special kind of cream soup containing a large proportion of solid food cut rather coarsely.

Clear Soup is made with meat or vegetable broth for flavor or with tomato juice.

TIPS

To de-salt over-salted soup, place a slice of raw potato into it and allow to boil for a short time; remove potato.

To remove grease from soup, place a leaf of lettuce on the hot soup; remove before serving.

Use a bouillon cube for extra flavor when adding water to canned or homemade soup.

Add a package of dehydrated chicken to chicken stock to make it more flavorful.

GARNISHES:

croutons
chopped parsley, chives or dill
chopped celery, green pepper or
   onion tops
dollop of whipped cream
Parmesan cheese
carrot gratings
tiny bite-size cereals toasted in a
   little butter
popped corn, especially in pea or
   corn soups

thinly sliced olive rings
chopped bacon
chopped walnuts, pecans or
   toasted almonds

For Clear Soup: lemon slices, avocado slices, chives, tiny meatballs or dumplings.

For Cream Soups: shredded cheese, toasted almonds, croutons and sour cream.

For Chowders or Meat Soups: crisp bacon, corn chips and lemon slices.

For Chilled Soups: sour cream, cucumber slices, parsley and dill.

ACCOMPANIMENTS

crisp crackers
oven hot toast cut in dainty sizes
relish trays
cheese pastry
bread sticks
cheese spread toast: Blend 2
   parts cream cheese with 1 part
   Roquefort cheese and mix with
   a little milk. Spread on hot
   buttered toast.

TASTY CANNED SOUP
   COMBINATIONS:
Use 1 can of each soup

Chicken and Cream of Asparagus
Cream of Mushroom and Cream
   of Chicken
Tomato Soup and Consommé
Tomato Soup and Clam Chowder
Cream of Pea and Chicken with
   Rice
Chicken Noodle and Vegetable

Broccoli Soup

Serves: 4
Preparing: 20 min
Cooking: 10-15 min

1 cup *(237 ml)* chicken stock
1 pkg frozen broccoli
1 medium onion, sliced
1 medium carrot, sliced
1 small stalk celery with leaves,
  sliced

1 clove garlic, minced
1 tsp *(5 ml)* salt
generous pinch of cayenne
  pepper
½ cup *(118 ml)* cream

Simmer broccoli, onion, carrot, celery and garlic in chicken stock for 10 minutes. Add salt and cayenne pepper and blend. Add cream last. Serve hot or cold.

Potato Soup With Sour Cream

Can do ahead

Yield: 1½ qts (1.42 l)
Preparing: 10 min
Cooking: 20-30 min

2 cups *(474 ml)* potatoes, diced
1 cup *(237 ml)* boiling water
1 tsp *(5 ml)* salt
1 small onion, sliced

½ tsp *(2.5 ml)* pepper
2 cups *(474 ml)* sour cream
minced parsley for garnish

Combine first 5 ingredients and cook together for 15 to 20 minutes. Add cream and cook until potatoes are tender. Serve hot.

Corn Chowder

Can do ahead

Serves: 8 to 10
Preparing: 20 min
Cooking: 20 min

1½ cups *(355 ml)* potatoes, diced
6 slices bacon, chopped
1 Tb *(15 ml)* dried chopped onion
4 cups *(946 ml)* milk
1 can, 1 lb *(454 g)* creamed corn

1 can, 10¾ oz *(305 g)* mushroom
  soup
1½-2 tsp *(7.5-10 ml)* salt
dash of pepper

Cook potatoes in ½ cup (118 ml) boiling water, with 1 tsp (5 ml) salt, until tender — about 15 minutes. Do not drain. Cook bacon in skillet til crisp. Remove bacon and cook re-constituted onion in drippings til tender, not brown. Add all ingredients except bacon. Heat thoroughly and stir often to prevent scorching. Garnish chowder with crumbled bacon when served.

Cucumber-Spinach Soup

Serves: 6-8
Preparing: 30-40 min

1 bunch scallions, sliced
2 Tb *(30 ml)* butter
4 cups *(946 ml)* cucumbers, diced
3 cups *(710 ml)* chicken broth
1 cup *(237 ml)* spinach, chopped

½ cup *(118 ml)* potatoes, sliced
½ tsp *(2.5 ml)* salt
lemon juice to taste
pepper to taste
1 cup *(237 ml)* light cream

Sauté scallions in butter until soft. Add cucumbers, chicken broth, spinach, potatoes, salt, lemon juice and pepper. Simmer until potatoes are tender. Put in blender and add cream. Cool and serve in chilled bowls with slices of cucumber.

Kathy's Spinach Soup

Good luncheon dish for the gals!
Serve with hot rolls and fruit salad

Can do ahead

Serves: 4
Preparing: 30 min
Cooking: 10 min

4 Tb *(60 ml)* butter
2 Tb *(30 ml)* flour
2 cups *(474 ml)* milk
½-1 cup *(118-237 ml)* cream
1 cup *(237 ml)* cooked spinach,
  drained

1 bouillon cube
1½ Tb *(22.5 ml)* sherry
1 small onion stuck with two
  whole cloves
salt and pepper
dash nutmeg

Put butter, flour, 1 cup (237 ml) of the milk, cream and spinach in the blender for 5 seconds. Place mixture in top of double boiler, heat quickly, and add bouillon cube and most of remaining milk. Stir over hot water until creamy. Add sherry and onion, and simmer for 10 minutes. If too thick, add a little more milk — season with salt, pepper, and a dash of nutmeg. Remove onion and serve.

Gazpacho

Must do ahead

Yield: 1 qt *(946 ml)*
Preparing: 20 min
Chilling: 4 hrs

1 cup *(237 ml)* **tomato, peeled and finely chopped**
½ cup *(118 ml)* **green pepper, finely chopped**
½ cup *(118 ml)* **celery, finely chopped**
½ cup *(118 ml)* **cucumber, finely chopped**
¼ cup *(59 ml)* **onion, finely chopped**
2 tsp *(10 ml)* **parsley, snipped**

1 tsp *(5 ml)* **chives, chopped**
1 small clove **garlic, minced**
2-3 Tb *(30-45 ml)* **wine vinegar**
2 Tb *(30 ml)* **olive oil**
1 tsp *(5 ml)* **salt**
¼ tsp *(1.25 ml)* **black pepper, freshly ground**
½ tsp *(2.5 ml)* **Worcestershire sauce**
2 cups *(474 ml)* **tomato juice**
croutons

Combine ingredients in bowl. Cover and chill thoroughly, at least 4 hours. Serve in chilled cups. Top with croutons.

Minestrone Alla Fiorentina

Can do ahead

Yield: 5 qts *(4.74 l)*
Preparing: 50 min
Cooking: 15 min

4 slices **bacon, diced**
1 large **onion, chopped** OR 1 cup *(237 ml)* **frozen onion, chopped**
2 cups *(474 ml)* **potatoes, diced**
1 cup *(237 ml)* **celery, diced**
1 cup *(237 ml)* **carrots, diced**
2 cans, 13 oz *(369 g)* **condensed beef broth**
2 soup cans **water**

1 can, 16 oz *(454 g)* **whole tomatoes**
1 can, 8 oz *(227 g)* **tomato sauce**
2 cans, 20 oz *(567 g)* **white kidney beans**
1 cup *(237 ml)* **elbow macaroni, tubettini** OR **ditalini**
salt

Cook bacon in kettle or large saucepan until golden. Add onion; sauté one minute. Add potatoes, celery and carrots; cook 5 minutes, stirring occasionally. Add broth, water, tomatoes and tomato sauce; bring to boil; cover and simmer 25-30 minutes or until vegetables are tender. Add kidney beans and pasta; cook 15 minutes. Season to taste with salt. Serve in warmed soup bowls.

Zucchini Soup

Can do ahead

Serves: 2-3
Preparing: 3 min
Cooking: 10 min

2 zucchini, sliced
1½ cups *(355 ml)* chicken broth
salt and pepper
1 medium onion, sliced

1 Tb *(15 ml)* butter
1¼ tsp *(6.2 ml)* curry powder
sour cream

Cook the zucchini in the broth until tender, about 10 minutes. Season with salt and pepper. Sauté onion in butter and when wilted, add curry powder. Blend onion and zucchini mixture in blender. Serve with a dollop of sour cream.

Note: My chicken broth consists of 2 packages of Herb Ox Instant Chicken Broth dissolved in the 1½ cups (355 ml) water.

Variation: Substitute dill for curry powder.

Cream Of Cauliflower Soup

Can do ahead

Serves: 4-6
Preparing: 15 min
Cooking: 15 min

1 pkg, 10 oz *(284 g)* frozen
  cauliflower
1 can, 10¾ oz *(305 g)* cream of
  potato soup, undiluted
2 cups *(474 ml)* milk

1 tsp *(5 ml)* dry mustard
3 Tb *(45 ml)* butter OR margarine,
  melted
1 Tb *(15 ml)* chives, chopped
salt and pepper to taste

Cook cauliflower according to package directions and drain. Combine cauliflower along with all ingredients except the chives in a blender and blend until smooth. Add chives and heat well. Season to taste.

Lazy Day Vegetable Soup

Can do ahead
Can freeze

Serves: 8
Preparing: 15 min
Cooking: 25 min

1½ lb *(680 g)* ground beef
1 onion, chopped
salt and pepper
1 can cream of mushroom soup

1 can cream of celery soup
3 cans, 12 oz *(355 ml)* V-8 juice
1 pkg, 10 oz *(284 g)* frozen mixed
  vegetables

Brown ground beef and onion. Add remaining ingredients and cook until all vegetables are tender.

Cream Of Artichoke Soup

Can do ahead

Serves: 4 large servings
Preparing: 30 min
Cooking: 10 min

1 can, 14 oz *(397 g)* artichoke
  hearts, reserve juice
¼ cup *(59 ml)* butter
2 Tb *(30 ml)* onion, finely chopped
2 Tb *(30 ml)* flour
½ cup *(118 ml)* milk
1 can, 14 oz *(397 g)* chicken broth

3 egg yolks
½ cup *(118 ml)* cream
1 tsp *(5 ml)* lemon juice
¼ tsp *(1.25 ml)* nutmeg
salt
chopped fresh parsley

Sauté butter and onions until transparent. Add flour, sautéing until light brown. Using a mixer, blend milk, juice from artichokes and chicken broth into flour mixture. Bring to a boil. In a separate bowl, mix egg yolks, and cream. Continue using mixer and add yolk/cream mixture to boiling soup. Lower heat, add lemon juice and nutmeg. Continue using mixer until blended. Add cut up artichokes, parsley and salt. Serve warm. This will keep in refrigerator several days.

Chilled Tomato-Orange Soup

Must do ahead

Serves: 8
Preparing: 30 min
Cooking: 50 min
Chilling: 2-3 hrs

5 cups *(1.18 l)* V-8 juice
1 bay leaf
1 tsp *(5 ml)* sugar
6 Tb *(90 ml)* butter
5 Tb *(75 ml)* flour

1 cup *(237 ml)* chicken broth
2 oranges
½ lemon
1 cup *(237 ml)* heavy cream
chopped parsley for garnish

Simmer V-8 juice, bay leaf, and sugar for 30 minutes over low heat. Strain. Heat the butter in a large saucepan and blend in the flour, cooking and stirring for 2 minutes. Mixture should be smooth but do not let brown. Add chicken broth and strained V-8 juice. Bring to boil and simmer 20 minutes. Shred outer rind of oranges coarsely and boil for 1 minute. Drain rind and refresh in cold water. Squeeze oranges and lemon and combine juices. This should measure about ⅔ cup (158 ml). Remove soup from heat. Add fruit juice and most of the shredded rind. Cool and add the cream. Chill 2 or 3 hours. Serve very cold garnished with rind and chopped parsley.

Chicken Gumbo

Can do ahead

Serves: 6
Preparing: 30 min
Cooking: 2½ hrs
Chilling: 2 hrs

1 whole broiler-fryer chicken
1 tsp *(5 ml)* Accent
4 cups *(946 ml)* water
1 medium onion, sliced

4 celery tops
1 tsp *(5 ml)* salt
¼ tsp *(1.25 ml)* pepper

Put chicken in large pot with remaining ingredients. Bring to a boil. Cover tightly. Reduce heat and simmer 1 hour or until tender. Remove from heat. Strain broth. Refrigerate chicken and broth at once. When chicken is cool, remove meat from bones. Cut in large pieces. Skim fat from stock. Reserve chicken and stock.

TO PREPARE GUMBO

3 Tb *(45 ml)* butter
1 medium onion, chopped
1 green pepper, chopped
1 cup *(237 ml)* celery, chopped
2 Tb *(30 ml)* flour
1 bay leaf
½ tsp *(2.5 ml)* dried leaf thyme

1 tsp *(5 ml)* Accent
1 tsp *(5 ml)* salt
¼ tsp *(1.25 ml)* pepper
2 cans, 1 lb *(454 g)* tomatoes
1 tsp *(5 ml)* Worcestershire sauce
1 pkg, 10 oz *(284 g)* frozen okra, thawed

Heat butter in a large pot. Add onion, green pepper, and celery. Cook, stirring occasionally, about 5 minutes. Blend in flour. Gradually add reserved stock and cook stirring occasionally until mixture comes to a boil. Add remaining ingredients except okra. Bring to a boil. Reduce heat and simmer 1 hour. Add okra and reserved chicken pieces. Simmer 15 minutes longer.

Cream Of Peanut Soup

Serves: 10-12
Preparing: 15-20 min

1 medium onion, chopped
2 ribs of celery, chopped
¼ cup *(59 ml)* margarine
3 Tb *(45 ml)* flour
2 qt *(1.89 l)* chicken broth

2 cups *(474 ml)* smooth peanut butter
1¾ cups *(414 ml)* light cream (half and half)
chopped peanuts

Sauté onions and celery in margarine only until soft. Stir in flour well. Add chicken broth; bring to a boil. Remove from heat; rub through sieve. Add peanut butter and cream, blending well. Heat and garnish with peanuts.

Soupe Au Pistou

Can partially do ahead

Serves: 8
Preparing: 20 min
Cooking: 30 min

2 qts *(1.89 l)* chicken broth — may substitute 7 chicken bouillon cubes with 2 qts *(1.89 l)* water
3 medium potatoes, peeled and cut in small cubes
½ lb *(227 g)* fresh green beans, cut up, OR 1 can cut green beans
3 carrots, peeled and sliced
1 medium onion, chopped
1 tsp *(5 ml)* salt
¼ tsp *(1.25 ml)* pepper
½ lb *(227 g)* zucchini or crookneck squash, sliced, OR 1 pkg, 10 oz *(284 g)* frozen zucchini, sliced

1 can, 16 oz *(454 g)* kidney OR navy beans, drained
2 cloves garlic, mashed
1 can, 6 oz *(170 g)* tomato paste
1 tsp *(5 ml)* dried basil
½ cup *(118 ml)* Parmesan cheese, grated
½ cup *(118 ml)* parsley, chopped, OR ¼ cup *(59 ml)* dried parsley flakes
¼ cup *(59 ml)* olive oil

Combine chicken broth, potatoes, green beans, carrots, onions, salt and pepper in a large pot or Dutch oven. Bring to a boil and then back to simmer for 10 minutes. Add zucchini and kidney or navy beans. Cook 10 minutes or until tender. Meanwhile, prepare sauce: mix garlic, tomato paste, basil, cheese and parsley. Using wire whip, gradually beat in oil until mix is thick sauce. Just before serving, stir sauce into hot soup and heat through quickly. Vegetable-broth mix can be cooked ahead of time then reheated before serving, adding tomato sauce just before serving.

Vichyssoise

Should do ahead 1 day

Yield: 2 qts *(1.89 l)*
Preparing: 30 min
Cooking: 2 hrs

3-4 cups *(710-946 ml)* peeled potatoes, sliced OR diced
3 cups *(710 ml)* yellow onions, thinly sliced

1 qt *(946 ml)* water
1 Tb *(15 ml)* salt
1 cup *(273 ml)* heavy cream

Simmer vegetables, water and salt together until tender. Strain and purée them in the blender. Save strained liquid and add approximately half of the liquid to puréed vegetables. Stir in heavy cream, over-salt slightly and chill. Serve in chilled soup cups and garnish with chives. You may use part chicken stock and part water to cook vegetables. Better if allowed to stand overnight.

Parisian Onion Soup

Can do ahead

Serves: 10
Preparing: 20 min
Cooking: 10 min

6 large white onions, thinly sliced
½ cup *(118 ml)* butter (no
  substitutes)
6 cups *(1.42 l)* chicken stock
½ tsp *(2.5 ml)* salt
⅛ tsp *(.6 ml)* pepper

6 slices French bread, lightly
  toasted
¼ cup *(59 ml)* Swiss cheese,
  grated
¼ cup *(59 ml)* Parmesan cheese,
  grated

Brown onions in butter **slowly** in 3 quart (2.84 l) pot until tender. Add stock and seasonings. Heat. To serve, place chunk of lightly toasted French bread in each bowl, sprinkle with Swiss cheese. Pour soup over and sprinkle the Parmesan cheese on top.

Split Pea Soup

Can do ahead
Can freeze

Serves: 4-6
Soaking: overnight
Preparing: 20 min
Cooking: 2 hrs

1 pkg, 16 oz *(454 g)* split peas
1 large onion, sliced
4 ribs celery with leaves, sliced
1 carrot, sliced
1 potato, diced

1 Tb *(15 ml)* tomato paste
1 ham hock
1 Tb *(15 ml)* salt
1 bay leaf

Rinse peas and soak overnight in 1 quart (946 ml) water. Combine remaining ingredients in 3 quart (2.84 l) kettle and bring to a boil. Skim off foam. Simmer for 2 hours, stirring frequently. Run through food mill and serve.

Secret Company Soup

Can do ahead
Can freeze

Serves: 8
Preparing: 10 min
Cooking: 10 min

2 cans, 10¾ oz *(305 g)* tomato
  soup
½ can, 10¾ oz *(305 g)* pea soup
1 can, 10¾ oz *(305 g)* bouillon
  soup

1 cup *(237 ml)* evaporated milk
1 can, 10¾ oz *(305 g)* cream of
  shrimp soup
¾ cup *(177 ml)* cooking sherry

Heat all ingredients except sherry; add that just before serving.

Manhattan Clam Chowder

Can do ahead

Serves: 6
Preparing: 15 min
Cooking: 35 min

4 slices bacon
6 medium potatoes, diced
2 onions, chopped
2 cups *(474 ml)* water

2 cans tomatoes
1 bottle clam juice and 2 cans
minced clams OR 1½ doz fresh
clams and juice

Fry bacon and remove. Reserve 2 tablespoons (30 ml) of grease in pan. Put in potatoes, onions, tomatoes and water. Let it cook for a few minutes in the bacon grease then transfer to a large saucepan and let it cook until the potatoes are done. Add clam juice and clams and just heat. You do not need to cook the clams — they will get tough. Serve with crumbled bacon on top of each serving.

Robert E. Lee Clam Chowder

Can do ahead

Serves: 6
Preparing: 20 min
Cooking: 30 min

¼ cup *(59 ml)* margarine
2 cans clams, drained, reserving
juice
1 Tb *(15 ml)* paprika
½ cup *(118 ml)* onions, diced
1½ cups *(355 ml)* half and half
1½ cups *(355 ml)* milk

1 - 2 Tb *(15-30 ml)* cornstarch
clam juice
2 potatoes, cooked and diced
1 tsp *(5 ml)* thyme
2 Tb *(30 ml)* Worcestershire sauce
dash Tabasco

Combine margarine, clams, paprika and onions and cook 10 minutes. Blend half and half, milk, cornstarch and clam juice well and add to cooked mixture. Then add potatoes, thyme, Worcestershire and Tabasco.

She-Crab Soup

Serves: 10-12
Preparing: 5 min
Cooking: 10 min

1 can, 10¾ oz *(305 g)* tomato soup
2 cans, 10¾ oz *(305 g)* celery soup
1 can she crab soup
3 soup cans milk
1 pkg whipped cream cheese with
chives

Accent
salt to taste
1 cup *(237 ml)* sherry
1 lb *(454 g)* deluxe crab meat

Heat the above slowly until the cream cheese is melted. Add Accent and a little salt. Add sherry and crabmeat the last few minutes. Heat — DO NOT BOIL.

Charleston She-Crab Soup

Can partially do ahead

Serves: 4-6
Cooking: 30 min

1 Tb *(15 ml)* **butter**
1 qt *(946 ml)* **milk**
¼ pt *(118 ml)* **whipped cream, whipped**
few drops of onion juice
⅛ tsp *(.6 ml)* **mace**
⅛ tsp *(.6 ml)* **pepper**
½ tsp *(2.5 ml)* **Worcestershire sauce**

1 tsp *(5 ml)* **flour**
2 cups *(474 ml)* **white crab meat and crab eggs (hard boiled yolk of eggs, crumbled may be substituted for crab eggs)**
½ tsp *(2.5 ml)* **salt**
4 Tb *(60 ml)* **dry sherry**

Melt butter in top of double boiler; blend with flour until smooth. Add milk gradually, stirring constantly; to this add crabmeat and eggs and all seasonings except sherry. Cook slowly over hot water for 20 minutes. To serve, place 1 tablespoon (15 ml) sherry in individual bowls, add soup, top with cream. Sprinkle with paprika or chopped parsley.

Shrimp Gumbo

Serves: 3-4
Preparing: 40 min
Cooking: 25-30 min

1 lb *(454 g)* **raw shrimp, fully cleaned**
2 cups *(474 ml)* **fresh OR frozen okra, chopped**
⅓ cup *(79 ml)* **shortening, melted**
⅔ cup *(158 ml)* **green onions and tops, chopped**
3 cloves garlic, chopped

1½ tsp *(7.5 ml)* **salt**
¼ tsp *(1.25 ml)* **pepper**
2 cups *(474 ml)* **hot water**
1 cup *(237 ml)* **canned tomatoes**
2 whole bay leaves
2 drops Tabasco
1½ cup *(355 ml)* **cooked rice**

Sauté okra in shortening until it appears dry — about 10 minutes. Add onion, garlic, salt, pepper, and shrimp. Cook about 5 minutes. Add water, tomatoes, and bay leaves. Cover and simmer 20 minutes. Remove bay leaves and add Tabasco. Place rice in bottom of soup bowls — fill with gumbo.

To fix ahead — leave shrimp out and do everything else. When time to serve, sauté shrimp in margarine or oil and add to other and heat. Shrimp must not be overcooked.

Oyster Stew

Should do ahead

Serves: 4
Preparing: 20 min

1½ Tb *(22.5 ml)* **flour**
1½ tsp *(7.5 ml)* **salt**
2 Tb *(30 ml)* **cold water**
1 pt *(474 ml)* **oysters and their liquid**

¼ cup *(59 ml)* **butter**
2 Tb *(30 ml)* **parsley, chopped**
3 cups *(710 ml)* **milk, scalded**
1 cup *(237 ml)* **cream, scalded**

Make a paste by blending flour, salt and water. Stir paste into oysters and liquid. Add butter and parsley. Simmer over low heat about 5 minutes, stirring, until the edges of the oysters curl. Add scalded milk and cream to oyster mixture. Remove from heat and cover; let stand 12 to 15 minutes to flavor. Reheat if necessary.

Mexican Chili
Very Mexican

Must do ahead
Can freeze

Serves: 15-18
Soaking: overnight
Preparing: 2½ hrs
Cooking: 3-4 hrs

2 lbs *(908 g)* **red beans**
3 lbs *(1.4 kg)* **ground meat**
2 cans, 8 oz *(227 g)* **tomato sauce**
4 cans, 6 oz *(170 g)* **tomato paste**
2 large **onions, chopped**
2 buds **garlic, chopped**
¾ tsp *(3.7 ml)* **red pepper**
1 medium **green pepper, chopped**

2 Tb *(30 ml)* **oregano**
2 Tb *(30 ml)* **cumin**
4 Tb *(60 ml)* **chili powder**
2 Tb *(30 ml)* **Italian seasoning**
2 Tb *(30 ml)* **cracked black pepper**
salt to taste
3 cans, 4 oz *(113 g)* **mushrooms**

Soak beans overnight. Pour off water, then cover beans with fresh water. Add salt and cook until nearly done. Pour off water. Cover with fresh water. Add meat and other ingredients, except mushrooms and season to taste. Stir frequently and simmer 3-4 hours. Add mushrooms at last before nearly ready to serve. Better if made the day before and reheated. Great with a salad and garlic bread.

Chili

Can do ahead
Can freeze

2½ lbs *(1.1 kg)* **ground chuck**
4 small onions *(egg size)*
2 cans, 16 oz *(454 g)* **tomatoes, cut
up**
1 can, 15 oz *(425 g)* **tomato sauce**
1 can, 12 oz *(340 g)* **tomato paste**

½ pack of small bag of dry pinto
beans
3 Tb *(45 ml)* **chili powder**
½ pack chili seasoning
1 tsp *(5 ml)* **salt**
1½ cups *(355 ml)* **water**

Brown meat in heavy skillet. Add all ingredients in large pot; mix thoroughly. Bring to boil; simmer several hours, approximately 6 hours, unless you soak the pintos overnight, then possibly 4 hours.

Brunswick Stew I
Good for cold winter lunches
or light winter suppers

Must do ahead

½ lb *(227 g)* **potatoes, diced**
1 lb *(454 g)* **onions, sliced**
2 lb *(908 g)* **chicken, cooked**
¾ lb *(340 g)* **stew beef**
6 slices bacon
1 can, 27 oz *(766 g)* **tomatoes**
1½ tsp *(7.5 ml)* **salt**
½ tsp *(2.5 ml)* **lemon pepper**

1½ tsp *(7.5 ml)* **Worcestershire
sauce**
1 pod red pepper
black pepper
1 can, 1 lb 12 oz *(794 g)*
cream-style corn
1 can, 1 lb 12 oz *(794 g)* **butter
beans**

Mix all but corn and butterbeans. Simmer for several hours in a large, heavy pot. Add butter beans the last hour of cooking and the corn the last half hour. Stir often after adding corn.

Variation: Add 2½ cups (592 ml) fresh okra or one No. 2 can of okra.

Brunswick Stew II

Can do ahead
Can freeze

Yield: 10-12 qts (9.5-9.9l)
Preparing: 12 hr
Cooking: 5-6 hr each day

5-6 lb *(2.3-2.7 kg)* **hen**
5-6 chicken breasts
salt and pepper corns
celery and celery leaves
onions
MBT instant chicken and beef
broth (if needed)

3 lb *(1.4 kg)* **chuck roast**
marrow bones
carrots
celery
bay leaf
parsley

FIRST DAY: Cook hen and chicken breasts almost covered with water and seasoned with salt, peppercorns, celery, celery leaves, and onions for 3-4 hours. Also cook chuck roast and marrow bones covered with water and seasoned with onions, carrots, celery, bay leaf, peppercorns and parsley for 5-6 hours. Let both cook down to the point where they are fairly concentrated and have plenty of flavor. If needed, add instant chicken or beef broth to respective broths. Strain and chill. Discard all seasonings and cut up beef and chicken.

1-1½ qts *(946 ml-1.42 l)* **potatoes,**
diced
several cups mashed potatoes
2 lbs *(908 g)* **lima beans, shelled**
6 qts *(5.68 l)* **tomatoes, peeled and**
cut up (about 32 large
tomatoes) OR canned
2 cans, 15 oz *(425 g)* **tomato sauce**
1 qt *(946 ml)* **onions, chopped**
1 pt *(474 ml)* **celery, chopped**
2 qts *(1.89 l)* **Silver Queen corn,**
about 18 ears

3-4 bay leaves
pinch of oregano
chicken fat
4 Tb *(60 ml)* **butter**
2 Tb *(30 ml)* **sugar**
salt and pepper
Worcestershire sauce
lemon juice
Samson's sauce
Tabasco sauce

SECOND DAY: Skim fat off broths saving chicken fats and discarding beef fat. Mix broths in a very large pot with meats. Add potatoes, lima beans, tomatoes, tomato sauce, onions, and celery. Cook for 5-6 hours or until vegetables blend together and it looks like Brunswick Stew. During the last hour of cooking, add remaining ingredients.

Cassoulet Du Midi

The greatest of French stews.

Can do ahead
Can freeze

Serves: 8-10
Preparing: 1 hr
Cooking: 6 hrs

1 pt *(474 ml)* **navy beans**
water
8 peppercorns and salt to taste
½ **bay leaf**
¼ **tsp** *(1.25 ml)* **thyme**
4 good sized onions, quartered
½ **lb** *(227 g)* **veal**
½ **lb** *(227 g)* **lean pork**

butter OR olive oil
1 clove of garlic
dry white wine
6 little link sausages, cooked and
  cut in thirds
2 slices of bacon, diced
½ **lb** *(227 g)* **mushrooms**
2 Tb *(30 ml)* **catsup**

Soak beans overnight in water. In morning drain and put in bean pot or earthenware casserole along with bay leaf, thyme, peppercorns and onions. Cover this with boiling water. Put lid on and bake all day very slowly in a 225° (107° C) oven adding enough water or wine from time to time to keep the beans covered. Add salt to taste. A couple of hours before dinner cut up veal and pork, and mushrooms if fresh, and sauté in plenty of butter or olive oil to which garlic bud has been added. When tender, cover veal and pork in pan with dry American white wine and simmer for 30 minutes, adding enough wine to keep this covered. At end of simmering time (or 2 hours before serving time) pour meat and wine mixture into bean pot. Add sausages, bacon and mushrooms (if canned add 2 Tb (30 ml) of catsup). Return to oven and forget about it until time to serve.

Hamburger-Vegetable Soup

Can do ahead
Can freeze

Serves: 6-8
Preparing: 15 min
Cooking: 2-3 hrs

1½ **lbs** *(680 g)* **ground chuck,**
  browned and drained
2 onions, chopped
1 can, 16 oz *(454 g)* **okra**
1 can, 16 oz *(454 g)* **Mitchell's**
  small white corn
1 can, 16 oz *(454 g)* **butter beans**

1 can, 16 oz *(454 g)* **tomatoes**
2 cans tomato soup
1½ **soup cans water**
salt and pepper to taste
garlic salt
1 Tb *(15 ml)* **chili powder**
1 Tb *(15 ml)* **oregano**

Brown meat and drain. Add other ingredients. Let simmer about 2-3 hours. May use crock pot.

Tips For Sandwiches

Garnishes for Open-Faced Sandwiches:

sprigs of parsley or watercress
slice of pimento
hard boiled egg slices
dash of paprika
olives

Easy Sandwich Combinations:

Quince jelly and minced ham on rye bread.

Peanut butter combined with applesauce and chopped celery.

Apple butter mixed with grated sharp cheese.

Grated raw carrots mixed with finely chopped salted peanuts and mayonnaise.

Crabmeat, chopped celery, lemon juice and mayonnaise.

Mashed sardines and hard boiled eggs mixed with salt and mayonnaise.

Ground cooked ham, beef or luncheon meat mixed with chopped pickle, mustard and mayonnaise.

Deviled ham chopped with hard boiled eggs and mixed with chopped pickle and a dash of Worcestershire sauce.

The Basics:

PIMENTO CHEESE

8 oz *(227 g)* sharp cheddar cheese, grated
1 medium onion, grated
1 tsp *(5 ml)* Worcestershire sauce
1 jar, 4 oz *(113 g)* pimento, chopped and liquid
3-4 Tb *(45-60 ml)* mayonnaise
¼ tsp *(1.25 ml)* cayenne pepper
⅛ tsp *(.6 ml)* salt

Blend with electric mixer on high speed until light and fluffy. Refrigerate.

EGG SALAD

6 hard boiled eggs, chopped
½ cup *(118 ml)* celery, chopped
⅓ cup *(79 ml)* sweet pickle relish
½ cup *(118 ml)* mayonnaise
¾ tsp *(3.7 ml)* salt
pepper to taste

Mix ingredients well and refrigerate.

HAM SALAD

1 cup *(237 ml)* cooked ham, ground
2 tsp *(10 ml)* mustard
4 Tb *(60 ml)* mayonnaise
2 Tb *(30 ml)* onion, minced
2 Tb *(30 ml)* Worcestershire sauce
Accent, salt and pepper to taste
4 Tb *(60 ml)* green pepper, chopped (optional)

Mix well and chill. Spread on buttered bread.

Easy Spreads:

CREAM CHEESE/OLIVE/BACON

2 pkgs, 3 oz *(85 g)* cream cheese
8 slices bacon, cooked and crumbled
½ cup *(118 ml)* olives, chopped

EGG AND BACON

hard boiled eggs, chopped
fried bacon, crumbled
salt and mayonnaise
a little minced onion if desired

CHEESE/TUNA

½ pt *(237 ml)* Miracle Whip
½ lb *(227 g)* Velveeta cheese
1 can, 6½ oz *(184 g)* tuna

Heat cheese and Miracle Whip in double boiler until cheese melts. Add tuna; mix, cool, and refrigerate.

For The Lunch Box

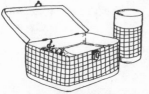

Include a protein-rich food such as peanut butter, meat, eggs or cheese.

Carrots, celery, green pepper, cucumbers — something crisp.

Fruit, cookies, cake, nuts or potato chips may be included as a treat; also banana nut bread or oatmeal cookies or bars.

Extras for sandwiches, such as pickles and tomatoes should be wrapped separately and added when ready to eat.

Spread both slices of bread with butter or margarine to keep bread from becoming soggy if using a moist filling; however, this is not necessary when using peanut butter or cream cheese.

Many sandwiches can be frozen, so make a batch, wrap individually and keep in the freezer up to 1 month. Add to lunch box frozen and it will thaw by lunch time.

Avoid freezing sandwiches with mayonnaise.

AVOID THE MONOTONY OF PEANUT BUTTER AND JELLY

**fried chicken legs
cream cheese and drained
   crushed pineapple
peanut butter and banana
liverwurst
corned beef
bacon, peanut butter and
   mayonnaise on whole wheat
chopped chicken, celery, sweet
   pickle and mayonnaise
tuna, celery and mayonnaise
cream cheese and marmalade
cream cheese and olive (green or
   ripe)
cucumber
asparagus and mayonnaise
pimento cheese and chopped
   pecans**

Full Meal Muffins

**English muffins
cream cheese, softened
tomatoes
asparagus spears
garlic salt**

**pepper
oregano
onion, minced
American cheese slices
sour cream**

Spread muffins with cream cheese. Top with a slice of tomato and 3 asparagus spears. Sprinkle each with a dash of: garlic salt, pepper, oregano and onion. Put on a cookie sheet, cover with foil and bake at 375° (191° C) for 25 minutes. Remove foil, cover each muffin with a slice of cheese and return to the oven for 2-3 minutes to melt the cheese. Top with sour cream and serve.

Sandwich In Foil

Can do ahead   Preparing: 20 min
Can freeze   Baking: 15 min

½ cup *(118 ml)* margarine
3 Tb *(45 ml)* mustard
1 Tb *(15 ml)* poppy seed
1 Tb *(15 ml)* Worcestershire sauce

small amount of onion, grated
3 slices boiled ham
2 slices Swiss cheese
onion OR sesame buns

Make dressing of first five ingredients and spread on both sides of bun. Put ham and cheese on bun and wrap in foil. Bake in 400° (204° C) oven for 10-15 minutes.

Stuffed Tuna Burgers

Can do ahead   Serves: 6-8
Can freeze   Preparing: 25 min
       Baking: 30 min

4 oz *(113 g)* American cheese,
    diced
3 eggs, hard-boiled and chopped
1 can, 7 oz *(198 g)* chunk tuna,
    drained and rinsed
½ cup *(118 ml)* mayonnaise
2 Tb *(30 ml)* green pepper,
    chopped

2 Tb *(30 ml)* onion, chopped
2 Tb *(30 ml)* olives, chopped
2 Tb *(30 ml)* sweet pickle, chopped
6-8 onion rolls, hotdog OR
    hamburger buns

Combine all ingredients except rolls and mix well. Spread mixture on rolls, wrap in foil, and heat at 350° (177° C) 30 minutes.

Wineburgers

Can do ahead   Serves: 4-5
Can freeze   Preparing: 15 min
       Cooking: 30 min

1 lb *(454 g)* ground beef
1 onion, chopped
2 Tb *(30 ml)* butter
¼ tsp *(1.25 ml)* pepper
½ tsp *(2.5 ml)* salt

1 can, 10¾ oz *(305 g)* tomato soup
⅓ cup *(79 ml)* red wine
1 tsp *(5 ml)* Worcestershire sauce
buns

Brown hamburger and onion in butter. Add remaining ingredients and simmer about 30 minutes. Serve on toasted buns.

Denver Brunch Sandwiches

Can partially do ahead

Serves: 6
Preparing: 5 min
Baking: 35 min

6 eggs
⅓ cup *(79 ml)* milk
½ cup *(118 ml)* Miracle whip
½ lb *(227 g)* bacon, cooked and
  crumbled OR ham, diced

¼ cup *(59 ml)* pimento, chopped
¼ tsp *(1.25 ml)* salt
dash of pepper
1 bell pepper, cut into 6 rings

Beat together eggs and milk. Stir in remaining ingredients except bell pepper. Pour into greased 8 inch (20.32) square pan. Place pepper rings separately on top of mixture. Set this pan into a pan of water and bake at 350° (177° C) for 35 minutes. Cut into squares, using 1 pepper ring per square. To serve, spread toast slices with additional Miracle Whip; top with lettuce and tomato and the squares of cooked mixture. Garnish with bacon.

Spicy Hot Beef Sandwiches

Serves: 6
Preparing: 5 min
Cooking: 30 min

1½ lbs *(680 g)* ground beef
½ cup *(118 ml)* onion, chopped
1 cup *(237 ml)* celery, chopped
2 Tb *(30 ml)* butter OR oil
2 Tb *(30 ml)* brown sugar
1½ tsp *(7.5 ml)* salt

½ bottle chili sauce
2 Tb *(30 ml)* vinegar
¼ cup *(59 ml)* green pepper,
  chopped
hamburger buns

Brown beef, onions, and celery in oil in large frying pan. Add rest of ingredients and simmer until thick and well blended. Spoon over hot buns.

Ham, Cheese And Olive Spread On Seeded Buns

Can do ahead
Keeps several days

Serves: 8
Preparing: 15 min

½ lb *(227 g)* ham, chopped
½ lb *(227 g)* mild cheddar cheese,
  grated
½ cup *(118 ml)* stuffed olives,
  chopped

¼ cup *(59 ml)* onions, chopped
2 hard-boiled eggs, chopped
½ cup *(118 ml)* chili sauce
salt and pepper
8 buns, halved

Mix ingredients and spread on cut side of buns. Broil until cheese is completely melted.

Corned Beef Sandwiches

Must do ahead
Can freeze

Serves: 8
Preparing: 20 min
Cooking: 25-30 min

¾ lb *(340 g)* **canned corned beef**
¼ lb *(113 g)* **American cheese,**
 cubed
2 eggs, hard boiled and cubed
½ **small onion, chopped and**
 sautéed

½ **green pepper, chopped and**
 sautéed
¼ cup *(59 ml)* **mayonnaise**
¼ cup *(59 ml)* **chili sauce**
buns

Mix all ingredients. Put on buns, wrap in foil, and let set for 4-6 hours.
Bake at 350° (177° C) for 25-30 minutes. Can be frozen and used
straight from freezer to oven.

Pizza Burgers

Can do ahead

Yield: 8

1 lb *(454 g)* **ground beef**
1 tsp *(5 ml)* **salt**
1 tsp *(5 ml)* **oregano**
1 medium onion, chopped
1 tsp *(5 ml)* **Worcestershire**
 sauce

½ **cup** *(118 ml)* **catsup**
1 Tb *(15 ml)* **mustard**
8 English muffin halves
Mozzarella cheese strips

Mix beef, salt, oregano, onion, catsup, Worcestershire, and mustard
lightly. Shape into 8 thin patties and place on top of English muffin
halves. Place in broiler rack and locate pan so that meat will be 4
inches from broiler unit. Broil 4-5 minutes, remove to add cheese
strips and return to broiler for another 4-5 minutes.

Sloppy Joes

Can do ahead
Keeps several days

Serves: 8-10
Preparing: 10 min
Cooking: 15 min

1 cup *(237 ml)* **onions, grated**
3 Tb *(45 ml)* **butter**
1 lb *(454 g)* **ground beef**
2 Tb *(30 ml)* **prepared mustard**

1 Tb *(15 ml)* **vinegar**
1 Tb *(15 ml)* **sugar**
½ **cup** *(118 ml)* **catsup**
hot dog OR hamburger buns

Sauté onions in butter; add ground beef and cook until done. Add rest
of ingredients except buns and cook until heated and blended. Serve
on buns.

Barbeque Beef Sandwiches

Can do ahead

Yields: 6 sandwiches
Preparing: 20 min
Cooking: 3 hr

1 lb *(454 g)* stew beef, trimmed
and cut in 1″ cubes
2 Tb *(30 ml)* oil

1¼ cups *(296 ml)* barbeque sauce
hamburger buns

Brown beef well on all sides in oil. Add barbeque sauce and simmer about 3 hours. Add water as necessary to keep it from drying out. When done, the meat should be stringy and falling apart. Spoon onto buttered hamburger buns.

Rye Bread Open-Face Sandwich
Good for lunch — a real meal

Serves: 2 slices per person

rye bread
mayonnaise
lettuce
tomato

Swiss cheese
baked ham
Russian dressing

Allow 2 slices of bread per person. Cover slice of bread with mayonnaise, a thin slice of lettuce, a thin slice of tomato, a slice of Swiss cheese and a thin slice of baked ham. Pour Russian dressing on top. It is runny, so serve it with a fork.

Open Face Sandwich

Preparing: 5 min
Cooking: 15 min

Holland rusk bread slices
tomato slices
cold, canned asparagus
hard-boiled egg, sliced

bacon, cooked and crumbled
chives
Seven Seas Russian dressing

On each slice of Holland rusk, layer the ingredients in the order listed. Bake at 350° (177° C).

Hot Vegetable Sandwiches

Serves: 6
Preparing: 45-60 min
(with food processor - 30 min)

½ cup *(118 ml)* **cabbage, minced**
½ cup *(118 ml)* **carrots, minced**
½ cup *(118 ml)* **green pepper, minced**
½ cup *(118 ml)* **celery, minced**
½ cup *(118 ml)* **radishes, minced**
½ cup *(118 ml)* **red onion, minced**

6 slices white bread
6 cups *(1.42 l)* **cheddar cheese, grated**
½ cup *(118 ml)* **beer**
white pepper to taste
cayenne pepper to taste

Mince all vegetables and combine in a bowl. Lightly toast and butter the bread. Put ½ cup of the vegetable mixture on each toasted slice of bread. In a saucepan melt the grated cheese, beer, and seasonings, stirring constantly. Put sandwiches on a baking sheet and divide the sauce among them. Broil 3 minutes or until cheese is lightly browned and bubbly.

Chilled Reuben Sandwiches
Unusual, but tasty flavor

Can do ahead

Yields: 6-8
Preparing: 20 min

1 can, 16 oz *(454 g)* **sauerkraut, drained well**
1 ctn, 8 oz *(227 g)* **sour cream**
garlic salt to taste
pepper to taste
1 pkg, 6 oz *(170 g)* **aged Swiss cheese, sliced**

1 pkg, 8 oz *(227 g)* **boiled ham, sliced**
1 loaf pumpernickel bread
olives for garnish, optional

Mix drained sauerkraut with sour cream until well blended. Add garlic salt and pepper to taste. Refrigerate. When ready to make sandwich, layer accordingly: slice of pumpernickel, ham, cheese, sauerkraut mixture and pumpernickel. Cut in half and garnish with a toothpick and olive on top. If traveling, wrap individually with clear plastic wrap. Serve with potato chips and cold beverage.

Crab Sandwich

Serves: 4
Preparing: 15 min
Baking: 20 min

2 pkg, 3 oz *(85 g)* cream cheese, softened
¼ cup *(59 ml)* butter, softened
1 Tb *(15 ml)* lemon juice
1 Tb *(15 ml)* onion, minced
1 tsp *(5 ml)* Worcestershire sauce

1 cup *(237 ml)* or more crabmeat
Holland rusk or English muffins
tomatoes, sliced
bacon, cooked
Old English cheese slices

Mix all ingredients together and form into 4 to 6 patties. On Holland Rusk or ½ English muffin place 1 slice tomatoes. Then put crabmeat patty on tomato slice. Top each patty with 2 strips of cooked bacon and a slice of Old English cheese. Anchor with toothpicks. Bake 15-20 minutes at 350° (177° C).

Curry Ripe Olive Sandwich

Can do ahead
Keeps several days

Serves: 6
Preparing: 20 min
Broiling: 6 min

2 cups *(474 ml)* ripe olives, chopped (2 cans, 7 oz *(198 g)*)
1 cup *(237 ml)* green onions, thinly sliced
3 cups *(710 ml)* American cheese

1 cup *(237 ml)* mayonnaise
½ tsp *(2.5 ml)* salt
½ tsp *(2.5 ml)* curry powder
6 English muffins

Mix thoroughly all ingredients except muffins. Split muffins and toast backs lightly. Pile mixture high on muffins and place under broiler until puffy and brown. This will also make 3-4 dozen canapes on melba toast rounds.

SANDWICHES

Hot Chicken Salad Sandwiches

Good for bridge luncheon

Serves: 6
Preparing: 30 min
Baking: 15 min

1½ cups *(355 ml)* **chicken, cooked and diced**
¾ cup *(177 ml)* **celery, diced**
2 Tb *(30 ml)* **onion, minced**
½ cup *(118 ml)* **mayonnaise**
½ cup *(118 ml)* **pecans, chopped (optional)**

1 Tb *(15 ml)* **lemon juice**
½ tsp *(2.5 ml)* **salt**
1 can, 10¾ oz *(305 g)* **cream of chicken soup**
3 **hamburger-type buns**

Combine all ingredients except buns. Put in 2 quart casserole and heat 15 minutes in 400° (204° C) oven. Butter and lightly toast bun halves. Put ample serving on each half. Eat with fork since salad is rather soupy.

Chicken Luncheon Sandwich

Delightful treat!!!

Can be done ahead, the day before and finish day of serving

Serves: 4-6
Preparing: 25 min
Cooking: 15 min
Baking: 25 min

1 can, 10¾ oz *(305 g)* **mushroom soup**
1 Tb *(15 ml)* **onion, minced**
1 jar, 2 oz *(57 g)* **pimento, chopped**
1½ cups *(355 ml)* **chicken, diced**
3 Tb *(45 ml)* **flour**
¾ cup *(177 ml)* **milk**

8 **bread slices, crusts removed**
2 **eggs, slightly beaten**
3 Tb *(45 ml)* **milk**
2 cups *(474 ml)* **potato chips, crushed**
½ cup *(118 ml)* **slivered almonds**

Mix soup, onion, pimento, and chicken in saucepan. Blend flour with milk and add to soup. Cook, stirring constantly, until thick. Chill. Place four slices of bread in a 9 x 9 inch pan. Spread chicken mixture on top. Cover with remaining bread. Chill several hours or overnight. Mix eggs and milk. Cut sandwiches into halves. Dip both sides of sandwich in mixture and then in crushed potato chips. Arrange on buttered cookie sheets and top with almonds. Bake 350° (177° C) for 25 minutes. Serve with a tossed salad and a rich or light, cool dessert!

Party Sandwiches

Freeze fresh bread to trim crust more easily.

Prepare fillings before trimming crust so you can work fast.

Spread slices of bread with butter or margarine to prevent sogginess.

Spread filling all the way to the edge to prevent dry edges.

To store prepared sandwiches, place in a pan or box lined with waxed paper. Separate layers with waxed paper and cover with a damp towel.

Moist prepared sandwiches can be frozen for two weeks. Most meat fillings, cream cheese and sour cream fillings freeze well. Avoid fresh vegetable fillings and fillings containing mayonnaise or salad dressing.

If using a design that needs to be cut, cut before thawing. Thaw in wrapper about 2 hours.

OTHER SUGGESTIONS FOR PARTY SANDWICHES:

Pimento Cheese
Egg Salad
Ham Salad
Cream Cheese and Olive

Cucumber (add green food
  coloring)
Tuna
Chicken Salad

CHECKERBOARD

| **Step 1** | **Step 2** | **Step 3** |

1. Make stack of 2 slices whole wheat and 2 slices white bread, using 1 or more spreads between slices. Pressing stack together, trim crusts and cut into ½" slices.
2. Stack 3 slices, making sure that white and whole wheat strips alternate. Spread 1 or more fillings between slices.
3. Securely wrap sandwiches in plastic and chill several hours. Cut in ½" slices. Cover sandwiches with waxed paper and damp towel, and refrigerate until serving time.

RIBBON

| Step 1 | Step 2 | Step 3 |

1. Make stack with 3 slices of whole wheat and 2 slices of white bread, using 1 or more spreads between the slices. Firmly press stack together, and trim crusts.
   OR
2. Securely wrap stack in plastic before chilling 2 hours or more. Slice stack in ½" strips.
3. Slice each strip into halves or thirds before serving. Unless sandwiches are to be served immediately, cover with waxed paper and damp towel. Store in refrigerator.

PINWHEEL

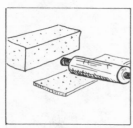

| Step 1 | Step 2 | Step 3 |

1. Trim off crust of loaf of unsliced bread. Cut loaf lengthwise into ¼" slices. Flatten each slice with rolling pin, and spread with softened butter and filling of your choice.
2. Pickles, Vienna sausage, frankfurter or olives may be placed across end of slice if desired. Roll up slice tightly and wrap in plastic wrap. Chill several hours or overnight.
3. Before serving, cut chilled rolls into ½" slices. Unless serving immediately, cover pinwheels with waxed paper and damp towel. Refrigerate until serving.

Asparagus Sandwiches

Must serve immediately

Preparing: 10 min
Baking: 10 min

sandwich bread
mayonnaise

asparagus spears, well-drained
melted butter

Trim crusts from bread slices and roll flat with rolling pin. Spread with mayonnaise and place an asparagus spear on each slice, roll and fasten with a toothpick. Brush with butter and brown at 350° (177° C) about 10 minutes.

Ham Spread For Sandwiches

Try this for a party or use the recipe for leftover ham

Can do ahead

Yields: 6 sandwiches
Preparing: 15 min

1, 6¾ oz *(191 g)* **Hormel Tender**
  Chunk ham
2, 3 oz *(170 g)* **blocks of cream**
  cheese, softened
2 Tb *(30 ml)* **mayonnaise**

cheese slices OR grated Swiss
  cheese
buns OR bread
seasoned salt to taste

Break up ham with fork. Blend in cream cheese, seasoned salt and mayonnaise. Spread on bread and top with a slice of cheese. This is also good on crackers. If using Swiss cheese, grate and mix in with ham.

Congealed Sandwich Spread

Must do ahead

Preparing: 30 min
Chilling: overnight

2 cups *(474 ml)* **mayonnaise**
dash of salt
1 cup *(237 ml)* **celery, chopped**
1 green pepper, chopped
2 tomatoes, chopped

1 onion, chopped
1 envelope gelatin
¼ cup *(59 ml)* **cold water**
½ cup *(118 ml)* **boiling water**

Add mayonnaise and dash of salt to chopped vegetables. Dissolve gelatin in cold water, then add boiling water to gelatin. Combine vegetable mixture and gelatin mixture. Refrigerate overnight. Spread on sandwiches.

Saturday Night Spread

Can do ahead
Can freeze

Serves: 6-8
Preparing: 15 min
Cooking: 30 min

1 lb *(454 g)* ground beef
½ cup *(118 ml)* onion, chopped
2 Tb *(30 ml)* catsup (or more)
2 tsp *(10 ml)* mustard
½ tsp *(2.5 ml)* salt and pepper

¼ tsp *(1.25 ml)* chili powder
1 can, 10¾ oz *(305 g)* chicken
   gumbo soup
hamburger buns

Let meat simmer; add onion; then add remaining ingredients. Simmer for 30 minutes. Serve on hamburger buns.

Ripe Olive Sandwich

2 pkgs, 3 oz *(85 g)* cream cheese
1 can, 3¼ oz *(92 g)* ripe olives,
   chopped
½ cup *(118 ml)* pecans, chopped

2 tsp *(10 ml)* onion, grated
3-4 Tb *(45-60 ml)* mayonnaise
1 tsp *(5 ml)* Worcestershire sauce

Mix well and spread on white or whole wheat bread. Delicious cut into finger-tip sandwiches for hors d'oeuvres.

Braunschweiger Sandwich Spread

½ cup *(118 ml)* fresh mushrooms,
   chopped
1 Tb *(15 ml)* butter, melted
2 rolls, 4 oz *(113 g)*
   braunschweiger, softened to
   room temperature

2 Tb *(30 ml)* mayonnaise
½ tsp *(2.5 ml)* Worcestershire
   sauce
salt as desired

Sauté mushrooms in butter until tender. Remove from heat and allow to cool slightly. Add remaining ingredients to mushrooms and mix well.

Shrimp Spread

1 can, 4½ oz *(127 g)* shrimp,
   drained
1 pkg, 3 oz *(85 g)* cream cheese,
   softened
1 small onion, grated

large dash of Worcestershire
   sauce
2 tsp *(10 ml)* mustard sauce
garlic powder to taste

Mash shrimp and add remaining ingredients; beat well. Chill to blend flavors.

Breads

Breads

Tips For Breads

To make bread crusty, brush top and sides with an egg white diluted with 1 Tb water 5 minutes before the end of baking. Cool loaves in a draft.

Use slightly beaten egg white, egg yolk, or whole egg to brush over top of biscuits or rolls just before baking.

To prevent a lump in the center of a quick bread, cut vertically down the center of the dough when it starts to rise during baking.

Use moderately warm, not hot milk or water; if too hot, the milk may kill the yeast; if too cool, the yeast may not dissolve completely.

Scald milk to lukewarm to destroy enzymes which make doughs hard to handle and sticky.

Cut candied fruit in strips or in petals and arrange in design on frosted breads.

Form design with red or green cherry rings. Use with or without nut meat halves, as desired.

Place ½ tsp (2.5 ml) of jam, jelly, or marmalade on top of each muffin before baking.

Sprinkle caraway, poppy, or sesame seed over dough which has been formed into desired shapes and brushed with butter.

Before scalding milk, rinse pan with cold water to prevent sticking.

Fresh bread keeps its shape if cut with a hot knife.

Milk makes finer textured bread and adds nutrients; water makes coarser bread and crisper crust.

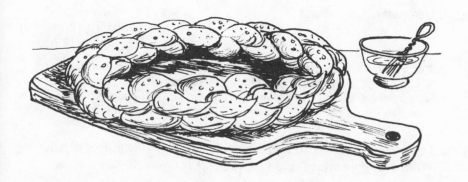

Frosting And Glazes For Breads

FROSTING:

1 cup *(237 ml)* confectioner's
  sugar
1 Tb *(15 ml)* butter OR margarine,
  softened
1-2 Tb *(15-30 ml)* milk

GLAZE:

1 cup *(237 ml)* confectioner's
  sugar
2-3 Tb *(30-45 ml)* milk

Combine all ingredients in a small bowl until smooth. Add more milk, a drop at a time, until spreading or drizzling consistency. Fruit juices can be substituted for milk and add food coloring accordingly.

VARIATIONS:

Almond: add ¼ tsp (1.25 ml) almond extract.

Chocolate: add 1 Tb (15 ml) cocoa.

Coffee: add ½ tsp (2.5 ml) instant coffee.
Mocha: add 1 Tb (15 ml) cocoa and ½ tsp (2.5 ml) instant coffee.

Orange OR lemon: add ¼ tsp (1.25 ml) grated peel and use fruit juice in place of milk.

Rum OR brandy: add ¼ tsp (1.25 ml) rum or brandy flavoring or 1 tsp (5 ml) rum or brandy.

Spice: add ¼ tsp (1.25 ml) cinnamon and a dash of nutmeg.

Vanilla: add ½ tsp (2.5 ml) vanilla.

Spreads For Breads

Garlic Bread

Can partially do ahead

Serves: 10-12
Preparing: 20 min
Baking: 10-12 min

1 cup *(237 ml)* butter, softened
¼ cup *(59 ml)* parsley, chopped
¼ cup *(59 ml)* grated Parmesan
  cheese
1 clove garlic, crushed

2 tsp *(10 ml)* dried marjoram
  leaves
½ tsp *(2.5 ml)* pepper
2 loaves of French bread

Make garlic butter. Cut bread diagonally. Spread with garlic butter. Wrap in aluminum foil. Bake at 425° (218° C) for 10-12 minutes.

Herbed Bread Spread

Can do ahead
Can freeze

Yield: 1 loaf
Preparing: 10 min
Baking: 25 min

1 loaf unsliced bread
¾ cup *(177 ml)* soft butter
½ tsp *(2.5 ml)* dried savory
¼ tsp *(1.25 ml)* salt

dash cayenne
¼ tsp *(1.25 ml)* paprika
½ tsp *(2.5 ml)* thyme

Cut all crusts, except bottom, off bread. Cut ¾ inch thick slices, not all the way through. Spread all sides of slices with mixture of remaining ingredients. Bake in 375° (191° C) oven for 20-30 minutes or until crusty brown.

Spread Variations
Dress up breads with a special spread or topping

FLUFFY ORANGE SPREAD

¼ cup *(59 ml)* orange juice
2 pkgs, 3 oz *(85 g)* cream cheese
1 Tb *(15 ml)* sugar
1 Tb *(15 ml)* orange peel, grated

Beat orange juice and cream cheese until smooth and creamy. Add sugar and orange peel and continue beating until well blended. Nice with fruit or nut bread.

COFFEE CHEESE SPREAD

2 pkgs, 3 oz *(85 g)* cream cheese
1 egg yolk
¼ cup *(59 ml)* confectioner's sugar
¼ tsp *(1.25 ml)* instant coffee

Combine all ingredients and beat until light and fluffy. Good for nut or raisin breads.

OLIVE SPREAD

½ cup *(118 ml)* butter, softened
2 Tb *(30 ml)* milk OR cream
2 Tb *(30 ml)* stuffed green olives, thinly sliced.

Mix well. Good for tea sandwiches.

CHERRY CHEESE SPREAD

1 pkg, 3 oz *(85 g)* cream cheese
1 Tb *(15 ml)* maraschino cherries, chopped
1 tsp *(5 ml)* milk

Whip cream cheese and milk until fluffy. Fold in cherries. Nice for holiday fruit breads.

CREAMY FRUIT SPREAD

Mix sour cream with strawberry preserves, orange marmalade or blackberry preserves. Use on your choice of bread.

Breakfast Bread

Can do ahead
Can freeze

Yield: 3 loaves
Preparing: 2 hr 45 min
Baking: 40 min

¾ **cup** *(177 ml)* **sugar**
1 **cup** *(237 ml)* **shortening**
1 **cup** *(237 ml)* **boiling water**
1½ **Tb** *(22.5 ml)* **salt**

3 **eggs**
2 **pkgs, ¼ oz** *(7 g)* **yeast**
1 **cup** *(237 ml)* **warm water**
6 **heaping cups plain flour**

Dissolve sugar, shortening and salt in boiling water. Soften yeast in warm water. Add slightly beaten eggs to first mixture; add yeast mixture then beat in flour. Let rise in bowl until doubled in size. Divide dough into 3 greased loaf pans. Cover, let rise again, and bake at 300° (149° C) for 40-45 minutes. Will keep for about 5 days.

This bread has a cakelike texture and is not suitable for sandwiches. It is delicious buttered and toasted for breakfast.

Sausage Casserole Bread

Can do ahead

Yield: 1 loaf
Preparing: 25 min
Baking: 30 min

1 **lb** *(454 g)* **sausage**
½ **cup** *(118 ml)* **onion, chopped**
¼ **cup** *(59 ml)* **Parmesan cheese**
½ **cup** *(118 ml)* **Swiss cheese,**
   grated
1 **egg, beaten**

¼ **tsp** *(1.25 ml)* **Tabasco**
1½ **tsp** *(7.5 ml)* **salt**
2 **Tb** *(30 ml)* **parsley, chopped**
2 **cups** *(474 ml)* **Bisquick**
⅔ **cup** *(158 ml)* **milk**
¼ **cup** *(59 ml)* **mayonnaise**

Brown sausage and onion. Drain very well. Combine browned mixture with cheeses, egg and seasonings. Make dough and divide in half. Layer dough, meat mixture, then dough in a greased loaf pan. Brush top with beaten egg yolk. Bake at 400° (204° C) for 30 minutes.

Oatmeal Bread

Can do ahead
Can freeze

Yield: 3 loaves
Preparing: 20 min
Rising: 3½ hrs
Baking: 30 min

2 cups *(474 ml)* **boiling water**
1 cup *(237 ml)* **oatmeal**
1 Tb *(15 ml)* **yeast**
¼ cup *(59 ml)* **warm water**
1 Tb *(15 ml)* **flour**
pinch of sugar

1 tsp *(5 ml)* **salt**
2 Tb *(30 ml)* **oil**
¼ cup *(59 ml)* **honey**
5-6 cups *(1.18-1.42 l)* **unbleached white flour**

Pour boiling water over 1 cup (237 ml) oatmeal. Dissolve yeast in ¼ cup (59 ml) warm water with 1 Tb flour and pinch of sugar. Stir and leave until bubbly. When oatmeal is lukewarm add 1 tsp (5 ml) salt, 2 Tb (30 ml) oil and ¼ cup (59 ml) honey. Add yeast mixture. Stir in flour gradually. Turn out on floured board and knead until smooth. Let rise in greased bowl in warm place until double in bulk. Punch down, knead again thoroughly. Let rise again until double and punch down. Divide into loaves. Let rise in pans. Bake at 350° (177° C) for 30 minutes. Makes 3 medium loaves.

Banana Bread

Can do ahead
Can freeze

Yield: 1 lb (454 g) loaf
Preparing: 20 min
Baking: 1¼ hr

½ cup *(118 ml)* **butter OR margarine, softened**
1 cup *(237 ml)* **sugar**
2 **eggs**
1 cup *(237 ml)* **ripe bananas, mashed**
1 tsp *(5 ml)* **lemon juice**

2 cups *(474 ml)* **flour, sifted**
1 Tb *(15 ml)* **baking powder**
½ tsp *(2.5 ml)* **salt**
1 cup *(237 ml)* **pecans OR walnuts, chopped**
1 tsp *(5 ml)* **vanilla**

Cream shortening and sugar together; beat eggs until light and add. Press bananas through sieve and add lemon juice; blend with creamed mixture. Add vanilla. Sift flour, baking powder and salt together and mix quickly into banana mixture. Add nuts. Bake in greased loaf pan at 350° (177° C) about 1¼ hours.

Cheese Poppy Seed Bread

Moist and tasty

Must do ahead
Can freeze

Yield: 2 loaves
Preparing: 25 min
Baking: 25-35 min

½ cup *(118 ml)* shortening
2 eggs, beaten
1 cup *(237 ml)* milk
3 cups *(710 ml)* biscuit mix

2 cups *(474 ml)* sharp cheddar
cheese, grated
2 Tb *(30 ml)* poppy seeds
2 Tb *(30 ml)* dried minced onion

Melt the shortening. Add eggs, milk and melted shortening to biscuit mix, cheese, poppy seeds and onion. Mix until dry ingredients are moistened. Grease and flour 2 regular sized loaf pans. Spread the dough in the pans. Bake in the oven at 375° (191° C). Check after 25 minutes. Continue baking until browned and done.

Easy French Bread

Can do ahead
Can freeze

Yield: 2 long loaves or
4 dinner-size loaves
Preparing: 80 min
Rising: 1½ hrs
Baking: 20 min

1 pkg, ¼ oz *(7 g)* dry yeast
1½ cup *(355 ml)* warm water
1 Tb *(15 ml)* sugar

1½ tsp *(7.5 ml)* salt
1 Tb *(15 ml)* shortening
4 cups *(946 ml)* flour

Sprinkle yeast into ½ cup (118 ml) warm water; stir until dissolved. In a large bowl dissolve sugar and salt in 1 cup (237 ml) warm water. Add shortening and yeast mixture. Add flour and stir to mix well. Dough should be quite stiff. If necessary, add a bit more flour to make it stiff. Work through dough with spoon at 10 minute intervals for 5 consecutive times. (Set oven timer and come back to stir — otherwise leave it alone at this point). Turn dough out onto lightly floured surface and divide in half. Shape into 2 balls. Let rest 10 minutes. Roll each ball into 9 inch x 12 inch (22.86 x 30.48 cm) rectangle. Then roll firmly, as for a jelly roll, starting with the long side. Pinch edges to seal. If smaller loaves are desired, cut each loaf in half and seal ends by pinching. Place on greased cookie sheet, seam side down. Score top with sharp knife in about 3 places. Cover with a towel and place in warm, draft-free place for 1½ hours to rise. Bake at 375° (191° C) for 10 minutes (or until barely brown). At this point it may be frozen. When ready to serve, slice ¾ way through and butter between slices. Then bake at 375° (191° C) about 7-10 minutes.

Yulekaka (Norwegian Bread)

Great toasted with soups!

Yield: 2 loaves
Preparing: 1 hr, 15 min
Rising: 2½-3½ hrs
Baking: 25-30 min

1 pkg, ¼ oz *(7 g)* **dry yeast**
¼ cup *(59 ml)* **warm water**
¼ cup *(59 ml)* **butter**
⅓ cup *(79 ml)* **sugar**
2 tsp *(10 ml)* **salt**
½ tsp *(2.5 ml)* **ground cardamon**
1 cup *(237 ml)* **milk, scalded**
½ cup *(118 ml)* **cold water**

1 **egg**
1 cup *(237 ml)* **chopped cherries
OR mixed candied fruit**
1 cup *(237 ml)* **light OR dark
raisins**
5 to 5½ cups *(1.18-1.30 l)* **all
purpose flour**

Soften yeast in warm water. In large mixing bowl, combine butter, sugar, salt, cardamon, and milk. Add cold water. Cool to lukewarm. Stir in egg, cherries, raisins, and yeast. Gradually add flour to form stiff dough. Knead on floured surface until smooth and satiny, 5 to 7 minutes. Place in greased bowl, turning dough to grease all sides. Cover; let rise in warm place until doubled, 1½ to 2 hours.

Divide dough in half. Shape into round loaves and place on greased cookie sheet. Cover. Let rise again in warm place until doubled, 1 to 1½ hours. Bake at 350° F (177° C) for 25 to 30 minutes until golden brown. Spread while warm with Vanilla Glaze. Decorate with candied cherries and nuts.

Variation: Shape into 3 loaves and place in greased 1 pound (454 g) coffee cans or star or ring molds.

VANILLA GLAZE:

1 cup *(237 ml)* **confectioner's
sugar**
2 to 3 Tb *(30-45 ml)* **milk**

In small mixing bowl, combine all ingredients; blend until smooth. Add more milk, a few drops at a time, until of spreading consistency or drizzling consistency.

Variation: Fruit juices may be substituted for milk; add food coloring if desired.   •

115

Dilly Bread

Can do ahead
Can freeze

Serves: 12
Preparing: 14 min
Rising: 1 hr 45 min
Baking: 40-50 min

1 pkg, ¼ oz *(7 g)* **dry yeast**
¼ **cup** *(59 ml)* **warm water**
1 **cup** *(237 ml)* **cottage cheese**
2 **Tb** *(30 ml)* **sugar**
2 **tsp** *(10 ml)* **dill seed**
¼ **tsp** *(1.25 ml)* **baking soda**

1 **Tb** *(15 ml)* **butter or margarine**
1 **Tb** *(15 ml)* **instant minced onion**
1 **tsp** *(5 ml)* **salt**
1 **egg, unbeaten**
2½-3 **cups** *(591-710 ml)* **flour**
coarse salt

Soften yeast in warm water. Heat cottage cheese to lukewarm. Combine with all other ingredients, except flour, in mixing bowl. Add flour to form a stiff dough. Beat well. Cover and put in warm place; let rise until light and double in size, about 1 hour. Stir down. Turn into a well-greased loaf pan or 8 inch (20.32 cm) round glass soufflé or 1½ quart (1.42 l) casserole (pretty this way for company on a buffet table). Let rise in warm place for 30-40 minutes. Bake in 350° (177° C) oven for 40-50 minutes or until golden brown. Brush with butter and sprinkle with coarse salt all over the top. Good served hot — or let it cool and toast.

Cranberry And Cheese Bread

Can do ahead
Can freeze

Yield: 1 loaf
Preparing: 15 min
Baking: 60 min

1½ **cups** *(355 ml)* **cranberries,**
   halved or chopped coarse in
   blender
1¼ **cup** *(296 ml)* **sugar**
2 **cups** *(474 ml)* **flour**
1 **Tb** *(15 ml)* **baking powder**
½ **tsp** *(2.5 ml)* **salt**
½ **cup** *(118 ml)* **walnuts, chopped**

2 **tsp** *(10 ml)* **orange peel, grated**
¾ **cup** *(177 ml)* **sharp cheddar**
   cheese, finely grated
1 **egg, slightly beaten**
1 **cup** *(237 ml)* **milk**
¼ **cup** *(59 ml)* **butter, melted and**
   cooled

Mix cranberries and ½ cup (118 ml) sugar. Combine flour, ¾ cup (177 ml) sugar, baking powder and salt. Mix cranberries, nuts, orange peel, and cheese. Beat egg with milk and butter; add to mixture. Stir just until mixed; **don't over mix.** Put in 9 x 5 x 2 inch (22.86 x 12.70 x 7.62 cm) pan buttered on bottom only. Bake at 350° (177° C) for 1 hour.

Date-Nut Pumpkin Bread

Can do ahead
Can freeze

Yield: 1 large bundt pan
Preparing: 45 min
Baking: 50-60 min

1 cup *(237 ml)* butter OR margarine
2½ cups *(592 ml)* sugar
4 eggs
2 cups *(474 ml)* canned pumpkin
   (1 lb *(454g)* can)
3 cups *(710 ml)* flour, sifted
1 tsp *(5 ml)* salt

2 tsp *(10 ml)* baking powder
½ tsp *(2.5 ml)* soda
1 Tb *(15 ml)* cinnamon
1 8 oz *(227 g)* pkg dates, diced
½ cup *(118 ml)* raisins
1 cup *(237 ml)* pecans, chopped

Cream butter and sugar. Add eggs, one at a time, beating well. Add and mix pumpkin. Sift dry ingredients together. Add to mixture and mix well. Add dates, raisins, and pecans. Mix well. Grease all containers well. (You may use coffee cans, peanut cans, small cans, loaf pans of any size.) Fill ¾ full of batter. Bake at 375° (191° C) for 50-60 minutes or less if using smaller container. (May use bundt pan and bake 45 minutes.)

Lemon Bread

Can do ahead
Can freeze

Yield: 2 loaves
Preparing: 25 min
Baking: 1 hr

1 cup *(237 ml)* margarine
2 cups*(474 ml)* sugar
4 eggs
3 cups *(710 ml)* flour, sifted
½ tsp *(2.5 ml)* salt
½ tsp *(2.5 ml)* soda

1 cup *(237 ml)* buttermilk
grated rind of 1 lemon
1 cup *(237 ml)* nuts, chopped
juice of 3 lemons
1 cup *(237 ml)* confectioner's
   sugar

Cream margarine and sugar. Add eggs one at a time and blend. Sift together flour, salt, and soda. Add alternately with buttermilk, lemon rind, and chopped nuts. Pour into 2 greased loaf pans (22.86 x 12.70 x 7.62 cm). Bake 1 hour at 350° (177° C). While bread bakes, combine lemon juice and confectioner's sugar. When bread is baked, pour lemon syrup over hot bread.

Magic Marshmallow Crescent Puffs

Can do ahead

Yield: 16
Preparing: 30 min
Baking: 10-15 min

¼ cup *(59 ml)* sugar
1 tsp *(5 ml)* cinnamon
2 cans, 8 oz *(227 g)* Pillsbury
  Refrigerator Quick Crescent
  Dinner Rolls
16 large marshmallows
¼ cup *(59 ml)* butter OR
  margarine, melted

½ cup *(118 ml)* confectioner's
  sugar
½ tsp *(2.5 ml)* vanilla
2-3 tsp *(10-15 ml)* milk
¼ cup *(59 ml)* chopped nuts,
  optional

Combine sugar and cinnamon. Separate rolls into 16 triangles. Dip a marshmallow in butter, then roll in sugar-cinnamon mixture. Wrap a triangle around each marshmallow, completely covering marshmallow and squeezing edges of dough tightly to seal. Dip in butter and place, butter side down, in deep muffin cups. Place pan on foil or cookie sheet during baking to prevent spillage. Bake at 375° (191° C) 10-15 minutes. Remove from pans immediately. Make glaze of confectioners sugar, vanilla and milk. Drizzle over rolls and sprinkle with nuts, if desired.

Blueberry-Nut Freezer Bread

Can do ahead
Can freeze

Yield: 2 loaves
Preparing: 20 min
Baking: 40-45 min

3 cups *(710 ml)* flour
2 tsp *(10 ml)* baking powder
1 tsp *(5 ml)* baking soda
½ tsp *(2.5 ml)* salt
⅔ cup *(158 ml)* corn oil
1⅓ cups *(316 ml)* sugar
4 eggs

½ cup *(118 ml)* milk
1½ tsp *(7.5 ml)* lemon juice
1 cup *(237 ml)* crushed pineapple,
  drained
2 cups *(474 ml)* blueberries, fresh
  or canned
1 cup *(237 ml)* pecans, chopped

Sift flour with baking powder, soda and salt; set aside. In large bowl, combine oil, sugar, eggs, milk, lemon juice and pineapple. Mix thoroughly. Add dry ingredients and beat until thoroughly blended. Fold in blueberries and nuts. Pour dough into 2 greased and floured loaf pans. Bake at 350° (177° C) for 40-45 minutes or until tests done. Remove from pans at once and cool on rack.

Cottage Cheese Bread

Can do ahead
Can freeze

Yield: 1 loaf
Preparing: 1½-2 hrs
Rising: 1½ hr
Baking: 40-45 min

1 pkg, ¼ oz *(7 g)* **yeast**
¼ cup *(59 ml)* **warm water**
½ ctn, 8 oz *(227 g)* **cottage cheese**
2 Tb *(30 ml)* **sugar**
2 Tb *(30 ml)* **oil**

1 tsp *(5 ml)* **salt**
1 **egg**
2 cups *(474 ml)* **unbleached flour**
¼ tsp *(1.25 ml)* **soda**

Dissolve yeast in warm water. Blend in other ingredients **less** 1 cup (237 ml) flour and the soda. Let rise till double (about 1½ hrs). Work in the last cup of flour and soda on board until smooth. Bake at 300° (149° C) for 40 to 45 minutes.

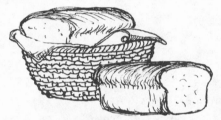

Sweet Roll Dough

Basic recipe used in a home economics class to demonstrate making tea rings, stollen, and dinner or luncheon rolls

Can freeze

Preparing: 3½ hrs.
Baking: 12 to 15 min

½ cup *(118 ml)* **warm water, not hot — 110 to 115°**
2 pkgs, ¼ oz *(7 g)* **dry yeast**
1½ cups *(354 ml)* **milk, lukewarm**
½ cup *(118 ml)* **sugar**

2 tsp **salt**
2 **eggs**
½ cup *(118 ml)* **shortening, soft**
7 to 7½ cups *(1.65-1.77 l)* **flour**

In bowl, dissolve yeast in water. Measure flour and sift. Add milk, sugar, salt, egg, shortening and half of flour to yeast. Mix with spoon until smooth. Add enough remaining flour to handle easily. Turn onto lightly floured board; knead until smooth (5 minutes). Round up in greased bowl, bring greased side up. Cover with cloth. Let rise in warm place, 85°, (29° C) until double, about 1½ hours. Punch down, let rise again until almost double, about 30 minutes. Shape dough as desired — just follow the following sketches and directions. Let rise until light, 15 to 20 minutes. Preheat oven to 400° (204° C). Bake 12-15 minutes in lightly greased pan. Can freeze. Reheat in foil paper, dull side on the outside of rolls.

119

Variation Of Roll Shapes

For all twisted shapes, dough must be rolled into a 12 inch oblong and less than ½ inch thick. After that brush with melted butter. Fold in half and cut into strips ½ inch wide and 6 inches long.

Parkerhouse Rolls
Dough must be rolled out to ¼″ thick, cut with a biscuit cutter and brushed with melted butter. Use back of knife to make a crease for each roll, then fold over so top slightly overlaps bottom and pinch edges together at crease. Place rolls close together in a greased pan.

Crescent Rolls
Dough must be rolled out to ¼ inch thick in a 12 inch circle. Cut into 16 pie-shaped pieces. Start rolling each piece from the larger end to the point. Place on greased baking sheet, point underneath.

Cloverleaf Rolls
Form small 1 inch balls from dough and place three balls in greased muffin cup.

Butter Fluffs
Roll dough into 9-inch rectangle, ⅛ inch thick. Brush with soft butter. Cut 6 long strips 1½ inches wide and stack all six one on top of the other evenly. 1-inch pieces are to be cut and placed cut side down in greased muffin cups.

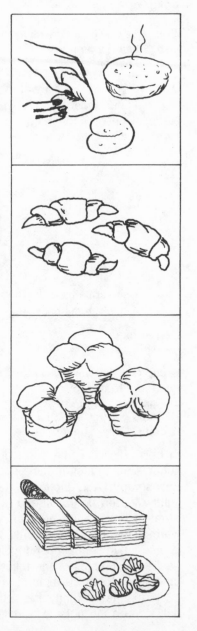

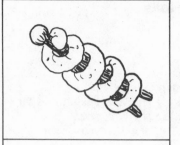

Clothespin Crullers
Grease clothespins and wrap strips of dough around until edges barely touch. After baking give a twist and pull out clothespin. Fill with jelly or fruit fillings.

Knots
Take a strip of dough, twist slightly and tie in a knot. Place on baking sheet.

Figure 8's
Roll long strip and twist into a figure eight. Pinch ends together and place on greased baking sheet.

Twists
Do the same as the figure 8's but add an extra twist before placing on greased baking sheet.

Snails
Roll long strip and twist slightly. Place one end on greased baking sheet and wind around in circle form, tucking other end underneath.

Buttermilk Rolls

Must do ahead
Can freeze

Yield: 2½ doz
Preparing: 20 min
Baking: 15 min

1 pkg, ¼ oz *(7 g)* dry yeast
2 cups *(474 ml)* buttermilk
5 cups *(1.18 l)* sifted flour, more if
  needed
3 Tb *(45 ml)* sugar

1 tsp *(5 ml)* salt
¼ tsp *(1.25 ml)* baking powder
¼ tsp *(1.25 ml)* soda
4 Tb *(60 ml)* Crisco

Heat buttermilk to lukewarm and dissolve yeast in it. Sift dry ingredients and cut in shortening; add buttermilk-yeast mixture and mix well. Cover and store in refrigerator overnight. About 1½ hours before serving, shape into rolls and let rise. Bake at 400° (204° C) for about 15 minutes.

Rum Rolls

Can do ahead
Can freeze

Yield: 2 doz
Preparing: 2½ hrs
Rising: 1¾ hrs
Baking: 15-20 min

3-3¼ cups *(710 ml-769 ml)* flour
1 pkg, ¼ oz *(7 g)* yeast
1 cup *(237 ml)* milk
6 Tb *(90 ml)* margarine
⅓ cup *(79 ml)* sugar
½ tsp *(2.5 ml)* salt
1 egg
2 Tb *(30 ml)* butter OR margarine,
  melted

1 cup *(237 ml)* brown sugar
1 cup *(237 ml)* raisins
1¼ cup *(296 ml)* powdered sugar,
  sifted
1½ tsp *(7.5 ml)* rum flavoring
1½-2 Tb *(22.5-30 ml)* hot water

Mix 2 cups (474 ml) flour and yeast together with hands. Heat milk, margarine, sugar and salt until warm stirring constantly until margarine melts. Add to dry mixture in bowl and beat 3 minutes with mixer. Add egg and beat 1 minute more. Stir in remaining flour to make soft dough. Turn out and knead about 5 minutes. Cover in bowl and let rise 1 hour. Turn out and shape into 2 balls. Cover and let rest 5 minutes. Roll into two rectangles; brush with butter. Combine brown sugar and raisins and sprinkle over dough. Roll up like jelly roll and cut in ¾ inch slices. Place in 24 muffin pans or 2 round or square 9 inch pans. Let rise 45 minutes. Bake at 375° (191° C) for 20 minutes. Remove rolls from pan and spoon or brush on frosting made by combining powdered sugar, rum flavoring and hot water.

Hot Rolls Or Buns

Must do ahead
Can freeze

Yield: 60-80
Preparing: 30 min
Rising: 3 hrs
Baking: 20-25 min

1 cup *(237 ml)* Crisco
4 Tb *(60 ml)* sugar
1 cup *(237 ml)* water
1½ Tb *(22.5 ml)* salt
2 pkgs dry yeast

2 eggs, beaten
1 cup *(237 ml)* milk
5 cups *(1.18 l)* flour
1-3 cups *(237-711 ml)* extra flour
1 cup *(237 ml)* margarine, melted

In a saucepan, heat Crisco, sugar, water and salt, stirring until sugar dissolves and Crisco melts; cool. Soften yeast in ¼ cup (59 ml) warm water in large bowl; add cooled Crisco, then eggs, then milk. Using a mixer, gradually add flour. After about 4 cups (946 ml) you will probably have to use a spoon. Turn out and knead, adding flour as needed, about 1 cup (237 ml) more. Put in greased bowl, turning once to grease all sides; cover and let rise 1-2 hours until double in bulk. Turn out on floured board; divide dough in thirds. Cover and let rest 5 minutes. With each third, pinch off 11-14 pieces and form each into a ball. Place balls in 3 round, greased cake pans. Cover and let rise 1 hour. Put spoonfuls of melted margarine over rolls while they are rising (and **also** when almost done in oven but not yet brown). The more the better — this is the secret of their great taste. Bake at 375° (191° C) for 20-25 minutes.

Refrigerator Rolls — Without Eggs

Can do ahead
Can freeze

Yield: 4 doz large or 9 doz small
Preparing: 1 hr
Rising: 3 hrs
Baking: 15-20 min

1 qt *(946 ml)* milk
1 cup *(237 ml)* sugar
1 cup *(237 ml)* shortening
1 pkg, ¼ oz *(7 g)* yeast
¼ cup *(59 ml)* water

9 cups *(2.13 l)* all purpose flour,
   sifted before measuring
1 Tb *(15 ml)* salt
1 tsp *(5 ml)* soda
2 tsp *(10 ml)* baking powder

Scald milk with sugar and shortening. Cool to lukewarm, then add yeast dissolved thoroughly in lukewarm water. Add 8 cups (1.89 l) of the flour. Beat thoroughly. Let rise until double in bulk, then add salt, soda, and baking powder. Add enough flour (the other cup) to make soft dough. Place in bowl, grease surface of the dough, cover and place in refrigerator. Make rolls as wanted. Bake on any type of baking sheet or in muffin cups at 425° (218°C). Dough will keep for a week or 10 days. You can halve this recipe, still using the entire package of yeast.

Popovers

Cannot do ahead

Yield: 8-10
Oven heating and pan heating: 20 min
Preparing: 5 min
Baking: 45 min

1 cup *(237 ml)* **flour**
1 cup *(237 ml)* **milk**
3 Tb *(45 ml)* **salad oil**

½ tsp *(2.5 ml)* **salt**
3 eggs

Preheat oven to 400° (204° C). Place all ingredients in a blender and blend (or use electric mixer). Place greased muffin tins in oven for 10 minutes. Pour batter into HOT muffin tins, filling each two-thirds full. Bake for 15 minutes; reduce heat to 350° (177° C) and continue baking for 30 minutes. **Do not open** oven door until cooking time is finished.

Swedish Tea Ring

Can do ahead
Can freeze

Yield: 2 large rings
Preparing: 35 min
Baking: 20-30 min

DOUGH:

2¼ cups *(533 ml)* **flour**
2 Tb *(30 ml)* **sugar**
1 tsp *(5 ml)* **salt**
½ cup *(118 ml)* **butter**
¼ cup *(59 ml)* **evaporated milk**

1 egg
¼ cup *(59 ml)* **raisins**
1 pkg, ¼ oz *(7 g)* **yeast**
¼ cup *(59 ml)* **warm water**

Soften yeast in ¼ cup (59 ml) warm water. Sift flour, sugar and salt into large bowl. Cut in ½ cup (118 ml) butter with pastry blender or fork until mixture is in fine particles. Add milk, egg, raisins and softened yeast. Mix well. Cover and chill at least 2 hours or overnight.

Divide dough in half. Roll out on floured surface. Spread with half of the filling. Roll up. Repeat with other half of dough. Shape each into ring or crescent on a greased cookie sheet. Snip outside edge of rings with scissors. Cut the ring ⅓ of the way through at 1 inch (2.54 cm) intervals, twisting to turn each section on its side. Let rise about 45 minutes to 1 hour or until double in bulk. Bake at 350° (177° C) for 20-30 minutes. Frost with glaze.

continued

FILLING I

¼ cup *(59 ml)* **butter, melted**
½ cup *(118 ml)* **brown sugar, firmly packed OR granulated sugar**
½ cup *(118 ml)* **nuts, chopped**

Brush rolled out dough with butter. Sprinkle with sugar, nuts and cinnamon.

FILLING II

1 can, 20 oz *(567 g)* **crushed pineapple, well drained**
¾ cup *(177 ml)* **sugar**
1 Tb *(15 ml)* **cornstarch**

Cook first 3 ingredients over medium heat until thick. Cool. Spread on rolled out dough.

GLAZE:

2 Tb *(30 ml)* **butter**
1 cup *(237 ml)* **powdered sugar, sifted**

½ tsp *(2.5 ml)* **vanilla**
1-2 Tb *(15-30 ml)* **evaporated milk**

Melt butter; mix with sugar and vanilla. Stir in milk until glaze is of spreading consistency.

Variation: Add a few drops of food coloring for holiday entertaining.

OPTIONAL: Garnish with red or green cherries and sliced almonds on top of icing.

COMMENT: This is a nice dough that needs no kneading and can be made up the day before and refrigerated or done the same day.

Orange Blossoms

Can do ahead
Can freeze

Yield: 5 doz
Preparing: 15 min
Baking: 10 min

½ cup *(118 ml)* **margarine**
1 cup *(237 ml)* **sugar**
3 **eggs**
½ cup *(118 ml)* **milk**

2 cups *(474 ml)* **flour**
2 tsp *(10 ml)* **baking powder**
1 tsp *(5 ml)* **vanilla**

Cream butter and sugar; add eggs and beat. Sift flour and baking powder together; add alternately with milk. Add vanilla. Bake in very small greased muffin pans at 350° (177° C) for 10 minutes.

ICING

1 **orange, juice and grated rind**
1 **lemon, juice and grated rind**

2 cups *(474 ml)* **confectioner's sugar, sifted**

Combine and stir until smooth. Dip muffins into icing as soon as they are removed from the oven. Dry on a rack. The secret is not to get too brown — just barely brown. If frozen, warm in foil to serve.

Oatmeal Muffins

Can do ahead

Yield: 1 doz
Preparing: 10 min
Baking: 15-20 min

Can freeze

1 cup *(237 ml)* **Quick Oats**
1 cup *(237 ml)* **butter OR sour milk***
1 egg
½ cup *(118 ml)* **brown sugar**

1 cup *(237 ml)* **flour**
½ tsp *(2.5 ml)* **salt**
1 tsp *(5 ml)* **baking powder**
½ tsp *(2.5 ml)* **soda**
½ cup *(118 ml)* **margarine, melted**

Soak oatmeal in milk for 1 hour; add egg and beat well. Add sugar and mix. Add flour sifted with salt, baking powder, and soda. Add cooled shortening. Bake in greased muffin pans at 400° (204° C) for 15-20 minutes.
*To Make Sour Milk:
1 cup (237 ml) sour milk — 1 Tb (15 ml) vinegar plus sweet milk to make 1 cup (237 ml).

Lemon Muffins

Can do ahead

Serves: 12-16
Preparing: 15 min
Baking: 15-20 min

Can freeze

1 cup *(237 ml)* **butter**
1 cup *(237 ml)* **sugar**
4 eggs, separated
2 cups *(474 ml)* **flour**

2 tsp *(10 ml)* **baking powder**
1 tsp *(5 ml)* **salt**
½ cup *(118 ml)* **fresh lemon juice**
2 tsp *(10 ml)* **lemon peel, grated**

Cream butter and sugar until smooth. Add egg yolks; beat until light. Sift flour with baking powder and salt; add alternately with lemon juice mixing thoroughly after each addition. DO NOT OVERMIX. Fold in stiffly beaten egg whites and the grated lemon peel. Fill buttered muffin pans ¾ full. Bake at 375° (191° C) about 20 minutes.

Apple Muffins

Can do ahead

Yield: 1 doz
Preparing: 15 min
Baking: 25 min

Can freeze

2 cups *(474 ml)* **flour**
¾ tsp *(3.75 ml)* **salt**
4 tsp *(20 ml)* **baking powder**
¼ cup *(59 ml)* **sugar**
¾ tsp *(3.75 ml)* **cinnamon**

¼ tsp *(1.25 ml)* **nutmeg**
1 egg, beaten
1 cup *(237 ml)* **milk**
⅓ cup *(79 ml)* **shortening, melted**
¾ cup *(177 ml)* **apples, chopped**

Sift dry ingredients; mix and add egg, milk, and shortening; stir until ingredients are just moistened. Add apples. Fill greased muffin pans ⅔ full. Bake at 400° (204° C) for 25 minutes.

French Breakfast Muffins

Can do ahead
Can freeze

Yield: 12
Preparing: 20 min
Baking: 20 min

5 Tb *(75 ml)* **margarine**
½ cup *(118 ml)* **sugar**
1 egg
1½ cups *(355 ml)* **flour**

2 tsp *(10 ml)* **baking powder**
¼ tsp *(1.25 ml)* **salt**
¼ tsp *(1.25 ml)* **nutmeg**
½ cup *(118 ml)* **milk**

Cream margarine and sugar. Add egg. Mix well. Add sifted dry ingredients alternately with milk. Fill greased muffin tins ⅔ full. Bake at 350° (177° C). This will make 12 regular size muffins which need to bake 20 to 25 minutes. Or 24 miniature muffins which need to bake 15 minutes. When done take out of pan immediately and coat.

COATING:

6 Tb *(90 ml)* **margarine, melted**
½ cup *(118 ml)* **sugar**
1 tsp *(5 ml)* **cinnamon**

Mix sugar and cinnamon. Roll hot muffins in butter, then sugar mixture. They can be reheated in foil if needed.

Bran Muffins

Can do ahead

Yield: 4 qts (3.79 l)
Preparing: 15 min
Baking: 15-20 min

4 cups *(946 ml)* **Kellogg's All Bran**
(soaked in 2 cups *(474 ml)*
boiling water)
2 cups *(474 ml)* **Nabisco 100%**
Bran (soaked in 1 qt *(946 ml)*
buttermilk)
1 cup *(237 ml)* **shortening**

3 cups *(710 ml)* **white sugar**
4 eggs, beaten
5 cups *(1.18 l)* **flour**
5 tsp *(25 ml)* **baking soda**
1 tsp *(5 ml)* **salt**
2 cups *(474 ml)* **raisins**

Cream shortening with sugar. Add eggs. Add Nabisco that has been soaked in buttermilk. Sift flour, soda and salt. Add to above mixture. Add All Bran until moist. Pour in raisins. Store covered in refrigerator (6 weeks if desired). Pour in muffin tins, two-thirds full. Bake 15-20 minutes at 400° (204° C). They are done when not moist or shiny on top.

Easy Biscuits

Can do ahead
Can freeze

Yield: 6 large biscuits
Preparing: 5 min
Baking: 10 min

1 cup *(237 ml)* **self-rising flour**
½ cup *(118 ml)* **milk**
2 Tb *(30 ml)* **mayonnaise**

Combine ingredients; put in small muffin tins. Bake at 400-425°
(204-218° C) 10 minutes.

Cheese Biscuits

Can do ahead
Can freeze

Yield: 2½ dozen
Preparing: 20 min
Baking: 12 min

¼ lb *(113 g)* **margarine**
¾ lb *(340 g)* **New York sharp
cheddar cheese, grated**
1½ cups *(355 ml)* **flour**

1 tsp *(5 ml)* **baking powder**
¾ tsp *(3.7 ml)* **salt**
dash of cayenne pepper
**olives, cooked sausage OR ham
bits**

Work margarine and cheese with hands; add other ingredients and
work until no longer sticky. Roll into small balls. Insert olives, sausage
or ham bits in middle of each biscuit. Bake at 350° (177° C) 10-15
minutes.

Beer Biscuits
Easy

Can do ahead

Yield: 24
Preparing: 5 min
Rising: 30 min
Baking: 10 min

2 cups *(474 ml)* **biscuit mix**
1 cup *(237 ml)* **beer, at room
temperature**

2 Tb *(30 ml)* **sugar**

Combine ingredients; let rise 30 minutes in greased muffin tins. Bake
10 minutes at 400° (204° C).

Buttermilk Biscuits

Can do ahead
Can freeze

Yield: 106 biscuits
Preparing: 10 min
Baking: 10 min

5 cups *(1.18 l)* self rising flour
2½ cups *(592 ml)* Crisco
1 tsp *(5 ml)* baking soda

2 cups *(474 ml)* buttermilk, at
room temperature
2 Tb *(30 ml)* sugar
1 pkg, ¼ oz *(7 g)* dry yeast

Combine flour and shortening. Dissolve soda in buttermilk; add sugar and yeast (dissolved in ¼ cup warm water). Add wet ingredients to flour mixture. Chill until cold. Roll out and cut. Bake at 400° (204° C) 10 minutes. To freeze, remove from oven when barely tan on bottom; cool and put in freezer.

Corn Bread

Serve immediately

Serves: 6
Preparing: 15 min
Baking: 18 min

1 cup *(237 ml)* white cornmeal
½ tsp *(2.5 ml)* baking soda
½ tsp *(2.5 ml)* salt

1 egg, beaten
1 cup *(237 ml)* buttermilk
1 Tb *(15 ml)* shortening, melted

Sift dry ingredients together. Mix egg and buttermilk and add to dry ingredients. Add shortening and pour into greased shallow pan. Bake in 450° (232° C) oven for 18 minutes.

Onion Cheese Corn Bread

Can do ahead
Can freeze

Serves: 6-8
Preparing: 15 min
Cooking: 5 min
Baking: 40 min

3 medium onions, sliced
3 Tb *(45 ml)* butter, melted
½ cup *(118 ml)* cheddar cheese,
grated

1 pkg, 8 oz *(227 g)* corn bread mix
1 cup *(237 ml)* creamed corn
½ cup *(118 ml)* sour cream

Preheat oven to 425° (218° C). Sauté onions in butter. Prepare mix, substituting corn for milk. Pour into metal 9 x 5 (22.86 x 12.70 cm) pan. Top with onions, sour cream, then cheese. Bake 40 minutes.

Cheese Spoonbread

Serve immediately

Serves: 8
Preparing: 20 min
Baking: 45 min
Cooking: 10 min

¾ cup *(177 ml)* **self-rising cornmeal**
1 tsp *(5 ml)* **salt**
⅛ tsp *(.6 ml)* **pepper**
1 Tb *(15 ml)* **sugar**

1 cup *(237 ml)* **water**
2 Tb *(30 ml)* **butter**
2 cups *(474 ml)* **milk**
½ lb *(227 g)* **sharp cheese, grated**
3 **eggs, beaten**

In a saucepan mix the first six ingredients and half the milk. Bring to a boil and cook, stirring until thick. Cut ⅔ of the cheese into cubes and stir into the cornmeal mixture. Add the rest of the milk and the eggs. Mix and pour into a 1½ quart (1.42 l) greased casserole. Slice the rest of the cheese and place gently on top. Bake at 325° (163° C) for 45 minutes.

COFFEE CAKES and BREAKFAST FOODS

Moravian Sugar Cake

Can do ahead
Can freeze

Yield: 7 cakes
Preparing: 45 min
Rising: 1½-2 hrs
Baking: 20 min

1½ cups *(355 ml)* **boiling water OR potato water**
¾ cup *(177 ml)* **shortening OR butter**
½ cup *(118 ml)* **sugar**

1 tsp *(5 ml)* **salt**
2 pkgs, ¼ oz *(7 g)* **yeast**
1 cup *(237 ml)* **potatoes, mashed**
2 **eggs, beaten**
6-7 cups *(1.42-1.66 l)* **flour**

Combine 2 cups (474 ml) flour and 2 packages yeast in large bowl. Combine sugar, salt, butter, potatoes, boiling water (120°-130°). Add flour and yeast and beat. Add eggs and beat with electric mixer until smooth. Add enough flour to form soft dough. Knead and add flour until smooth and elastic. Place in bowl and grease top, cover and let rise until double in bulk. Press into greased pans, about ¼ to ½ inch thick, let rise (I use 7 nine inch foil pans). When very light, punch holes about 1 inch apart in dough. Fill holes with butter, water and brown sugar that has been combined and heated. Bake at 350° (177° C) about 20 minutes. Do not overbake.

Quick Praline Coffee Cake

Can do ahead
Can freeze

Yield: 2 cakes
Preparing: 10 min
Baking: 25 min

1 pkg yellow cake mix
¼-½ cup *(59 ml-118 ml)* butter
1 lb *(454 g)* light brown sugar
2 Tb *(30 ml)* flour

2 eggs, beaten
1 tsp *(5 ml)* vanilla
1½ cup *(355 ml)* pecans, chopped
   coarsely

Prepare yellow cake mix according to directions. Pour batter into 2 greased and floured 13 x 9 (33.02 cm x 22.86 cm) pans. Bake at 350° (177° C) until done. Remove.

Melt butter in skillet. Mix light brown sugar, flour and eggs. Add to the butter in the skillet and cook 3 minutes over low heat. Remove from heat and stir in vanilla and pecans. Spread evenly over surface of the cooled cakes. Return cakes to oven and bake for 8 minutes at 400° (204° C) in order to set the topping. Cool. Cut in 1½ inch (3.81 cm) sizes.

Sour Cream Coffee Cake

Can freeze

Serves: 15
Preparing: 20 min
Baking: 40 min

½ cup *(118 ml)* shortening
1 cup *(237 ml)* sugar
2 eggs
2 cups *(474 ml)* sifted flour
1 tsp *(5 ml)* baking soda
1 tsp *(5 ml)* baking powder
½ tsp *(2.5 ml)* salt
1 tsp *(5 ml)* vanilla
1 cup *(237 ml)* sour cream

TOPPING:

1 cup *(237 ml)* pecans, chopped
¾ cup *(177 ml)* brown sugar
¼ cup *(59 ml)* white sugar
1 tsp *(5 ml)* cinnamon (or more)
Melted butter to glaze finished
   cake

Cream shortening and sugar well. Add eggs one at a time and mix well. Add dry ingredients, sour cream, and vanilla. Pour half in lightly greased 9 x 13 inch (22.86 x 33.02 cm) pan. Cover with half of the topping mix. Then pour on rest of the batter, then the rest of the topping. Bake for 40 minutes at 325° (163° C). Brush after baked with melted butter.

Yellow Coffee Cake

Can do ahead
Can freeze

Yield: 1 cake
Preparing: 20 min
Baking: 1 hr

1 box Duncan Hines yellow cake
  mix
3 eggs
1 8 oz *(227 g)* carton sour cream
½ cup *(118 ml)* oil

½ cup *(118 ml)* ginger ale
½ cup *(118 ml)* sugar
2 tsp *(10 ml)* cinnamon
1 cup *(237 ml)* nuts, chopped

Place cake mix, eggs, sour cream, oil and ginger ale in bowl; beat 2 minutes. Fold in sugar, cinnamon and nuts. Pour into well-greased and floured Bundt pan. Bake in preheated 350° (177° C) oven for 1 hour. Let cool 20 minutes. Remove from pan.

Butterscotch Buns

Can do ahead

Serves: 12-15
Preparing: 15 min
Baking: 30 min

½ cup *(118 ml)* nuts, chopped
2 pkgs canned biscuits
¼ cup *(59 ml)* margarine, melted
½ cup *(118 ml)* sugar

1 tsp *(5 ml)* cinnamon
1 pkg, 6 oz *(170 g)* butterscotch
  morsels
⅓ cup *(79 ml)* evaporated milk

Place nuts in greased pan. Dip biscuits in melted margarine; then sugar and cinnamon. Place on nuts. Bake at 400° (204° C) for 30 minutes. Melt morsels and milk over medium heat. Pour over hot biscuit buns and let stand for 5 minutes before serving.

Cinnamon Buns

Can do ahead

Yield: 18 buns
Preparing: 45 min
Rising: 2½ hrs
Baking: 25 min

2 pkgs, ¼ oz *(7 g)* yeast
½ cup *(118 ml)* very warm water
1 tsp *(5 ml)* sugar
½ cup *(118 ml)* milk
½ cup *(118 ml)* sugar

1½ tsp *(7.5 ml)* salt
¼ cup *(59 ml)* butter OR margarine
2 eggs
4½ cups *(1.06 l)* flour

continued

FILLING:

½ cup *(118 ml)* butter OR
  margarine, softened
1 cup *(237 ml)* brown sugar, firmly
  packed

1 cup *(237 ml)* raisins
½ cup *(118 ml)* walnuts, chopped
1 tsp *(5 ml)* ground cinnamon

Sprinkle yeast into very warm water. Stir in 1 tsp (5 ml) sugar and allow to stand 10 minutes or until mixture begins to foam. Heat milk, remaining sugar, salt and butter in a medium-sized saucepan, just until butter melts; pour into a large bowl and allow to cool slightly. Beat in eggs. Stir in foaming yeast. Beat in 2 cups (474 ml) flour until smooth. Stir in enough of remaining flour to make soft dough. Turn dough out onto lightly floured surface. Knead until smooth and elastic. Place dough in large greased bowl, turn over to bring greased side up. Cover. Let rise in warm place 1½ hours. Punch down and allow to rest 5 minutes. To make filling, combine softened butter and brown sugar until well blended; stir in raisins, nuts and cinnamon. Divide dough in half; roll out onto a 15 x 9 inch rectangle on a lightly floured surface. Spread half the filling mixture over the dough. Roll up (as with a jelly roll) starting with the short end. Cut into 9 equal slices. Place cut side down in 2 buttered 8 x 8 x 2 inch (20.32 x 20.32 x 5.08 cm) baking pans. Cover pans; let rise in a warm place 45 minutes or until double. Bake in moderate oven, 375° (191° C) for 25 minutes. Invert pans immediately onto wire rack. To serve, separate buns with two forks.

Doughnuts

Can do ahead
Can freeze

Yield: 2-2½ doz
Preparing: 20 min
Frying: 20 min

¾ cup *(177 ml)* sugar
2 Tb *(30 ml)* butter
2 eggs
2 tsp *(10 ml)* vanilla
¾ cup *(177 ml)* milk

5½ cups *(1.30 l)* flour
6 tsp *(30 ml)* baking powder
1 tsp *(5 ml)* nutmeg
oil
confectioner's sugar

Cream sugar, butter and eggs. Add vanilla and milk. Sift flour, baking powder and nutmeg together. Add flour, one cup (237 ml) at a time until 4 cups (946 ml) are used. Knead and roll in remaining flour. Roll ¼ inch (.64 cm) thick, deep fry, cool and toss in confectioner's sugar.

Crêpes

Can do ahead
Can freeze

Yield: 16
Preparing: 3-4 min per crêpe

1 cup *(237 ml)* flour
¼ cup *(59 ml)* butter OR
  margarine, melted and cooled
  OR ¼ cup *(59 ml)* oil
2 eggs
2 egg yolks
1½ cups *(355 ml)* milk

butter OR margarine, melted
strawberry preserves OR
  currant jelly
confectioner's sugar
for dessert crêpes, add 5 tsp *(25 ml)* sugar

Combine first 4 ingredients and ½ cup (118 ml) milk; beat until smooth. Beat in remaining milk. Cover and refrigerate at least 30 minutes. Heat an 8 inch (20.32 cm) skillet slowly. For each crêpe, brush skillet with butter, add 2 Tb (30 ml) batter and rotate pan quickly to completely cover the bottom. Cook until lightly browned; turn and brown other side. Put on wire rack. Keep warm in a 300° (149° C) oven while making the rest or serve immediately. Spread each crêpe with 1 Tb (15 ml) preserves and fold in half or roll. Sprinkle with confectioner's sugar.

VARIATIONS: (omit powdered sugar and preserves above)

1. Mix spinach, sour cream and grated onion. Top with Swiss cheese; put under broiler to melt cheese.
2. Mix cooked shrimp and mushrooms with a cream sauce. Brush crêpes with melted butter and broil lightly.
3. Mix cooked chicken and broccoli with cream of chicken soup. Fill crêpes and top with your favorite cheese sauce; broil until bubbly.
4. Mix cooked ham, mushroom pieces and hard boiled eggs with a cheese sauce. Reserve a little cheese sauce for the top and broil lightly.

Bran Waffles

Can do ahead

Yield: 4-5
Preparing: 15 min

1 cup *(237 ml)* sifted flour
¼ cup *(59 ml)* sugar
1 tsp *(5 ml)* baking powder
½ tsp *(2.5 ml)* soda
¼ tsp *(1.25 ml)* salt

1 cup *(237 ml)* buttermilk
2 eggs, separated
1 cup *(237 ml)* whole bran cereal
6 Tb *(90 ml)* butter OR margarine,
  melted

Sift together first 5 ingredients. Beat egg yolks and add to dry mixture along with buttermilk. Beat egg whites stiff and fold in with bran and butter. Bake in a preheated waffle iron.

Comment: This batter can also be used to make pancakes on a lightly greased griddle. Yields about 16 pancakes.

Grandmother's Waffles

Easy as Aunt Jemima and much tastier

Can do ahead
Can freeze

Serves: 4-5
Preparing: 5 min
Cooking: 5-7 min per waffle

2 eggs
2 cups *(474 ml)* **milk**
2 cups *(474 ml)* **flour**
6 Tb *(90 ml)* **Wesson oil**

1 tsp *(5 ml)* **salt**
1 tsp *(5 ml)* **sugar**
2 tsp *(10 ml)* **baking powder**

Preheat waffle iron. If iron is well seasoned, do not grease. If not seasoned, spray with Pam. Beat eggs. Add milk and remaining ingredients. Pour some batter in center and spread with knife (takes approximately 1 cup (237 ml) for a 3-section waffle iron grill combination). Cook until done. If making batter a day ahead, add another teaspoon (5 ml) baking powder right before cooking.

Variation: Can sprinkle each waffle with chopped pecans right after batter is poured, OR add 1 cup (237 ml) cheddar cheese, shredded, and ½ cup (118 ml) ham, finely diced to the batter before pouring.

Buttermilk Waffles

Can do ahead
Can freeze

Yield: 6 whole squares
Preparing: 20 min

3 cups *(710 ml)* **all purpose flour**
1 tsp *(5 ml)* **baking soda**

1 tsp *(5 ml)* **salt**
2 Tb *(30 ml)* **baking powder**

Sift flour before measuring, then sift with other dry ingredients.

3 eggs, beaten
3 cups *(170 ml)* **buttermilk**
1 stick *(118 ml)* **margarine, melted**

Add 1 cup *(237 ml)* buttermilk to beaten eggs — mix — then add ⅓ of flour mixture. Continue in this manner until all is mixed. Stir in melted margarine. This should be a thin batter. Bake on medium hot waffle iron until golden brown. A handful of cooked rice can be added to this batter for interesting texture and flavor.

Pancakes

Can do ahead

Yield: 12-14
Preparing: 15-20 min
Cooking: 3-5 min per cake

1½ cups *(355 ml)* **sifted flour**
1 tsp *(5 ml)* **salt**
3 Tb *(45 ml)* **sugar**
1¾ tsp *(8.75 ml)* **baking powder**

1-2 eggs
3 Tb *(45 ml)* **butter, melted**
1-1¼ cups *(237-296 ml)* **milk**

Sift the first 4 ingredients. Beat eggs lightly; add butter and milk. Blend with dry ingredients, but do not overbeat. Cook in greased or seasoned skillet over medium high heat.

VARIATIONS:

Apple: add 1 cup (237 ml) apple, finely chopped.

Blueberry: sprinkle about 1 Tb (15 ml) blueberries on each pancake after pouring on griddle.

Pineapple: add ½ cup (118 ml) crushed pineapple, well drained, to batter.

Herb/Cheese: add a little thyme and marjoram with 1 cup (237 ml) cheddar cheese, shredded.

Easy Cheese Pancakes

Yield: 10-12
Preparing: 10 min

1½ cups *(355 ml)* **milk**
1 egg
¾ cup *(177 ml)* **cottage cheese**
1½ cups *(355 ml)* **pancake mix**

2 Tb *(30 ml)* **butter OR margarine, melted**
1 tsp *(5 ml)* **orange peel, grated**

Put first 3 ingredients in blender and blend quickly to break up the cottage cheese. Pour into bowl and add pancake mix, stirring just to moisten. Add butter and orange peel. Bake on lightly greased griddle.

Jelly Pancakes

Serves: 4
Preparing: 15-20 min

1 cup *(237 ml)* **all purpose flour**
½ tsp *(2.5 ml)* **salt**
1 **egg**

1 cup *(237 ml)* **milk**
2 Tb *(30 ml)* **Crisco**

Heat Crisco in iron skillet. Have oil hot before pouring in some of the mixture. These are made similar to crêpes. Pour in a little batter and tilt skillet so that batter covers entire bottom of pan. Cook over medium high heat 1-2 minutes then flip to cook other side. Remove and spread with favorite jelly, roll up and sprinkle with powdered sugar.

Buckwheat Pancakes

Must do ahead

Yield: 36-40

2 cups *(474 ml)* **buckwheat**
¾ cup *(177 ml)* **flour**
1 tsp *(5 ml)* **salt**

4 cups *(946 ml)* **buttermilk**
1 tsp *(5 ml)* **soda**

Mix all ingredients, except soda, to make a smooth batter. Let stand at room temperature overnight. Divide batter in half. To one half, add the teaspoon of soda dissolved in a little warm water. Also, add enough buttermilk so batter will pour readily. Refrigerate other half of batter until needed — it will keep a few weeks. Half of this batter will yield about 18-20 pancakes.

French Toast

Serves: 4
Preparing: 5 min
Cooking: 5 min per slice

1-2 **eggs, beaten slightly**
½ tsp *(2.5 ml)* **salt**
⅔-1 cup *(158-237 ml)* **milk**

½ tsp *(2.5 ml)* **vanilla**
8 **slices bread**

Mix first 4 ingredients together and dip each bread slice into mixture. Brown the bread on each side on a hot, well buttered griddle. Serve hot, sprinkle with powdered sugar, cinnamon or syrup.

Orange French Toast

Great for company

Serves: 5
Preparing: 5 min
Cooking: 5 min

2 eggs, beaten
1 cup *(237 ml)* orange juice
10 slices raisin bread

1½ cups *(355 ml)* vanilla wafers,
crushed OR graham cracker
crumbs
butter OR margarine

Combine eggs and orange juice. Quickly dip bread into egg mixture then into crumbs. Fry on both sides in a tablespoon (15 ml) of butter until brown. Add additional butter each time more bread is added. Serve with butter and warm maple syrup.

Syrups For
Pancakes And Waffles

Applesauce Syrup

1 cup *(237 ml)* applesauce
1 jar, 10 oz *(284 g)* apple jelly
½ tsp *(2.5 ml)* cinnamon
dash of ground cloves
dash salt

Cook and stir until jelly melts and syrup is hot.

Orange Syrup

½ cup *(118 ml)* butter
1 cup *(237 ml)* sugar
½ cup *(118 ml)* frozen orange juice

Mix and bring just to boil.

Fruit Butter

½ lb *(227 g)* butter
½ tsp *(2.5 ml)* salt
2 tsp *(10 ml)* powdered sugar
¾ cup *(177 ml)* strawberries OR
blueberries

Whip butter; add remaining ingredients and blend until smooth. Cover and refrigerate.

Maple Syrup

1 cup *(237 ml)* light corn syrup
½ cup *(118 ml)* brown sugar
½ cup *(118 ml)* water
maple flavoring
1 Tb *(15 ml)* butter

Cook corn syrup, brown sugar and water until sugar dissolves. Add a few drops of flavoring and butter.

Preserve Syrup

1 cup *(237 ml)* apricot preserves
¼ cup *(59 ml)* honey
2 Tb *(30 ml)* water
⅛ tsp *(.6 ml)* cinnamon

Blend and heat. Do not allow to boil.

Honey Butter

½ cup *(118 ml)* butter, softened
½ cup *(118 ml)* honey

Beat until light and fluffy.

Eggs and Cheese

Eggs and Cheese

Egg-Seafood Roll

Excellent with garlic grits
and curried fruit for a brunch!

Can do ahead

Serves: 6-8
Preparing: 45 min
Cooking: 30 min

4 Tb *(60 ml)* **butter**
½ tsp *(2.5 ml)* **salt**
5 eggs, separated

½ cup *(118 ml)* **flour**
⅛ tsp *(.6 ml)* **white pepper**
2 cups *(474 ml)* **milk**

Preheat oven to 400° (204° C). Grease, line with wax paper, grease again, a jelly roll pan, then dust it with flour. Melt butter in sauce pan, blend in flour, salt and pepper, stirring in milk gradually. Bring to a boil, stir, and cook 1 minute. Beat egg yolks, adding a little hot sauce while beating. Mix all together and cook stirring over medium heat 1 minute longer. DO NOT BOIL! Cool to room temperature.* Beat egg whites until stiff and fold into cooled sauce. Pour into jelly roll pan and bake 25 to 30 minutes until puffed and brown. Turn onto clean towel immediately. Carefully pull off wax paper. Spread with filling and roll from long side with the aid of the towel putting on serving platter with seam side down.

*May be done to this point the day before.

FILLING:

2 Tb *(30 ml)* **butter**
1 pkg *(283 g)* **frozen chopped spinach, cooked and drained**
3 cans, 4½ oz *(127 g)* **shrimp**
1 scant tsp *(5 ml)* **dill**

4 green onions, chopped
1 can, 3 oz *(85 g)* **mushrooms, drained**
2 pkg, 3 oz *(85 g)* **cream cheese**
salt and pepper to taste

Melt butter in skillet, cook onions until tender. Add mushrooms, shrimp, spinach, dill, and cream cheese. Season to taste. Spread in above before rolling it up. Filling may be made 1-2 days ahead and refrigerated. If refrigerated, bring to room temperature or warm slightly before spreading.

Egg Brunch

Good served with tomato aspic, cheese grits casserole
or stewed apples

Can do ahead

Serves: 10-12
Preparing: 30 min
Baking: 1 hr

4 slices bacon, cut up
½ lb *(227 g)* dried beef, cut
coarsely
2 cans, 3 oz *(85 g)* sliced
mushrooms
¼ cup *(59 ml)* butter
½ cup *(118 ml)* flour

1 qt *(946 ml)* milk
pepper to taste
16 eggs
¼ tsp *(1.25 ml)* salt
1 cup *(237 ml)* evaporated milk
¼ cup *(59 ml)* butter

To make sauce, sauté bacon until almost done. Add dried beef, mushrooms and ¼ cup (59 ml) butter. While still hot, add flour and milk. Add pepper, but no salt. Stir until thickened and smooth. Mix eggs with salt and evaporated milk and scramble in ¼ cup (59 ml) butter. Butter 3 qt (2.8 l) flat casserole. Place small amount of sauce in bottom, then a layer of eggs, layer of sauce, another layer of eggs and top with sauce. Garnish the top with mushrooms, if desired. Heat, covered, for one hour in 275° (135° C) oven. This may be fixed day before, refrigerated and heated when needed.

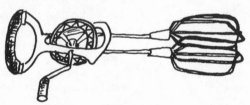

Eggs Royal Casserole

Good for weekend guests on Sunday morning

Can do ahead

Serves: 6
Preparing: 20 min
Baking: 55-60 min

2 cups *(474 ml)* croutons, herb
seasoned
1 cup *(237 ml)* cheese, shredded
4 eggs, slightly beaten
2 cups *(474 ml)* milk

½ tsp *(2.5 ml)* salt
½ tsp *(2.5 ml)* mustard
⅛ tsp *(.6 ml)* onion powder
½ tsp *(2.5 ml)* pepper
10 slices bacon, cooked

Combine croutons and cheese and put in the bottom of a greased 2 quart (1.89 l) casserole. Mix other ingredients until well blended; pour over croutons and cheese. Crumble bacon on top. Bake at 325° (163° C) for 55-60 minutes. May be made the night before.

Eggs Goldenrod

Can do ahead

Serves: 6-8
Preparing: 20-30 min
Cooking: 15 min

2 cups *(474 ml)* **medium cream
  sauce: see p. 234**
6 **hard-boiled eggs, sieved OR
  grated**

1 tsp *(5 ml)* **Worcestershire sauce**
1 tsp *(5 ml)* **salt**
½ tsp *(2.5 ml)* **pepper**
1 dash **hot pepper sauce**

Grate eggs into hot, but not boiling, white sauce. Add seasonings and adjust to taste. Thin with additional milk if necessary. Serve over hot toast. Pretty garnished with paprika and parsley for brunch.

Ham And Egg Brunch

Can partially do ahead

Serves: 4
Preparing: 20 min
Baking: 10-15 min

4 **slices of ham OR Canadian
  bacon**
8 **eggs**
¼ **cup** *(59 ml)* **butter**
¼ **cup** *(59 ml)* **flour**

1 cup *(237 ml)* **milk**
½ cup *(118 ml)* **chicken stock**
½ cup *(118 ml)* **Vermouth**
Parmesan cheese

Place slices of ham in four small baking dishes. Break 2 eggs on top of each one. Melt butter in sauce pan and stir in flour. Blend in milk, stock, and Vermouth. Season with salt and pepper. Pour over eggs and top with parmesan cheese. Bake at 400° (204° C) for 10-15 minutes (until eggs are set).

E
G
G
S

A
N
D

C
H
E
E
S
E

Canadian Egg Scramble

Must do ahead

Serves: 10
Preparing: 30 min
Chilling: 30 min
Baking: 30 min

1 cup *(237 ml)* **Canadian bacon,**
   diced
½ cup *(118 ml)* **green onion,**
   chopped
3 Tb *(45 ml)* **butter**
12 eggs, beaten

1 can, 3 oz *(85 g)* **sliced**
   mushrooms, drained
4 tsp *(20 ml)* **butter, melted**
2¼ cups *(532 ml)* **bread crumbs**
⅛ tsp *(.6 ml)* **paprika**

In large skillet cook Canadian bacon and onion in 3 Tb (45 ml) butter until onion is tender. Add eggs and scramble until just set. Fold mushrooms and cooked eggs into cheese sauce. Turn into 12 x 7 x 2 inch (30.48 x 17.78 x 5.08 cm) baking dish. Combine remaining melted butter, crumbs and paprika; sprinkle atop eggs. Cover, chill until 30 minutes before serving. Bake uncovered in 350° (177° C) oven for 30 minutes.

CHEESE SAUCE:

2 Tb *(30 ml)* **butter**
2 Tb *(30 ml)* **flour**
½ tsp *(2.5 ml)* **salt**

⅛ tsp *(.6 ml)* **pepper**
2 cups *(474 ml)* **milk**
1 cup *(237 ml)* **cheese, shredded**

Melt butter, blend in flour, salt and pepper. Add milk. Cook and stir until bubbly. Stir in cheese until melted.

French Stuffed Eggs

Can do ahead

Serves: 6
Preparing: 45 min

6 hard-cooked eggs
½ cup *(118 ml)* **cooked shrimp,**
   diced
3 Tb *(45 ml)* **mayonnaise**

½ tsp *(2.5 ml)* **salt**
dash of pepper
6 crisp lettuce leaves
parsley

Cut eggs in half lengthwise. Remove yolks. Mash yolks of 4 eggs; add shrimp, mayonnaise and seasonings. Refill egg whites with mixture. Place on lettuce leaves on serving platter. Force remaining egg yolks through a fine sieve and sprinkle over stuffed eggs. Garnish with parsley.

Omelet

2 eggs   **desired seasoning**
2 Tb *(30 ml)* **water**

Using a fork, beat the above together. For two omelets, double the ingredients. If making a batch, allow 2 eggs per person.

You will need a heavyweight 10 inch (25.4 cm) pan, preferably teflon-coated, or a regular omelet pan. Be sure your pan is very hot. Add a tablespoon (15 ml) of butter and move around the pan quickly so it does not burn. Add egg mixture quickly — it should make bubbles if your pan is hot enough. As soon as it bubbles, draw the egg away from the sides into the center, using a spatula. At the same time, tilt the pan so that the raw egg can go over to the edge of the pan. When omelet is moist but does not run, add filling of your choice, putting it on half of the omelet only. Using spatula, fold the unfilled side of the omelet all the way over. Start sliding omelet out of the pan onto a plate and when part of it is barely on the plate, turn it upside down. This will hide any tears you made on the unfilled side.

SUGGESTED FILLINGS:

vegetables such as frozen
  artichokes, asparagus, carrots,
  broccoli, green pepper
cheese and onion
ham and Swiss cheese
sausage, onions and potatoes
shrimp and spinach

shrimp and snow peas
asparagus and mushrooms
broccoli and bacon
tomatoes and mozzarella with
  oregano
bananas or strawberries with sour
  cream

Easy Eggs Benedict

Serves: 6
Preparing: 15 min
Cooking: 10 min

1 can, 10¾ oz *(305 g)* **cream of
  chicken soup**
¼ cup *(59 ml)* **mayonnaise**
⅓ cup *(79 ml)* **milk**
1 Tb *(15 ml)* **lemon juice**

6 cooked ham slices
**3 English muffins, split and
  toasted**
6 eggs, poached

In saucepan, combine soup, mayonnaise, milk and lemon juice. Heat; stir now and then. Meanwhile, place a slice of ham on each muffin half; top with egg. Pour sauce over eggs. Very nice for brunch, luncheon or dinner. Fruit and asparagus are nice accompaniments.

Curried Eggs

Can do ahead

Serves: 6
Preparing: 15 min

6 hard boiled eggs
¼ tsp *(1.25 ml)* **mustard**
⅛ tsp *(.6 ml)* **salt**
½ tsp *(2.5 ml)* **vinegar**

2 Tb *(30 ml)* **mayonnaise**
1 tsp *(5 ml)* **onion, chopped**
English muffins

Slice eggs lengthwise, remove yolks and mix with remaining ingredients except muffins.

CREAM SAUCE:

2½ Tb *(37.5 ml)* **flour**
2½ Tb *(37.5 ml)* **butter**
1¼ cups *(296 ml)* **milk**

1 chicken bouillon cube
¼ tsp *(1.25 ml)* **curry powder**

Combine flour, butter and milk over medium heat to make a medium thick sauce. Add bouillon and curry. Arrange eggs in a shallow, greased baking dish and pour sauce over eggs.

TOPPING:

4 slices bread, cubed
1½ Tb *(22.5 ml)* **butter**
1 Tb *(15 ml)* **onion, chopped**

Toast bread cubes and toss with butter and onion. Put on top of casserole and bake at 350° (177° C) for 15 minutes or until crumbs are brown. Serve on toasted English muffins. Triple for 16 people.

Eggs In A Basket
Nice for a brunch dish or a midnight breakfast

Can partially do ahead

Serves: 18
Preparing: 1 hr
Baking: 30 min

3 pkgs frozen patty shells (18)
18 eggs

18 slices Canadian bacon, fried
Hollandaise sauce

Bake patty shells according to package directions, undercooking just slightly so not very brown. Cool, cut off tops and scoop middle dough out, being careful not to puncture sides of baskets. Line baskets on a large cookie sheet. Crack a raw egg into each. Bake at 300° (149° C) 30 minutes or until egg is set. Eggs can be put into shells one hour before baking. Serve each basket on slice of Canadian bacon and top with Hollandaise sauce.

Sausage-Egg Casserole

Must do ahead

Serves: 6
Preparing: 30 min
Chilling: overnight
Baking: 1½ hrs

8 slices bread, cubed
2 cups *(474 ml)* sharp cheese, grated
3 lbs *(1.4 kg)* link sausages, cut in thirds OR 1½ lbs *(680 g)* bulk sausage

4-6 eggs
2½ cups *(592 ml)* milk
¾ tsp *(3.7 ml)* dry mustard
½ cup *(118 ml)* additional milk
1 cup *(237 ml)* mushroom soup

Place bread cubes in a 9 x 13 inch (22.86 x 33.02 cm) casserole. Brown and drain sausage. Put cheese on bread; then the sausage. Beat eggs with mustard and the 2½ cups (592 ml) milk and pour over casserole. Refrigerate overnight. When ready to bake, dilute soup with the half cup of milk and pour over casserole. Bake at 300° (149° C) for 1½ hours.

Cheese Mold With Asparagus

Serves: 6
Preparing: 25 min
Baking: 40-50 min

2 cups *(474 ml)* milk
8 oz *(227 g)* Swiss cheese, cubed
½ tsp *(2.5 ml)* salt
½ tsp *(2.5 ml)* Worcestershire
dash of cayenne pepper

2 Tb *(30 ml)* butter
4 eggs
1 pkg, 10 oz *(284 g)* frozen asparagus, cooked and drained

Heat oven to 325° (163° C). Scald milk; reduce heat to low, add cheese, salt, Worcestershire, pepper and butter. Stir until cheese has melted. Cool. In a bowl, beat eggs gradually adding the cheese mixture, beating constantly. Pour into a well-greased 4 cup (946 ml) ring mold. Put mold in a deep baking pan and add enough boiling water to come as high as the mixture in the mold. Cover mold with foil loosely and bake 45 to 50 minutes. Be sure that a knife comes out clean when inserted, then loosen and unmold. Place asparagus spears in the center.

Baked Eggs For Two

Must serve immediately

Serves: 2
Preparing: 10 min
Baking: 15-20 min

¼ cup *(59 ml)* plain croutons
1 Tb *(15 ml)* margarine, melted
2 eggs

1 Tb *(15 ml)* Swiss cheese, grated
2 Tb *(30 ml)* chopped ham

Toss croutons with butter. Add eggs, sprinkle with salt and pepper, add cheese and ham. Pour into custard cups or a 1 quart (946 ml) baking dish and bake at 350° (177° C) 15-20 minutes.

Egg Casserole
Different and easy to prepare

Can do ahead
Can freeze

Serves: 8-10
Preparing: 15 min
Baking: 20 min

28-30 saltine crackers, crumbled
2 cups *(474 ml)* sharp cheddar
   cheese, grated
6 eggs, beaten

½ cup *(118 ml)* margarine, melted
salt and pepper
3 cups *(710 ml)* milk

Put saltines in buttered 8 x 12 inch (20.32 x 30.48 cm) casserole dish. Combine remaining ingredients and pour over saltines. Bake at 400° (240° C) 20 minutes.

Myrtle P's Eggs

Must do ahead

Serves: 18
Preparing: 30 min
Chilling: overnight
Baking: 30-40 min

15 slices bread, cubed
1 lb *(454 g)* Velveeta cheese
1 cup *(237 ml)* margarine, melted

1 cup *(237 ml)* butter, melted
8 eggs
4 cups *(946 ml)* milk

Grease a 3-quart (2.84 l) casserole and line with bread cubes. Melt margarine and cheese; pour over bread cubes. Beat eggs, milk and melted butter. Pour over casserole and refrigerate overnight. Bake at 350° (177° C) for 30-40 minutes or until set.

CHEESE DISHES

Cheese Cloud

Can do ahead

Serves: 6
Preparing: 25 min
Standing: 60 min
Baking: 60 min

12 slices day-old white bread
½ lb *(227 g)* Cheddar cheese,
  sliced
4 eggs
2½ cups *(592 ml)* milk

½ tsp *(2.5 ml)* prepared mustard
1 Tb *(15 ml)* onion, grated
¼ tsp *(1.25 ml)* salt
dash of cayenne pepper
1 tsp *(5 ml)* seasoned salt

Trim crusts from bread and arrange 6 slices in bottom of a 12 x 8 x 2 inch (30.48 x 20.32 x 5.08 cm) greased baking dish. Cover with cheese slices then with remaining bread slices. Beat eggs, add milk, mustard, onion and seasonings. Pour over casserole and let stand at room temperature for 1 hour. May be prepared a day before and refrigerated overnight. Bake at 350° (163° C) for 1 hour. Serve immediately.

Lennox Rarebit

Serve immediately

Serves: 4
Preparing: 15 min
Cooking: 10 min

1 Tb *(15 ml)* butter
¾ cup *(177 ml)* milk
6 eggs, slightly beaten
1 Tb *(15 ml)* salt
few grains of cayenne pepper

¼ tsp *(1.25 ml)* black pepper
¼ - ½ tsp *(1.25-2.5 ml)*
  Worcestershire sauce
1 pkg, 8 oz *(227 g)* cream cheese

Melt butter in the top of a double boiler. Add milk, eggs, and seasonings. Cook like scrambled eggs until nearly done, then add cream cheese, worked until soft. Do not cook too dry. Serve on toast.

Quiche Lorraine

Can do ahead
Can freeze

Serves: 4-6
Preparing: 30 min
Baking: 25-30 min

**6-8 slices bacon, cut in ¼" (.64 cm)
pieces, browned
1 8"(20.32 cm) pastry shell,
preferably puff pastry
1 cup** (237 ml) **Gruyére cheese,
sliced OR Swiss**

**3 large eggs
1¼-1½ cups** (296-355 ml) **heavy
cream
¼ tsp** (1.25 ml) **salt
pinch of pepper and nutmeg
1-2 Tb** (15-30 ml) **butter, cut in bits**

Partially cook pastry shell on buttered pan. Spread bacon on bottom of pastry shell alternately with cheese. Beat eggs, cream and seasonings well and pour into shell within ⅛ inch (.32 cm) from top. Dot with butter. Bake at 375° (191° C) in upper third of oven 25-30 minutes until quiche has puffed and browned. Serve warm or cold.

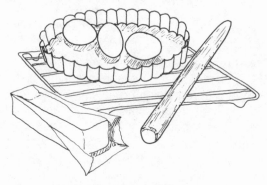

Crabmeat Quiche

Serve immediately

Serves: 4
Preparing: 30 min
Cooking: 5 min
Baking: 25-30 min

2 Tb (30 ml) **shallots, chopped
3 Tb** (45 ml) **butter
2 cups** (474 ml) **crabmeat
⅛ tsp** (.6 ml) **salt
2 Tb** (30 ml) **dry sherry**

**3 eggs
1 cup** (237 ml) **cream
1 Tb** (15 ml) **tomato paste
9 inch** (22.86 cm) **pastry shell
Swiss cheese, grated**

Sauté shallots in butter. Add crabmeat and cook over low heat for several minutes. Add salt and sherry. Set aside. Beat eggs until fluffy and add cream and tomato paste. Blend in crab mixture and pour into pastry shell. Sprinkle with grated Swiss cheese over top. Bake 25-35 minutes in upper third of preheated oven at 375° (191° C). Serve immediately.

Cheese Casserole

Can do ahead

Serves: 8
Preparing: 15 min
Baking: 1 hr

1 can, 4 oz *(113 g)* **green chilies**
1 lb *(454 g)* **Monterey Jack cheese, grated**
1 lb *(454 g)* **cheddar cheese, grated**
4 **egg whites, stiffly beaten**

4 **egg yolks**
⅔ cup *(158 ml)* **evaporated milk**
1 Tb *(15 ml)* **flour**
½ tsp *(2.5 ml)* **salt**
¼ tsp *(1.25 ml)* **pepper**
sliced tomatoes for top

Chop chilies in large bowl. Combine cheese and chilies and place in a 9 x 13 inch (22.86 x 33.02 cm) buttered casserole. In a small bowl combine egg yolks, milk, flour, salt, and pepper. Fold in beaten egg whites. Pour on top of cheese and chilies in a 2 quart (1.89 l) casserole, and push with a fork. Bake at 350° (177° C) for 30 minutes. Take out and put tomatoes on top. Bake another 30 minutes. Serve with green salad and French bread.

Country Noodle Casserole

Can do ahead

Serves: 12
Preparing: 35 min
Baking: 30-40 min

½ lb *(227 g)* **bacon, fried and crumbled**
1 pkg **fine egg noodles, cooked and drained**
3 cups *(680 ml)* **cottage cheese**
3 cups *(680 ml)* **sour cream**
2 cloves **garlic, crushed**
2 **onions, minced**

2 Tb *(30 ml)* **Worcestershire sauce**
dash of Tabasco
4 tsp *(20 ml)* **salt**
3 Tb *(45 ml)* **horseradish**
1 cup *(237 ml)* **Parmesan cheese, grated**
extra sour cream

Combine cottage cheese, sour cream, garlic, onions, Worcestershire, Tabasco, salt, horseradish, and ¾ cup (177 ml) Parmesan cheese. Add noodles and bacon and toss. Put in buttered 3½ quart (3.21 l) casserole. Cover and bake at 350° (177° C) for 30-40 minutes. Remove cover and sprinkle with ¼ cup (59 ml) of the Parmesan cheese and and broil until golden. Serve with rest of cheese and extra sour cream.

Almond Poppy Seed Noodles

Serve immediately

Serves: 8
Preparing: 20 min

1 cup *(237 ml)* **margarine**
1½ cups *(355 ml)* **blanched**
  slivered almonds, chopped

½ cup *(118 ml)* **poppy seeds**
¾ tsp *(3.7 ml)* **salt**
2 pkg, 8 oz *(227 g)* **noodles**

Melt margarine slowly so that it does not brown. Add almonds and sauté slowly until golden. Stir in poppy seeds and salt. Cook noodles according to package directions; drain. Turn back into pan in which they were cooked, pour almond mixture on them; mix lightly.

Garlic Grits

Can do ahead
Can freeze

Serves: 6-8
Preparing: 12 min
Baking: 45 min

4½ cups *(1.06 l)* **water**
1 cup *(237 ml)* **quick grits**
1 tsp *(5 ml)* **salt**
1 cup *(237 ml)* **margarine**

1 garlic cheese roll
2 eggs
½ cup *(118 ml)* **milk**
crackers, crushed OR paprika

Pour grits into salted boiling water. Cook. Add margarine and cheese roll. Beat eggs and milk and stir into grits. Pour into margarine greased 1½ quart (1.42 l) casserole. Top with crackers or paprika. Bake 45 minutes at 350° (177° C).

Fried Grits
Good way to use leftover grits

Must partially do ahead

Serves: 6
Preparing: 5-10 min
Chilling: 1-2 hrs
Cooking: 10 min

1 cup *(237 ml)* **grits**
4 cups *(946 ml)* **water**

flour
eggs, beaten

Cook grits according to package directions. Pour cooked grits into an 8½ x 4½ inch (21.59 x 11.43 cm) loaf pan and chill. When cold, cut into ½ inch (1.27 cm) slices. Dip slices in flour, then into beaten eggs, and back into flour again. Pan fry in small amount of fat until golden brown.

Meats

Meats

Tips For Meats

BEEF

Baste meat with a paint brush.

Add a grated, raw potato to each pound of ground meat for juicy hamburgers.

Put a strip of bacon on the bottom of your meat loaf pan to keep it from sticking.

Tenderize meat with a few drops of vinegar — no change in taste — will start the cooking faster, too.

Best to thaw meats in refrigerator (keep wrapped), or you will lose more juice. After thawing, bring them to room temperature for perfect cooking.

Place a piece, or two, of dry bread under the broiler pan. It soaks up the fat drippings and reduces smoking and fire.

Uncooked steaks, chops, small roasts can be held under good refrigeration for 2-3 days — larger roasts, slightly longer. Ground or cubed meat and variety meats should be cooked within 24 hours, after purchase.

After cooking, meat should be allowed to stand at room temperature only about an hour — cooked roasts and larger cuts of meat, if unsliced, will hold 4 days under good refrigeration.

Let a cooked roast stand 10-15 minutes at room temperature before carving — a large roast, 30 minutes.

One pound ground meat makes 4 servings when shaped into a loaf or 4 large meat balls.

Eye-appealing garnishes for seafood and beef — lemon cups filled with tartar sauce, cranberry sauce or chutney in peach halves, mincemeat baked in orange cups and small pickled beets stuffed with cream cheese.

Cut meats that are small in diameter (tenderloins, etc.) on the diagonal to make each serving larger.

Allow ½ lb meat (with bone) per serving.

Salt meat only after it is ¾ cooked. Allow ¾ tsp of salt for 1 pound of ground meat and 1 tsp salt for 1 pound solid meat.

LIVER

All liver is tender; overcooking toughens it. Beef and pork liver are more nutritious than calves liver, and far less costly.

TURKEY

For best flavor, choose turkey weighing 10 pounds or over. A frozen bird weighing up to 10 pounds will thaw in refrigerator in 1 day; over 10 pounds, in about 2 days.

Allow about 1 pound for each serving. Decrease amount by about ¼ pound for bird weighing 20 pounds or over.

M
E
A
T
S

POULTRY

Poultry is very perishable. To store in refrigerator, cover raw poultry tightly. Raw poultry keeps about 2 days. Cooked poultry will keep about 5 days. (Stuffing should be removed and stored separately).

Poultry may be stuffed the night before roasting, as long as both the bird and the stuffing are first well chilled.

Do not keep poultry frozen for more than six months.

Poultry can be skinned and boned easily if slightly frozen.

Before baking or frying chicken, marinate overnight in buttermilk, sour milk or sour cream.

Allow 1 pound of chicken (including bones) per serving.

Do not let cooked chicken stand at room temperature. Refrigerate, covered, and use in less than 3 days.

Soaking chicken in salt water before flouring to fry seals the juices in and keeps out grease.

VEAL

Veal is infant beef and similar to young chicken. The two are interchangeable in recipes.

Avoid overcooking veal as it dries and toughens readily.

To flatten veal for escallops pound it with the flat side of a heavy pot.

HAM

The butt end of a ham has more bone in proportion to lean meat. It is a little more tender than the shank end, and also is more expensive.

Allow about 3 ounces of boneless, cooked ham per person.

Soak country cured or home cured ham 8-12 hours in cold water before roasting.

Bake hams about 20 minutes per pound.

Baste ham with wine, ginger ale, fruit juices, cider, honey, or maple syrup. They penetrate very slightly.

Cut diagonal gashes in fat of ham slices, every inch or so, to prevent curling while cooking.

Coca Cola is a great baste for ham.

GRAVY

Freeze leftover gravy in an ice cube tray. When frozen, transfer to a plastic bag.

Instant potato makes a great thickening for stews and gravies — will not lump.

Gravy made with cornstarch as a thickening agent, instead of flour, can be reheated many times without causing the grease to separate.

For sour cream gravy, slowly blend in 1 cup sour cream for 1½-2 cups stock.

Easy Way To Cook A Roast

Preparing: 5 min
Baking: 2 hrs

Preheat oven to 500° (260° C). Put uncovered roast in pan and cook:

5 minutes per lb for rare
6 minutes per lb for medium
7 minutes per lb for well done

Turn oven off and do not open for 2 hours. Perfect every time! This is a good way to cook rump roast or any tender cut roast.

Marinated Chuck Roast

Must do ahead

Serves: 4-6
Preparing: 20 min
Marinating: 90 min
Baking: 30 min on grill

3-5 lb *(1.4-2.3 kg)* **chuck roast**
½ cup *(118 ml)* **strong coffee**
½ cup *(118 ml)* **soy sauce**
1 Tb *(15 ml)* **Worcestershire sauce**

1 Tb *(15 ml)* **vinegar**
1 Tb *(15 ml)* **sesame seeds**
1 large onion, chopped
meat tenderizer

Rub roast with butter, pierce and sprinkle with meat tenderizer. Combine remaining ingredients and marinate at least 45 minutes on each side. Delicious grilled or broiled. Cook to desired doneness.

Beef Tender

Must do ahead

Serves: 6
Preparing: 10 min
Marinating: 24 hrs
Roasting: 25-30 min

1 large beef filet-3 lb *(1.4 kg)*
(allow ½ lb *(227 g)* per person)

MARINADE:
1 cup *(237 ml)* **soy sauce**
1 cup *(237 ml)* **olive oil**
1 cup *(237 ml)* **sherry**

6 cloves garlic, chopped
1 tsp *(5 ml)* **Tabasco**
dash of pepper

Marinate filet for 24 hours. Turn several times during this 24 hour period. Remove and dry — rub with oil — roast on broiling rack at 475° (246° C) for 25 minutes (very rare); 28 to 30 minutes (rare). Baste with marinade 3 to 4 times — allow to cool for 10 minutes before slicing.

Beef Paprika
Serve over noodles or rice

Serves: 4
Preparing: 20 min
Baking: 2 hrs

2 lbs *(908 g)* round steak,
  cut in 2″ *(5.08 cm)* cubes
1 garlic clove, minced
6 large slices of onion
¼ cup *(59 ml)* butter

1 tsp *(5 ml)* salt
¼ tsp *(1.25 ml)* pepper
1 Tb *(15 ml)* paprika
2½ cups *(592 ml)* water
3 Tb *(45 ml)* cornstarch

Sauté the garlic with onions in butter. Add meat, brown well. Add salt, pepper, paprika and water. Simmer 2 hours until tender. Add cornstarch mixed with 2 Tb (30 ml) water. Stir until thick and serve.

Quick Cheese Steaks
Great quick family meal

Can do ahead

Serves: 4-6
Preparing: 10 min
Cooking: 5 min
Baking: 1 hr

2 Tb *(30 ml)* onion, grated
1 Tb *(15 ml)* shortening
4-6 cubed steaks
1 can, 10½ oz *(298 g)* tomato soup

1 tsp *(5 ml)* sugar
¼ tsp *(1.25 ml)* basil
1 tsp *(5 ml)* salt
¼ cup *(59 ml)* Parmesan cheese

Cook onion in melted shortening; add steaks, and cook until brown. Add other ingredients except cheese. Put into a 2 quart (1.89 l) casserole and cover tightly. Let cool; then seal and freeze. To bake, remove from freezer, thaw and bake at 350° (177° C) for 1 hour or until steaks are tender. Sprinkle with cheese before serving.

Liver

Serves: 4
Preparing: 1 hr, 15 min
Cooking: 2 min

4 slices calves' liver
milk
salt and pepper
½ cup *(118 ml)* butter

2½ Tb *(37.5 ml)* lemon juice
¾ cup *(177 ml)* fresh parsley
4 servings of rice, cooked
bacon strips for garnish

Cover liver with milk and marinate for 1 hour. Cut into thin strips. Melt butter in skillet until sizzling but not brown. Add liver strips, salt and pepper, and cook 2 minutes, stirring constantly. Remove liver and place on top of rice. To the butter in the skillet, add lemon juice and parsley, mix and heat. Pour over liver and rice and garnish.

Country Style Steak

Can do ahead
Can freeze

Serves: 4
Preparing: 15 min
Cooking: 2-2½ hrs

1 lb *(454 g)* **cube steak**
2 or 3 **onions**
3 **beef bouillon cubes**
4 Tb *(60 ml)* **Crisco**

3 Tb *(45 ml)* **butter**
½ cup *(118 ml)* **flour**
1 tsp *(5 ml)* **Kitchen Bouquet**
diced potatoes and carrots
(optional)

Roll cube steak in flour. Brown thoroughly on both sides, adding onion and pepper to taste. When the meat is browned, remove from pan. Add the bouillon cubes to the hot grease and dissolve adding 1 cup (237 ml) water. Stir constantly with a whisk until well blended. Make a roux of butter and flour; add this mixture to the frying pan along with 1½ cups (355 ml) water. Stir very quickly until thickened, adding Kitchen Bouquet. Put meat back in the frying pan and simmer over low heat for 2-2½ hours, covered. If using the potatoes and carrots, add 45 minutes before meat is done. If more flavor is desired, add one more cube of bouillon.

Stuffed Round Steak

Serves: 6
Preparing: 20-25 min
Baking: 1½ hrs

DRESSING:
3½ cups *(828 ml)* **dry bread cubes**
¾ tsp *(3.7 ml)* **leaf sage**
½ cup *(118 ml)* **butter, melted**
garlic salt to taste

pepper to taste
1 medium size **onion, cut fine**
3 **celery stalks, cut in**
  small pieces

Mix all ingredients together and reserve.

STEAK:
2 slices **round steak**
  ½'' *(1.27 cm)* **thick**
flour

dry mustard
oil
1 can, 10¾ oz *(305 g)* **mushroom**
  soup, (optional)

Cover each slice of steak with a small amount of flour. Sprinkle a little dry mustard over flour. Pound this in well with the edge of a saucer or wooden meat hammer. Spread dressing over each slice of steak and roll up. Brown the two rolls in a small amount of vegetable oil or Crisco. Place in roaster and bake until tender, about 1½ hours at 325° (163° C). To make especially good, put mushroom soup over the meat when you put it in the roaster.

Filet Of Boeuf With Perigueux Sauce

(Beef Sauté with Sauce)
Fabulous meal

Can partially do ahead

Serves: 12
Preparing: 1½ hrs
Cooking: 15-20 min

SAUCE:
1 lb *(454 g)* **fresh mushrooms,
sliced**
6 Tb *(90 ml)* **butter**
6 Tb *(90 ml)* **green onions, minced**
½ tsp *(2.5 ml)* **salt**
pinch of pepper
½ cup *(118 ml)* **Madeira or dry
white vermouth**

1½ cups *(355 ml)* **canned beef
bouillon**
2 cups *(474 ml)* **whipping cream**
2 Tb *(30 ml)* **cornstarch, blend with
2 Tb** *(30 ml)* **of the whipping
cream**

Sauté the mushrooms until lightly brown (4 to 5 minutes). Add onion, cook a minute longer and add seasoning. Set this aside. In another skillet, pour wine and bouillon in and rapidly boil it down until there is about ⅓ cup (79 ml) of liquid remaining. Beat in the cream, then the cornstarch mixture. Simmer a minute then add sautéed mushrooms and simmer a little more. Sauce should be lightly thickened.

BEEF SAUTÉ:
5 lbs *(2.3 kg)* **filet of beef**   2 Tb *(30 ml)* **cooking oil**
4 Tb *(60 ml)* **butter**

Remove fat from filet and cut into pieces 2″ (5.08 cm) wide and ½″ (1.27 cm) thick. Put butter and oil in skillet and sauté a few pieces of beef at a time 2 or 3 minutes The beef should be brown on the outside, but the inside should be red. When all beef has been sautéed, season with salt and pepper and drain excess fat from pan. Pour the cream and mushroom sauce over the beef. As sauce is basted over the beef, add 4 Tb (60 ml) butter and mix until butter melts and is absorbed. Place in casserole or serving dish and garnish with parsley.

Tenderloin Tips With Mushrooms

Serves: 6-8
Preparing: 20 min
Simmering: 1½ hrs

1½ lb *(680 g)* **sirloin tip roast
cut in ½" *(1.27 cm)* cubes**
2 tsp *(10 ml)* **salt**
⅛ tsp *(.6 ml)* **pepper**
3 Tb *(45 ml)* **flour**
4 Tb *(60 ml)* **oil**

¾ cup *(177 ml)* **tomato puree**
1½ cups *(355 ml)* **bouillon**
2 oz *(59 ml)* **Burgundy wine**
4 oz *(113 g)* **mushrooms, sliced**
2 oz *(59 ml)* **butter**

Sprinkle salt and pepper over meat. Dredge meat with flour. Sear meat in hot oil for 20 minutes. Add puree and bouillon. Simmer for 1½ hours or until tender. Sauté mushrooms in butter for 10 minutes. Add mushrooms and wine to meat mixture before serving. May be served on rice, noodles, or toast.

Barbequed Beef Brisket

Must do ahead
Can freeze

Serves: 6
Preparing: 10 min
Marinating: 2 hrs
Baking: 3½ hrs

1 cup *(237 ml)* **catsup**
1 cup *(237 ml)* **water**
1 Tb *(15 ml)* **dried onion,
minced**
2 Tb *(30 ml)* **vinegar**

1 Tb *(15 ml)* **horseradish**
1 Tb *(15 ml)* **mustard**
1 tsp *(5 ml)* **salt**
¼ tsp *(1.25 ml)* **pepper**
4 lb *(1.8 kg)* **beef brisket**

Mix first eight ingredients. Place beef (fat side up) in casserole. Pour mixture over and refrigerate several hours. Bake in 300° (149° C) oven for 3 to 3½ hours. This is good for cold beef sandwiches, too.

Chipped Beef Casserole
Nice for a brunch

Serves: 3-4
Preparing: 15 min
Cooking: 1 hr

1 can **cream of mushroom soup**
1 pkg **chipped beef**

1 cup *(237 ml)* **cheddar cheese**
2 **eggs, beaten**

Mix together and put in a casserole. Set casserole in pan of hot water. Cook in preheated 350° (177° C) oven for 1 hour.

Spare Ribs

Substantial, a good family fare

Can do ahead

Serves: 4
Preparing: 20 min
Marinating: 2 hrs
Cooking: 1-1½ hrs

4 lbs *(1.8 kg)* ribs
4 lemons and juice
4 oranges and juice
2 cups *(474 ml)* honey
2 Tb *(30 ml)* dry mustard

1 cup *(237 ml)* catsup
2 Tb *(30 ml)* horseradish
1 Tb *(15 ml)* Worcestershire
sauce
salt and pepper to taste

Marinate 2 hours in sauce. Then cook in sauce 1-1½ hours over medium-low heat. Stir occasionally to prevent sticking.

Moussaka

For eggplant lovers, it's a real treat

Can do ahead
Can freeze

Serves: 6-8
Preparing: 1 hr
Baking: 30 min

1 lb *(454 g)* ground beef
1 cup *(237 ml)* onion, chopped
1 clove garlic, crushed
1 cup *(237 ml)* tomato sauce
1 pkg spaghetti sauce mix
¾ cup *(177 ml)* red wine
2 medium eggplants, peeled, sliced
¼'' thick

¼ cup *(59 ml)* salad oil
1 Tb *(15 ml)* butter, melted
1 Tb *(15 ml)* flour
1 cup *(237 ml)* evaporated milk
⅓ cup *(79 ml)* bread crumbs
1⅓ cups *(316 ml)* shredded
Monterey Jack cheese

MEAT SAUCE:
Brown ground beef. Add onion, garlic, salt, tomato sauce, spaghetti sauce and wine; simmer 15 minutes.

Cook eggplant in oil until light brown on both sides; drain.

WHITE SAUCE:
Add flour to butter in saucepan to make roux; add evaporated milk and stir until thickened.

To assemble: Line a greased 9 x 13 inch (22.86 x 33.02 cm) dish with bread crumbs. Place ⅓ of eggplant in dish. Spread half of meat mixture over eggplant. Sprinkle with ⅓ cup (79 ml) cheese. Repeat layers, ending with eggplant. Pour white sauce over this and top with rest of cheese (⅔ cup [158 ml]). Bake at 350° (177° C) for 30 minutes.

Joan's Marinade For Shish Kebabs

Must do ahead

Serves: 8-10
Preparing: 25 min
Marinating: 12-36 hrs
Grilling: 10-15 min

5½ lbs *(2.5 kg)* sirloin, cut in cubes
½ cup *(118 ml)* olive or salad oil
¼ cup *(59 ml)* soy sauce
½ cup *(118 ml)* Taylor N. Y. State
  claret or Burgundy
2 Tb *(30 ml)* candied ginger,
  finely chopped (optional)

2 cloves garlic, grated
2 Tb *(30 ml)* tomato sauce OR
  catsup
1 Tb *(15 ml)* curry powder
½ tsp *(2.5 ml)* black pepper

Mix all ingredients thoroughly; add no salt since soy sauce provides ample. Marinate meat in refrigerator 12 to 36 hours depending on how pungent you like it. Turn cubes several times for even flavor. When ready to grill, drain meat, arrange on skewers alternately with vegetables or fruit. Usually use quartered onions, green peppers, tomatoes, and top end of skewer with a large fresh button mushroom. Serve over browned rice.

Spicy Beef Kebabs

Must do ahead

Serves: 4
Preparing: 20 min
Grilling: 15 min

1 cup *(237 ml)* Burgundy
1 cup *(237 ml)* salad oil
2 Tb *(30 ml)* Worcestershire sauce
¼ cup *(59 ml)* catsup
2 Tb *(30 ml)* sugar
2 Tb *(30 ml)* vinegar
1 tsp *(5 ml)* marjoram

1 tsp *(5 ml)* rosemary
2 lbs *(908 g)* sirloin steak,
  cut into 1" *(2.54 cm)* squares
2 tomatoes, cut in wedges
melted butter
1 large onion

Combine Burgundy, salad oil, Worcestershire, catsup, sugar, vinegar, marjoram and rosemary. Add meat and marinate at least 4 hours in refrigerator. Quarter onion and separate sections. (I bake onions in toaster oven for about 20 minutes so they are not so strong tasting after broiling on grill.) Alternate meat and vegetables on skewers. Brush vegetables with butter. Grill 10-15 minutes over medium heat, basting with marinade and turning occasionally.

London Broil

Can partially do ahead

Serves: 4
Preparing: 15 min
Cooking: 10 min

flank steak
5 Tb *(75 ml)* **Worcestershire sauce**
5 Tb *(75 ml)* **catsup**
5 tsp *(25 ml)* **brown sugar**
10 Tb *(150 ml)* **red wine**

5 pinches dry mustard
1 can, 4 oz *(113 gr)* **sliced**
mushrooms, drained
5 Tb *(75 ml)* **butter, melted**

Broil flank steak to degree of doneness you like. Slice on the diagonal into fairly thin strips. Mix all the ingredients together and pour the sauce over the steak. Excellent served with rice casserole.

Teriyaki Steak

Must do ahead

Serves: 4-6
Preparing: 5-10 min
Marinating: all day
Cooking: 20-30 min

London broil
1 clove garlic
1-2 tsp *(5-10 ml)* **ginger**
1½ tsp *(7.5 ml)* **sugar**

1 Tb *(15 ml)* **cider vinegar**
½ cup *(118 ml)* **soy sauce**
4 Tb *(60 ml)* **dry white wine**
(I use vermouth)

Marinate London broil all day in sauce made with above ingredients. Cook on charcoal grill and cut in strips to serve.

Round Steak

Can do ahead

Serves: 4
Preparing: 20 min
Baking: 1½ hrs

4 slices bacon
2 medium onions, chopped
2 lbs *(908 g)* **round steak**
1½ Tbs *(22.5 ml)* **flour**
2 cups *(474 ml)* **beer**

1 small bay leaf
1 pinch thyme
1 garlic clove
1 Tb *(15 ml)* **sugar**
1 tsp *(5 ml)* **vinegar**

Cook bacon. Sauté onion in fat. Add and brown meat. Put flour over meat until absorbed. Add remaining ingredients. Bake 1½ hours at 325° (163° C).

Barbequed Beef

Can partially do ahead

Serves: 6-8
Preparing: 10 min
Cooking: 20 min

4 cups *(946 ml)* **cooked beef,**
  cut into 2" *(5.08 cm)*
  strips
¼ cup *(59 ml)* **vinegar**
1½ cups *(355 ml)* **water**
¼ cup *(59 ml)* **sugar**
4 tsp *(20 ml)* **prepared mustard**
2 medium onions, sliced
¼ tsp *(1.25 ml)* **pepper**

1 Tb *(15 ml)* **salt**
¼ tsp *(1.25 ml)* **cayenne pepper**
2 thick lemon slices
½ cup *(118 ml)* **margarine**
1 cup *(237 ml)* **catsup**
  OR chili sauce
3 Tb *(45 ml)* **Worcestershire**
  sauce

Combine all ingredients except beef, catsup or chili sauce and Worcestershire sauce. Simmer, uncovered, 20 minutes. Then add catsup or chili sauce, Worcestershire and beef strips. It's best to let this marinate several hours in the refrigerator, but it can be served immediately by heating until the beef is heated through.

Double recipe and freeze half in an oven proof dish. Reheat in slow oven and serve with rice.

Lady's Day-Out Casserole
Delicious and Easy

Can do ahead
Can freeze

Serves: 6
Preparing: 15 min
Cooking: 25 min
Baking: 45 min

2 cups *(474 ml)* **macaroni**
1 lb *(454 g)* **ground round**
2 medium onions, chopped
1½ tsp *(7.5 ml)* **salt**
½ tsp *(2.5 ml)* **pepper**

1 jar, 15 oz *(425 g)* **spaghetti**
  sauce with mushrooms
1 lb *(454 g)* **tomatoes**
½ lb *(227 g)* **extra sharp**
  cheese, grated

Cook macaroni as directed on package; drain. Brown meat and onions; add salt, pepper, spaghetti sauce and tomatoes. Simmer 20 minutes. Place half the macaroni in 2½ quart (2.4 l) casserole. Cover with half the meat mixture, then half the cheese. Repeat layers. Bake uncovered in 350° (177° C) oven 45 minutes.

Smothered Hamburger Steaks

Can do ahead

Can freeze

Serves: 4
Preparing: 5 min
Cooking: 10 min
Baking: 30 min

1 lb *(454 g)* ground chuck
OR round
½ cup *(118 ml)* water
1 Tb *(15 ml)* hamburger
seasoning
¼ tsp *(1.25 ml)* ground black pepper

¼ cup *(59 ml)* dry bread
crumbs
1-1½ cups *(237-355 ml)* water
1 pkg brown gravy mix
1 can, 8 oz *(227 g)*
onion rings

Mix first 5 ingredients. Shape into 4 large patties and brown on both sides. Remove patties and add water (1-1½ cups) to drippings, then add gravy mix. Bring to a boil. Add onions. Place patties in square 8x8x2 inch (20.32 x 20.32 x 5.08 cm) dish. Cover and bake at 350° (177° C) for 30 minutes.

Hamburger Roll (Meatloaf)
With Mushroom-Rice Filling

Serves: 8
Preparing: 30 min
Cooking: 1 hr, 15 min

½ cup *(118 ml)* long grain rice
2 eggs
3 slices of bread made into
crumbs (use blender)
¼ cup *(59 ml)* milk
½ lb *(227 g)* mushrooms,
sautéed in butter

2 lbs *(908 g)* ground chuck
¼ cup *(59 ml)* catsup
1½ tsp *(7.5 ml)* salt
3 Tbs *(45 ml)* parsley, minced
pepper to taste
1 medium onion, chopped

Cook rice as directed and let cool. In a large bowl, beat eggs slightly. Add bread crumbs and milk and set aside. Add sautéed mushrooms and chopped parsley to cooled rice.

Mix onion, beef, catsup in bread crumbs, add salt and pepper and blend gently but thoroughly. On a sheet of tin foil, pat out meat mixture to form a rectangle about 9 x 12 x ¾ inches (22.86 x 30.48 x 1.91 cm) thick. Spread the rice and mushroom mixture over meat leaving a 1 inch border. Roll meat up as for jellyroll. Take meat roll on foil and place into a loaf pan and fold foil around to store until time to cook or use other greased oven-to-table pan. Bake at 350° (177° C) for one hour and fifteen minutes.

Manicotti

Can do ahead
Can freeze

FILLING:

Serves: 6
Preparing: 30 min
Baking: 30 min

12 manicotti shells, cooked	1 pkg frozen spinach, thawed,
¼ cup *(59 ml)* butter	drained and chopped
¼ cup *(59 ml)* onion, chopped	½ cup *(118 ml)* cottage cheese
1 clove garlic, mashed	2 eggs
1 lb *(454 g)* ground beef	1 tsp *(5 ml)* salt

Sauté butter, onion, and garlic. Add ground beef and brown, then remove from heat, add spinach, cottage cheese, eggs and salt.

SAUCE I:

¼ cup *(59 ml)* butter, melted	1½ cup *(355 ml)* milk
¼ cup *(59 ml)* flour	¼ cup *(59 ml)* parsley, chopped
2 cubes chicken bouillon	

Blend flour and bouillon with melted butter. Stir in milk and parsley. Heat to boiling and cook 1 minute.

SAUCE II: Mix spaghetti sauce and basil and set aside.

1 jar, 15½ oz *(440 l)* Ragu	2 tsp *(10 ml)* basil leaves
spaghetti sauce with	Parmesan
mushrooms	Mozzarella

Fill each shell with ¼ cup (59 ml) filling. Place in a 3 quart (2.8 l) oblong dish, buttered. Pour first sauce over shells, then second sauce. Sprinkle with Parmesan and shredded Mozarella cheese. Bake at 350° (177° C) for 30 minutes.

Beef Stroganoff

Can partially do ahead

Serves: 10
Preparing: 20 min
Cooking: 45-60 min

¾ cup *(177 ml)* margarine	2 cans undiluted consommé
1 cup *(237 ml)* onion, chopped	3 Tb *(45 ml)* lemon juice
3 lbs *(1.4 kg)* round steak,	9 Tb *(135 ml)* red wine
thinly sliced, floured	3 cans, 4 oz *(113 g)* mushrooms
salt and pepper to taste	1 pint *(711 ml)* sour cream
1 tsp *(5 ml)* crushed rosemary	

Sauté onion in margarine. Add meat, brown. Add salt and pepper, rosemary, liquid and then mushrooms. Simmer for 10-15 minutes. Thicken with flour if necessary. Add sour cream just before serving.

Meatball Casserole

This proves Mother is a good cook!

Can partially do ahead

Serves: 6
Preparing: 30 min
Baking: 20 min

1 lb *(454 g)* ground beef
¼ cup *(59 ml)* onion, chopped
1 Tb *(15 ml)* parsley, chopped
6 Tb *(90 ml)* sour cream
1 tsp *(5 ml)* salt
¼ tsp *(1.25 ml)* pepper
1 can, 10 oz *(284 g)* cream of
celery soup

1 can, 16 oz *(454 g)* sliced
carrots
1 can, 15 oz *(425 g)* sliced
potatoes, drained
OR 2 carrots and 1 potato,
pared, sliced, and cooked
instead of canned vegetables
1 can biscuits (8)

Mix beef, onion, parsley, 3 Tb (45 ml) sour cream, salt and pepper. Shape in 1 inch (2.54 cm) balls. Place in shallow baking dish (11 x 7 inch) (29.94 x 17.78 cm). Bake 10-12 minutes in 450° (232° C) oven. Mix soup, 3 Tb (45 ml) sour cream, drained carrots plus ½ can of their liquid (or cooking liquid if fresh are used) and potatoes. Pour over meat balls. Top with canned biscuits. Bake 15-20 minutes in hot oven to brown biscuits.

Zucchini Ground Meat Casserole

A good choice for a casual buffet dinner party

Serves: 8-10
Preparing: 30 min
Baking: 20-30 min

1½ lb *(680 g)* ground chuck
OR lamb, browned
2 medium onions, chopped
1 can, 16 oz *(454 g)* tomatoes
1 can, 8 oz *(227 g)* tomato sauce
1 can, 6 oz *(170 g)* tomato paste
1 tsp *(5 ml)* garlic salt
½ tsp *(2.5 ml)* oregano

1 tsp *(5 ml)* salt
1 cup *(237 ml)* cheddar cheese,
grated
4 zucchini, steamed and
sliced thick
1 pkg, 8 oz *(227 g)* Mozzarella
cheese
¼ cup *(59 ml)* Parmesan cheese

Mix all ingredients except zucchini and cheeses. Simmer 10 minutes. Remove from heat. Add cheddar cheese. Simmer 10 minutes more. Grease 2 quart (1.89 l) casserole. Layer half of zucchini, all of sauce, then rest of zucchini. Top with Parmesan cheese and strips of Mozzarella cheese. Bake 350° (177° C) for 20-30 minutes.

Pasta Griffiana
Ideal for a buffet

Can do ahead
Can freeze

Serves: 10
Preparing: 30 min
Baking: 25-35 min

2 lbs *(908 g)* ground beef,
  browned in olive oil
1 large onion, chopped
1 small bell pepper, chopped
2 tsp *(10 ml)* chili powder
2 tsp *(10 ml)* black pepper
½ tsp *(2.5 ml)* garlic, minced
pinch of nutmeg

1 can, 1 lb 13 oz *(822 g)*
  tomatoes, chopped
⅓ cup *(79 ml)* olives chopped
sharp cheddar and Swiss cheese
1 pkg, 8 oz *(227 g)* thin
  spinach noodles, cooked
mushrooms, if desired

Combine first 9 ingredients to make sauce. In casserole, layer spinach noodles, sauce and cheese, ending with sauce and cheese topping. Heat in a 350° (177° C) oven until bubbly approximately 25-35 minutes.

Sweet And Sour Meat With Cabbage
Easy . . . and such a different flavor

Serve immediately

Serves: 4
Preparing: 10 min
Cooking: 20 min

1 lb *(454 g)* ground beef
1 small onion
1 cup *(237 ml)* catsup
¼ cup *(59 ml)* water
2 Tb *(30 ml)* sugar
2 Tb *(30 ml)* cider OR wine
  vinegar

¼ tsp *(1.25 ml)* cloves
1 bay leaf
5 cups *(1.18 l)* coarsely sliced
  cabbage strips

In a large frying pan, brown meat and onion. Drain off fat. Add catsup, water, vinegar, sugar, cloves and bay leaf. Blend well. Arrange cabbage on top of meat mixture. Cover and cook over low heat about 20 minutes, or until cabbage is limp. It is the steam from the meat mixture which cooks the vegetable. Remove top and stir cabbage into meat and sauce before serving.

Steak Siciliano

Must do ahead

Preparing: 10 min
Marinating: 24 hrs
Broiling: 30 min

**1 top round steak, cut 1½" (3.81
 cm) thick**

SAUCE:
1 cup (237 ml) **port wine**
1 small clove garlic, minced
1 Tb (15 ml) **Worcestershire sauce**
1 small onion, minced
1 tsp (5 ml) **salt**
¼ tsp (1.25 ml) **pepper**

2 Tb (30 ml) **horseradish**
2 Tb (30 ml) **parsley, minced**
2 Tb (30 ml) **prepared mustard**
1 Tb (15 ml) **sugar**
2 Tb (30 ml) **butter**

Heat all sauce ingredients; cool. Put meat in shallow pan; pour sauce over it; refrigerate 24 hours, turning once. To cook meat: scrape off marinade, separating solids from liquids; put meat on oven rack near top level; broil 15 minutes on first side, basting with sauce; turn and pour solids on top and broil 15 minutes, basting. Remove, baste again and slice in thin diagonal strips across grain of meat.

Easy Lasagna

Can do ahead

Serves: 8-10
Preparing: 20 min
Baking: 1 hr

2½ lbs (1.1 kg) **ground beef**
1 large onion, chopped
salt and pepper to taste
Worcestershire sauce
**3 cans Hunt's tomato herb
 sauce**
1 pkg, 16 oz (454 g) **wide flat
 egg noodles, cooked, drained**

**1 large carton creamed cottage
 cheese**
1-2 cups (237-474 ml) **sour
 cream**
1 lb (454 g) **sharp cheese,
 grated**

Brown meat and onions, then drain. Add salt, pepper and a dash of Worcestershire. Add tomato sauce and simmer 30 minutes. Mix noodles, cottage cheese and sour cream and salt to taste. In a 3 quart (2.8 l) casserole, layer noodle mixture and meat sauce, beginning with noodles and ending with sauce. Top with cheese. Cover and bake 1 hour or until bubbly at 350° (177° C).

Rolled Lasagna

Can do ahead
Can freeze

Serves: 6-8
Preparing: 35 min
Cooking: 20-30 min
Baking: 40 min

**12 lasagna noodles, cooked according to directions; drain and
return to kettle and cover with cold water.**
1 pkg, 8 oz *(227 g)* **Mozzarella cheese**

FILLING:

1 carton, 1 lb *(454 g)* **cream-style
cottage cheese**
1 pkg, 3 oz *(85 g)* **cream cheese**
2 eggs

¼ cup *(59 ml)* **parsley,
chopped**
1 tsp *(5 ml)* **basil, crumbled**
½ tsp *(2.5 ml)* **salt**

Combine cottage cheese and cream cheese. Beat in eggs. Add
parsley, basil and salt.

SAUCE:

1 lb *(454 g)* **ground beef**
1 garlic clove, minced
1 can, 6 oz *(170 g)* **tomato paste**
1 can, 1 lb *(454 g)* **tomatoes OR
3 tomatoes and ½ cup** *(118 ml)* **water**

1 tsp *(5 ml)* **salt**
¾ tsp *(3.7 ml)* **pepper**
½ tsp *(2.5 ml)* **oregano**

Brown beef and garlic; drain grease. Add tomato paste, tomatoes,
salt, pepper and oregano. Cover and simmer 20 minutes.

Preheat oven to 350° (170° C).

Drain noodles, one at a time, on paper towels, spreading each with ¼
cup *(59 ml)* of filling. Roll up each noodle and place seam side down in
a 9″ x 13″ inch (22.86 x 33.02 cm) baking dish. After all noodles are
complete, spoon the sauce over, cover, and bake 40 minutes. Then
uncover and top with slices of Mozzarella cheese and bake a few
minutes longer until the cheese melts.

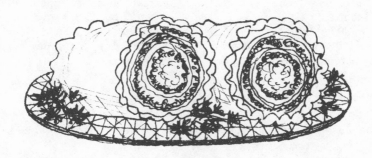

Apple Stuffed Pork Tenderloin

Can partially do ahead

Serves: 6-8
Preparing: 20 min
Cooking: 1½ hrs

PORK TENDERLOIN:

2 1 lb. *(454 g)* whole pork
   tenderloins
salt and pepper to taste

1 cup *(237 ml)* apple juice
4 slices bacon, halved

Cut each tenderloin lengthwise, NOT QUITE THROUGH; flatten out. Sprinkle generously with salt and pepper. Prepare stuffing.

APPLE STUFFING:

⅓ cup *(79 ml)* apple juice
1 Tb *(15 ml)* butter
1 tsp *(5 ml)* sage
¾ cup *(177 ml)* tart apples,
   chopped and unpared

½ cup *(118 ml)* onion, chopped
¾ cup *(177 ml)* packaged herb-
   seasoned stuffing

Heat apple juice with butter and sage. Stir in remaining ingredients. Spread stuffing over one flattened loin; top with second one; skewer shut. Place all stuffed loins in a shallow baking pan. Pour the 1 cup (237 ml) apple juice over meat and lay bacon strips on top. Roast uncovered at 350° (177° C) for 1½ hours or until well done (no pink). Remove skewers. Make gravy from pan drippings.

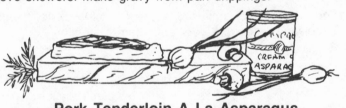

Pork Tenderloin A La Asparagus

Must serve immediately

Serves: 4
Preparing: 20 min
Cooking: 40-45 min

8 pieces pork tenderloin
   about 2 lbs *(908 g)*
2 Tb *(30 ml)* butter
1 can, 10¾ oz *(305 g)* cream of
   asparagus soup
¼ cup *(59 ml)* milk

½ cup *(118 ml)* chopped onion
1 can, 3 oz *(85 g)* sliced
   mushrooms, drained
½ tsp *(2.5 ml)* curry powder
dash pepper

Pound meat to flatten. In skillet brown meat lightly in butter; set aside. In same skillet, blend together soup and milk; stir in remaining ingredients. Return meat to skillet, cover and simmer 40-45 minutes (until meat is tender). Serve sauce on top of meat.

Apricot-Stuffed Pork Chops

Serve immediately

Serves: 6
Preparing: 20 min
Cooking: 40 min

6 pork rib chops, 1 inch
(2.54 cm) thick
salt and pepper to taste
1 can, 17 oz (482 g) apricot
halves
¼ cup (59 ml) catsup

2 Tb (30 ml) cooking oil
1 Tb (15 ml) lemon juice
2 Tb (30 ml) onion, chopped
½ tsp (2.5 ml) dry mustard
½ cup (118 ml) syrup from
canned apricot halves

Cut pocket in each chop, cutting from fat side almost to the bone edge. (Your butcher may do this for you.) Season cavity with a little salt and pepper. Drain apricots, reserving ½ cup (118 ml) syrup. Place two apricot halves in pocket of each chop. Cut up remaining apricots; set aside. Grill chops over medium coals for 35 minutes, turning once. Meanwhile, in saucepan combine catsup, oil, lemon juice, onion, dry mustard, reserved syrup and cut up apricots. Heat to boiling; reduce heat and simmer 15 minutes. Cook chops 5 minutes more, brushing often with mixture. Pass remaining sauce when serving chops.

Sweet And Sour Pork

Can do ahead

Serves: 8
Preparing: 1 hr
Cooking: 35 min

1½ lb (680 g) pork tenderloin,
cut in bite-sized pieces
¼ cup (59 ml) cooking oil
2 green peppers, cut in strips
1 can, 2 lb (908 g) pineapple
chunks
¾ cup (177 ml) brown sugar

½ cup (118 ml) white vinegar
3 Tb (45 ml) molasses
3 tomatoes, finely chopped OR
1 can, 1 lb (454 g) tomatoes
1 cup (237 ml) water
2 Tb (30 ml) cornstarch, mixed
with ¼ cup (59 ml) water

Brown pork well in 1″ (2.54 cm) oil, removing pieces as they are done. Combine green pepper, pineapple chunks, brown sugar, vinegar, molasses, tomatoes and water. Simmer together 5 minutes. Stir in cornstarch mixed with water. Cook and stir until thickened. Add browned pork cubes to sauce and cook 30 minutes.

Veal Rolls Continental

Unusual tasty meal with gourmet flare

Can partially do ahead

Serves: 8
Preparing: 2 hrs
Baking: 45 min

MEAT:

8 pieces of veal, cut as
  for Scallopini about 7″ x 4″
  (17.78 x 10.16 cm), ¼″ (.64 cm)
  thick
pepper
1 can, 4½ oz (128 g) deviled ham
8 Tb (120 ml) Ricotta OR Pot
  cheese

4 tsp (20 ml) onion, grated
2 eggs, slightly beaten
bread crumbs
4 Tb (60 ml) butter
¼ cup (59 ml) undiluted beef
  consommé

Sprinkle each piece of veal with pepper. Spread with deviled ham leaving ¼″ (.64 cm) border all the way around. Next spread each piece with 1 Tb (15 ml) Ricotta or Pot cheese and ½ tsp (2.5 ml) grated onion. Roll up jelly-roll fashion and secure with toothpicks. Dip in egg and coat with bread crumbs. Heat the butter in skillet and sauté rolls until golden all over. Drain on paper towels. Remove toothpicks. Transfer to a shallow casserole. Add consommé. Cover and bake in moderately low oven 325° (163° C) for 45 minutes.

SAUCE:

1 Tb (15 ml) butter, melted
8 scallions, chopped
1 cup (237 ml) mushrooms, sliced
2 cloves garlic, peeled and
  crushed
1 cup (237 ml) undiluted beef
  consommé

3 drops liquid pepper
  seasoning (Tabasco sauce)
1 Tb (15 ml) cornstarch
2 Tb (30 ml) cold water
2 Tb (30 ml) dry Marsala

Melt butter in saucepan; add scallions, mushrooms and garlic. Cook 5-7 minutes. Add consommé, cover and simmer until mushrooms and scallions are tender. Season with liquid pepper. Mix cornstarch and water to a smooth paste. Add to vegetable mixture. Cook and stir until smooth and thickened. When veal rolls are tender, drain liquid from casserole into sauce. Add Marsala if you like. Pour over rolls. Serve with rice, salad and dinner rolls.

Veal Casserole

Delicious with a raw spinach salad

Serves: 6
Preparing: 30-40 min
Baking: 1½ hrs

1½ lbs *(680 g)* **veal cutlets,**
    ¼'' *(.64 cm)* **thick**
1½ tsp *(7.5 ml)* **paprika**
3 Tb *(45 ml)* **flour**
1 tsp *(5 ml)* **salt**
1½ cups *(355 ml)* **beef gravy**

2 cups *(474 ml)* **wide noodles,**
    cooked
½ lb *(227 g)* **Swiss cheese,**
    sliced
¼ cup *(59 ml)* **butter**
½ cup *(118 ml)* **light cream**
2 tsp *(10 ml)* **chives, chopped**

Cut the veal into serving pieces. Place a slice of cheese on half of the veal pieces and top with a second piece of veal. Press the edges together. Combine flour, paprika and salt and coat the veal. Brown veal well in butter and remove from the skillet. Add gravy and cream to the skillet and simmer 5 minutes. Arrange alternate layers of noodles, sauce and veal in a buttered 2 quart (1.8 l) casserole. Sprinkle with chives, cover and bake at 375° (191° C) for 1½ hours.

Variation: Can add ½ cup (118 ml) white wine when adding gravy and
    cream. Can also add ½ lb (227 g) cooked ham cut in chunks
    and slightly browned when layering.

Veal In Lemon Sauce

Serves: 4
Preparing: 30 min

1 lb *(454 g)* **veal scallops**
¼ cup *(59 ml)* **flour**
1½ tsp *(7.5 ml)* **salt**
¼ tsp *(1.25 ml)* **black pepper,**
    freshly ground

2 Tb *(30 ml)* **olive oil**
2 Tb *(30 ml)* **butter**
2 Tb *(30 ml)* **lemon juice**
2 Tb *(30 ml)* **parsley, minced**

Pound veal very thin. Dip slices in mixture of flour, salt and pepper. Heat oil and butter; brown veal on both sides. Have veal flat in a single layer. When browned and tender, remove and pour off the fat. Add lemon juice and parsley to the pan, return the veal and heat, stirring to coat the veal thoroughly.

French Ham

An exotic twist to ordinary ham

Can do ahead

Serves: 6
Preparing: 20 min
Cooking: 10 min

3 lb *(1.4 kg)* **boned ham, cooked**
2 Tb *(30 ml)* **butter, melted**
1½ Tb *(22.5 ml)* **oil**
2 Tb *(30 ml)* **green onions**
  OR shallots, minced
⅔ cup *(158 ml)* **Madeira OR port**

3 Tb *(45 ml)* **cognac**
2 cups *(474 ml)* **whipping cream**
2 Tb *(30 ml)* **Dijon mustard**
1 Tb *(15 ml)* **tomato paste**
pepper

Slice ham into ¼″ (.64 cm) thick slices, trim off fat, cut into serving pieces and dry on paper towel. Brown slices lightly on each side in butter and oil and set aside, saving butter mixture. Pour all but 1 Tb (15 ml) of sautéing fat out of skillet; stir in onions and cook slowly until tender, pour in the wine and cognac and scrape up the drippings, stirring until all is mixed well. Then boil rapidly until the liquid is reduced to about a quarter cup (59 ml). Next mix the mustard, tomato paste and 2 Tb (30 ml) of cream together. Add the rest of the cream to the wine mixture. Beat in the mustard mixture and simmer slowly until the sauce has thickened slightly and been reduced. Add pepper and correct seasonings. Do not over-salt. Return ham slices to sauce, bake with sauce. This is now ready for serving but is better if made ahead — even the day before — and then reheated at a low simmer gently until ham is heated through. Serve with French bread to get up the last bites of sauce.

Golden Glazed Ham Steak

Can do ahead

Serves: 6
Preparing: 10 min
Baking: 1 hr

1 one inch *(2.54 cm)* **thick sliced**
  fully-cooked ham (1½ lbs *(680 g)* **))**
¾ cup *(177 ml)* **brown sugar,**
  firmly packed
1 Tb *(15 ml)* **cornstarch**

¼ tsp *(1.25 ml)* **ginger**
1 can, 8½ oz *(241 g)* **crushed**
  pineapple, not drained
1 Tb *(15 ml)* **lemon juice**

Slash fat edge of ham in several places. Place in shallow baking dish. Blend together sugar, cornstarch and ginger; add undrained pineapple and lemon juice. Heat to boiling, stirring constantly. Pour over ham. Bake in 325° (163° C) oven for 1 hour.

Roast Stuffed Lamb

Perfect entrée for formal dinner party

Can do partially ahead

Serves: 8
Preparing: 1 hr
Roasting: 2 hrs approx

1 5-6 lb *(2.3-2.7 kg)* **leg of lamb, boned**

Remove all fat and fell from lamb. It is best to bone your lamb from inside the meat as opposed to cutting down to the bone and cutting around it. This takes much longer but is well worth the trouble so the outside meat is not pierced. Trim excess meat from bone end reserving this meat for the stuffing. Do not remove entire end flap. Allow enough to pull up over end to enclose opening after stuffing.

STUFFING:

¾ **cup** *(177 ml)* **bread crumbs**
2 Tb *(30 ml)* **milk**
2 Tb *(30 ml)* **onion**
2 Tb *(30 ml)* **butter**
1 cup *(237 ml)* **lean raw lamb (from trimmings)**

¼ **cup** *(59 ml)* **pork fat or suet**
1 garlic clove, mashed
¼ **tsp** *(1.25 ml)* **ground rosemary**
¼ **tsp** *(1.25 ml)* **salt**

Sauté onion in butter to soften. Combine bread crumbs and milk, working into a paste. Pour out excess liquid. In food processor or grinder, grind lamb with suet. Add lamb, onions and remaining ingredients to bread crumb mixture. Push this stuffing into opening where bone was. Close opening, using skewers as you would for a turkey and lacing with string.

MUSTARD COATING:

½ **tsp** *(2.5 ml)* **ground rosemary**
1 garlic clove, mashed
1 Tb *(15 ml)* **soy sauce**

½ **cup** *(118 ml)* **Dijon mustard**
4 Tb *(60 ml)* **olive oil**

Mix rosemary, garlic, soy sauce, and mustard with a wire whisk. Slowly beat in oil to make sauce.

Coat entire lamb with mustard sauce reserving 2-3 Tb (30-45 ml) for a gravy. For a medium rare lamb, roast to a temperature of 140° (60° C) on your meat thermometer. This is 1½-2 hours in a 350° (177° C) oven. To make a sauce or gravy, remove meat from pan and remove excess fat, reserving in case you need more later. Sprinkle 2-3 Tb (30-45 ml) flour in roasting pan on stove top burner. Stir, scraping up coagulated juices and add 1-2 cups (237-474 ml) water plus reserved mustard coating. Stir constantly until thickened. Strain if desired and serve.

Marty's Marinated Boned Leg Of Lamb

Must do ahead

Preparing: 5 min
Marinating: 24 hrs
Cooking: on grill

1 leg of lamb, boned
2 cups *(474 ml)* **dry red wine**

1 cup *(237 ml)* **French dressing**

Marinate lamb for 24 hours in wine and French dressing in refrigerator. Cook on charcoal grill to desired doneness. Serve with spinach and mandarin orange salad and wild rice.

Armenian Lamb

The seasoning will convert anyone
who does not like lamb to a lamb lover

Can do ahead

Serves: 10-12
Preparing: 30 min
Baking: 20 min per lb

leg of lamb
6-8 cloves of garlic,
  peeled, then sliced in half
⅓ - ½ cup *(79-118 ml)* **flour**

⅛ tsp *(.6 ml)* **salt**
⅛ tsp *(.6 ml)* **pepper**
2 tsp *(10 ml)* **ground ginger**

With sharp knife slit six to eight slashes at random into each side of leg, then insert garlic clove slices in each so clove is inside meat. Mix flour and seasonings well. Transfer leg to roasting rack, moisten each side of lamb with quite damp paper towel then pat on as much of flour mixture as will stay on, on both sides, ending with the rounded side up. Scatter remainder of flour mixture in roasting pan. Roast at 350° (177° C) for 20 minutes per pound. Should be well done and skin crisp around the bone.

Lamb gravy: Pour off excess oil and fat, then make usual gravy with flour and water, scraping up browned flour from pan bottom as part of your flour.

Let roast sit 20 minutes to half hour before slicing. Serve with mint jelly as side dish.

MEAT SAUCES

Barbeque Sauce

Must do ahead

Yield: 3 cups (710 ml)
Preparing: 5 min
Cooking: 20 min

½ cup *(118 ml)* **vinegar**
¾ cup *(177 ml)* **water**
2 Tb *(30 ml)* **sugar**
3 Tb *(45 ml)* **dry onion soup
  mix**
1 tsp *(5 ml)* **salt**

pepper to taste
⅛ tsp *(.6 ml)* **cayenne pepper**
1 Tb *(15 ml)* **prepared mustard**
¼ cup *(59 ml)* **butter**
1 thick lemon slice
½ cup *(118 ml)* **catsup**

Mix all ingredients except catsup and bring to a boil. Add the catsup and simmer for 20 minutes. Excellent for chicken and hamburgers. You may prepare the sauce a day in advance and marinate the chicken.

Orange Sauce (For Pork Chops)
Delicious

Serve immediately

Yield: ½ cup (118 ml)
Preparing: 10 min
Cooking: 5-8 min

5 Tb *(75 ml)* **granulated sugar**
1½ tsp *(7.5 ml)* **cornstarch**
¼ tsp *(1.25 ml)* **salt**
¼ tsp *(1.25 ml)* **cinnamon**
10 cloves

2 tsp *(10 ml)* **orange rind,
  grated**
½ cup *(118 ml)* **orange juice**
4 orange slices, halved

Twenty minutes before chops are done cook sugar, cornstarch, salt, cinnamon, cloves, orange rind with ½ cup (118 ml) orange juice, stirring until thickened and clear. Add orange slices, cover pan, remove from heat. Garnish platter with glazed orange slices and spoon some of the orange glaze over each chop.

179

Raisin Sauce For Ham

Can do ahead

Yield: 3 cups (710 ml)
Preparing: 10 min
Cooking: 13 min

1¾ cup *(414 ml)* water
½ cup *(118 ml)* sugar
6 cloves
½ cup *(118 ml)* seedless raisins
2 Tb *(30 ml)* vinegar
2 Tb *(30 ml)* butter

grated rind of lemon
1 Tb *(15 ml)* cornstarch
1½ Tb *(22.5 ml)* prepared mustard
1 Tb *(15 ml)* currant jelly
⅓ cup *(79 ml)* port wine

Combine water, sugar, raisins, cloves and boil 10 minutes. Combine other ingredients with first mixture. Simmer 3 minutes.

Accompaniment For Ham

Can do ahead

Serves: 4-6
Preparing: 15 min

½ pt *(237 ml)* whipping cream
2 Tb *(30 ml)* mayonnaise
2 Tb *(30 ml)* horseradish
½ tsp *(2.5 ml)* prepared mustard

dash of salt
1 pkg, 3 oz *(85 g)* lime jello
1 cup *(237 ml)* boiling water

Beat cream and add mayonnaise, horseradish, mustard and salt. Dissolve jello in water; cool and add to above mixture. Chill. Serve as a salad or as a garnish for buffet supper, cut in small squares arranged on plate displayed with cold meats.

Sauce For Grilled Lamb Chops

⅓ cup *(79 ml)* currant jelly
⅓ cup *(79 ml)* mint sauce

⅓ cup *(79 ml)* chili sauce

Combine the above and heat. Serve over grilled chops. This makes enough for 6 to 8 lamb chops.

Hunter's Sauce

Yield: 1 cup (237 ml)
Preparing: 10 min

½ cup *(118 ml)* pepper jelly
¼ cup *(59 ml)* catsup
¼ cup *(59 ml)* port wine

½ Tb *(7.5 ml)* Worcestershire
sauce
2 Tb *(30 ml)* butter

Mix well over low heat and serve warm with any wild game.

Béarnaise Sauce
For beef ... or fish

Yield: 1 cup (237 ml)

3 sprigs tarragon, finely
  chopped
3 sprigs chervil, finely
  chopped
2 shallots, finely chopped
4 peppercorns, crushed
¼ cup *(59 ml)* tarragon vinegar
¼ cup *(59 ml)* white wine

3 egg yolks
1 Tb *(15 ml)* water
½ lb *(227 g)* butter,
  divided in three
salt to taste
pinch of cayenne pepper
1 Tb *(15 ml)* meat extract

Combine three sprigs of tarragon and chervil and two shallots, all finely chopped, four peppercorns, crushed, and one fourth cup each of tarragon vinegar and white wine in a heavy bottomed sauce pan. Cook the mixture over high heat until the volume is reduced by one third. Strain the mixture and set aside.

Put three egg yolks and one tablespoon of water in a bowl, set in a pan of hot water and gradually beat in the strained vinegar. Stir the mixture briskly over very low heat with a wire whisk until it is light and fluffy. Divide one half pound of butter at room temperature into three portions. Add the first portion, stirring constantly until the sauce is thick and smooth. Stir in the second and third portions, stirring after each addition until the sauce is thick and glossy. Season with salt to taste and a pinch of cayenne and add three sprigs each of tarragon and chervil, both finely chopped. Finish the sauce with one tablespoon of meat extract.

Hot Mustard Sauce
Delicious on sandwiches or as a sauce for meat

Can do ahead

Standing: overnight
Preparing: 30 min
Cooking: 20 min

2 cups *(474 ml)* dry mustard
2 cups *(474 ml)* vinegar
3 eggs

1 egg yolk
2 cups *(474 ml)* sugar

Stir mustard and vinegar until well mixed; cover and set aside overnight. The next day, add eggs and egg yolk, well beaten, and sugar. Cook over low heat in a 2 quart (1.8 l) double boiler, stirring constantly, until the consistency of custard — about 20 minutes. Let cool and refrigerate. Will keep indefinitely in refrigerator.

Creamy Mustard Sauce

Can do ahead

Yield: 1¼ cup (296 ml)
Preparing: 5 min

½ **cup** *(118 ml)* **mayonnaise**
½ **cup** *(118 ml)* **sour cream**

¼ **cup** *(59 ml)* **mustard**

Jezebel's Sauce For Ham

Can do ahead

Yield: 4 cups (946 ml)
Preparing: 10 min

1 jar, 10 oz *(284 g)* **pineapple**
  preserves
1 jar, 10 oz *(284 g)* **apple jelly**
1 jar, 8 oz *(227 g)* **hot mustard**

½-1 jar, 5 oz *(70-140 g)* **prepared**
  horseradish
salt and pepper
  to taste

Mix all ingredients in electric mixer. Will keep indefinitely in refrigerator.

Teriyaki Sauce

Can do ahead

Yield: 1¼ cup (296 ml)
Preparing: 5 min

1 cup *(237 ml)* **soy sauce**
1 Tb *(15 ml)* **sake**
  (OR any liquor)
⅓ **cup** *(79 ml)* **sugar**

1 Tb *(15 ml)* **ginger**
1 clove garlic, grated
¼ **cup** *(59 ml)* **onion, grated**

Mix ingredients well. Use with thinly sliced flank steak, ribs or chicken. Marinate meat 1 hour before broiling. Baste meat with sauce while broiling.

Mint Sauce For Lamb

½ **cup** *(118 ml)* **vinegar**
¼ **cup** *(59 ml)* **powdered sugar**
  or more

½ **cup** *(118 ml)* **mint leaves,**
  chopped fine

Heat vinegar and sugar together and pour over mint leaves. Let stand for 1 hour or longer.

Marinade For Chicken And Beef

Can do ahead

Yield: 4½ cups (1.06 l)
Preparing: 5 min
Marinating: overnight

1½ cups *(355 ml)* salad oil
¾ cup *(177 ml)* soy sauce
¼ cup *(59 ml)* Worcestershire
sauce
2 tsp *(10 ml)* dry mustard
2¼ tsp *(11.25 ml)* salt

1 tsp *(5 ml)* pepper
1½ cup *(355 ml)* wine vinegar
1½ tsp *(7.5 ml)* dry parsley
flakes
⅓ cup *(79 ml)* lemon juice
2 cloves garlic

CHICKEN: Marinate chicken breasts overnight, turning occasionally. Grill over charcoal.

BEEF: May use London broil. Marinate overnight and grill over charcoal fire. Keeps up to 6 weeks in the refrigerator and may be reused.

Sour Cream And Walnut Sauce

Blend sour cream with prepared horseradish, chopped walnuts and salt and pepper to taste. Serve with roast beef or fish.

Cumberland Sauce

Serve with ham, Cornish hens or pheasant

Can do ahead

Yield: 2½ cups (592 ml)
Preparing: 15 min
Cooking: 30-40 min

peel from ½ orange and
½ lemon
4 Tb *(60 ml)* currant jelly
1 cup *(237 ml)* port wine
juice of 1 orange and ½ lemon
1 tsp *(5 ml)* dry mustard
1 Tb *(15 ml)* light brown sugar

¼ tsp *(1.25 ml)* powdered ginger
dash cayenne pepper
½ cup *(118 ml)* white
raisins
½ cup *(118 ml)* blanched, slivered
almonds

With sharp knife remove thin peel without any white pulp, cut into tiny slivers, put into cold water and bring to boil. Drain and repeat three times. Melt currant jelly in top of double boiler. Add ½ cup (118 ml) port, peels, orange and lemon juice, mustard, sugar, ginger and cayenne. Bring to a boil on low direct heat. Put over boiling water to keep hot. Meanwhile boil raisins in ½ cup (118 ml) port until plump. Add to sauce. Add almonds last. This recipe is from Oregon and is really delicious over baked ham.

Meatball Sauce

Can do ahead
Can freeze

Yield: 3 cups (710 ml)
Preparing: 10 min
Cooking: 10 min

½ cup *(118 ml)* **onion, diced**
2 Tb *(30 ml)* **butter**
1 cup *(237 ml)* **canned tomato soup**
2 cups *(474 ml)* **cocktail OR barbecue sauce**

2 Tb *(30 ml)* **brown sugar**
1 Tb *(15 ml)* **vinegar**
1 Tb *(15 ml)* **Lea & Perrins Worcestershire sauce**
1 Tb *(15 ml)* **mustard**
Italian seasoning to taste

Combine all and heat to bubble. Add meatballs or cut up hot dogs. If frozen, reheat before adding to chafing dish.

Horseradish Whip
Delicious with roast beef

Can do ahead

Yield: ¾ cup (177 ml)
Preparing: 5 min

6 Tb *(90 ml)* **prepared horseradish**
½ cup *(118 ml)* **sour cream**

½ tsp *(2.5 ml)* **salt**
freshly ground pepper to taste

Whip horseradish and sour cream. Add salt and pepper. Serve with cold cuts of meat.

Spaghetti Meat Sauce

Can do ahead

Yield: 12 cups (2.84 l)
Preparing: 15 min
Cooking: 45-55 min

1 cup *(237 ml)* **onion, chopped**
2 cloves **garlic, minced**
1 lb *(454 g)* **ground beef**
2 **Italian sausages, skinned and chopped**
2 cans, 2 lb 3 oz *(992 g)* **tomatoes**
2 cans, 6 oz *(170 g)* **tomato paste**

1 Tb *(15 ml)* **sugar**
1 Tb *(15 ml)* **oregano**
1 Tb *(15 ml)* **basil**
1 Tb *(15 ml)* **salt**
½ tsp *(2.5 ml)* **pepper**
¼ cup *(59 ml)* **Parmesan cheese, grated**

Place onion, garlic, beef and sausage in large skillet. Brown beef and sausage. Pour off all but 2 tablespoons (30 ml) of fat in skillet. Stir in tomatoes, tomato paste, sugar, oregano, basil, salt and pepper. Simmer, uncovered, stirring frequently for 45 minutes or until sauce thickens. Stir in Parmesan cheese; cool.

Freeze in plastic containers in measured recipe portions.

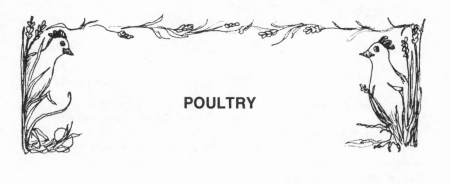

POULTRY

Spanish Rice With Chicken

Can do ahead

Serves: 8
Preparing: 40 min
Baking: 50 min

3 slices bacon, cut into
  small squares
2 cups *(474 ml)* onion, chopped
3 cloves garlic, minced
2 green peppers, chopped
1 lb *(454 g)* Spanish OR Italian
  sweet sausage
½ lb *(227 g)* Spanish OR Italian
  hot sausage
4 cups *(946 ml)* chicken stock
salt and pepper

12 stuffed green olives
1 tsp *(5 ml)* whole saffron, crushed
  OR ½ tsp *(2.5 ml)* powdered
  saffron
3 lbs *(1.4 kg)* chicken pieces
1 Tb *(15 ml)* paprika
¼ cup *(59 ml)* olive oil
2 cups *(474 ml)* uncooked rice
1 cup *(237 ml)* green peas, cooked
pimento for garnish

Combine bacon, onion, garlic and green peppers in a skillet. Add sausages and brown until onions are wilted and sausages cook slightly. Slice sausages into half-inch (1.27 cm) lengths. Spoon mixture, draining off grease, into a 5 quart (4.73 l) Dutch oven or casserole dish. Add a sprinkle of salt and pepper, the olives and the saffron. Add ¼ cup (59 ml) of stock. Sprinkle chicken with salt, pepper and paprika. Brown in olive oil and add to casserole. Add rice and remaining stock to casserole and cover. Bake at 400° (204° C) for 35 to 40 minutes, stirring once during baking. If rice begins to dry out, add more stock. When rice is tender, uncover, reduce heat to 300° (149° C) and add peas. Cook 10 minutes longer. Garnish with chopped pimento before serving.

NOTE: This is not as complicated as it may sound, and it is a great company dinner. It can be made ahead and baked at the last minute. All it needs is bread and perhaps a salad to complete the meal. It is quite colorful and attractive to serve.

Chicken Piquant

Can do ahead

Serves: 4
Preparing: 15 min
Baking: 1½ hrs

chicken parts, enough for
  4 people
1 lb (454 g) fresh mushrooms,
  sliced
¾ cup (177 ml) rosé wine
¼ cup (59 ml) soy sauce
2 Tbs (30 ml) olive oil

2 Tbs (30 ml) brown sugar
4 Tbs (60 ml) water, mixed
  with 2 Tbs (30 ml) cornstarch
1 garlic clove, crushed
¼ tsp (1.25 ml) oregano
rice

Place sliced mushrooms in bottom of a casserole. Top with chicken
pieces. Mix all other ingredients and pour over the chicken. Bake
uncovered in a 350° (177° C) oven for 1½ hours. Serve with rice.

Chicken Coronation

Can do ahead

Serves: 6
Preparing: 20 min
Cooking: 1 hr

1 hen, stewed, boned
  and chopped
1 can, 17 oz (482 g) apricots,
  drained

curry to taste
mayonnaise

Purée apricots in blender jar. Combine with curry and mayonnaise;
mix with chicken. Serve cold.

Chicken Chop Sticks
Very easy - children like this

Can do ahead

Serves: 4
Preparing: 10 min
Baking: 30 min

1 can, 5 oz (142 g) Chinese
  chow mein noodles
2 cans, 10¾ oz (305 g) cream
  of mushroom soup

1 cup (237 ml) cashew nuts,
  chopped
2 cups (474 ml) chicken, chopped
butter

Put a layer of noodles (¾ of can) in a 2 quart (1.89 l) casserole.
Combine soup, nuts and chicken; pour over noodles. Top with rest of
noodles, dot with butter and bake at 300° (149° C) 30 minutes.

Chicken Tetrazzini

Serves: 8-10
Preparing: 1 hr
Cooking: 45 min
Baking: 30 min

4-5 lb *(1.8-2.3 kg)* **boiled chicken**
½ lb *(227 g)* **macaroni**
½ lb *(227 g)* **fresh mushrooms,**
  sautéed
3 Tb *(45 ml)* **butter OR chicken fat**
2 Tb *(30 ml)* **flour**
2 cups *(474 ml)* **chicken broth**
seasoning

1 cup *(237 ml)* **heavy cream**
2 Tb *(30 ml)* **sherry**
½ cup *(118 ml)* **almonds,**
  blanched and shredded
  (optional)
grated Parmesan cheese

Cook chicken. Cut the meat in shreds (there should be about 2-3 cups). Cook macaroni in salted, boiling water; drain. Add sautéed mushrooms. Make a sauce of butter or chicken fat, flour, broth and seasonings. Remove from heat and add cream and sherry. Add ½ of sauce to the chicken. Add ½ of sauce to the macaroni and mushrooms. Place the macaroni in a greased baking dish. Make a hole in center and add chicken. Sprinkle top with grated Parmesan cheese. Bake in moderate oven 375° (191° C) until lightly browned. You may add ½ cup blanched and shredded almonds.

Chicken In Orange Sauce

Can do ahead

Serves: 6
Preparing: 15 min
Baking: 45-60 min

6 **chicken breasts**
¼ cup *(59 ml)* **butter, melted**
2 Tb *(30 ml)* **flour**
¼ tsp *(1.25 ml)* **cinnamon**
¼ tsp *(1.25 ml)* **ginger**

1½ cups *(355 ml)* **orange juice**
½ cup *(118 ml)* **white raisins**
1 can, 11 oz *(312 g)* **mandarin**
  oranges, drained
½ cup *(118 ml)* **slivered almonds**

Salt chicken and brown well in butter. Remove from skillet. To drippings in pan, add flour and spices. Slowly stir in orange juice. Cook over medium heat until thick. Add chicken pieces, raisins, oranges and almonds. Cook over low heat 45 minutes to 1 hour. Good served with rice or rice pilaf.

TOPPING

1 can, 11 oz *(312 g)* **Mandarin**
  oranges, drained
1 jar, 10 oz *(284 g)* **orange**
  marmalade

¼ cup *(59 ml)* **Grand Marnier**
  liqueur

Combine and heat. Spoon over chicken before serving.

Chicken Chasseur Casserole

Serves: 4-6
Preparing: 20 min
Cooking: 15 min

1 can, 3 oz *(85 g)* mushrooms,
   drained
½ green pepper
¾ cup *(177 ml)* water
1 onion, chopped
2 garlic cloves
4 Tb *(60 ml)* margarine
½ cup *(118 ml)* red wine
1 can, 6 oz *(170 g)* tomato
   paste

1½ tsp *(7.5 ml)* fine herbs
   OR Beau Monde seasoning
1 envelope brown gravy mix
½ cup *(118 ml)* white raisins
sliced ripe olives
almonds, chopped
bite size chicken breast
   pieces (about 4 large
   breasts, cooked)
rice (I cook instant in
   chicken broth)

Make chasseur sauce by sautéing onions, garlic, green pepper and fresh or canned, drained mushrooms. Add gravy mix to water — add to above. Add wine and tomato paste and herbs. Cook until semi-thick. Add cooked chicken. Before serving on rice, add ½ cup sliced ripe olives and almonds.

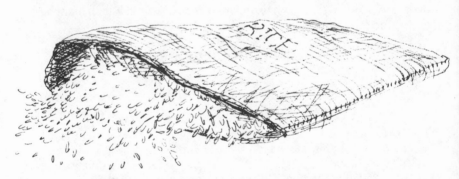

Chicken With Sausage And Mushrooms

Can do ahead
Can freeze

Serves: 6-8
Preparing: 30-35 min
Baking: 30 min

1 chicken, boiled and cut
   in large pieces
1 lb *(454 g)* Neese's hot sausage,
   cooked and drained
1 small box Uncle Ben's Long
   Grained and Wild Rice, cooked

1 can, 10¾ oz *(305 g)*
   mushroom soup
1 can, 6 oz *(170 g)* mushrooms,
   sliced (do not drain)

Mix all ingredients in shallow 2-3 quart (1.89-2.84 l) casserole and bake at 350° (177° C) for 30 minutes.

Chicken Cannelloni
An elegant dinner!

Can partially do ahead

Serves: 6-8
Preparing: 15 min
Cooking: 10 min

4 whole chicken breasts,
  split and boned
4 slices Mozarrella cheese
4 green onions, chopped
8 mushrooms, sliced
3 tomatoes, seeded, chopped OR
  2 lb *(908 g)* can Italian
  plum tomatoes

Dijon mustard
about 1 cup *(237 ml)* vermouth
Italian seasoning to taste
salt and pepper
flour
olive oil
parsley

Pound chicken breasts flat. Sprinkle with salt, pepper, and Italian seasoning. Spread with mustard. Put slices of cheese on and roll up. Salt, dredge in flour and sauté in olive oil. Remove. Sauté mushrooms, onions and tomatoes in oil and season. Put chicken back in and add vermouth. Simmer a few minutes, sprinkle with parsley.

Serve with buttered spaghetti, green salad, and wine.

Sweet And Sour Chicken

Can do ahead

Serves: 6
Preparing: 15 min
Baking: 1 hr

1 3-4 lb *(1.4-1.8 kg)* chicken cut
  in serving pieces
1 can, 8¼ oz *(234 g)* crushed
  pineapple
2 Tb *(30 ml)* cornstarch
¾ cup *(177 ml)* sugar

½ cup *(118 ml)* soy sauce
¼ cup *(59 ml)* vinegar
½ tsp *(2.5 ml)* ground ginger
¼ tsp *(1.25 ml)* pepper
1 clove garlic, minced

Place chicken pieces skin side down in shallow 9 x 13 inch (22.86 x 33.02 cm) baking dish. Drain pineapple, reserve 2 Tbs (30 ml) of juice. Combine cornstarch, reserved pineapple juice, sugar, soy sauce, vinegar, garlic, ginger and pepper in large saucepan. Cook over medium heat, stirring constantly until sauce thickens and bubbles. Pour over chicken. Bake at 400° (204° C) for 30 minutes, basting several times. Turn chicken, spread with pineapple, spoon sauce over all. Bake 30 minutes longer or until chicken is tender.

Parmesan Chicken

Can do ahead

Serves: 6-8
Preparing: 20 min
Baking: 45-60 min

2 cups *(474 ml)* **bread crumbs**
¾ cup *(177 ml)* **Parmesan cheese**
2 tsp *(10 ml)* **salt**
½ tsp *(2.5 ml)* **pepper**

¼ cup *(59 ml)* **parsley, chopped**
1 lb *(454 g)* **butter**
8 **chicken breasts**

Combine first 5 ingredients. Melt butter and soak each breast in it for 5 minutes. Roll and press cheese mixture on each piece and put in 8 x 12 x 2 inch (20.32 x 30.48 x 5.08 cm) dish. Pour remaining butter on top. Bake uncovered at 325° (163° C) for 45 minutes to 1 hour.

Chicken In A Blanket
Elegant company entree

Can partially do ahead

Serves: 6
Preparing: 20 min
Baking: 20 min

FILLING:

1 pkg, 3 oz *(85 g)* **cream
  cheese, softened**
2 Tb *(30 ml)* **margarine**
2 cups *(474 ml)* **cooked chicken,
  chopped**
¼ tsp *(1.25 ml)* **salt**

⅛ tsp *(.6 ml)* **pepper**
2 Tb *(30 ml)* **milk**
2 Tb *(30 ml)* **chives, chopped**
2 Tb *(30 ml)* **onion, minced**
2 Tb *(30 ml)* **pimento, minced**
1 pkg **Italian crescent rolls**

Blend cream cheese and margarine. Add other ingredients, except rolls. Combine 2 rolls and arrange in flat rectangle; place 2 Tb (30 ml) filling on each rectangle; bring ends together to form square and pinch to hold together. Bake at 350° (177° C) 20 minutes.

SAUCE:

1 can, 10¾ oz *(305 g)* **cream
  of mushroom soup**
1 ctn, 8 oz *(227 g)* **sour cream**
¼ cup *(59 ml)* **milk**

salt and pepper to taste
4 oz *(113 g)* **mushrooms,
  sliced and sautéed**

Combine all ingredients, heat and pour over hot chicken in blankets.

Katherine's Company Chicken

Can do ahead

Serves: 6
Preparing: 30 min
Baking: 20-25 min

1 stewing chicken, cooked
1 pkg Pepperidge Farm
  pastry shells, defrosted
2 Tb *(30 ml)* butter
3 Tb *(45 ml)* flour
1 cup *(237 ml)* light cream

½ cup *(118 ml)* dry white wine
heavy dash of pepper
¼ tsp *(1.25 ml)* salt
½ cup *(118 ml)* chicken broth
¼ tsp *(1.25 ml)* paprika
1 can, 6 oz *(170 g)* mushrooms

Stew the chicken and cut up in big lumps. Reserve broth. Defrost the pastry shells. Make a thick sauce from remaining ingredients, adding the broth and wine last. Roll out each pastry shell separately between two sheets of waxed paper. Mix enough sauce with chicken to moisten. Put a generous spoonful in each rolled-out shell. Take each side up and pinch closed. (Be careful not to let tops mix with sauce or it will not stay closed.) Bake according to pastry directions. Cool 15 minutes. Serve with extra sauce poured over top. Can make chicken mixture ahead.

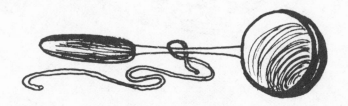

Chicken And Spaghetti

Serves: 10-15
Preparing: 30 min
Cooking: 1 hr, 45 min

1 hen about 6 lbs *(2.7 kg)* OR
  the equivalent in fryers
4 large onions, chopped fine
4 large bell peppers,
  chopped fine
2 cups *(474 ml)* celery,
  chopped fine

1 pkg, 10 oz *(284 g)*
  spaghettini
1 large can pimento
1 large can mushrooms
1 lb *(454 g)* Kraft
  American cheese

Cook hen in seasoned water until tender and, when cool, remove chicken from bones. Cook spaghettini in 1 quart (946 ml) of the chicken stock. Simmer onion, peppers and celery in some additional stock until tender. Mix all together and add cheese and stir until all cheese is melted. Season to taste with salt and pepper.

Chicken Casserole

Must do ahead
Refrigerate overnight

Serves: 6 - 8
Preparing: 20 min
Baking: 40 min

2 cups *(474 ml)* **cooked chicken,**
  diced
1 cup *(237 ml)* **rice, cooked**
1 small onion, chopped
¼ cup *(59 ml)* **sliced almonds,**
  browned a little
¾ cup *(177 ml)* **celery, chopped**
½ cup *(118 ml)* **Duke's mayonnaise**

1 tsp *(5 ml)* **salt**
2 Tbs *(30 ml)* **lemon juice**
2 eggs, hardboiled and sliced
1 small can water chestnuts,
  drained
1 can cream of mushroom soup
1 cup *(237 ml)* **buttered**
  bread crumbs

Mix all ingredients except bread crumbs and put in 2 quart (1.8 l)
greased casserole. Refrigerate overnight. Before cooking, put buttered bread crumbs on top. Bake 30 to 40 minutes at 350° (177° C).

Chicken Divan

A good luncheon casserole

Can do ahead
Can freeze

Serves: 6
Preparing: 30 min
Baking: 45 min

2 pkgs, 10 oz *(284 g)* **frozen**
  broccoli
6 boned chicken breasts, cooked
garlic salt
butter
¼ cup *(59 ml)* **American cheese,**
  grated
toasted slivered almonds

1 can cream of chicken soup
1 cup *(237 ml)* **sour cream**
3 Tb *(45 ml)* **milk**
1 cup *(237 ml)* **cheese,**
  grated (or more)
3 Tb *(45 ml)* **sherry**
paprika

Cook broccoli according to package directions. Place a layer of
broccoli and a layer of chicken pieces in casserole, sprinkle all over
with garlic salt and chunks of butter. Cover lightly with ¼ cup (59 ml)
grated cheese and sprinkle with almonds. Mix soup, sour cream, milk,
1 cup (237 ml) of grated cheese and sherry together in a saucepan
and heat. Pour over chicken and broccoli. Sprinkle with more almonds
and paprika. Bake at 375° (191° C) for 45 minutes.

Hot Chicken Soufflé

Must do ahead

Serves: 12
Preparing: 30 min
Chilling: overnight
Baking: 50 min

**16 slices bread, buttered
and crust removed
7 cups** *(1.66 l)* **chicken, chopped
½ cup** *(118 ml)* **pimento, chopped
½ cup** *(118 ml)* **onion, chopped
½ cup** *(118 ml)* **celery, chopped
1 cup** *(237 ml)* **mayonnaise**

1½ tsp *(7.5 ml)* **salt
pepper to taste
5 eggs, well beaten
4 cups** *(946 ml)* **milk
1 can cream of mushroom soup
2 cups** *(474 ml)* **American cheese,
grated**

Cube 8 of 16 bread slices and place in bottom of 3 quart (2.84 l) pyrex dish. Mix together next 5 ingredients and spread over bread. Crumble remainder of bread on top. Combine salt, pepper, eggs and milk. Pour over casserole carefully. Cover with foil and place in refrigerator overnight. The next day, spread mushroom soup over top. Bake at 350° (177° C) for 40 minutes. Take out and cover with cheese. Bake 10 more minutes.

Hot Chicken Salad

Great for bridge luncheon or Friday night get-together

Can do ahead

Serves: 6-8
Preparing: 1½ hrs
Baking: 20 min

1 cup *(237 ml)* **celery, chopped
½ cup** *(118 ml)* **mayonnaise
1 Tb** *(15 ml)* **lemon juice
1 can cream of chicken soup,
undiluted
½ cup** *(118 ml)* **water chestnuts,
sliced**

3 cups *(710 ml)* **chicken, chopped
3 hard boiled eggs, grated
salt
pepper
Parmesan cheese**

Mix in a large bowl and pour into a 2 quart (1.8 l) casserole and top with Parmesan cheese. Bake at 400° (204° C) for 20 minutes. Can be put in individual soufflé dishes. Serves nicely with grapefruit salad topped with honey dressing.

Vinegar Chicken
Easy and different

Can be done ahead

Serves: 4
Preparing: 20 min
Baking: 2 hrs

1 chicken, cut up
½ cup *(118 ml)* **butter**
1 cup *(237 ml)* **vinegar**

1 medium red pepper pod, broken
up

Brown chicken very well in butter. Pour the vinegar into the drippings, add red pepper and pour over the chicken that has been placed in small covered roaster. Cover and cook 1½-2 hours at 325° (163° C). Baste often and uncover last 30 minutes. Chicken browns more quickly if butter is very hot before putting chicken in skillet. It splatters terribly so I use a lid or piece of foil to cover while browning.

Chicken Curry
Excellent for a ladies luncheon

Can do ahead
Can freeze

Serves: 6
Preparing: 15-20 min
Baking: 20-30 min

⅔ cup *(158 ml)* **butter**
3 cups *(710 ml)* **raisin bran**
2 tsp *(10 ml)* **salt**
2 Tb *(30 ml)* **flour**
¼ tsp *(1.25 ml)* **pepper**
2 cups *(474 ml)* **half and half**
cream

2 Tb *(30 ml)* **flaked coconut**
2½ cups *(592 ml)* **turkey OR**
chicken, chopped
2 Tb *(15-30)* **chutney,**
(optional)
1-2 Tb *(15-30 ml)* **curry or to taste**

Melt ⅓ cup (79 ml) butter. Add raisin bran and 1 tsp (5 ml) salt. Combine. Melt other ⅓ cup (79 ml) butter. Blend in flour, 1 tsp (5 ml) salt, pepper and curry. Stir in half and half. Cook over low heat until thick. Fold in chicken, coconut and chutney. Line shallow 1½-2 quart (1.42-1.89 l) casserole with raisin bran and fill with chicken mixture. Bake at 350° (177° C) until hot and bubbly.

Orange Duck

Serve immediately

Serves: 6
Preparing: 45 min
Cooking: 3 hrs

3 domestic (not wild) ducks
6 Tb *(90 ml)* **chopped onion**
salt and pepper
⅓ cup *(79 ml)* **Burgundy**
1 Tb *(15 ml)* **wine vinegar**

1 Tb *(15 ml)* **sugar**
½ cup *(118 ml)* **sauterne**
½ cup *(118 ml)* **orange juice**
2 Tb *(30 ml)* **grated orange peel**

Salt and pepper inside of each duck; put 2 Tb (30 ml) chopped onion inside each duck. Pour Burgundy over ducks. Bake at 450° (232° C) 35 minutes; reduce heat to 325° (163° C) and bake 2 hours. Meanwhile make sauce: heat wine vinegar and sugar to caramel stage and clear; add sauterne, orange juice and grated peel and heat until dissolved. In the last hour of cooking ducks, pour half the sauce over ducks. Pour rest of sauce over ducks 30 minutes later. Serve with orange gravy below.

ORANGE GRAVY:

liver from duck, minced
3 Tb *(45 ml)* **butter**
3 Tb *(45 ml)* **brandy**
2 Tb *(30 ml)* **grated orange peel**
¼ tsp *(1.25 ml)* **garlic salt**
2 Tb *(30 ml)* **flour**
2 tsp *(10 ml)* **catsup**
⅛ tsp *(.6 ml)* **pepper**

1 can, 10 oz *(284 g)* **condensed chicken broth**
⅓ cup *(79 ml)* **Burgundy**
¼ cup *(59 ml)* **orange marmalade**
¼ cup *(59 ml)* **orange juice**
2 oranges, peeled and sectioned

Brown liver well in 2 Tb (30 ml) butter; remove from heat. Heat brandy in saucepan, then ignite; slowly pour over liver; remove liver when fire is out and liver is very fine. In brandy add other Tb (15 ml) butter, grated peel and garlic salt; sauté 3 minutes; remove from heat. Stir in flour, catsup and pepper until well blended. Gradually stir in chicken broth, Burgundy, marmalade and orange juice. Put back on stove; bring to boil, stirring occasionally 15 minutes. At serving time, add chopped liver and orange sections to sauce; reheat and pour over ducks. The leftover gravy is for the table.

Chicken-Fried Rice Special

A complete entree

Must do ahead

Serves: 4-6
Preparing: 30-35 min
Chilling: 1 hr

3 Tb *(45 ml)* peanut oil
1-2 filet chicken breasts, cooked and chopped
half small head of cabbage, chopped
2 Tb *(30 ml)* soy sauce
¼ tsp *(1.25 ml)* garlic powder
¼ tsp *(1.25 ml)* curry powder
¼ tsp *(1.25 ml)* Chinese 5-spice powder

3-4 scallions, chopped
2 stalks celery, chopped
1 tsp *(5 ml)* sesame oil
⅔ cup *(158 ml)* uncooked rice
2 Tb *(30 ml)* peanut oil
½ tsp *(2.5 ml)* salt
1½ cups *(355 ml)* boiling water
1 bouillon cube

Stir-fry chopped scallions, cabbage and celery quickly in oil. Mix vegetables, chicken, sesame oil, and spices in a bowl. Cover and refrigerate one hour or more. Cook rice in hot oil until brown. Add salt, water and bouillon cube. Cover; cook 15 minutes. Add chicken mixture, cook 5 minutes more, adding water if necessary. Add soy sauce to taste. Good served with stir-fried vegetables.

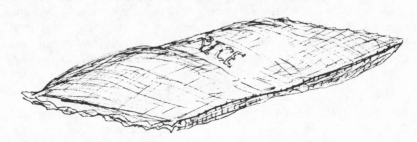

Saucy Spring Bake

Wonderful for a Brunch

Serves: 4
Preparing: 5 min
Baking: 20 min

1 pkg, 10 oz *(284 g)* frozen asparagus, cooked and drained
1 pkg, 6 oz *(170 g)* sliced Canadian bacon

2 cans, 10½ oz *(297 g)* chicken a la king — OR homemade
1 cup *(237 ml)* French fried onions

In shallow baking dish arrange asparagus. Top with bacon. Pour a la king over it. Bake at 400° (204° C) for 15 minutes. Top with onions and bake 5 minutes more.

TURKEY AND DRESSINGS

Different Way To Cook A Turkey

Place the turkey on a rack in the roaster pan with the breast side down. Put the turkey in a cold oven and turn the oven on to 500° (260° C) and cook for 20 minutes. At the end of the 20 minutes turn the oven down to 350° (177° C) and cook the turkey for 18 minutes per pound. The last hour of cooking, turn the turkey over so that the breast side is up.

Turkey Cantonese
Good way to use leftover turkey

Can do ahead
Can be frozen without noodles

Serves: 8
Preparing: 25 min
Baking: 50 min

2 cups *(474 ml)* **white rice, cooked**
1 cup *(237 ml)* **celery, chopped**
½ cup *(118 ml)* **green pepper, chopped**
½ cup *(118 ml)* **green onion, chopped**
1 can, 1 lb *(454 g)* **bean sprouts, drained well**
1 can, 5 oz *(142 g)* **water chestnuts, drained and sliced**
3 cups *(710 ml)* **turkey, cooked, coarsely chopped and firmly packed**

1 can, 10¾ oz *(305 g)* **cream of mushroom soup**
1 soup can, 10¾ oz *(305 g)* **plus ½ cup *(118 ml)* turkey broth**
3 Tb *(45 ml)* **soy sauce**
¾ tsp *(3.7 ml)* **salt**
½ tsp *(2.5 ml)* **pepper**
1 can, 3 oz *(85 g)* **chow mein noodles**

Mix together first seven ingredients. In separate bowl, combine next five ingredients; mix well. Add to turkey mixture and combine thoroughly. Pour into buttered 3 quart (2.84 l) dish. Top with noodles. Bake in 350° (177° C) oven for 50 minutes. If to be frozen, add noodles after thawing and before baking.

197

Turkey Stuffing

Can do ahead
Can freeze

Serves: 6
Preparing: 15 min
Baking: 30 min

1 cup *(237 ml)* onions, chopped
1 tsp *(5 ml)* brown sugar
1 cup *(237 ml)* parsley, chopped
1 cup *(237 ml)* carrots, chopped
1 cup *(237 ml)* celery, chopped
1 cup *(237 ml)* mixed nuts,
    coarsely chopped
2 cups *(474 ml)* Pepperidge Farm
    stuffing

1 small apple, chopped
1 tsp *(5 ml)* Beau Monde
    seasoning
1 tsp *(5 ml)* Accent
1 tsp *(5 ml)* salt
1 tsp *(5 ml)* pepper
½ cup *(118 ml)* melted butter

Chop onion and let stand in brown sugar. Chop parsley, carrots, celery, apple, nuts. Add dry seasonings to bread crumbs. Fork onions out of their juice and add to crumbs. Add other chopped ingredients and mix well using a wooden spoon. When all ingredients are mixed thoroughly, add melted butter. Heat, covered, in shallow 2 quart (1.89 l) pyrex dish at 350° (177° C) until hot through.

Oyster Dressing

Can do ahead

Yield: 6 cups (1.42 l)
Preparing: 30 min
Baking: 1 hr

1½ cups *(355 ml)* onion, chopped
1½ cups *(355 ml)* celery, chopped
6 Tb *(90 ml)* margarine
6 Tb *(90 ml)* oil
6-8 slices bread, broken
    into small pieces
3 Tb *(45 ml)* parsley, minced
salt and pepper

¾ tsp *(3.7 ml)* thyme
¾ tsp *(3.7 ml)* sage
¾ tsp *(3.7 ml)* marjoram
¾ tsp *(3.7 ml)* oregano
1½ cups *(355 ml)* oysters,
    chopped
2 eggs, optional

Slowly cook onions and celery, covered, in margarine and oil until soft and yellow. Add bread and the remaining ingredients (add oysters last). Stuff the turkey or put into a buttered casserole dish and bake at 350° (177° C) for 1 hour.

Cornbread Dressing

Can do ahead
Can freeze

Serves: 12-16
(enough for large turkey)
Preparing: 25 min
Baking: 45 min

2 cups *(474 ml)* onion, chopped
2 cups *(474 ml)* celery with
tender leaves, chopped
1 cup *(237 ml)* oil — OR mixture
of oil, chicken, and bacon fat
1 cup *(237 ml)* sliced fresh OR
canned mushrooms
12 squares *(3x3x1")* cornbread,
crumbled
12 saltines, crumbled

1½ cups *(355 ml)* Brazil nuts,
chopped
1 cup *(237 ml)* parsley with
tender stems, minced
1 Tb *(15 ml)* fresh rosemary,
minced
1 Tb *(15 ml)* fresh thyme,
minced
salt and pepper to taste
2 hard boiled eggs, chopped
(optional)

Sauté onion in part of oil until limp. Remove to large mixing bowl. Sauté mushrooms and celery until tender crisp in the remaining oil. Mix with onion. Add other ingredients — cornbread, saltines, nuts, parsley, rosemary, thyme, salt (go slow on salt because of saltines), and pepper to taste.

If you want to freeze part of the mixture — remove some now. Add eggs, mix and put into pyrex baking dish 2" deep. Cover with foil. Bake at 400° (204° C) for ½ hour. Remove foil and bake until very hot, about 10-15 minutes. If dressing seems too dry, sprinkle with a little chicken stock. Serve with a bowl of gravy.

Frozen dressing: Thaw, add some fresh raw chopped celery and some hard cooked egg and bake.

Cranberry-Pecan Stuffing

Can do ahead
Can freeze

Serves: 6
Preparing: 1 hr
Baking: 30-40 min

1 pkg, 7 oz *(198 g)* cube stuffing
1 cup *(237 ml)* onions, chopped
1 cup *(237 ml)* mushrooms, sliced
½ cup *(118 ml)* pecans, chopped
½ cup *(118 ml)* parsley, chopped

1 cup *(237 ml)* butter OR
margarine
1 cup *(237 ml)* cranberries,
cut in half
3 Tb *(45 ml)* sugar

Prepare stuffing according to package directions. Meanwhile, sauté onions, mushrooms and pecans in butter for 5 minutes. Combine cranberries and sugar. Add all ingredients to stuffing, stirring only to blend. Place in 1½ quart (1.42 l) casserole and bake covered last 30 minutes of roasting time.

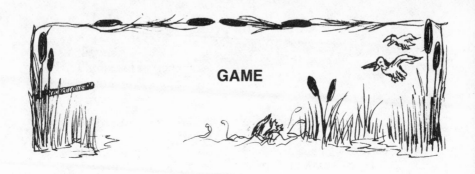

GAME

Fruit-Filled Ducks

I suggest a soup and an apple and onion casserole to accompany this and Coffee Pumpkin Flan for dessert. Good wine to accompany this — Geurey-Chambertin 1967

Serves: 6
Preparing: 45 min
Baking: 2 hrs

Two 4-5 lb *(1.8-2.3 kg)* **ducks, cleaned and oven ready**
½ cup *(118 ml)* **onion, chopped**
½ cup *(118 ml)* **butter**
1 cup *(237 ml)* **celery, chopped**
2 cups *(474 ml)* **apples, chopped and cored**
1 **orange**
1 **lemon**
2 **eggs, lightly beaten**

½ cup *(118 ml)* **dry white wine**
4 cups *(946 ml)* **soft bread crumbs**
salt and freshly ground pepper to taste
1 Tb *(15 ml)* **parsley, chopped**
½ tsp *(2.5 ml)* **rosemary**
⅛ tsp *(.6 ml)* **mace**
2 cups *(474 ml)* **shelled filberts**

Preheat oven to 275° (135° C). Spread filberts in a shallow pan and toast in the oven about 20 minutes or until tender and the skins start to crack. Place the nuts in a clean towel and roll back and forth to remove skins. (They do not have to be eliminated completely.) Heat ¼ cup (59 ml) butter in a skillet and sauté the onion and celery until tender. Combine filberts, onion mixture and apples in a large bowl. Grate and add orange and lemon rinds. Remove white skins of orange and lemon and discard. Section both orange and lemon and add to bowl. Increase oven heat to 425° (218° C). Stir in parsley, white wine, eggs and spices. Add bread crumbs. Toss to mix and stuff both ducks. Place on a rack in a shallow roasting pan. Brush ducks with remaining ¼ cup (59 ml) of butter. Roast at 425° (218° C) for 30 minutes. Reduce oven heat to 375° (191° C) and continue cooking 1½ hours or until ducks no longer drip pink liquid when pierced in thigh.

Easy Wild Duck

Can partially do ahead

Serves: 6
Preparing: 10 min
Baking: 3 hrs

3 wild ducks
3 apples, quartered
3 onions, quartered
salt and pepper

12 slices bacon
1 can, 12 oz *(340 g)* **orange**
    juice concentrate

Put apples and onions in ducks' cavities. Salt and pepper outside of ducks; cover each breast with 2 slices bacon and secure with tooth-picks. Line bottom of roaster with heavy aluminum foil. Pour orange juice over ducks. Cover and bake with vent open at 350° (177° C) for 3 hours.

Gourmet Duck

Can do ahead

Serves: 3 (one duck)
Preparing: 30 min
Cooking: 2 hrs

2 ducks
2 Irish potatoes OR turnips
1 Tb *(15 ml)* **flour**
1 cup *(237 ml)* **rice water**

1 cup *(237 ml)* **rice water, reserved**
    from cooking wild rice below
½ cup *(118 ml)* **stuffed olives,**
    chopped

Parboil ducks with Irish potatoes or turnips until ducks are very tender (this removes the game flavor). Remove ducks from stock, saving 1 cup (237 ml) stock. Remove skin and bones from ducks, leaving meat in as large pieces as possible. In frying pan, brown flour; add stock, rice water, ducks and olives (you may also want to add a small amount of olive juice). Cook until gravy thickens.

SERVING SUGGESTIONS: Serve on a large platter centered with a mold of wild rice. Pour the ducks and gravy around the rice mold. This is an unusual method of cooking ducks and never fails to elicit comments.

Doves

Unusual taste but very good

Can do ahead

Preparing: 20 min
Cooking: 2 hrs, 15 min

doves
flour
salt
pepper

corn oil
¾ cup *(177 ml)* **water**
¾ cup *(177 ml)* **pineapple juice**

Wash and dry thawed doves. Roll in mixture of flour, salt and pepper. Brown in small amount of corn oil. After browning, add water and pineapple juice to doves. Steam for approximately 2 hours. Keep checking to make sure there is juice and water in the pan. If gravy is desired, add the juice from the pan to flour in the usual manner of making gravy.

Marinated Doves

Must do ahead

Serves: 4
Preparing: 25 min
Marinating: overnight
Baking: 1½-2 hrs

12 doves
1½ cups *(355 ml)* **salad oil**
½ cup *(118 ml)* **vinegar**
½ cup *(118 ml)* **red wine**
2-3 bay leaves
1 onion, sliced
1 clove garlic, minced
1 tsp *(5 ml)* **Worcestershire**
  sauce

salt and pepper
½ cup *(118 ml)* **butter**
3 Tb *(45 ml)* **flour**
1 onion, chopped
2 bouillon cubes OR 1 can,
  10 oz *(284 g)* **bouillon**
2 cups *(474 ml)* **boiling water**
salt and pepper

Combine first nine ingredients and marinate doves in it 7-8 hours or overnight. Brown doves in butter over high heat until brown on all sides. Add flour and onion to drippings and stir until flour is brown. Dissolve bouillon cubes in boiling water and slowly add to roux. Stir until smooth. Put doves in roaster and cover with gravy. Bake in 225° (107° C) oven 3-4 hours or until tender.

Sautéed Doves

Makes a delicious gravy to serve over wild rice

Can do ahead

Serves: 6
Preparing: 15 min
Cooking: 35-60 min

6 doves, split
½ cup *(118 ml)* **butter**
1 cup *(237 ml)* **vermouth OR dry**
  white wine
¼ cup *(59 ml)* **onion, minced**

2 Tb *(30 ml)* **celery leaves,**
  minced
salt
½ tsp *(2.5 ml)* **tarragon**

Sauté doves in butter 5 minutes or until lightly browned. Add wine, onion, celery leaves and salt. Cover and simmer over low heat 20 minutes. Add tarragon and simmer, uncovered, 15 minutes.

Wild Game Pie

Serve immediately

Serves: 4
Preparing: 30 min
Baking: 1 hr

15 doves OR 18 quail (could
  use 3 lb *(1.4 k)* **chicken)**
1 Tb *(15 ml)* **celery seed**
½ cup *(118 ml)* **margarine**
black pepper
1 cup *(237 ml)* **flour**
1 Tb *(15 ml)* **baking powder**
  (recommend Rumford)

1 cup *(237 ml)* **milk**
1 can *(305 g)* **cream of celery**
  soup
1 can *(305 g)* **chicken broth**
  soup
½ can *(153 g)* **of broth that**
  birds have been cooked in

Cook birds covered with water and celery seeds. Remove from broth when tender — approx. 1 hr (when removing meat from bones, breast will separate from bones). Put meat in a 13 x 7 inch (33.02 x 17.78 cm) dish. Melt margarine and pour over meat. In small mixing bowl, sift flour with baking powder and pepper. Blend in milk until smooth (mixture becomes fluffy); spread flour mixture over meat. While making flour mixture, heat soup to boiling and pour over flour mixture which has been poured over birds. Bake at 425° (218° C) for 15 minutes, then at 350° (177° C) for approximately 45 minutes or until crust is brown.

Wild Goose

This is a no-fail recipe

Can do ahead

Serves: 2
Baking: approx 50 min

1 wild Canada goose
salt, pepper, cinnamon
¾ cup (177 ml) **red wine vinegar**

½ cup (118 ml) **peanut oil**
¾ cup (177 ml) **cooking sherry**

Sprinkle salt, pepper and cinnamon over entire goose. Rub into skin. Combine vinegar, oil, and sherry and pour over goose with breast down. Bake at 450° (232° C) 40 minutes with top on roaster. Take top off, broil 8 minutes. Turn goose breast side up and broil 8 minutes.

SAUCE:

Pour off oil, add flour to make a very thin sauce. Pour over thinly sliced goose.

Roast Pheasant With Cumberland Sauce

Can do ahead

Serves: 2-3 per pheasant
Preparing: 15 min
Baking: 1½-2 hrs

PHEASANT:
pheasants
bread
onions
celery

bacon
1 can, 10¾ oz (305 g) **chicken**
broth

Make a regular dressing with plain bread, onions and celery — not too spicy as it will overpower the bird. Cover breast with several slices of bacon and then cover with one can undiluted chicken broth. Bake at 350° (177° C) for 1½-2 hours, basting frequently. Serve with Cumberland sauce (p. 183).

Marinated Quail

Quick and tasty

Can do ahead

Serves: 3
Preparing: 2 min
Marinating: 30 min
Cooking: 1 hr

4 quail
2 Tb *(30 ml)* Kitchen Bouquet
oil for browning

1 can, 6 oz *(170 g)* frozen
orange juice concentrate
2 Tb *(30 ml)* flour

Brush quail with Kitchen Bouquet. Let stand about ½ hour. Brown on all sides in small amount of oil. Add the orange juice concentrate and one can, 6 oz (170 g) water. Cover and cook over low heat about one hour. Mix flour with a little water and use to thicken sauce for gravy.

Quail Baked In Wine

The white wine makes the difference

Can do ahead

Serves: 6
Preparing: 30 min
Cooking: 30 min

6 quail
2 small onions, chopped
2 whole cloves
1 tsp *(5 ml)* peppercorns
2 cloves garlic, chopped
½ bay leaf
½ cup *(118 ml)* butter

2 cups *(474 ml)* white wine
½ tsp *(2.5 ml)* salt
¼ tsp *(1.25 ml)* pepper
cayenne pepper
1 tsp *(5 ml)* chives
2 cups *(474 ml)* evaporated milk

Sauté onions, cloves, peppercorns, garlic, bay leaf in butter. Add quail and brown. Add wine, salt, pepper, cayenne pepper, chives and simmer 30 minutes. Remove quail to serving dish, strain sauce and add milk. Heat to boiling and pour over quail.

Roast Loin Of Venison

Serves: 4-6
Preparing: 30 min
Baking: 55-60 min

1 3-4 lb *(1.4-1.8 k)* **venison loin**
salt and pepper
2 small onions stuck with
1 clove each
1 cup *(237 ml)* **orange juice**
½ cup *(118 ml)* **butter OR**
margarine, melted

1 tsp *(5 ml)* **rosemary**
½ cup *(118 ml)* **tart currant**
OR spiced grape jelly
1 Tb *(15 ml)* **grated lemon peel**
1 Tb *(15 ml)* **flour**

Season loin all over with salt and pepper. Place in 450° (232° C) oven for 15 minutes to sear and seal in juices. Add onions, orange juice, butter and rosemary. Cover. Lower heat to 325° (163° C) and roast about 10 minutes per pound. Baste frequently with pan juices. Meanwhile, melt jelly and add lemon peel. About 10 minutes before meat is done brush meat with jelly mixture. Remove meat when done. Strain 2 cups (474 ml) of remaining liquids and heat in saucepan. Sprinkle flour in and heat, stirring until thickened. Serve as gravy.

Venison

Must do ahead

Preparing: 30 min
Roasting: 30 min per lb

venison
water to cover
½-1 cup *(118-237 ml)* **vinegar**
2 onions, cut

salt and pepper
flour
oil

Soak venison overnight in water, vinegar and onions. In morning, take out of solution and dry well. Salt and pepper it, rub a little flour on it; brown on stove in hot oil. Place in broiling pan, put in 300° (149° C) oven. Cover with barbeque sauce; cook 30 minutes per lb — do not cover roast.

BARBECUE SAUCE:

½ cup *(118 ml)* **onions, minced**
1½ cups *(355 ml)* **tomato catsup**
2 Tb *(30 ml)* **vinegar**
¼ cup *(59 ml)* **margarine, melted**
¼ cup *(59 ml)* **Worcestershire**
sauce
¼ cup *(59 ml)* **prepared mustard**

⅓ cup *(79 ml)* **lemon juice**
1 cup *(237 ml)* **meat stock OR**
2 beef bouillon cubes dis-
solved in 1 cup hot water
1 tsp *(5 ml)* **celery seed**
¼ tsp *(1.25 ml)* **Hot Pete sauce**

Seafood

Seafood

Seafood Tips

Quantity of seafood per serving:

1 lb (454 g) whole fish — as it comes from the catch.

¾ lb (340 g) drawn fish — eviscerated. Scales, fins and tail removed.

½ lb (227 g) dressed fish — entrails and scales removed and usually the head, fins and tail. Ready to cook.

⅓ lb (142 g) fish steaks — sliced from a large fish such as tuna. Cross-section cuts of dressed fish.

⅓ lb (142 g) fish filets — boned, dressed, halves of fish too small to be cut into steaks.

Oysters and shrimp — allow 6-12 per person (less if used as an appetizer).

Clams — allow 6 per serving.

Raw shrimp (average for 3 or 4 servings):
very small shrimp — allow 40
large shrimp — allow 25-30
jumbo shrimp — allow 16-25

Lobster — allow ¾ to 1 pound (340-454 g) per person; one live 1¼ lb (567 g) lobster yields one serving.

Fresh fish and shellfish keep in the refrigerator for 1 or 2 days.

Cooked fish, shellfish, chowders, bisques keep for 3 days.

Leftover fish deteriorates quickly.

Seafood can be frozen for 6 months. Never re-freeze fish. Once thawed, treat it as fresh fish and cook immediately.

Filet fish when they are half frozen, then keep filets fresh in ice water.

Frozen shrimp should be ivory-colored, not white. If they are white, they have suffered freezer burn.

To eliminate the odor when boiling seafood, add celery leaves to the water.

Get your grill very hot before cooking fish; it will not stick if hot enough.

Oysters, clams and shrimp should not be cooked too long as it toughens them and destroys the flavor.

Fish should always be cooked until well done, that is, when the flesh separates easily from the bone.

Large, fleshy fish are better broiled than baked. Small fish are better fried.

When selecting fish, the flesh should be firm and adhere to the bone; eyes should be clear; gills bright red and the skin shiny with tightly clinging scales.

Bluefish In Sauce

Can partially do ahead

Serves: 4
Preparing: 10 min
Cooking: 30 min

2 lbs *(908 g)* **bluefish filets**
½ cup *(118 ml)* **mayonnaise**
1½ cups *(355 ml)* **sour cream**

2 Tb *(30 ml)* **chopped chives**
3 Tb *(45 ml)* **lemon juice**
salt and pepper to taste

Place filets in buttered baking dish. Mix sour cream, mayonnaise, chives, lemon juice, salt and pepper. Spread over fish. May do ahead earlier in day and refrigerate. Bake at 375° (191° C) for about 30 minutes.

Bluefish Chanticleer

Serves: 4
Preparing: 15 min
Marinating: 4-5 hrs
Broiling: 5-7 min
Baking: 10-15 min

2 lbs *(908 g)* **bluefish filets,**
  skinned
salt and pepper
½ cup *(118 ml)* **olive oil**
2 Tb *(30 ml)* **lemon juice**
¼ cup *(59 ml)* **shallots, chopped**
  OR spring onions
2 Tb *(30 ml)* **parsley, chopped**
3-4 Tb *(45-60 ml)* **Dijon mustard**
½ cup *(118 ml)* **bread crumbs**

1 tsp *(5 ml)* **fresh tarragon,**
  minced*
1 tsp *(5 ml)* **fresh thyme,**
  minced*
1 tsp *(5 ml)* **fresh rosemary,**
  minced*
¼ cup *(59 ml)* **Gruyère cheese,**
  grated
***with dried herbs mix 1 tsp**
  (5 ml) **of the 3 herbs**

Season fish with salt and pepper, then marinate in a mixture of olive oil, lemon juice, shallots and parsley for 4 to 5 hours. Transfer fish to a baking dish and lightly coat top surface of filets with mustard. Mix together bread crumbs and herbs and spread mixture over fish. Dot with butter and sprinkle on grated Gruyère. Cook under broiler 5 to 7 minutes until topping is golden brown. Transfer dish to oven, lower temperature to 425° (218° C) and bake until fish tests done, another 10 to 15 minutes.

Stuffed Flounder

Serves: 5-6
Preparing: 20-25 min
Baking: 30 min

1 large flounder, about 5 lbs
(2.3 kg)
½ cup (118 ml) green onions,
chopped
¼ cup (59 ml) butter
2 Tb (30 ml) parsley, chopped

⅓ cup (79 ml) bread crumbs
2 hard-boiled eggs, chopped
½ lb (227 g) crab meat
½ tsp (2.5 ml) pepper
1 tsp (5 ml) salt
dash Tabasco

Prepare fish for cooking. Slit a pocket in the back of the fish using a sharp knife. Brown onion in butter; add parsley, bread crumbs, eggs, crab meat and seasonings. Mix well and stuff in the pocket you slit in the fish. Brush fish with melted butter and sprinkle with paprika. Bake 30 minutes at 375° (191° C).

Baked Filet Of Flounder

Serves: 4
Preparing: 10 min
Baking: 30 min

fish filets
1 lemon
⅛ tsp (.6 ml) oregano
2 Tb (30 ml) dry parsley
2 Tb (30 ml) dry onion

2 Tb (30 ml) celery, chopped
salt and pepper to taste
slivered almonds to taste
dot with margarine (at
least 2 Tb (30 ml))

Rub fish with lemon wedge, or sprinkle with small amount of lemon juice and rub in. Place fish in buttered baking dish and sprinkle with remaining ingredients, except margarine. Dot with margarine. Bake at 325° (163° C) for 30 minutes or until fish cakes easily.

S
E
A
F
O
O
D

Simple Filet Of Sole

Good served with dry white wine

fish filets
dry white wine
salted water
lime juice

onion pulp
almonds, chopped
parsley, chopped
Parmesan cheese, freshly grated

Poach filets in half wine and half salted water. Drain. Brush filets with lime juice mixed with onion pulp (½ cup — (118 ml) lime juice to 1 tsp — (5 ml) onion pulp). Brown almonds in a little butter. Season filets and spread nuts on evenly and thinly. Brown quickly under broiler. Dust with parsley and cheese.

Filet Of Sole Veronique

Can do partially ahead

Serves: 6
Preparing: 30 min
Cooking: 15 min

1½ lbs (680 g) thawed frozen
  OR fresh fish filets
1 tsp (5 ml) salt
⅛ tsp (.6 ml) pepper
1 Tb (15 ml) butter OR margarine
¼ cup (59 ml) onion, chopped
1 clove garlic

½ cup (118 ml) dry white
  wine OR chicken broth
1 tsp (5 ml) fresh lemon juice
¼ cup (59 ml) light cream
1 egg yolk
1 tsp (5 ml) flour
2 cups (474 ml) fresh seedless
  grapes

Sprinkle fish with salt and pepper. Roll up and fasten with toothpicks. Set aside. Melt butter in a 10-inch (25.4 cm) skillet, add onion, cook until tender. Spear garlic on toothpick and put in skillet with wine (broth) and lemon juice. Arrange fish in skillet. Cover and simmer 5-10 minutes or until fish flakes. Remove fish to serving platter and keep warm. Discard garlic. Strain liquid in skillet. Pour strained liquid back into skillet. Blend in cream and egg yolk. Sprinkle flour over liquid in skillet and stir to blend. Cook over medium heat stirring constantly, until thickened and smooth. Add grapes and heat them through. Pour sauce over fish.

Fish Filets Deluxe

Can do ahead

3 Tb *(45 ml)* **onion, chopped**
2 Tb *(30 ml)* **margarine**
½ cup *(118 ml)* **long grain
rice, uncooked**
1 cup *(237 ml)* **water**
1 chicken bouillon cube
½ tsp *(2.5 ml)* **salt**
1 can, 3 oz *(85 g)* **button
mushrooms, drained**

8 fish filets
3 Tb *(45 ml)* **margarine**
3 Tb *(45 ml)* **flour**
1½ cups *(355 ml)* **milk**
½ cup *(118 ml)* **dry white wine**
paprika
1 pkg, 4 oz *(113 g)* **Swiss
cheese, shredded**

Brown onion in the 2 Tb (30 ml) of margarine with the rice; stir often for 8 minutes. Add water, bouillon cube and salt. Bring this to a boil, cover and stir for 25 minutes until rice is dry and fluffy. Add mushrooms. Place fish in a casserole and cover with the above mixture. In a saucepan, melt the other 3 Tb (45 ml) of margarine and stir in the flour. Add milk and wine. Cook until thick. Pour this over the fish. Bake uncovered at 400° (204° C) for 35 minutes. Sprinkle with paprika and cheese and bake 10 minutes more.

Mackerel Steaks

Can partially do ahead

**4 pieces heavy duty
aluminum foil**
½ cup *(118 ml)* **onion, chopped**
½ cup *(118 ml)* **green pepper,
chopped**
2 Tb *(30 ml)* **butter**

½ cup *(118 ml)* **catsup**
½ tsp *(2.5 ml)* **garlic salt**
bay leaf
4 mackerel steaks
salt and pepper

Cook onion and green pepper in butter. Add seasonings and simmer 10-15 minutes. Place fish in foil. Pour one-fourth of the sauce over each. Fold tightly using a "drug store wrap." Bake in shallow pan for 20 minutes at 500° (260°C).

Trout With Lemon Parsley Butter

Serves: 2
Preparing: 10 min
Baking: 10-20 min

1 trout, well-cleaned,
  not boned
flour

salt and pepper
salad oil

Preheat oven to 450° (232° C). Dip the whole fish in flour seasoned with salt and pepper. Put a ¼ inch (.64 cm) layer of salad oil in an oven-proof serving dish. Place in the oven. When the oil is hot, lay the fish in it and bake 10 to 20 minutes, turning after one side has cooked in the oil approximately 7 minutes. Serve with Lemon Parsley Butter.

LEMON PARSLEY BUTTER:

½ cup *(118 ml)* butter
1 tsp *(5 ml)* parsley, minced

juice of half lemon
salt and pepper

Cream butter with the parsley, lemon juice, salt and pepper. Serve on top of fish or to the side.

Shrimp And Vegetable Creole
Great to freeze for unexpected guests

Can do ahead
Can freeze

Serves: 8-10
Preparing: 45 min
Cooking: 15-20 min

2 lbs *(908 g)* shrimp
1 cup *(237 ml)* each of the
following diced vegetables:
  carrots, celery, green beans,
  onions, green pepper
1 can, 4-6 oz *(113-170 g)* mushrooms
paprika
cayenne pepper

1 can, 8 oz *(227 g)* tomato sauce
1 can tomato paste
1 can consommé
Sauce 'n Gravy flour
½ cup *(118 ml)* sherry
1 cup *(237 ml)* sour cream
(optional)

Cook the shrimp with a bay leaf, a little vinegar and salt. Sauté vegetables in butter until just crunchy. Add some paprika and cayenne pepper to taste. Cook for a few minutes, then add consommé, tomato sauce and tomato paste. In a cup, mix together Wondra flour and a little water. Use to thicken sauce to desired consistency. Mix in sherry and simmer ten minutes. Add shrimp and sour cream and keep warm. Do not boil after adding sour cream. Serve over rice.

Curried Shrimp With Green Grapes

Can do ahead

Serves: 6
Preparing: 30 min

¼ cup *(59 ml)* **butter**
¼ cup *(59 ml)* **flour**
1½ tsp *(7.5 ml)* **curry powder**
1 Tb *(15 ml)* **onion, chopped**
2 cups *(474 ml)* **milk OR 1 cup**
  (237 ml) **milk, 1 cup** *(237 ml)*
  shrimp stock

1 tsp *(5 ml)* **salt**
⅛ tsp *(.6 ml)* **black pepper**
1½ cups *(355 ml)* **cooked shrimp**
  OR 2 cans, 6¾ oz *(191 g)*
  shrimp
1½ cups *(355 ml)* **seedless green**
  grapes
chow mein noodles OR rice

Melt butter in sauce pan. Remove from heat and blend in flour, curry powder and onion. Stir and cook 1 minute. Gradually add milk, stir and cook until medium thickness. Add salt, pepper and shrimp. Add grapes. Heat only until hot. Serve over chow mein noodles or rice.

Shrimp Creole For Twenty-Five

With tossed salad & bread, a complete buffet

Can do ahead
Can freeze

Serves: 25
Preparing: 15 min
Cooking: 10-12 hrs

1 Tb *(15 ml)* **bacon grease**
½ cup *(118 ml)* **margarine**
3 large **onions, chopped**
4 cloves **garlic, minced**
2 large **green peppers,**
  chopped
1 cup *(237 ml)* **celery, chopped**
1 bunch **parsley, chopped**
3 cans, 29 oz *(857 ml)* **tomatoes**
1 can, 46 oz *(1.35 l)* **tomato**
  juice

1 can, 6 oz *(177 ml)* **tomato**
  paste
1 bottle, 16 oz *(454 g)* **catsup**
sugar to taste
salt and pepper to taste
Worcestershire sauce to taste
Tabasco to taste
pinch of thyme
1 **bay leaf**
10 lb *(4.6 kg)* **shrimp, cleaned**

Melt bacon grease and margarine. Brown onions, garlic, peppers, celery and parsley. Add tomatoes, tomato juice, tomato paste and catsup. Let sauce cook the better part of the day. Add seasonings. Add shrimp about one hour before removing from heat. Allow to stand in sauce several hours before serving. Heat about 20 minutes to serve.

Shrimp Nantua

Can do ahead
Can freeze

Serves: 8-10
Preparing: 30 min
Cooking: 15 min

5 lbs *(2.3 kg)* **shrimp, boiled,**
  shelled, deveined
⅓ cup *(79 ml)* **butter**
2 Tb *(30 ml)* **flour**
1 Tb *(15 ml)* **tomato paste**

2½ cups *(592 ml)* **whipping cream**
1½ cups *(355 ml)* **tomatoes**
salt
cayenne pepper
Holland rusks

Melt butter and blend in flour. Add shrimp and sauté for 5 minutes. Add tomato paste and cream. Simmer until thickened. Add seasonings. Skin, seed and dice tomatoes. Add. Lightly toast rusks, allowing 1 to 2 per person. Pour shrimp mixture over rusks and serve.

Scampi

Can do ahead

Serves: 2
Preparing: 25 min
Baking: 15 min

1 lb *(454 g)* **shrimp**
½ cup *(118 ml)* **butter**
1 cup *(237 ml)* **olive oil**
salt

pepper
minced parsley
1 Tb *(15 ml)* **lemon juice**
2 **cloves garlic, pressed**
  OR minced

Remove shell from raw shrimp. Slit to butterfly and remove vein. Combine remaining ingredients and dip shrimp in mixture. Place in broiler pan and pour rest of mixture over. Run under broiler in bottom of oven for 15 minutes. Allow 1 lb shrimp per 2 people. Recipe doubles easily. Serve with lemon rice.

Shrimp Tempura

Can do partially ahead

Serves: 2
Preparing: 30 min
Frying: 10 min

1 lb *(454 g)* **shrimp**
lemon juice
1 cup *(237 ml)* **flour**

1 **egg**
1 tsp *(5 ml)* **baking powder**
milk

Clean and dry uncooked shrimp. May leave tails on and butterfly if desired. Sprinkle with lemon juice. This may be done ahead, covered and stored in refrigerator overnight. Combine flour, egg, and enough milk to make a fairly thick batter. Dip shrimp and place on wax paper to allow excess batter to run off. This may be done 1 to 2 hours ahead. Fry in shallow fat until golden brown.

Crab Imperial

Can do ahead

Serves: 6
Preparing: 20 min
Baking: 30 min

1½ lb *(680 g)* white lump
  crab meat
1 green pepper, chopped fine
2 Tb *(30 ml)* butter
1 small jar chopped pimento
1 tsp *(5 ml)* Worcestershire sauce

1 tsp *(5 ml)* salt
½ tsp *(2.5 ml)* dry mustard
1 cup *(237 ml)* mayonnaise
sharp cheese, grated
paprika

Sauté green pepper in butter until soft but not brown; cool thoroughly. Mix green pepper, pimento, salt, dry mustard, Worcestershire sauce and mayonnaise gently with crab meat. Put in baking shells, sprinkle with grated cheese and paprika. Bake 30 minutes at 350° (177° C).

Crab And Spinach Loaf

Must do ahead

Serves: 4
Preparing: 30 min
Baking: 60 min

1 can, 7½ oz *(212 g)* Alaska King
  crab OR 1 pkg, 6-8 oz *(170-227 g)*
  Alaska King crab
1 pkg, 10 oz *(284 g)* frozen,
  chopped spinach
2 tsp *(10 ml)* lemon juice
2 Tb *(30 ml)* onion, minced

¼ tsp *(1.25 ml)* salt
1 beaten egg
¼ cup *(59 ml)* cottage cheese
2 Tb *(30 ml)* Parmesan cheese,
  grated
1 pkg of Pepperidge Farm
  patti shells, thawed

SAUCE:

1 can condensed cream of
  mushroom soup
¼ cup *(59 ml)* milk
1 can drained mushrooms

1 Tb *(15 ml)* pimento
  chopped
2 Tb *(30 ml)* sherry

Drain crab and slice. Cook spinach as directed. Drain well. Combine crab, spinach, lemon juice, onion, salt, egg, cottage cheese, and Parmesan cheese. Roll out patti shells together into a rectangle. Spread the filling over the dough. Roll up, sealing ends and place in well greased 9x5x3 inch (22.86 x 12.70 x 7.62 cm) loaf pan. Bake in 375° (191° C) oven approximately 1 hour. Combine and heat remaining 5 ingredients for sauce.

Almond Crab Casserole

Can do ahead
Can freeze

Serves: 8
Preparing: 20-25 min
Baking: 45 min

1 cup *(237 ml)* **crab meat**
1 cup *(237 ml)* **shrimp**
2 cans **cream of mushroom soup**
1 cup *(237 ml)* **celery, sliced fine**

¼ cup *(59 ml)* **onion, minced**
1 can, 3 oz *(85 g)* **chow mein noodles**
1 pkg, 2 oz *(57 g)* **almonds, shaved OR chopped**

Combine all ingredients and top with almonds in greased casserole. Dust lightly with paprika. Bake 45 minutes at 350° (177° C).

Crab Meat Maryland

Can do ahead
Can freeze

Serves: 6
Preparing: 15 min
Cooking: 10 min
Baking: 20 min

¼ cup *(59 ml)* **butter**
3 Tb *(45 ml)* **flour**
2 cups *(474 ml)* **milk**
2 Tb *(30 ml)* **onion, minced**
½ tsp *(2.5 ml)* **celery salt**
⅛ tsp *(.6 ml)* **orange rind, grated**
1 Tb *(15 ml)* **parsley, minced**
1 Tb *(15 ml)* **green pepper, minced**
1 **pimento, minced**

dash **Tabasco**
2 Tb *(30 ml)* **sherry**
1 **egg, beaten**
1 tsp *(5 ml)* **salt**
pinch of **pepper**
3 cups *(710 ml)* **crab meat, cooked, fresh, canned OR frozen**
½ cup *(118 ml)* **soft bread crumbs**
1 Tb *(15 ml)* **butter, melted**
paprika

Melt butter in double boiler; stir in flour, then milk, cooking over boiling water and stirring until thickened. Stir in next seven ingredients. Remove from heat. Add sherry. Stir some of sauce slowly into beaten egg, then stir all back into sauce. Add salt, pepper, and crab meat. Turn into greased 1½ quart (1.42 l) casserole. Combine crumbs and melted butter; sprinkle over casserole, then add paprika. Bake at 350° (177° C) 20 minutes or until bubbly and brown. When preparing for guests, make sauce early in day and add crab meat just before putting in oven.

Polly's Crab And Asparagus Casserole

Can do ahead

Serves: 4-6
Preparing: 20 min
Baking: 30 min

2 pkgs, 10 oz *(283 g)* frozen
  asparagus
1 lb *(454 g)* deluxe crab meat
4 Tb *(60 ml)* butter
4 Tb *(60 ml)* flour
1 tsp *(5 ml)* salt
1 tsp *(5 ml)* dry mustard
¼ tsp *(1.25 ml)* pepper

1 pt *(474 ml)* half and half
4 Tb *(60 ml)* lemon juice
¾ cup *(177 ml)* cheddar cheese,
  grated
1½ cup *(355 ml)* fresh bread
  crumbs
3 Tb *(45 ml)* butter, melted

Cook asparagus until a little tender, but slightly undercooked. Lay in bottom of a buttered casserole. Place crabmeat over it. Make a sauce from the 4 Tb (60 ml) butter, flour, salt, dry mustard, pepper, half and half, lemon juice, and cheese. Cook until it thickens. Pour this sauce on asparagus and crab meat. Cover with fresh bread crumbs mixed with the 3 Tb (45 ml) of melted butter. Bake at 350° (177° C) for 30 minutes.

Crêpes With Crab, Almonds And Water Chestnuts

Can do ahead
Can freeze

Serves: 8
Preparing: 45 min
Cooking: 10-15 min
Baking: 20 min

1 lb *(454 g)* crab meat
2 cans, 5 oz *(142 g)* water
  chestnuts
1 cup *(237 ml)* blanched almonds
1 cup *(237 ml)* thick white sauce
1 cup *(237 ml)* onions, chopped

½ cup *(118 ml)* butter
½ cup *(118 ml)* white wine
¼-½ tsp *(1.25-2.5 ml)* ginger
¼-½ tsp *(1.25-2.5 ml)* nutmeg
¼-½ tsp *(1.25-2.5 ml)* pepper
crepes

Sauté onions in butter until limp and add crab meat and wine. Cook until reduced by half. Combine white sauce and seasonings. Add to crab meat mixture and cook until thickened. Add almonds and water chestnuts. Put a spoon or two of filling in each crêpe and roll. Place seam side down in buttered casserole. Bake 375° (191° C) for 20 minutes. If you desire to freeze, freeze filling and crêpes separately.

Variation: Add curry to seasonings.

219

Deviled Crab

Can do ahead
Can freeze

Serves: 6
Preparing: 30 min
Baking: 20-25 min

4 Tb *(60 ml)* butter
1 medium onion, finely chopped
2 large mushrooms, chopped
½ green pepper, chopped
¼ tsp *(1.25 ml)* salt
½ tsp *(2.5 ml)* dry mustard
⅛ tsp *(.6 ml)* pepper
1 Tb *(15 ml)* Worcestershire
  sauce

dash of Tabasco
2 Tb *(30 ml)* flour
1 cup *(237 ml)* hot milk
1 cup *(237 ml)* hot clam juice
  (or broth)
2 egg yolks, well beaten
1 lb *(454 g)* lump white crab meat

Sauté onion, mushrooms, and green pepper in butter. Add salt, pepper and dry mustard, Worcestershire sauce and Tabasco. Then add flour, hot milk, hot clam juice, and well beaten egg yolks. Cook together for 10 minutes in double boiler (til thickened). Stir constantly. Add crab meat that has been thoroughly picked for cartilage and cook for 5 minutes more. Remove from heat and place in individual casseroles or crab shells. Before serving, reheat in oven at 350° (177° C).

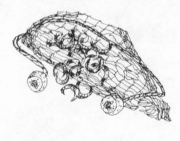

Salmon Cheese Casserole

Serve immediately

Serves: 4-6
Preparing: 15 min
Baking: 1 hr

1½ cups *(355 ml)* milk
2 Tb *(30 ml)* butter
3 eggs, beaten
1 cup *(237 ml)* soft bread crumbs
2 Tb *(30 ml)* onion, minced

2 Tb *(30 ml)* parsley
pepper and paprika to taste
1½ cups *(355 ml)* sharp cheese,
  shredded
2 cups *(474 ml)* salmon

Heat milk and butter. Stir together hot milk, beaten eggs, bread crumbs, onion, parsley, seasonings and cheese. Remove all skin and bones from salmon. Fold into above mixture. Place in 1½ quart (1.42 l) casserole. Place in pan of water. Bake at 350° (177° C) for 1 hour or until set.

Salmon Mousse

Must do ahead

3 Tb *(45 ml)* flour
3 Tb *(45 ml)* powdered sugar
2 tsp *(10 ml)* Dijon mustard
2 tsp *(10 ml)* salt
4 eggs
1½ cups *(355 ml)* milk
½ cup *(118 ml)* tarragon vinegar

3 Tb *(45 ml)* butter, melted
2 envelopes plain gelatin
¼ cup *(59 ml)* cold water
3 cups *(710 ml)* flaked salmon
1 cup *(237 ml)* whipping cream,
  whipped

Mix flour, sugar, mustard, salt in top of double boiler. Add eggs and whisk until smooth. Add milk. Stir in vinegar slowly or it will curdle. Mix well. Cook over hot water until thickened, stirring constantly. Add butter. Soften gelatin in cold water; add to hot mixture. Stir until gelatin is completely dissolved. Add salmon. Chill. Stir occasionally. When slightly thickened, fold in whipped cream. Turn into a 2 quart (1.8 l) mold (fish mold if you have one), rinsed with cold water. Chill until firm. Unmold on lettuce. Serve with "Cucumber-Dill Sauce."

If served in the shape of a fish, decorate with pimento, olive and thin slices of radishes set in appropriate place for eyes, scales, etc.

CUCUMBER-DILL SAUCE:

Must do ahead

Serves: 6-8
Preparing: 45 min
Chilling: 3-4 hrs

1 cucumber, peeled and seeded
salt
1 Tb *(15 ml)* lemon juice OR
  tarragon vinegar

1 tsp *(5 ml)* dill weed
1 tsp *(5 ml)* chopped chives
¼ tsp *(1.25 ml)* white pepper
1 cup *(237 ml)* sour cream

Shred cucumber with coarse grater. Sprinkle with salt and let stand at room temperature for 1 hour. Drain thoroughly. Combine with remaining ingredients. Chill.

Easy Salmon Patties

Can do ahead

Serves: 6-8
Preparing: 15 min
Cooking: 5 min

1 can, 15-16 oz *(454 g)* pink
  salmon
1 egg
⅓ cup *(79 ml)* onion, minced

½ cup *(118 ml)* flour
1½ tsp *(7.5 ml)* baking powder
1½ cup *(355 ml)* shortening
tartar sauce, for serving

Drain salmon and set aside 2 Tb (30 ml) salmon juice. Mix the salmon, egg and onion until sticky. Stir in flour. Add baking powder to salmon juice. Stir into salmon mixture, and form into small patties. Fry until golden brown in hot shortening (about 5 minutes).

Tuna-Cashew Casserole

Can do ahead

Serves: 5-6
Preparing: 15 min
Baking: 20-40 min

1 jar, 3 oz *(85 g)* chow mein
  noodles
1 can, 10¾ oz *(305 g)* cream
  of mushroom soup, undiluted
¼ cup *(59 ml)* water
1 can, 7 oz *(198 g)* tuna

¼ lb *(113 g)* cashew nuts
1 cup *(237 ml)* celery,
  finely diced
¼ cup *(59 ml)* onion, minced
dash of salt
dash of pepper

Preheat oven to 325° (163° C). Set aside ½ cup (118 ml) chow mein noodles. In a 1½ quart (1.42 l) casserole, combine remaining ingredients. Sprinkle with reserved noodles. Bake, uncovered, at 325°-375° (163°-191° C) for 20 to 40 minutes.

Tuna Florentine

Can do ahead

Serves: 4
Preparing: 15 min
Baking: 20 min

1 pkg, 10 oz *(284 g)* frozen
  chopped spinach, cooked and
  well drained
1 can, 7 oz *(198 g)* tuna, flaked
⅓ cup *(79 ml)* bread crumbs
1 Tb *(15 ml)* lemon juice

½ tsp *(2.5 ml)* salt
dash pepper
dash nutmeg
½ cup *(118 ml)* mayonnaise
grated Parmesan cheese

Blend all ingredients, except cheese, together thoroughly. Place in individual baking dishes or 9 inch (22.86 cm) pie pan. Sprinkle well with cheese. Bake in 350° (177° C) oven for 20 minutes.

Scalloped Oysters De Luxe

Serve immediately

Serves: 6-8
Preparing: 5 min
Baking: 30 min

1 cup *(237 ml)* **bread crumbs**
2 cups *(474 ml)* **cracker crumbs**
1 cup *(237 ml)* **butter, melted**
1 qt *(946 ml)* **oysters**

salt and pepper to taste
4 Tb *(60 ml)* **cream**
¾ to 1 cup *(177-237 ml)* **oyster liquor**

Examine oysters for shells. Combine bread and cracker crumbs and mix with melted butter. Put a thin layer in the bottom of dish and cover with a layer of oysters. Season with salt and pepper. Add half of cream and oyster liquor. Repeat and cover the top with remaining crumbs. Bake for 30 minutes at 450° (232° C). Never have more than 2 layers of oysters.

Oyster And Rice Casserole
Elegant company dish

Can partially do ahead

Serves: 4
Preparing: 30 min
Baking: 30 min

1 cup *(237 ml)* **brown OR wild rice, cooked**
¼ cup *(59 ml)* **butter**
2 cups *(474 ml)* **fresh mushrooms, sliced OR 1 can, 8 oz *(227 g)* mushrooms, drain and reserve liquid**

½ cup *(118 ml)* **green pepper, chopped**
1 cup *(237 ml)* **chablis OR sauterne**
2 cups *(474 ml)* **oysters**

Melt butter in large skillet and add mushrooms and green pepper. Brown lightly over moderate heat. Salt and pepper to taste. Add liquid from mushrooms, if using canned, and wine. Simmer 15 minutes and mix with cooked rice. Spread this mixture in a shallow 2 quart (1.89 l) casserole dish. Dip oysters into melted butter and arrange on top of rice. Bake in moderate oven 350° (177° C) for 30 minutes.

Oyster Loaf

Must do ahead

Serves: 6
Preparing: 15 min
Baking: 30 min

3 doz oysters
3 small loaves of French
   bread

1 garlic clove
4 Tb *(60 ml)* butter, melted
milk

Split bread lengthwise; scoop out soft centers and use as crumbs. Rub inside of loaves with cut garlic, then brush with butter. Drain oysters and save the liquid. Sauté oysters in butter for 5 minutes. Stuff loaves and fill in with crumbs and enough liquid to moisten. Wrap loaves in cheese cloth that has been dipped in milk. Bake at 350° (177° C) for 30 minutes.

Scalloped Oysters And Ham

Can do ahead

Serves: 4-6
Preparing: 10 min
Baking: 20 min

½ cup *(118 ml)* margarine, melted
4 cups *(946 ml)* soft bread
   crumbs
1¼ tsp *(6.25 ml)* salt
¼ tsp *(1.25 ml)* pepper

1 Tb *(15 ml)* lemon juice
1-2 pts *(474-946 ml)* oysters
¼ cup *(59 ml)* heavy cream OR
   half and half
Smithfield ham

In an 8 x 12 inch (20.32 x 30.48 cm) baking dish, layer buttered bread crumbs, then oysters with salt, pepper and lemon juice. Repeat layers ending with crumbs on top. Pour cream over mixture. Bake at 450° (232° C) for 20 minutes. Serve with thin slices of Smithfield ham.

Lobster Casserole

Serves: 4-6
Preparing: 15 min
Baking: 45 min

2 Tb *(30 ml)* butter
2 Tb *(30 ml)* flour
½ tsp *(2.5 ml)* salt
⅛ tsp *(.6 ml)* pepper
1 cup *(237 ml)* milk
dash of nutmeg
½ tsp *(2.5 ml)* paprika
2 egg yolks, slightly beaten

1 cup *(237 ml)* sharp OR extra
sharp cheddar cheese,
shredded
2 cans, 6 oz OR 8 oz *(170-227 g)*
button mushrooms
1 lb *(454 g)* lobster meat,
canned or fresh
¼ cup *(59 ml)* sherry

Combine butter, flour, salt, pepper and milk; cook until thickened. Add nutmeg and paprika. Add egg yolks; cook about 3 minutes. Add ½ cup (118 ml) cheese, mushrooms, lobster and sherry. Place in a greased 1½ quart (1.42 l) casserole. Sprinkle remaining cheese over top. Bake at 350° (177° C) for 45 minutes or until cheese is melted and slightly bubbly.

Lobster Thermidor

Easily doubled for guests

Can do ahead

Serves: 2
Preparing: 35-40 min
Baking: 15 min

2 medium or large lobster
tails
5 Tb *(75 ml)* butter
4 Tb *(60 ml)* flour
½ tsp *(2.5 ml)* paprika
½ tsp *(2.5 ml)* dry mustard
¼ tsp *(1.25 ml)* salt
dash of cayenne

1 cup *(237 ml)* light cream
1 can, 4 oz *(113 g)* chopped
mushrooms, drained
4 Tb *(60 ml)* dry sherry
¼ cup *(59 ml)* Parmesan cheese,
grated
cracker crumbs

Boil lobsters, cool, and cut into bite sized chunks. Save shells to stuff. In a skillet, sauté lobster in 4 Tb (60 ml) of the butter for two minutes; stir in flour, paprika, mustard, salt and cayenne; cook stirring constantly until bubbly. Stir in cream; continue cooking and stirring until mixture boils for 1 minute. Remove from heat and stir in sherry and mushrooms. Spoon into lobster shells. Melt the other tablespoon of butter in a saucepan; add cracker crumbs and cheese; toss lightly to mix and sprinkle over filling in the shells. Bake in a hot oven 425° (218° C) for 15 minutes or until filling is hot and crumb topping is golden.

Coquilles St. Jacques

Serves: 6-7
Preparing: 25 min
Baking: 5-10 min

1½ lbs *(680 g)* **scallops, preferably
North Carolina scallops**
2 sprigs fresh thyme OR
½ tsp *(2.5 ml)* **dried thyme**
1 bay leaf
1 sprig parsley
8 peppercorns
salt to taste

½ cup *(118 ml)* **water**
½ cup *(118 ml)* **dry white wine**
7 Tb *(105 ml)* **butter**
3 Tb *(45 ml)* **flour**
2 egg yolks
1 tsp *(5 ml)* **lemon juice**
cayenne pepper
Parmesan cheese

Preheat oven to 400° (204° C). Combine first eight ingredients in a small saucepan and bring to a boil. Cover and simmer exactly 2 minutes. Remove the parsley, bay leaf and thyme and drain, but reserve the cooking liquid. Let the scallops cool. If North Carolina scallops are used, leave whole and set aside. If large scallops are used, slice thinly and set aside. In another saucepan, melt 2 Tb (30 ml) of the butter and stir in the flour with a wire whisk. When blended, add the scallop liquid — about 1½ cups (355 ml) — stirring vigorously. Remove the sauce from the heat and beat vigorously with an electric beater. Add the remaining butter, a little at a time very gradually. Beat in the egg yolks and continue beating until cool. Add the lemon juice and cayenne. Spoon a little of the mixture into 12-16 small scallop shells or 6-8 large scallop shells or ramekins. Top with equal parts of scallops. Cover with the remaining sauce and sprinkle with Parmesan cheese. Bake 5-10 minutes, or until bubbling and golden brown. If necessary, glaze at the last minute under the broiler. Although the sauce is very rich, small portions make a great appetizer.

Harold's Delight

Can do ahead
Can freeze

Serves: 8 plus
Preparing: 40 min
Baking: 30-40 min

¼ cup *(59 ml)* butter
1 stalk celery, chopped
½ green pepper, chopped
¼ cup onion, chopped
2 cups *(474 ml)* rice, cooked
2¼ cups *(534 ml)* milk
3 Tb *(45 ml)* butter
3 Tb *(45 ml)* flour
1 can tuna, drained

1 cup *(237 ml)* crabmeat OR
lobster
1 cup *(237 ml)* shrimp
1 cup *(237 ml)* mayonnaise
½ jar, 4 oz *(113 g)* pimento,
chopped
corn flakes OR bread crumbs
1 can cream of mushroom soup

Melt butter in saucepan; add celery, green pepper and onion, cover and simmer until tender. Make a white sauce with the milk, 3 Tb (45 ml) butter and flour. To the white sauce, add the tuna, crabmeat, shrimp, mayonnaise, pimento and the sautéed vegetables. Put cooked rice in the bottom of a 2 quart (1.89 l) pyrex dish and pour the white sauce mixture over. Can freeze at this point. Cover with crushed corn flakes — approximately 1 cup (237 ml). Bake at 325° (163° C) for 30-40 minutes. Partially dilute the mushroom soup and put over the top of each serving.

Wild Rice Seafood Casserole

Can partially do ahead

Serves: 18
Preparing: 35 min
Baking: 40 min

2 cups *(474 ml)* wild rice
cooked
2 cups *(474 ml)* shrimp, cooked
2 cups *(474 ml)* crab meat
2 cups *(474 ml)* white rice,
cooked
2 cans, 10¾ oz *(305 g)* cream of
mushroom soup
1 small green pepper, minced
salt, pepper, and Accent
to taste

2 cans, 4 oz *(113 g)* mushrooms
1 cup *(237 ml)* cheese, grated
1 cup *(237 ml)* bread crumbs,
buttered
1 can, 16 oz *(454 g)* bean
sprouts
1 cup *(237 ml)* celery, diced
1 small onion, minced

Combine the two rices after cooking. Sauté celery, green pepper, onion and mushrooms in butter. Mix with rice, shrimp, crab, bean sprouts, and mushroom soup. Put in buttered 3 quart (2.81 l) baking dish. Sprinkle with cheese and crumbs. Bake in pan of water in 350° (177° C) oven for 40 minutes.

S
E
A
F
O
O
D

Seafood Casserole

May do ahead
Can freeze

Serves: 4-6
Preparing: 20 min
Baking: 30-40 min
till bubbly

4 Tb *(60 ml)* **butter**
4 Tb *(60 ml)* **flour**
2 cups *(474 ml)* **milk**
1½ tsp *(7.5 ml)* **salt**
¼ tsp *(1.25 ml)* **black pepper**
dash of red pepper

2 eggs, beaten
4 oz *(113 g)* **sharp cheese,**
   cubed
¾ cup *(177 ml)* **crab meat**
¾ cup *(177 ml)* **shrimp, cooked**
1 cup *(237 ml)* **bread crumbs**

Mix butter, flour, milk, salt and pepper in a saucepan. Cook and stir until thick. Add eggs and cheese. Stir until cheese is melted. Add crab meat and shrimp. Pour into one large 2½ quart (2.37 l), or 4 to 6 individual buttered casseroles. Top with buttered bread crumbs and grated cheese if desired. Bake 450° (232° C) until brown and hot. Good served in pastry shells.

May be made ahead and refrigerated or frozen. In this case, add crumbs just before putting into oven and bake at 350° (177° C).

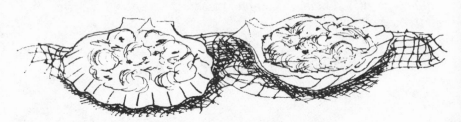

Shrimp And Crab Casserole
Excellent for guests

Can do ahead
Can freeze

Serves: 8
Preparing: 20 min
Baking: 20 min

2 lbs *(908 g)* **cooked shrimp**
2 lbs *(908 g)* **crab meat, picked**
2 medium onions, chopped fine
2 medium green peppers,
   chopped fine
1 large stalk celery, chopped
   fine

1½ pts *(710 ml)* **mayonnaise**
1 bottle Durkee's dressing
salt, pepper, Tabasco
   to taste
bread crumbs

Mix all ingredients except bread crumbs in a 13 x 8 x 2 inch (33.02 x 20.32 x 5.08 cm) casserole dish. Spread toasted bread crumbs on top. Bake at 400° (204° C) for 20 minutes.

SAUCES

Litchfield Pink Sauce
Good with all seafood

Can do ahead

Serves: 8-10
Preparing: 10 min

1 Tb *(15 ml)* **tomato paste**
1 pimento, diced
pinch dried tarragon
pinch basil

1 cup *(237 ml)* **mayonnaise**
lemon juice to taste
chopped chives to garnish

Combine tomato paste, pimento and spices. Blend together with mayonnaise and lemon juice. Top with chopped chives.

Sauce Bonne Femme

Yield: ⅔ cup (158 ml)
Preparing: 10 min

2 Tb *(30 ml)* **butter**
1½ Tb *(22.5 ml)* **flour**
3 Tb *(45 ml)* **heavy cream**

1 Tb *(15 ml)* **dry white wine**
½ cup *(118 ml)* **hollandaise sauce**

Melt butter and add flour to make a roux. Add cream and wine and cook very slowly, adding salt and pepper to taste. Remove from heat and stir in warm hollandaise sauce. Blend well and serve with fish or vegetables.

Boiled Shrimp Sauce

Can do ahead

Yield: Enough for
2 lbs (908 g) of shrimp
Preparing: 10 min

1 cup *(237 ml)* **mayonnaise**
⅓ cup *(79 ml)* **chili sauce**
1 Tb *(15 ml)* **onion, grated**
2 Tb *(30 ml)* **lemon juice**

½ tsp *(2.5 ml)* **Worcestershire**
sauce
1 Tb *(15 ml)* **celery, chopped**

Tartar Sauce Supreme

Must do ahead

Yield: 1 cup (237 ml)

1 cup *(237 ml)* **mayonnaise**
1½ Tb *(22.5 ml)* **pickles,**
  minced or grated
1½ Tb *(22.5 ml)* **parsley, minced**
1½ Tb *(22.5 ml)* **capers**

1½ Tb *(22.5 ml)* **onion,**
  minced OR grated
1½ Tb *(22.5 ml)* **green olives,**
  minced

Combine all ingredients and let sit several hours prior to serving.

Remoulade Sauce I

Can do ahead

Yield: 1½ cups (355 ml)

1 cup *(237 ml)* **mayonnaise**
dash of Angostura bitters
twist of lemon peel (zest)
1 Tb *(15 ml)* **ground mustard**
  seed
1 Tb *(15 ml)* **prepared horseradish**
Tabasco to taste

2 tsp *(10 ml)* **catsup OR**
  tomato paste
¼ tsp *(1.25 ml)* **filé**
¼ tsp *(1.25 ml)* **Lawry's**
  seasoned salt
½ tsp *(2.5 ml)* **paprika**

Blend all ingredients and serve with cooked shrimp.

Remoulade Sauce II

1 cup *(237 ml)* **homemade**
  mayonnaise
3 shallots, finely chopped
  OR 1 large garlic clove,
  finely chopped
1 Tb *(15 ml)* **parsley, finely**
  chopped
1 tsp *(5 ml)* **Dijon mustard**

1 Tb *(15 ml)* **capers, chopped**
1 hard-cooked egg, finely
  chopped
1 Tb *(15 ml)* **fresh tarragon,**
  chopped OR 1 tsp *(5 ml)*
  dry tarragon

Blend all ingredients thoroughly and season if necessary with salt, lemon juice or vinegar. Allow to stand at least an hour or more before serving.

Vegetables

Vegetables

Tips

POTATOES

Look for sound, smooth potatoes with shallow eyes and few blemishes.

Avoid potatoes with large cuts or green patches on the skin. The green areas taste bitter.

Choose potatoes approximately the same size so that they will cook in the same amount of time.

Potatoes should be stored in a cool, dark, dry place.

To freeze potatoes, cook them in their jackets. Cool, then wrap in foil.

To renew potatoes that have been stored for some time, peel and cut them in quarters. Boil them in a mixture of half milk and half water.

Three medium-size baking potatoes weigh about one pound.

For mashed potatoes, one pound makes about 4 servings.

For French-fried potatoes, one pound yields about 4 to 5 servings.

For potato salads, one pound yields about 2 cups (474 ml) of cubes or slices.

To shorten the baking time, cut potatoes in half lengthwise and place cut-side down on a lightly greased baking sheet. Bake at 425° (218° C) for 35 minutes.

To shorten the baking time, boil potatoes for 5 minutes in salted water. Cool slightly; dry, and bake at 425° (218° C) for about 35 minutes or until tender.

Reheat baked potatoes by dipping in very hot water and baking again at 325° (163° C).

MUSHROOMS

Mushrooms are at their best and least expensive during the winter months. They should be white with firm, closed caps.

If using mushrooms the day they are purchased, they may be refrigerated in their container. If they are to be stored for longer periods of time, put in an airtight container.

To prepare mushrooms, rinse briefly or wipe with a damp paper towel. Trim off any unappetizing brown spots but do not peel. If tips of stems are dry, cut off a slice.

When using canned mushrooms in a recipe, use the liquid if possible, or reserve it for soups or sauces.

One pound of fresh mushrooms equals 20 to 24 medium mushrooms.

One pound of fresh mushrooms, sliced and cooked, equals one 8 oz (227 g) can of sliced mushrooms.

Two ounces (57 g) dried mushrooms soaked in 1½ cups (355 ml) water equals 1⅓ cups (316 ml) chopped mushrooms and liquid.

233

One pound of fresh mushrooms equals 20 to 24 frozen. Do not go by weight.

VEGETABLE SAUCES

If Hollandaise curdles, gradually beat one well-beaten egg yolk into the mixture or add 1 Tb (15 ml) boiling water to mixture.

VEGETABLES

A little vinegar or lemon juice added to potatoes to be mashed just before draining off water will make them beautifully white.

To peel tomatoes easily, dip for a few seconds into boiling water.

When cooking vegetables, remember to boil all vegetables that grow above the ground without being covered. The flavor and color will be much better.

Weep no more, my lady! An unlighted kitchen match held between your teeth while working with onions will dissipate the onion fumes.

To remove onion odor from your hands, rub them with celery.

Add a little milk to the water in which cauliflower cooks; this makes the flowerets especially white.

To seed and juice a tomato: remove the core, pierce inside several times with sharp knife, then squeeze like a dish rag over a bowl.

A bit of sugar when cooking tomatoes heightens flavor.

White onions are milder than yellow ones.

Fresh herbs are only half as potent as dried herbs, so use twice the amount.

A small pinch of baking soda will preserve the color of fresh vegetables.

Don't add salt to the water when cooking corn, it toughens it. Add salt when serving.

To prevent a rubbery taste in white sauces, always bubble flour and butter at least one minute before adding milk. Always stir with a wooden spoon.

Put a piece of bread on top of pan when cooking cabbage or cauliflower to prevent unpleasant odor.

HOW TO MAKE CREAM SAUCE:

Light Cream Sauce: Use 1 Tb (15 ml) each of butter or margarine and 1 Tb (15 ml) flour to 1 cup (237 ml) milk.

Medium Cream Sauce: Use 2 Tb (30 ml) each of butter and 2 Tb (30 ml) flour to 1 cup (237 ml) milk.

Heavy Cream Sauce: Use 3 Tb (45 ml) each butter and flour to each cup of milk.

To Make The Sauce: Melt butter in saucepan over low heat. Stir in flour and blend until smooth. Add milk gradually, stirring constantly until smooth and well blended. Season to taste with salt and pepper. Always remember to keep the butter and flour in the same proportion.

VEGETABLE SAUCES

Savory Walnut Topping

Yield: ¾ cup
Preparing: 15 min

¼ cup *(59 ml)* butter OR margarine
½ cup *(118 ml)* walnuts, coarsely
chopped
1 cup *(237 ml)* bread crumbs, soft

¼ tsp *(1.25 ml)* dillweed, rosemary
oregano, OR other herb

Melt butter in a skillet. Add walnuts, bread crumbs and herbs, stirring constantly until lightly toasted. Sprinkle crumbs over hot, well-drained, cooked vegetables.

Lemon Crumb Vegetable Topping

Yield: ½ cup (118 ml)
Preparing: 15 min

3 Tb *(45 ml)* butter OR margarine
6 Tb *(90 ml)* coarse dry bread
crumbs
⅛ tsp *(.6 ml)* salt

⅛ tsp *(.6 ml)* pepper
1 tsp *(5 ml)* lemon rind,
grated

Melt butter in a skillet. Add bread crumbs, salt, and pepper; stir over low heat until lightly toasted. Stir in lemon rind, mixing well. Sprinkle over hot, well-drained, cooked vegetables.

Sauce Merlaise

Can do ahead

Yield: 2 cups (474 ml)
Preparing: 15 min
Cooking: 5 min

1 cup *(237 ml)* mayonnaise
1 cup *(237 ml)* sour cream
grated rind and juice of
1 lemon
½ tsp *(2.5 ml)* prepared mustard

2 oz *(57 g)* sharp cheddar
cheese
¼ cup *(59 ml)* milk
scattering of cayenne pepper

Melt cheese in milk at low heat stirring constantly. Remove from heat and add remaining ingredients. Refrigerate — it will keep for days. May be heated very gently — not to boiling point — for use on hot vegetables. Excellent chilled and used as a dip.

Cheese Sauce For Potatoes

Must do ahead

Yields: 1½ cup (355 ml)
Preparing: 5 min

1 cup *(237 ml)* mayonnaise
½ cup *(118 ml)* soft butter
¼ cup *(59 ml)* onion, minced

½ tsp *(2.5 ml)* Tabasco
½ cup *(118 ml)* Parmesan cheese

Mix and store in refrigerator at least two days ahead of time and serve at room temperature on baked potatoes.

Sauce For Vegetables

Yield: 1 cup (237 ml)
Preparing: 5-10 min

½ pt *(237 ml)* sour cream
juice of ½ lemon
1 Tb *(15 ml)* wine vinegar
1 Tb *(15 ml)* horseradish
cayenne pepper to taste

1½ tsp *(7.5 ml)* salt
1 tsp *(5 ml)* dry mustard
½ tsp *(2.5 ml)* paprika
1 tsp *(5 ml)* onion juice

Mix all of the above well and serve over vegetables.

Chef's Cheese Sauce For Potatoes

Serves: 5-6
Preparing: 15 min

½ cup *(118 ml)* sour cream
¼ cup *(59 ml)* butter OR
  margarine, softened
1 cup *(237 ml)* sharp cheddar
  cheese, shredded OR grated

2 Tb *(30 ml)* green onions,
  chopped
4 slices bacon, crumbled

Combine sour cream, butter, cheese, bacon and onions; mix well. Serve on hot baked potatoes.

Cheesy Herb Topping

Yield: 1½ cups
Preparing: 10 min

½ cup *(118 ml)* herb-seasoned
  stuffing mix
2 Tb *(30 ml)* butter OR margarine,
  melted

1 cup *(237 ml)* pasteurized
  processed American cheese

Crush stuffing mix; toss with melted butter. Sprinkle over hot cooked vegetables or casseroles. Top with shredded cheese.

Blender Hollandaise Sauce

Yield: ¾ cup (177 ml)
Preparing: 10 min

½ cup *(118 ml)* butter
3 egg yolks
2 Tb *(30 ml)* lemon juice

pinch cayenne
dash salt

In saucepan, heat butter until very hot, but do not let it brown. Into blender container put egg yolks, lemon juice, cayenne and salt. Cover. Press mix button. As soon as blades reach full speed, remove inner cap of cover and pour in hot butter.

Herb Butter

½ cup *(118 ml)* butter OR
margarine, melted
2 Tb *(30 ml)* parsley,
finely chopped
1 Tb *(15 ml)* chives, snipped

½ tsp *(2.5 ml)* dried tarragon
leaves
2 Tb *(30 ml)* lemon juice

In a small bowl combine all of the above and mix until well blended. To serve, drain asparagus, spoon herb butter over and serve immediately.

Fried Artichokes

A different way to serve artichokes

Serves: 6-8
Preparing: 50 min

4 medium artichokes
1 egg
½ cup *(118 ml)* milk
½ cup *(118 ml)* biscuit baking
mix
¼ cup *(59 ml)* flour
1½ tsp *(7.5 ml)* double-acting
baking powder

1 tsp *(5 ml)* salt
½ tsp *(2.5 ml)* garlic powder
¼ cup *(59 ml)* onion, finely
chopped
1 Tb *(15 ml)* parsley, chopped
vegetable oil for deep-fat
frying

Wash and drain artichokes. Cut off top half and trim stem. Snip off all outer leaves down to the pale green leaves. Slice them in half lengthwise. Cut each half into quarters; remove the thistle portion. In a small bowl, blend together egg and milk. Stir in biscuit mix, flour, baking powder, salt and garlic powder until well mixed. Fold in onion and parsley. Dip artichoke pieces in batter to thinly coat. Fry in a deep-fat fryer or in 2″ (5.08 cm) of vegetable oil heated to 350° (177° C) in a saucepan, a few at a time for 6 to 8 minutes. Remove, drain and sprinkle with salt. Serve hot.

Artichoke Casserole

A special treat

Can do ahead

Serves: 4-6
Preparing: 20 min
Baking: 20 min

2 pkgs, 9 oz *(255 g)* **frozen artichokes, cooked, drained**
1 chicken bouillon cube
½ cup *(118 ml)* **hot water**
2 Tb *(30 ml)* **margarine**
2 Tb *(30 ml)* **flour**

½ cup *(118 ml)* **milk**
½ cup *(118 ml)* **Swiss cheese, grated**
1 Tb *(15 ml)* **sherry (optional)**
¼ tsp *(1.25 ml)* **salt**

Put artichokes in buttered 2 quart (1.89 l) casserole. Dissolve bouillon cube in hot water. Melt margarine in saucepan; blend in flour, then gradually add milk and bouillon water. Cook until thickened, stirring constantly. Remove from heat and add half of the cheese, stirring until cheese is melted. Add sherry and salt. Pour sauce over artichokes and sprinkle with remaining cheese. Bake at 375° (191° C) 15-20 minutes.

Artichoke-Mushroom Casserole

An elegant gourmet treat

Can do ahead
Can freeze

Serves: 6-8
Preparing: 25 min
Baking: 30 min

2 cans, 14 oz *(397 g)* **artichokes, drained**
1 lb *(454 g)* **fresh mushrooms, sliced**
6 Tb *(90 ml)* **butter**

1 cup *(237 ml)* **sour cream**
1 tsp *(5 ml)* **Worcestershire sauce**
pinch of dried parsley
bread crumbs

Put artichokes in casserole dish. Sauté mushrooms in butter 10 minutes; drain (save butter in pan) and add mushrooms to artichokes. Put sour cream in pan with butter; blend well. Add seasonings and parsley. Pour over artichokes and mushrooms. Top with bread crumbs. Bake at 350° (177° C) 30 minutes or until bubbly.

Asparagus And Nut Casserole

Can do ahead
Can freeze

Serves: 4
Preparing: 15 min
Baking: 20 min

3 Tb *(45 ml)* butter
3 Tb *(45 ml)* flour
1 cup *(237 ml)* milk
½ tsp *(2.5 ml)* salt
dash of pepper

2 cans, 14½ oz *(411 g)*
Del Monte asparagus
1 pkg, 3 oz *(85 g)* almonds,
slivered
1 cup *(237 ml)* sharp New York
cheese, grated (or more)

Melt butter and blend in flour. Add milk, salt and pepper and cook. Add cheese and stir constantly until blended. Line a 1 quart (946 ml) casserole with a layer of asparagus, almonds, and then sauce. Continue until dish is full, topping with almonds. Bake uncovered at 350° (177° C) for 20 minutes or until bubbly.

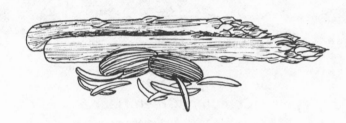

French Green Beans In Sauce
Good company dish

Can do ahead

Serves: 8
Preparing: 25 min
Baking: 25 min

2 Tb *(30 ml)* butter
1 tsp *(5 ml)* sugar
½ tsp *(2.5 ml)* salt
1 Tb *(15 ml)* dehydrated Lipton
onion soup
⅛ tsp *(.6 ml)* pepper

1 carton, 8 oz *(227 g)* sour cream
5 slices Swiss cheese,
crumbled
3 cans French style beans,
drained
buttered bread crumbs

Stir and mix all ingredients except beans over low heat. Stir until smooth. Mix with beans and pour into a greased 3-quart (2.84 l) casserole. Top with buttered bread crumbs and bake at 325° (163° C).

Sweet And Sour Green Beans

Must do ahead

Serves: 6
Preparing: 15 min
Marinating: several hrs or overnight
Baking: 45 min

2 cans, 15½ oz *(439 g)* **French cut beans**
1 medium onion, cut in rings
8 strips bacon

½ cup *(118 ml)* **slivered almonds**
6 Tb *(90 ml)* **sugar**
6 Tb *(90 ml)* **vinegar**

Drain beans and put in 1½ quart (1.42 l) casserole dish. Place separated onion rings over beans. Fry bacon strips and save drippings. Cut the strips in halves or quarters and lay over onion rings. Sprinkle almonds over bacon. Add sugar and vinegar to bacon drippings and heat. Pour over casserole. Marinate several hours or overnight. Bake 45 minutes at 350° (177° C).

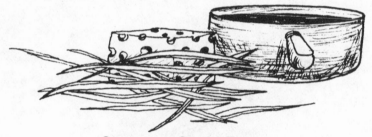

Company Green Beans
Delectable and imaginative

Can do ahead

Serves: 6-8
Preparing: 20 min
Cooking: 15 min
Baking: 30 min

½ cup *(118 ml)* **onion, sliced**
2 Tb *(30 ml)* **butter**
1 Tb *(15 ml)* **parsley, chopped**
2 Tb *(30 ml)* **flour**
1 tsp *(5 ml)* **salt**
½ tsp *(2.5 ml)* **lemon peel, grated**
1 cup *(237 ml)* **sour cream**

½ cup *(118 ml)* **sharp cheese, grated**
5 cups *(1.18 l)* **canned green beans**
1 cup *(237 ml)* **water chestnuts, sliced**
2 Tb *(30 ml)* **butter, melted**
½ cup *(118 ml)* **cracker crumbs**

Sauté slightly the onion and parsley in 2 Tb (30 ml) butter. Add the flour, salt, and lemon peel. Blend. Remove from heat and add sour cream, cheese, beans, and water chestnuts. Place in 2 quart (1.89 l) casserole. Mix 2 Tb (30 ml) melted butter with cracker crumbs. Place on top and bake at 350° (177° C).

Dinner Baked Beans

Can do ahead

Serves: 6
Preparing: 10 min
Baking: 2½-3 hrs

3 cups *(710 ml)* **canned pork**
  and beans
2 pieces of bacon
1 onion, diced
2 tsp *(10 ml)* salt

1 tsp *(5 ml)* **ginger**
¾ cup *(177 ml)* **brown sugar**
1 tsp *(5 ml)* **mustard**
1 cup *(237 ml)* **maple syrup**

Combine all ingredients except bacon in an oven proof pot, thoroughly mixing. Top with bacon strips. Cover. Bake at 300° (149° C) for 2½ to 3 hours. Stir every half hour. If beans get too dry, add ½ cup (118 ml) mixture of catsup and water. Bake uncovered for last 30 minutes.

Marinated Mixed Bean Casserole
Tangy and flavorful

Must do ahead

Serves: 8-10
Preparing: 20 min
Cooking: 20 min
Baking: 1 hr

8 slices bacon
4 onions, chopped fine
1 cup *(237 ml)* **brown sugar**
½ cup *(118 ml)* **cider vinegar**
1 tsp *(5 ml)* **dry mustard**
½ tsp *(2.5 ml)* salt
1 can, 28 oz *(794 g)* **pork**
  and beans

1 can, 16 oz *(454 g)* **red**
  kidney beans
1 can, 16 oz *(454 g)* **green**
  limas, partially drained
1 can, 16 oz *(454 g)* **white**
  limas, partially drained

Fry bacon until crisp. Remove and break into small pieces. Sauté onions in bacon fat. Add sugar, vinegar, mustard and salt to onion mixture. Cook 20 minutes. Carefully fold in beans and bacon. Marinate 6-12 hours. Bake at 350° (177° C) for 1 hour.

VEGETABLES

Cold Beets In Mustard Dressing

Can do ahead

Serves: 4
Preparing: 10 min
Marinating: 10-15 min

1 can, 1 lb *(454 g)* **beets,**
  drained
1 Tb *(15 ml)* **olive oil**
1 Tb *(15 ml)* **vinegar**

1 tsp *(5 ml)* **Dijon mustard**
½ tsp *(2.5 ml)* **thyme and**
  basil, mixed
salt and pepper to taste

Pour dressing over beets and marinate at room temperature 10-15 minutes. This is also good served on toothpicks as an hors d'oeuvre.

Sour Cream Beets
Very good, easy party fare

Can do ahead

Serves: 4-5
Preparing: 15 min

¼ cup *(59 ml)* **sour cream**
1 Tb *(15 ml)* **vinegar**
¾ tsp *(3.7 ml)* **sugar**
½ tsp *(2.5 ml)* **salt**

½ tsp *(2.5 ml)* **onion, grated**
dash cayenne pepper
2½ cups *(592 ml)* **cooked beets,**
  cut in cubes

Mix first 6 ingredients well. Carefully stir in beets. Heat slowly stirring often. Serve warm or cold.

Caroline's Broccoli Casserole

Can do ahead

Serves: 6-8
Preparing: 20 min
Baking: 1 hr

2 cans, 10¾ oz *(305 g)*
  cream of mushroom soup
1 jar, 8 oz *(227 g)* **Cheese Whiz**
½ cup *(118 ml)* **butter**
  OR margarine
¾ cup *(177 ml)* **celery, chopped**

¾ cup *(177 ml)* **onion, chopped**
2 cups *(474 ml)* **Minute Rice,**
  uncooked
1 can **mushrooms, drained**
2 pkgs, 10 oz *(284 g)* **frozen**
  broccoli spears, thawed

Mix soup, cheese and butter or margarine in saucepan and cook over very low heat to melt cheese. Stir to mix well, then add other ingredients; pour into greased 2 quart (1.89 l) casserole dish. Bake at 325° (163° C) until bubbly, then reduce heat to 300° (149° C) and continue cooking until most of moisture is gone, about 45 minutes to 1 hour.

Creamy Broccoli And Zucchini

Serves: 4-6
Preparing: 20-25 min

2 cups *(474 ml)* fresh broccoli,
  chopped
2 cups *(474 ml)* unpared zucchini,
  chopped
½ cup *(118 ml)* onion, chopped
1 clove garlic, minced
2 Tb *(30 ml)* butter OR
  margarine
3 Tb *(45 ml)* all-purpose flour
2 Tb *(30 ml)* parsley, snipped

½ tsp *(2.5 ml)* salt
½ tsp *(2.5 ml)* dried oregano,
  crushed
¾ cup *(177 ml)* milk
1½ cups *(355 ml)* Ricotta OR
  cream-style cottage cheese
8 oz *(227 g)* spinach noodles,
  cooked, drained, and buttered
Parmesan cheese

In medium saucepan, cook broccoli and zucchini together, covered, in a small amount of boiling salted water until tender, about 8 to 10 minutes; drain well. In large saucepan, cook onion and garlic in butter until onion is tender but not brown. Blend in flour, parsley, salt, and oregano. Add milk all at once. Cook and stir until thickened and bubbly. Add Ricotta cheese. Cook and stir until cheese is nearly melted. Stir in cooked vegetables. Heat through. Serve over hot cooked spinach noodles. Pass Parmesan cheese.

Stafford's Broccoli Supreme

Can do ahead

Serves: 4-6
Preparing: 30 min
Baking: 25 min

1 pkg, 10 oz *(284 g)* frozen
  chopped broccoli OR 2 cups
  (474 ml) of fresh
3 carrots, sliced
1 can, 14 oz *(397 g)* artichoke
  hearts, drained and quartered
1 can, 10¾ oz *(305 g)* cream
  of mushroom soup
½ cup *(118 ml)* mayonnaise

2 eggs, slightly beaten
1 tsp *(5 ml)* lemon juice
1 tsp *(5 ml)* Worcestershire
  sauce
1 cup *(237 ml)* sharp
  cheddar cheese, shredded
bread crumbs
¼ cup *(59 ml)* butter OR
  margarine, melted
garlic salt

Cook broccoli in a small amount of boiling water just until tender; drain and set aside. Cook carrots until tender in a small amount of boiling water; drain and set aside. Place artichokes in a buttered 9 inch (22.86 cm) casserole. Combine soup, mayonnaise, eggs, lemon juice and Worcestershire sauce. Mix well. Combine soup mixture, broccoli and carrots. Pour over artichokes, sprinkle with bread crumbs and cheese, then with garlic salt. Bake at 350° (177° C) for 25 minutes.

Pineapple Carrots

Serves: 8
Preparing: 35 min

2 pkgs, 16 oz *(454 g)* carrots,
sliced
1 tsp *(5 ml)* salt
2 cups *(474 ml)* boiling water
½ cup *(118 ml)* sugar
4 tsp *(20 ml)* cornstarch

1 can, 6 oz *(177 ml)* pineapple
juice
2 Tb *(30 ml)* butter OR
margarine
2 Tb *(30 ml)* fresh mint
leaves, chopped

Combine carrots, salt and water in a saucepan. Cover and simmer 25 minutes; drain. Combine sugar, cornstarch and pineapple juice. Cook, stirring constantly, over medium heat until sauce thickens and boils for 3 minutes. Add butter and stir until melted. Stir in carrots and mint.

Heavenly Carrots

Can do ahead

Serves: 6
Preparing: 10 min
Baking: 20-25 min

4 cups *(946 ml)* sliced carrots,
cooked
1½ cups *(355 ml)* croutons
1¼ cups *(296 ml)* sharp cheddar
cheese, shredded
2 eggs, beaten

¼ cup *(59 ml)* half and half
¼ cup *(59 ml)* margarine, melted
1 tsp *(5 ml)* Worcestershire
sauce
1 tsp *(5 ml)* salt

Place carrots in a buttered 1½ quart (1.42 l) casserole. Stir in croutons and cheese. Combine remaining ingredients and pour over carrot mixture. May be refrigerated at this point until ready to bake. Bake uncovered at 400° (204° C) for 20 minutes or until brown.

Corn In Sour Cream

Can do ahead

Serves: 8
Preparing: 20 min
Baking: 20 min

2 Tb *(30 ml)* onion, chopped
2 Tb *(30 ml)* butter
1 cup *(237 ml)* sour cream
2 cans, 12 oz *(340 g)* whole
kernel corn, drained

½ lb *(227 g)* bacon, cooked
and crumbled
2 Tb *(30 ml)* ripe olives, sliced
(optional)

Cook onion in butter until tender. Add sour cream gradually, stirring well. Add corn and bacon. Bake at 325° (163° C) 20 minutes.

Scalloped Corn And Tomatoes

A delicious company dish

Can do ahead
Can freeze

Serves: 8-10
Preparing: 30 min
Cooking: 5 min
Baking: 30 min

1 cup *(237 ml)* **onion, thinly sliced**
¼ cup *(59 ml)* **margarine**
2 lb *(908 g)* **tomatoes,**
   peeled and chopped
2 tsp *(10 ml)* **sugar**
2 tsp *(10 ml)* **salt**
1 tsp *(5 ml)* **dried marjoram**
   leaves

¼ tsp *(1.25 ml)* **pepper**
2 pkgs, 10 oz *(284 g)* **frozen**
   shoe peg corn, thawed
2 Tb *(30 ml)* **margarine**
2 cups *(474 ml)* **fresh bread**
   crumbs
2 tsp *(10 ml)* **parsley, chopped**

Sauté onion in margarine about 5 minutes until tender and golden. Stir in next five ingredients; combine with corn. Put in 2 quart (1.89 l) casserole. To make topping, melt margarine; stir in crumbs and parsley. Sprinkle over corn mixture just before baking. Bake uncovered at 350° (177° C) 30 minutes or until hot and crumbs are brown.

Cauliflower And Tomatoes Au Gratin

Serves: 8-10
Preparing: 20 min
Baking: 20 min

2 cups *(474 ml)* **water**
1¼ tsp *(6.25 ml)* **salt**
2 lbs *(908 g)* **cauliflower,**
   cut into flowerets
⅓ cup *(79 ml)* **margarine**
1 cup *(237 ml)* **Swiss cheese,**
   grated

½ cup *(118 ml)* **fine dry**
   bread crumbs
½ tsp *(2.5 ml)* **celery salt**
⅛ tsp *(.6 ml)* **pepper**
3 medium **tomatoes, peeled,**
   seeded and cut into ½"
   (1.27 cm) **strips**

Bring water and 1 tsp (5 ml) salt to a boil. Add cauliflower, cover and return to a boil. Reduce heat and cook about 15 minutes or until tender. Drain and set aside. In a saucepan, melt margarine; stir in cheese, bread crumbs, celery salt, ¼ tsp (1.25 ml) salt and pepper. Sprinkle half of crumb mixture over bottom of a shallow 1½ quart (1.42 l) baking dish. Arrange cauliflower and tomatoes over crumbs. Bake at 375° (191° C) about 20 minutes until golden brown.

Scalloped Celery

Can do ahead

Serves: 6-8
Preparing: 20 min
Baking: 20-30 min

4 cups *(946 ml)* celery,
    coarsely chopped
¼ cup *(59 ml)* almonds,
    slivered and blanched
1 can, 6 oz *(170 g)* water
    chestnuts, sliced
½ cup *(118 ml)* mushroom pieces

5 Tb *(75 ml)* butter
3 Tb *(45 ml)* flour
½ cup *(118 ml)* half and half cream
1 cup *(237 ml)* chicken broth
½ cup *(118 ml)* dry bread crumbs
½ cup *(118 ml)* Parmesan cheese

Boil celery for five minutes. Drain, then mix with almonds, chestnuts and mushrooms. Melt the butter in a saucepan, add the flour and cook roux until it bubbles; add the cream and chicken broth; cook until thick. Blend celery mixture into the sauce, then pour into ovenproof casserole. Top with bread crumbs and cheese. Bake at 375° (191° C) 15 minutes or until hot and bubbly.

Cucumber Delight

Serve immediately

Preparing: 20 min

medium-size cucumbers
cold water
vinegar
salt

milk
egg, beaten
bread crumbs
1 tsp *(5 ml)* thyme (optional)

Peel and slice cucumbers ¼ inch (.64 cm) thick. Soak cucumber slices in a mixture of cold water, vinegar and salt for 1 hour. Dry in a cloth. Dip slices into milk; then egg. Roll in fine bread crumbs. Cook in deep fat until brown.

Sweet And Sour Cucumbers

Can do ahead

Serves: 4
Preparing: 10 min
Soaking: 2 hrs

2 medium cucumbers, sliced
    thin
1 medium onion, sliced
    thin

¾ cup *(177 ml)* half and half
    OR heavy cream
¼ cup *(59 ml)* vinegar
sugar, sweeten to taste

Soak sliced cucumbers in cold salted water for several hours; drain well. Combine cucumbers and onions and put in a bowl. Mix cream, vinegar and sugar; pour over cucumbers and onions.

Stuffed Eggplant Creole

Can do ahead

Serves: 4-6
Preparing: 45 min
Baking: 45 min

2 lbs *(908 g)* **eggplant**
1½ tsp *(7.5 ml)* **salt**
2 Tb *(30 ml)* **bacon fat**
1 lb *(454 g)* **ground meat**
garlic salt
¼ cup *(59 ml)* **onion,**
  finely chopped
¼ cup *(59 ml)* **green pepper,**
  finely chopped

¼ cup *(59 ml)* **celery, finely**
  chopped
1 can, 1 lb *(454 g)* **tomatoes,**
  undrained
¼ tsp *(1.25 ml)* **thyme**
½ tsp *(2.5 ml)* **Tabasco**
½ cup *(118 ml)* **grape nut cereal**
¼ cup *(59 ml)* **Burgundy wine**
½ cup *(118 ml)* **bread crumbs**
¼ cup *(59 ml)* **butter, melted**

Wash eggplant; cut in half lengthwise. Add with ½ tsp (2.5 ml) salt to one inch boiling water in pan; simmer, covered, for 15 minutes. Drain and cool. Preheat oven to 375° (191° C). Carefully scoop out pulp from eggplant halves, leaving ¼ inch (.64 cm) thick shell. Dice pulp; set aside with shells. In bacon fat in large skillet sauté beef with garlic salt to taste until brown. Add onion, green pepper, celery; cook over low heat for about 5 minutes. Stir in tomatoes, 1½ tsp (7.5 ml) salt, thyme and Tabasco. Remove from heat. Add diced eggplant, grape nuts, and wine. Spoon meat mixture into eggplant shells. Place in shallow baking dish. Combine bread crumbs and butter; sprinkle over stuffed eggplant. Bake uncovered about 45 to 50 minutes or until hot and bubbly.

Fried Eggplant

Serve immediately

Serves: 8
Soaking: 1 hr
Preparing: 20-25 min

1 large eggplant
1 Tb *(15 ml)* **salt**
1½ cups *(355 ml)* **fine cracker**
  crumbs

2 eggs, well beaten
salad oil

Peel eggplant and cut into finger-size strips. Sprinkle with salt, cover with water and soak 1 hour. Drain and pat dry. Coat each piece with cracker crumbs, dip in egg and then coat again with crumbs. Fry in hot oil until golden brown.

Teriyaki Mushrooms

Can do ahead

Serves: 4-6
Preparing: 5 min

1 lb *(454 g)* **sliced mushrooms**
½ cup *(118 ml)* **teriyaki sauce**
½ cup *(118 ml)* **sherry**

salt and pepper
4 Tb *(60 ml)* **butter**

Marinate mushrooms in teriyaki and sherry for ½ hour. Sauté, along with juice in butter.

Scalloped Mushrooms

Can do ahead

Serves: 8-10
Preparing: 15 min
Baking: 35 min

1 lb *(454 g)* **fresh mushrooms,**
  cleaned and sliced
2 cups *(474 ml)* **soft bread crumbs**

½ cup *(118 ml)* **butter OR**
  margarine, melted
salt and pepper to taste
⅓ cup *(79 ml)* **dry white wine**

Place one-third of mushrooms in a buttered 1½ quart (1.42 l) casserole; cover with one-third of bread crumbs, and drizzle with one-third of butter; sprinkle with salt and pepper. Repeat with another third of mushrooms, bread crumbs, and butter; sprinkle with salt and pepper. Then cover with remaining third of mushrooms, and add wine. Cover and bake at 325° (163° C) for 25 minutes. Combine remaining third of butter and bread crumbs; spoon over mushrooms. Bake uncovered an additional 10 minutes or until lightly browned.

Baked Mushrooms With Cheese

Can do ahead

Serves: 6-8
Preparing: 20-25 min

1 lb *(454 g)* **fresh mushrooms**
2 shallots, finely chopped
½ cup *(118 ml)* **butter**
½ cup *(118 ml)* **sour cream**

4 oz *(113 g)* **sharp cheddar**
  cheese, grated
salt and pepper

Wash and slice mushrooms, removing ends of stems. Melt butter in skillet and add shallots and mushrooms. Cook slowly until tender. Add salt and pepper. Put in a casserole dish and cover with sour cream. Sprinkle with cheese and broil until lightly browned.

Steamed Fresh Mushrooms

Delicious with steak or hamburger

Serves: 6
Preparing: 15 min
Baking: 20 min

1 lb *(454 g)* **medium-size fresh mushrooms, washed and cut in half**
1 tsp *(5 ml)* **seasoned salt**
¼ tsp *(1.25 ml)* **paprika**

⅛ tsp *(.6 ml)* **pepper**
¼ cup *(59 ml)* **butter OR margarine**
2 Tb *(30 ml)* **dry sherry**
¼ cup *(59 ml)* **parsley, chopped**

Preheat oven to 400° (204° C). Place mushrooms in the center of a rectangle of heavy-duty foil 24 x 18 inches (60.96 x 45.72 cm). Sprinkle with seasoned salt, paprika and pepper. Dot with butter; sprinkle sherry all over. Bring long sides of foil together and fold three times and the ends twice to seal securely, but leave a little room for expansion. Place foil in a shallow baking pan and bake 20 minutes. Sprinkle with parsley when serving.

Stuffed Mushrooms

Can do ahead
Can freeze

Serves: 6-8
Preparing: 20-30 min
Baking: 15 min

1 pkg, 10 oz *(284 g)* **frozen, chopped spinach**
2½-3 doz **large fresh mushrooms**
½ cup *(118 ml)* **butter**
1 medium **onion, finely chopped**
¼-½ tsp *(1.25-2.5 ml)* **garlic powder**

½ cup *(118 ml)* **bread crumbs**
1 tsp *(5 ml)* **salt**
¼ tsp *(1.25 ml)* **pepper**
⅛ tsp *(.6 ml)* **dry mustard**
½ tsp *(2.5 ml)* **ground nutmeg**
1 cup *(237 ml)* **sour cream**
Parmesan cheese, grated

Cook spinach in unsalted water; drain thoroughly. Wash mushrooms and remove stems. Chop stems. Melt butter and sauté mushroom tops until thoroughly coated, 5 to 10 minutes. Remove caps from butter and place cap side down on baking tin. Sauté onions in butter. Add chopped mushroom stems and heat until tender. Add spinach and remaining ingredients except cheese. Mix well. Fill caps with spinach mixture. Sprinkle tops with cheese and bake for 15 minutes at 375° (191° C).

French Fried Green Pepper Rings

Can do ahead
Can freeze

Serves: 8
Preparing: 15 min
Cooking: 15 min

3 large green peppers
⅔ cup *(158 ml)* **seasoned bread crumbs**
½ cup *(118 ml)* **Parmesan cheese, grated**

2 eggs
2 cups *(474 ml)* **milk**
flour

Slice peppers into rings and remove seeds. Combine bread crumbs and cheese. Set aside. Combine eggs and milk. Place crumb mixture on sheet of wax paper and flour on another sheet of wax paper. Dip pepper rings one at a time in milk mixture then flour, back in milk mixture and finally in crumb mixture. Arrange on another sheet of wax paper. May be done in the morning and left unrefrigerated until evening meal. Fry in deep fat til golden brown. To freeze, fry partially, cool and bag.

VARIATION: Slice large bermuda onion and divide into rings. Omit cheese in bread crumbs.

Spring Onions

Serves: 4
Preparing: 10 min
Cooking: 10 min

24 spring onions

hollandaise sauce

Wash and trim stems and tips of onions. Tie in small bunches (6 per bunch) like fresh asparagus. Cover with boiling salted water; cook 10 minutes or until tender; drain well. Serve on toast and top with hollandaise sauce.

Curried Onions

Can do ahead

Serves: 6-8
Preparing: 10 min
Baking: 30 min

2 jars, 1 lb *(454 g)* **tiny whole onions, drained**
1 can, 10¾ oz *(305 g)* **cream of mushroom soup**
2 Tb *(30 ml)* **mayonnaise**

¼ tsp *(1.25 ml)* **curry powder**
½ cup *(118 ml)* **bread crumbs**
2 Tb *(30 ml)* **butter, melted**
2 Tb *(30 ml)* **parsley, chopped**

Place onions in casserole dish. Combine soup, mayonnaise and curry; spoon over onions. Toss bread crumbs in butter and parsley; sprinkle over casserole. Bake at 350° (177° C) 30 minutes.

Onion-Cheese Pie

For all quiche lovers

Serve immediately

Serves: 6
Preparing: 30 min
Baking: 35-40 min

1 medium size onion, thinly
  sliced
4 slices Swiss cheese
1 Tb *(15 ml)* flour
1½ cups *(355 ml)* milk

½ tsp *(2.5 ml)* salt
pinch of cayenne pepper
2 tsp *(10 ml)* butter, melted
4 eggs, beaten
pastry for 9″ *(22.86 cm)* pie

Cover bottom of pastry shell with onion, then cheese. Mix flour in small amount of milk until no longer lumpy, then stir in remaining milk. Add flour-milk mixture, salt, pepper and butter to eggs. Mix well; pour over cheese. Bake at 375° (191° C) for 35 to 40 minutes or until nicely browned and custard is set.

Onion Casserole

Serves: 6
Preparing: 15 min
Baking: 30-35 min

4 cups *(946 ml)* onion, thinly
  sliced
4 medium-size ripe tomatoes,
  peeled and sliced
1 tsp *(5 ml)* salt
¼ tsp *(1.25 ml)* pepper
½ tsp *(2.5 ml)* dried basil leaves

6 slices American cheese,
  cut in half
½ cup *(118 ml)* packaged bread
  crumbs
3 Tb *(45 ml)* butter OR
  margarine, melted

Preheat oven to 350° (177° C). Lightly grease a 1½ quart (1.42 l) casserole. Cook onion, covered, in one inch (2.54 cm) of boiling water 10 minutes; drain. Layer in casserole, half of tomatoes and half of onions. Sprinkle with half of the salt, pepper and basil. Top with half of cheese. Repeat. Toss bread crumbs with butter and sprinkle over cheese. Bake uncovered 30 to 35 minutes or until tomatoes are tender.

Joan's Green Pea Casserole

Can do ahead
  1 day

Serves: 8-10
Preparing: 20 min
Baking: 40 min

¼ cup *(59 ml)* **butter**
2 whole bay leaves
1 onion, finely chopped
2 garlic cloves
1 pkg almonds, blanched
  and sliced
2 cans, 6 oz *(170 g)* **mushrooms**
2 Tb *(30 ml)* **Worcestershire sauce**

3 pkgs, 10 oz *(284 g)* **frozen
  green peas**
1 can, 10¾ oz *(305 g)* **cream of
  chicken soup**
3 hard boiled eggs
2 cups *(474 ml)* **cheese, grated**
1 can pimento, chopped

Sauté butter, bay leaves, onion, garlic, almonds and mushrooms. Remove bay leaves and add remaining ingredients. Put in the refrigerator until ready to bake. Bake at 325° (163° C) for 40 minutes.

Company Peas

Can do ahead

Serves: 4
Preparing: 15 min

⅓ cup *(79 ml)* **onion, chopped**
2 Tb *(30 ml)* **butter**
1 can, 16 oz *(454 g)* **small peas,
  drained**
1 can, 3 oz *(85 g)* **sliced mushrooms**

1 tsp *(5 ml)* **sugar**
dash of thyme
½ tsp *(2.5 ml)* **salt**
dash of pepper

Cook onion in butter until tender but not brown. Stir in remaining ingredients and heat over low heat.

Pea And Asparagus Casserole

Can do ahead

Serves: 6
Preparing: 5 min
Cooking: 20 min

1 can, 17 oz *(482 g)* **peas**
1 can, 14½ oz *(411 g)* **asparagus**
1 can cream of mushroom
  soup
1 cup *(237 ml)* **cheese, grated**

Durkee's dressing
1 can, 8 oz *(227 g)* **water
  chestnuts**
cracker crumbs
salt and pepper

Drain vegetables. Mix with soup, cheese, Durkee's to taste, and water chestnuts. Season to taste. Cracker crumbs on top. Bake at 350° (177° C) until bubbly in a 2 quart (1.89 l) casserole.

Hash Brown Potato Hot Dish

Can do ahead
Can freeze

Serves: 8-10
Preparing: 20 min
Baking: 1 hr

4 cups *(946 ml)* **frozen hash browned potatoes**
⅓ cup *(79 ml)* **milk**
1 pkg, 8 oz *(227 g)* **cream cheese, cut up in bowl**

1 can, 10¾ oz *(305 g)* **cream of celery soup**
¼ cup *(59 ml)* **onion, chopped, green pepper (optional) pimento (optional) grated cheese**

Mix all together; pour in greased 9 x 13 inch (22.86 x 33.02 cm) casserole. Bake at 325° (163° C) 1 hour. Sprinkle cheese on top as you take out of oven.

Potato-Lima Bacon Patties

Serves: 4
Preparing: 30 min

2 slices bacon, cooked crisp
1 egg, beaten
⅓ cup *(79 ml)* lima beans, cooked
1 medium potato, cooked
¼ tsp *(1.25 ml)* instant onion

salt and pepper
⅓ cup *(79 ml)* tomato juice
grated cheese, optional
toast

Mash potato and limas together. Crumble bacon and add to beaten egg, together with the onion, salt and pepper. Form into balls or patties and cook in bacon drippings until crisp on both sides. Place patties on a piece of toast. Remove liquid bacon drippings from pan and heat tomato juice in pan, scraping and stirring — add grated cheese to patties if using, and then pour over hot tomato juice.

Potato Casserole

Can do ahead

Serves: 10-12
Preparing: 1 hr
Baking: 20 min

8-9 baking potatoes, baked
OR boiled, peeled
¼ cup *(59 ml)* hot milk
2 pkgs, 3 oz *(85 g)* cream cheese
1 cup *(237 ml)* sour cream
2 Tb *(30 ml)* butter

2 tsp *(10 ml)* onion salt
1 tsp *(5 ml)* salt
¼ tsp *(1.25 ml)* pepper
butter to dot
paprika

Cream potatoes with hot milk; add rest of ingredients and put in 2 quart (1.89 l) buttered casserole. Dot with butter and sprinkle paprika over top. Bake at 350° (177° C) until bubbly.

Sweet Potato Balls

Can do ahead
Can freeze

Serves: 8
Preparing: 20 min
Baking: 20 min

3 cups *(710 ml)* **sweet potatoes,
cooked and mashed**
¼ **cup** *(59 ml)* **butter**
¾ **cup** *(177 ml)* **light brown
sugar**

2 **Tb** *(30 ml)* **milk**
¼ **tsp** *(1.25 ml)* **salt**
8 **large marshmallows**
½ **cup** *(118 ml)* **crushed corn
flakes**

Combine first five ingredients. Cover marshmallows with potato mixture; roll each ball in corn flakes. Place in buttered baking dish; bake at 350° (177° C) until marshmallows begin to ooze, about 20 minutes.

Sweet Potatoes Supreme

Can do ahead

Serves: 4
Preparing: 10 min
Baking: 30 min

2 cups *(474 ml)* **sweet potatoes,
mashed**
2 **Tb** *(30 ml)* **cream**
2 **Tb** *(30 ml)* **butter, melted**
1 **tsp** *(5 ml)* **salt**

¼ **tsp** *(1.25 ml)* **paprika**
½ **cup** *(118 ml)* **brown sugar**
½ **cup** *(118 ml)* **butter**
1 **cup** *(237 ml)* **pecan halves**

Thoroughly mix first five ingredients; spread in greased casserole. Heat brown sugar and butter over low heat, stirring constantly until butter is **barely** melted (it is important to remove from heat at this stage or topping will harden when casserole is baked). Spread topping over potato mixture; cover with pecans. Bake in 350° (177° C) oven 30 minutes or until bubbly hot.

Sweet Potatoes With Orange Sauce

Serve this very rich and special dish
with turkey, lamb or pork

Can do ahead
Can freeze

Serves: 6-8
Preparing: 35 min
Baking: 30 min

2 cups *(474 ml)* OR 1 large can
cooked sweet potatoes
2 eggs, lightly beaten
1 cup *(237 ml)* brown sugar
1 cup *(237 ml)* milk
¼ cup *(59 ml)* butter, melted
1 tsp *(5 ml)* lemon rind

2 tsp *(10 ml)* lemon juice
¼ tsp *(1.25 ml)* ginger
¼ tsp *(1.25 ml)* cinnamon
½ tsp *(2.5 ml)* salt
½ cup *(118 ml)* nuts, chopped
several pecan halves for top
brown sugar for top

Combine first ten ingredients and mix well. Pour into large shallow, greased baking dish. Arrange pecan halves on top; sprinkle with additional brown sugar. Bake at 350° (177° C) 30 minutes. Serve warm orange sauce (below) over sweet potato pudding.

⅓ cup *(79 ml)* sugar
1 Tb *(15 ml)* cornstarch
⅛ tsp *(.6 ml)* salt
1 tsp *(5 ml)* orange peel,
grated

1 cup *(237 ml)* orange juice
1 Tb *(15 ml)* lemon juice
2 Tb *(30 ml)* butter
3 dashes Angostura bitters

Combine sugar, cornstarch and salt in saucepan. Add orange peel, orange juice and lemon juice; bring to boil and cook until thick. Remove from heat and stir in butter and bitters.

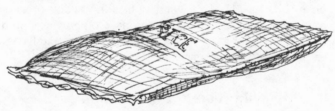

Rock Rice

Must do ahead

Serves: 10 or more
Preparing: 15 min
Baking: 20-30 min

2 cups *(474 ml)* rice, cooked
1½ sticks *(170 g)* butter
1 green pepper, chopped
1 bunch onions, chopped
2 cups *(474 ml)* celery, chopped

2 cans water chestnuts,
chopped
2 cans mushrooms, chopped
2 or 3 Tb *(30 or 45 ml)* soy
sauce

Cook vegetables in butter until clear. Mix together with rice. Let set in refrigerator overnight. Heat 20 minutes at 350° (177° C).

Armenian Rice Pilaf

Can do ahead

Serves: 6-8
Preparing: 15 min
Cooking: 30 min

¼ cup *(59 ml)* butter
½ onion, chopped
1-2 cloves garlic, crushed
2 chicken bouillon cubes
1 stalk celery, chopped

1 tsp *(5 ml)* salt
dash pepper
1 cup *(237 ml)* broken vermicelli
1 cup *(237 ml)* long grain rice
2¼ cup *(532 ml)* water

Melt butter and brown rice, celery, and onion in a 3-quart (2.84 l) saucepan. Add rest of the ingredients and bring to boil uncovered. Stir once. Cover and cook on low heat for 15 minutes. Remove from stove and let sit for 15 minutes.

Green Rice

Serves: 10-12
Preparing: 30 min
Baking: 30 min

1 cup *(237 ml)* onions, chopped
1 can cream of mushroom
   soup
1 cup *(237 ml)* uncooked rice
1½ cups *(355 ml)* sharp cheese,
   grated

2 pkgs, 10 oz *(284 g)* frozen
   chopped broccoli
½ cup *(118 ml)* milk
½ cup *(118 ml)* margarine
1 tsp *(5 ml)* salt
¼ tsp *(1.25 ml)* pepper

Cook rice in 2 cups (474 ml) water until done. Cook broccoli only slightly and drain. Sauté onions in margarine. Combine all ingredients, saving some cheese for top. Place in greased 3 quart (2.8 l) casserole and bake uncovered for 30 minutes at 325° (163° C).

Wild Rice With Consommé

Can do ahead

Serves: 8-10
Preparing: 30 min

½ cup *(118 ml)* onions,
   finely cut
¼ lb *(113 g)* hot sausage
1 cup *(237 ml)* wild rice
1 can, 10¾ oz *(305 g)* consommé

½ soup can water
1 large can mushrooms, sliced OR
   whole
½ cup *(118 ml)* celery,
   finely cut

Sauté onions and sausage; drain. Add to rest of ingredients; mix in greased casserole. Bake at 325° (163° C) 1½ hours. Great served with tenderloins, stuffed porkchops, veal, turkey, and chicken. Garnish with parsley in center.

Fried Rice

Serves: 8
Preparing: 20 min
Cooking: 5-10 min

1 cup *(237 ml)* rice, uncooked
3 slices bacon, fried and crumbled
1 medium onion, chopped and
  sautéed
3 eggs

1 Tb *(15 ml)* bacon drippings
4-6 Tb *(60-90 ml)* soy sauce
salt and pepper
pork or shrimp, optional

Cook rice. Scramble eggs in 1 Tb (15 ml) bacon drippings. Stir together all ingredients. Add chopped pork or shrimp if desired for main course.

Lemon Rice

Can do ahead

Serves: 4
Preparing: 5 min
Cooking: 25 min

2½ cups *(592 ml)* water
1 cup *(237 ml)* rice
1 tsp *(5 ml)* salt

1 Tb *(15 ml)* butter
2-3 Tb *(30-45 ml)* lemon juice
lemon rind, grated

Bring water to boil. Stir in rice, salt, butter and lemon juice; cover tightly and simmer until all water is absorbed (25 minutes). Sprinkle with lemon rind before serving.

Company Rice

Serves: 8-10
Preparing: 15 min
Baking: 50-60 min

1 cup *(237 ml)* regular rice,
  uncooked
1 cup *(237 ml)* onion, chopped
½ cup *(118 ml)* butter OR
  margarine, melted
½ cup *(118 ml)* seedless raisins

1 can, 4 oz *(113 g)* sliced
  mushrooms, drained
2 cans, 10½ oz *(298 g)* consommé
½ cup *(118 ml)* peanuts, chopped
½ cup *(118 ml)* celery, chopped

Lightly brown rice and onion in butter. Combine rice mixture, raisins, mushrooms, consommé, peanuts, and celery; mix well. Pour into a 2-quart (1.89 l) casserole. Bake uncovered at 350° (177° C) for 50 to 60 minutes or until rice is done.

Sweet-Sour Sauerkraut

Unusual combination

Can do ahead

Serves: 4
Preparing: 20 min
Cooking: 30 min

1 can, 16 oz *(454 g)* sauerkraut
water
½ cup *(118 ml)* butter
1 onion, sliced

1-2 Tb *(15-30 ml)* flour
2 Tb *(30 ml)* carraway seeds
2 Tb *(30 ml)* sugar
2 beef bouillon cubes

Cover sauerkraut with water. Boil. Drain off half of water and boil again. Add butter, onion, and flour and thicken on a low burner. Add carraway seeds, sugar and beef bouillion cubes. Simmer 30 minutes.

Spinach Madeleine

Can do ahead
Can freeze

Serves: 5-6
Preparing: 20 min
Cooking: 15 min

2 pkgs, 10 oz *(284 g)* frozen
   chopped spinach, cooked
4 Tb *(60 ml)* butter
2 Tb *(30 ml)* flour
2 Tb *(30 ml)* onion, chopped
½ cup *(118 ml)* evaporated milk
½ cup *(118 ml)* vegetable liquid
½ tsp *(2.5 ml)* black pepper

¾ tsp *(3.7 ml)* celery salt
¾ tsp *(3.7 ml)* garlic salt
salt to taste
1 roll, 6 oz *(170 g)* Jalapeno
   cheese, cut up
1 tsp *(5 ml)* Worcestershire sauce
cayenne pepper to taste

Drain and reserve liquid from cooked spinach. Melt butter in saucepan over low heat; add flour, stirring until blended and smooth but not brown. Add onion and cook until soft but not brown. Add liquids slowly, stirring constantly to avoid lumps. Cook until smooth and thick, stirring constantly. Add seasonings and cheese; stir until melted. This may be served immediately; however, flavor is improved if put in casserole, topped with buttered bread crumbs and kept in refrigerator overnight.

Spinach Elegante

Can partially do ahead

Serves: 6
Preparing: 10-15 min
Baking: 20 min

3 pkgs, 10 oz *(284 g)* frozen
chopped spinach
4 slices bacon, cooked and
crumbled
1 can, 6 oz *(170 g)* mushrooms,
drained, either chopped
OR sliced

¼ tsp *(1.25 ml)* dried marjoram,
crushed
1 cup *(237 ml)* sour cream
½ cup *(118 ml)* sharp cheddar
cheese, grated

Cook spinach according to package directions. Drain well. Spread on the bottom of a casserole dish and arrange bacon and mushrooms over the spinach. Sprinkle with pepper and marjoram. Bake at 325° (163° C) for 15 minutes. Cover with sour cream and cheese. Return to oven 5 minutes until cheese melts.

Buttered Sesame Spinach

Serves: 3-4
Preparing: 15 min

1 pkg, 10 oz *(284 g)* frozen spinach
2 Tb *(30 ml)* butter

salt and pepper
2 Tb *(30 ml)* sesame seeds

Cook spinach according to package directions; drain well. Add butter, salt and pepper to taste, and toss in sesame seeds. Serve warm.

Spinach And Artichokes En Casserole
Good even to non-spinach eaters

Can do ahead

Serves: 6
Preparing: 20 min
Cooking: 10 min
Baking: 25 min

1 pkg, 9 oz *(256 g)* frozen
artichoke hearts, cooked
and drained
2 pkgs, 10 oz *(284 g)* frozen
chopped spinach, cooked and
drained
½ cup *(118 ml)* butter, melted

1 pkg, 8 oz *(227 g)* cream cheese,
softened
1 tsp *(5 ml)* lemon juice
cracker crumbs
butter
water chestnuts (optional)

Place artichokes in greased casserole. Combine spinach, butter, cream cheese and lemon juice; pour over artichokes. Sprinkle with cracker crumbs and dot with butter. Bake at 350° (177° C) 25 minutes.

Delicious Squash Casserole

Serves: 6
Preparing: 15 min
Baking: 25-30 min

2 lbs *(908 g)* yellow squash,
sliced
¼ cup *(59 ml)* onion, chopped
1 can, 10¾ oz *(305 g)* cream
of chicken soup
1 cup *(237 ml)* sour cream

1 cup *(237 ml)* carrots, shredded
1 pkg, 8 oz *(227 g)* herb seasoning
stuffing mix
½ cup *(118 ml)* butter OR
margarine, melted

Cook squash and onion in boiling water for 5 minutes; drain. Combine soup and sour cream and stir in carrots. Fold in squash and onion. Combine stuffing mix and butter. Spread half of mixture in bottom of a 12 x 7½ x 2 inch (30.48 x 19.05 x 5.08 cm) baking dish. Spoon vegetable mixture on top. Sprinkle remaining stuffing over vegetables. Bake at 350° (177° C) for 25 to 30 minutes or until heated through.

Zucchini-Tomato Summer Casserole
A very tasty combination

Serves: 10
Preparing: 20 min
Cooking: 15 min
Baking: 20-30 min

10 zucchini squash
4 Tb *(60 ml)* olive oil
2 medium onions
1 garlic clove
2 Tb *(10 ml)* butter
2 Tb *(10 ml)* flour
1 cup *(237 ml)* milk

1 cup *(237 ml)* sour cream
salt and pepper
onion salt
2-3 Tb *(30-45 ml)* dill
2 tomatoes, peeled and cut in
eighths
bread crumbs

Scrub and parboil zucchini, adding 2 Tb (30 ml) olive oil to water. Drain and slice ¼ inch (.64 cm) thick. Sauté onions and garlic in 2 Tb (30 ml) olive oil and drain. Make a cream sauce in same pan using butter, flour, and milk. Add sour cream and seasonings. Stir in zucchini and tomatoes and put in casserole. Top with bread crumbs and heat til bubbly.

Zucchini Au Gratin

Serves: 6-8
Preparing: 20-25 min
Baking: 30-35 min

2 lbs *(908 g)* **zucchini**
3 Tb *(45 ml)* **olive oil**
1 cup *(237 ml)* **onions, minced**
2 Tb *(30 ml)* **flour**
salt and pepper
¼ tsp *(1.25 ml)* **savory**

½ cup *(118 ml)* **rice, cooked**
2½ cups *(592 ml)* **hot liquid**
  (zucchini juices)
⅔ cup *(158 ml)* **Parmesan**
  cheese, grated
2 Tb *(30 ml)* **olive oil**

Prepare and grate zucchini; toss with 1½ tsp (7.5 ml) salt and let drain in colander over bowl.* Heat 3 Tb (45 ml) olive oil in large skillet and slowly cook onions until translucent. Squeeze zucchini and pat dry. Increase heat under skillet with onions and brown them while stirring. Add zucchini. Cook and stir 5 minutes until zucchini is almost tender. Sprinkle on flour and stir to coat. Add hot liquid gradually while stirring. Add savory and cook until simmering and smooth. Remove from heat. Stir in rice and all but 2 Tb (30 ml) cheese. Put in buttered baking dish and sprinkle reserved cheese on top. Dribble the 2 Tb (30 ml) olive oil evenly over cheese. Bake at 425° (218° C) for a half hour or until rice has absorbed liquid and casserole is bubbling.

*Heat juices left in bowl under colander.

Marinated Garden Special

Serves: 6-8
Preparing: 25 min
Marinating: 6 hrs

6 Tb *(90 ml)* **lemon juice**
6 Tb *(90 ml)* **vinegar**
6 Tb *(90 ml)* **olive oil**
¼ cup *(59 ml)* **garlic salt**
⅔ cup *(158 ml)* **salad oil**
4 tsp *(20 ml)* **salt**
1 tsp *(5 ml)* **sugar**

dash of pepper
½ **head cauliflower**
3 **stalks celery, cut into**
  sticks
3-4 **carrots, cut into sticks**
10-15 **cherry tomatoes, halved**

Combine all ingredients except vegetables; mix well, and set aside. Cut cauliflower flowerets 1 inch (2.54 cm) from top of stalks; then cut into bite-size pieces. Arrange vegetables on a serving platter, and pour marinade over all. Marinate 6 hours before serving.

Tomatoes Stuffed With Mushrooms

Can do ahead

Serves: 8
Preparing: 20 min
Baking: 15 min

8 firm, ripe tomatoes
1½ lbs *(680 g)* mushrooms, sliced
½ cup *(118 ml)* butter OR
  margarine, melted
1 carton, 8 oz *(227 g)* sour cream
4 tsp *(20 ml)* all-purpose
  flour

1 pkg, 3 oz *(85 g)* Roquefort
  cheese
¼ tsp *(1.25 ml)* ground oregano
1 tsp *(5 ml)* parsley, chopped
2 Tb *(30 ml)* dry sherry
salt and pepper to taste
paprika

Cut a slice from top of each tomato; scoop out pulp, leaving shells intact. Invert tomatoes and drain. Sauté mushrooms in butter until tender; drain. Combine sour cream, flour, cheese, oregano, parsley, and sherry; cook over low heat until smooth and thickened, stirring constantly. Add mushrooms, salt, and pepper; stir well. Spoon mixture into tomato shells, and place in a shallow baking pan. Sprinkle with paprika. Bake 375° (191° C) for 15 minutes.

Cheese Stuffed Tomatoes
Good with beef

Can do ahead

Serves: 6-8
Preparing: 30 min
Baking: 15 min

1 Tb *(15 ml)* onion, chopped
½ cup *(118 ml)* butter
½ cup *(118 ml)* flour
2½ cups *(592 ml)* hot milk
salt, pepper, paprika
2 egg yolks

¼ cup *(59 ml)* cream
¾-1 cup *(177-237 ml)* Swiss OR
  Parmesan cheese
6-8 tomatoes, hollowed,
  drained and salted

Sauté onion in butter; stir in flour until smooth. Slowly stir in hot milk and cook and stir until thick — 10 to 20 minutes. Add salt, pepper and paprika to taste. Beat egg yolks with cream and stir into thick sauce. Cook almost to boiling, remove from heat and stir in cheese. Stuff tomatoes with mixture; bake at 425° (218° C) for 15 minutes.

Salads
and Fruits

Salads and Fruits

Tips For Salads

TOSSED SALADS

All uncooked materials must be crisp, cold and free from excess moisture. They should be artfully blended and served on chilled plates.

You need two or more greens for variety. Use materials that produce a contrast in texture, flavor and color.

Tear or shred greens, never cut them.

Fresh tomatoes will keep longer when stored upside down.

Watercress, parsley and mint keep well in airtight jars in the refrigerator. Wash, drain and dry well before storing.

MOLDED SALADS

One tablespoon (15 ml) of gelatin (1 envelope) sets 2 cups (474 ml) of liquid; never boil gelatin.

To unmold, dip mold in warm, but not hot, water to the depth of the gelatin. Loosen around the edge with a paring knife.

Rinse the serving dish with cold water. Do not dry the plate, then gelatin will slide easily.

Allow gelatin to set until it is the consistency of unbeaten egg whites before adding other ingredients.

Avoid loss of carbonation in bottled beverages that are used as the liquid in a gelatin salad. Pour the beverage down the side of the bowl; stir with an up and down motion.

For a quick chill, place gelatin mixture in freezer for 10 minutes or set the bowl in ice water and stir.

Avoid diluting the gelatin mixture by draining frozen or canned fruits thoroughly before adding.

QUICK TOPPINGS

Add 4 teaspoons (20 ml) of lemon juice to mayonnaise and place on top of a fruit salad.

Add ¼ cup (59 ml) lemon juice to 1 cup (237 ml) yogurt or sour cream for a nice salad dressing.

Add thin, sliced, raw zucchini or broccoli stem to a green salad and dress with Italian dressing.

Mix one 8 ounce (227 g) package of cream cheese with ⅓ cup (79 ml) fruit juice and 2 teaspoons (10 ml) grated fruit peel. This is good on a congealed fruit salad.

For fluffy fruit salad dressing, mix a cup (237 ml) of soft vanilla ice cream with 3 tablespoons (45 ml) of mayonnaise.

Tips For Fruit

Always remember that frozen fruits must be kept at 0° F and should not be re-frozen after thawing, especially if the package has been opened.

Ripen avocados, bananas, melons and pears at room temperature.

Store un-cut fresh pineapple in a cool place away from sunlight. After cutting, wrap and store in refrigerator up to 3-4 days.

One pound of apples (3 medium size) yields 3 cups (710 ml) pared or diced or sliced.

One quart of red cherries yields 2 cups (474 ml) of pitted cherries.

One pound of Tokay grapes yields 2¾ cups (650 ml) of seeded grapes.

One pound of cranberries yields 4 cups (946 ml) grated.

One medium lemon yields 2-3 Tb (30-45 ml) of juice. Five to eight medium lemons yields 1 cup (237 ml).

Stuff canned pears with cream cheese mixed with juice from pears; top with nuts.

Try curry sprinkled on apples, plums or thick slices of banana.

One medium orange yields 6-8 Tb (90-120 ml) of juice. Three to four medium oranges yield 1 cup (237 ml) of juice. One orange yields 1-2 Tb (15-30 ml) grated rind.

Apples will not crack while they are baking if you peel a 1 inch (2.54 cm) band around the middle or the top. Core apples; stuff the centers and add a little water to the pan and bake.

If fruits lack flavor, serve them or prepare them with candied peels, ginger or spices, or add a little lemon or lime juice to the cooked fruits.

Glaze cooked fruits with contrasting fruit jellies, especially apple or quince.

Fruits should be poached instead of stewed. Drop them into boiling liquid. Reduce the heat at once and simmer until barely tender. Drain immediately.

Almost any fruit may be broiled and served as garnish with meat or poultry.

Frost grapes with slightly beaten egg whites, sprinkle with sugar and let dry on rack to use as a salad garnish.

Parmesan cheese is good on top of most any fruit or fruit salad.

DRESSINGS

Julie's Honey Dressing

Yield: 2 cups (474 ml)
Preparing: 30 min

¼-⅓ cup *(59-79 ml)* **sugar**
1 tsp *(5 ml)* **dry mustard**
1 tsp *(5 ml)* **paprika**
1 tsp *(5 ml)* **celery seed**
¼ tsp *(1.25 ml)* **salt**

⅓ cup *(79 ml)* **honey**
⅓ cup *(79 ml)* **vinegar**
1 Tb *(15 ml)* **lemon juice**
1 tsp *(5 ml)* **onion, grated**
1 cup *(237 ml)* **salad oil**

Combine sugar, mustard, paprika, celery seed and salt. Stir in honey, vinegar, lemon juice and onion. Very slowly, pour salad oil into mixture, beating constantly with rotary or electric beater.

Citrus Dressing

Must do ahead

Yield: 1½ cups (355 ml)
Preparing: 15 min
Cooking: 5 min
Chilling: 2 hrs

1 **egg**
½ cup *(118 ml)* **sugar**
1 Tb *(15 ml)* **orange peel,
    grated**

2 tsp *(10 ml)* **lemon peel,
    grated**
2 Tb *(30 ml)* **lemon juice**
1 cup *(237 ml)* **heavy cream,
    whipped**

In saucepan or double boiler, beat egg. Add sugar, orange peel, lemon peel, and lemon juice. Cook and stir over low heat until thick, approximately 5 minutes. Cool well. Fold in whipped cream. Chill. You may use Cool Whip instead of cream if sugar is adjusted. Serve with fresh fruit and melon.

Minted Dressing For Fruit

Must do ahead

Yield: ½ cup (118 ml)
Preparing: 15 min

2 Tb *(30 ml)* **honey**
3 Tb *(45 ml)* **mint jelly**

juice and peel of 1 lime
juice of 1 lemon

Blend honey and jelly. Add grated lime peel and juices. Chill. Serve over fruit and decorate with mint leaves.

Celery Or Poppy Seed Dressing

Can do ahead

Yield: 1½ cups (355 ml)
Preparing: 10-15 min

⅓ cup *(79 ml)* sugar
1 Tb *(15 ml)* vinegar
1 tsp *(5 ml)* paprika
1 tsp *(5 ml)* salt

1 tsp *(5 ml)* onion juice
1 tsp *(5 ml)* dry mustard
1 tsp *(5 ml)* celery seed OR
1 Tb *(15 ml)* poppy seed

Combine all the above ingredients. Then add alternately until blended smoothly: 3 Tb *(45 ml)* vinegar
1 cup *(237 ml)* vegetable oil

Chill well. Serve as a dressing for fresh fruit.

Cottage Cheese Dressing

Yield: ¾ cup (177 ml)
Preparing: 5 min

⅓ cup *(79 ml)* cottage cheese
1 Tb *(15 ml)* honey

⅓ cup *(79 ml)* orange juice
pinch of salt

Blend all ingredients thoroughly. Good on vegetable or fruit salads.

Dressing For Fruit Salad

Must do ahead

Yield: 3 cups
Preparing: 10 min

1 cup *(237 ml)* sugar
1 cup *(237 ml)* oil
1 cup *(237 ml)* white vinegar

¼ tsp *(1.25 ml)* paprika
1 onion, quartered

Mix well and put in quart jar in refrigerator at least overnight. Stir before serving. Serves 20 or more. Very good over grapefruit and orange sections, strawberries and avocado.

Lemon Cream Dressing

2 cups *(474 ml)* sour cream
speck of salt

1 can, 6 oz *(170 g)* frozen
lemon juice concentrate

Blend well and serve with fruit salad.

Artichoke Salad Dressing

Can do ahead

Yield: 3 cups (710 ml)
Preparing: 5 min

1 pt *(474 ml)* **mayonnaise**
½ pt *(237 ml)* **sour cream**
2 Tb *(30 ml)* **lemon juice**

2 Tb *(30 ml)* **onion, grated**
1 tsp *(5 ml)* **curry powder**

Mix ingredients together and serve with cooked artichokes. Also good as a raw vegetable dip.

Quick Caesar Dressing

Great to keep on hand

Must do ahead

Yield: 1 cup (237 ml)
Preparing: 5 min

1 tsp *(5 ml)* **salt**
½ tsp *(2.5 ml)* **pepper**
¼ tsp *(1.25 ml)* **garlic powder**
1 tsp *(5 ml)* **Worcestershire sauce**
¼ cup *(59 ml)* **salad oil**

1 egg, coddled
½ cup *(118 ml)* **salad oil**
¼ cup *(59 ml)* **lemon juice**
¼ cup *(59 ml)* **Parmesan cheese, grated**

Combine first five ingredients in blender. Coddle egg 1 minute. Add and blend. Add remaining ingredients and blend. Refrigerate.

Avocado Dressing

A true West Coast dressing for tossed salad

Yield: 2½ cups (592 ml)
Preparing: 20 min
Chilling: 24 hrs

1 large avocado, very ripe
1 cup *(237 ml)* **mayonnaise**
½ cup *(118 ml)* **sour cream**
¼ cup *(59 ml)* **tarragon vinegar**
1 Tb *(15 ml)* **lemon juice**
1 small garlic clove, chopped or crushed

¼ cup *(59 ml)* **wine vinegar**
5 Tb *(75 ml)* **anchovy filets, well-rinsed, drained and chopped**
2 Tb *(30 ml)* **scallions, finely chopped**

Put all ingredients in blender and mix well. Chill 24 hours before serving.

Topaz Dressing For Fresh Fruit

Must do ahead

Yield: 2¼ cups (533 ml)
Preparing: 10 min

1 Tb *(15 ml)* orange rind, grated
¼ cup *(59 ml)* coconut, shredded

1 cup *(237 ml)* mayonnaise
½ cup *(118 ml)* heavy cream, whipped

Combine orange rind, coconut and mayonnaise. Fold in whipped cream. Sprinkle with additional coconut and orange rind, if desired. This is excellent with grapes, orange slices, blueberries, strawberries, cantaloupe, honeydew, and pineapple. Garnish with mint.

Vinaigrette Dressing

Yield: 3 cups (710 ml)

½ small onion, chopped
⅝ cup *(148 ml)* tarragon vinegar
a few tarragon leaves
1 Tb *(15 ml)* Dijon mustard
½ tsp *(2.5 ml)* Worcestershire sauce
dash of Tabasco sauce

1 large garlic clove
freshly ground pepper
1 whole egg
⅔ cup *(158 ml)* olive oil
1 beef bouillon cube
3 Tb *(45 ml)* boiling water
1⅓ cups *(316 ml)* salad oil
salt to taste

Put first 9 ingredients in the blender and blend well. Add olive oil slowly. Dissolve bouillon cube in boiling water and blend in quickly. Blend in salad oil, slowly, in a continuous stream. Taste before adding salt. Keep in covered jar in refrigerator. Serve over salad greens.

Colonial Manor Dressing

Must do ahead

Yield: 2½ cups (591 ml)
Preparing: 8 min

1 cup *(237 ml)* salad oil
⅓ cup *(79 ml)* vinegar
½ cup *(118 ml)* chili sauce
1 tsp *(5 ml)* Worcestershire sauce
1 medium onion, minced

½ cup *(118 ml)* sugar
1 tsp *(5 ml)* salt
1 clove garlic, minced
1 tsp *(5 ml)* bleu cheese
1 egg (optional)

Mix and let stand 1 week.

Creamy Roquefort Salad Dressing

Can do ahead   Yield: 2½ cups (592 ml)

2 cups *(474 ml)* sour cream
½ tsp *(2.5 ml)* each: garlic
  salt, celery salt, pepper
  and paprika

¼ cup *(59 ml)* mayonnaise
2 Tb *(30 ml)* vinegar
8 oz *(227 g)* Roquefort cheese,
  crumbled

Mix all ingredients except cheese, then carefully fold in cheese.

Hot Bacon Dressing

Can do ahead   Yield: 2½ cups (592 ml)

8 slices bacon, cut into
  small pieces
1½ cups *(355 ml)* sugar
3 tsp *(15 ml)* cornstarch

½ tsp *(2.5 ml)* salt
1 tsp *(5 ml)* dry mustard
1¼ cups *(296 ml)* water
½ cup *(118 ml)* cider vinegar

Fry bacon pieces until crisp; leave in pan undrained. Add water and vinegar to dry ingredients. Add to fried bacon pieces in pan and cook, stirring constantly, until it thickens. Use on endive, lettuce, cucumbers, cabbage or hot slaw.

Shallot Dressing
Good on tossed salad

Can do ahead   Yield: 1 cup (237 ml)

¾ cup *(177 ml)* vegetable oil
1 Tb *(15 ml)* olive oil
2 Tb *(30 ml)* wine vinegar
1 Tb *(15 ml)* sugar
¼ tsp *(1.25 ml)* Accent

4 Tb *(60 ml)* parsley, chopped
1 Tb *(15 ml)* tarragon
1 Tb *(15 ml)* chives
1 Tb *(15 ml)* dill
2 shallots, minced

Mix all ingredients in order given.

Cucumber Dressing

Must do ahead   Yield: 4 cups (946 ml)
                                Chilling: 3 hrs

1 small cucumber, peeled and
  chopped
1 small onion, chopped
lemon juice to taste

2 cups *(474 ml)* mayonnaise
green food coloring
seasoned salt to taste
Worcestershire sauce to taste

Combine all ingredients in blender, cover and blend well. Make sure that the consistency is smooth. Chill well.

French Dressing

Can do ahead

Yield: 2½ cups (592 ml)
Preparing: 10 min

1 cup *(237 ml)* **Mazola oil**
¼ cup *(59 ml)* **vinegar**
⅓ cup *(79 ml)* **sugar**
½ cup *(118 ml)* **catsup**
juice of 1 lemon

1 tsp *(5 ml)* **salt**
1 tsp *(5 ml)* **paprika**
1 small onion, grated
(optional)

Mix all ingredients together and shake well. Keeps indefinitely in the refrigerator. Also good as a marinade for artichoke hearts.

FRUITS

Coconut Fruit Bowl
Good with meat and poultry

Must do ahead

Serves: 8-10
Preparing: 10 min

1 can, 20 oz *(567 g)* **pineapple tidbits, drained**
1 can, 11 oz *(312 g)* **mandarin oranges, drained**
1 cup *(237 ml)* **seedless grapes**
1 cup *(237 ml)* **miniature marshmallows**

1 can, 3½ oz *(99 g)* **flaked coconut**
2 cups *(474 ml)* **dairy sour cream**
¼ tsp *(1.25 ml)* **salt**

Combine first 5 ingredients. Stir in sour cream and salt. Chill overnight.

Cranberry-Pineapple Salad
Colorful at Thanksgiving served in glass bowl

Must do ahead

Serves: 10-12
Preparing: 20 min

1 qt *(946 ml)* **raw cranberries**
1 cup *(237 ml)* **pineapple, crushed**
1 pkg, 1 lb *(454 g)* **miniature marshmallows**

1½ cups *(355 ml)* **sugar**
pinch of salt
½ pt *(237 ml)* **whipping cream**

Grind cranberries and drain pineapple. Mix together. Combine with marshmallows, sugar and salt. Whip cream and fold in with the above. Chill in covered bowl overnight.

Poached Plums With Brandy

Must do ahead

Serves: 4-6

¾ cup *(177 ml)* sugar
¼ cup *(59 ml)* water

1¼ lbs *(567 g)* medium-size
  plums, sliced (about 12)
2 Tb *(30 ml)* brandy

Bring water and sugar to a boil; add plums. Cover and simmer about 5 minutes. Stir in brandy and cook 5 minutes longer or until plums are tender. Chill overnight. Serve with custard sauce.

CUSTARD SAUCE: Yield: 1¼ cups (296 ml)

3 Tb *(45 ml)* sugar
dash of salt
3 egg yolks

1 cup *(237 ml)* half and half
⅛ tsp *(.6 ml)* vanilla

In a saucepan, heat sugar, salt and egg yolks. Blend in half and half, stirring constantly over low heat until the custard coats the back of a metal spoon. Stir in vanilla, then cool completely.

Apples In Sauterne
Refreshing dish

Can do ahead

Serves: 6
Preparing: 10 min
Cooking: 45 min

6 medium apples, peeled and
  cored
½ cup *(118 ml)* sauterne
1 Tb *(15 ml)* candied orange
  peel

½ tsp *(2.5 ml)* nutmeg
2 Tb *(30 ml)* orange juice
1 Tb *(15 ml)* lemon juice

Poach apples in wine and juices with orange peel and nutmeg. When apples are soft, take half of one and blend with pan juices in blender. Serve as a sauce for remaining solid apples with or without whipped cream.

Frosted White Grapes
Beautiful served around a baked ham!

Can do ahead

Serves: 4-6
Preparing: 10-12 min

2 medium bunches white
  seedless grapes

2 egg whites, beaten
1 cup *(237 ml)* granulated sugar

Remove grapes from large stems in little bunches. Beat egg whites until they form soft peaks. Dip grapes in egg whites. Lay them on waxed paper, sprinkle with sugar and chill. Keeps several days.

Oranges In Red Wine

Serve immediately

Serves: 4-6
Preparing: 10 min
Cooking: 15 min

1 cup *(237 ml)* **water**
¾ cup *(177 ml)* **sugar**
1 cup *(237 ml)* **red wine**
2 **cloves**

1 *(2.54 cm)* **vanilla bean**
1 *(2.54 cm)* **cinnamon stick**
4 **lemon slices**
6 **oranges, sectioned**

Bring water and sugar to a boil. Add red wine, cloves, vanilla bean, cinnamon stick and lemon slices. Boil 15 minutes. Strain and pour over sections of oranges.

Waldorf Salad

A wonderful addition to a brunch

Can do ahead

Serves: 6-8
Preparing: 15 min

⅓ cup *(79 ml)* **mayonnaise**
2 tsp *(10 ml)* **lemon juice**
dash of **salt**
2 cups *(474 ml)* **unpeeled red apples, diced**

1½-2 cups *(355-474 ml)* **celery, diced**
½ cup *(118 ml)* **walnuts, coarsely chopped**
raisins
lettuce leaves

In salad bowl blend mayonnaise, lemon juice and salt. Add apples, celery and walnuts and toss well. Serve on lettuce leaves.

Simple Salad

Quick and Easy

Must do ahead

Serves: 8-10
Preparing: 5 min

1 pkg, 3 oz *(85 g)* **orange jello, dry**
1 can, 11 oz *(312 g)* **mandarin oranges**
1 ctn, 12 oz *(340 g)* **cottage cheese**

1 can, 16 oz *(454 g)* **crushed pineapple, drained**
1 ctn, 9 oz *(255 g)* **Cool Whip**
nuts, optional

Mix dry jello with cottage cheese, then Cool Whip; blend well. Add oranges, pineapple, and nuts. Refrigerate several hours or overnight. Serve on beds of lettuce.

Pears In Port

Attractive and delicious

Can do ahead

Serves: 6
Preparing: 5 min
Cooking: 15 min

3 firm pears
½ cup *(118 ml)* **port OR**
Dubonnet
½ tsp *(2.5 ml)* **lemon peel,**
grated

4 Tb *(60 ml)* **honey**
2 Tb *(30 ml)* **lemon juice**
2 Tb *(30 ml)* **water**

Halve, peel, and core pears. Poach in wine and water with honey and lemon until tender. Chill and serve, with or without whipped cream.

Baked Peach Halves

Beautiful garnish for roasts

1 can peach halves
1 jar cherry OR strawberry
preserves

OR

1 can peach halves
1 bottle chutney

Fill peach halves with chutney or preserves. Bake at 300° (149° C) for 30 minutes. Good with lamb or pork.

Exotic Fruit

Colorful and tasty

Serves: 15
Cooking: 25 min

1 medium can sliced pineapple
1 jar apple rings
1 medium can apricot halves
1 medium can sliced peaches
1 can pear halves, sliced

½ cup *(118 ml)* **butter**
½ cup *(118 ml)* **brown sugar**
2 Tb *(30 ml)* **flour**
1 cup *(237 ml)* **sherry wine**

Drain all fruit; cut pineapple in halves. Arrange in alternate layers in a large, medium deep casserole. In top of double boiler, combine sugar, butter, flour, sherry and cook until smooth and thickened. Pour over fruit in casserole, cover and let stand in refrigerator overnight. Cook for 25 minutes, covered, at 350° (177° C) or until heated through. For 20 people, add an additional small can of pears.

CONGEALED SALADS

Daiquiri Fruit Salad

Must do ahead

Yield: 1½ qt (1.42 l) mold
Cooking: 10 min
Preparing: 1½ hrs

1½ cups *(355 ml)* crushed pineapple
1 pkg, 3 oz *(85 g)* lime OR
lemon gelatin
½ cup *(118 ml)* frozen limeade
concentrate, thawed

⅓ cup *(79 ml)* mayonnaise
2 cups *(474 ml)* whipped topping
OR whipped cream
2 medium bananas, sliced

Drain pineapple, reserving syrup. Add water to syrup to make 1 cup (237 ml). Bring to a boil; add gelatin and stir to dissolve. Add frozen limeade concentrate and mayonnaise; stir until well blended. Chill until slightly thickened but not set — about 45 minutes. Fold in pineapple and remaining ingredients. Pour into 1½ quart (1.42 l) ring mold. Freeze until firm — about 2 hours. To serve, unmold. Can be refrigerated as well.

TIPS:
Use 1 cup (237 ml) whipping cream, whipped and sweetened; or 1 pint (474 ml) frozen whipped topping, thawed.

For dessert, just add a dollop of whipped cream and garnish with a twist of lime or lemon.

Lemonade Salad

Serves: 6-8
Preparing: 10 min

1 envelope gelatin
¼ cup *(59 ml)* cold water
2 pkgs, 3 oz *(85 g)* cream cheese
3 Tb *(45 ml)* sugar

1 cup *(237 ml)* milk
½ cup *(118 ml)* boiling water
1 can, 6 oz *(170 g)* frozen
lemonade, thawed

Soften gelatin in cold water; dissolve in boiling water. Soften cream cheese and add sugar; add milk. Add cream cheese mixture to lemonade, then add gelatin. Pour into a 1-quart (946 ml) greased mold and chill.

Raspberry-Strawberry Sour Cream Salad

Must do ahead

Serves: 12
Preparing: 30 min

2 pkg, 3 oz *(85 g)* raspberry, lemon
or lime jello
2 cups *(474 ml)* boiling water
2 pkgs, 10 oz *(284 g)* frozen
strawberries

1 can, 20 oz *(567 g)* pineapple,
crushed
½ cup *(118 ml)* celery, chopped
½ cup *(118 ml)* pecans, chopped
½ pint *(237 ml)* sour cream

Dissolve jello in hot water. Add frozen berries. When berries thaw, add pineapple, celery, and nuts. Pour ½ of mixture in 13 x 9 inch (33 oz x 22.86 cm) pan or glass dish and chill. Whip sour cream and spread over firm gelatin. Pour in remaining mixture. Chill until firm.

Waldorf Cranberry Salad

Must do ahead

Serves: 6
Preparing: 15 min

1 pt *(474 ml)* cranberry juice
cocktail
1 pkg, 3 oz *(85 g)* lemon jello
¼ tsp *(1.25 ml)* salt

1 cup *(237 ml)* unpared apple,
chopped
½ cup *(118 ml)* celery, chopped
¼ cup *(59 ml)* pecans OR
walnuts, chopped

Heat 1 cup (237 ml) cranberry juice just to boiling. Dissolve gelatin in hot juice. Add remaining juice and salt. Chill until consistency of egg whites. Fold in celery, nuts and apples. Pour into six individual molds. Chill until firm.

Bing Cherry Salad

Must do ahead

Yield: 5 cups
Preparing: 25 min

1 pkg, 3 oz *(85 g)* black cherry
jello
¾ cup *(177 ml)* port

¾ can, 16½ oz *(468 g)* Bing
cherries pitted
¾ cup *(177 ml)* pecans, chopped

For the 2 cups (474 ml) liquid needed to make the jello, use wine and juice from the cherries and fill with water to 1¾ cup (414 ml) instead of 2 cups (474 ml). Cool until consistency of egg whites. Add cherries and nuts. Chill until congealed.

Heavenly Orange Fluff

Can do ahead

Serves: 12-14
Preparing: 10 min
Topping: 10 min

2 pkg, 3 oz *(85 g)* orange jello
2 cups *(474 ml)* hot water
1 can, 6 oz *(170 g)* frozen
  orange juice, undiluted

2 cans, 11 oz *(312 g)* mandarin
  oranges, drained
1 can, 16 oz *(454 g)* crushed
  pineapple, not drained

Dissolve jello in boiling water. Add orange juice, stirring until melted; cool. Add oranges and pineapple. Congeal in 13 x 9 inch pan (22.86 x 33.02 cm) or molds. Before serving mix topping and add on top of jello.

TOPPING:

1 pkg instant lemon pudding
1 cup *(237 ml)* milk

½ pt *(237 ml)* whipping cream
6 maraschino cherries

Beat pudding and milk until slightly firm, about 4 minutes. Whip cream. Fold into pudding mixture, spread on jello or dab on top of unmolded jello. Top with maraschino cherries, cut in half, and drained well on paper towels.

Comments: Can make one or two days in advance and refrigerate covered. Especially good when serving a chocolate dessert; nice combination.

Blueberry Salad
It's yummy

Must do ahead

Serves: 12
Preparing: 10-15 min

1 large box blackberry jello
1 can, 8 oz *(227 g)* crushed
  pineapple

1 can blueberries (packed in
  water if possible)

Reserving juice, drain pineapple and add blueberries. Add enough water to juice to make 2 cups (474 ml). Boil juice and add jello and 1½ cups (355 ml) cold water. Add blueberries and pineapple. Let stand overnight.

TOPPING:

1 pkg, 8 oz *(227 g)* cream
  cheese
½ pint *(237 ml)* sour cream

½ cup *(118 ml)* sugar
1 cup *(237 ml)* pecans

Cream and spread on top. Refrigerate before slicing.

Pineapple And Cheese Salad

Must do ahead

Serves: 6-8
Preparing: 30 min

1 cup *(237 ml)* **sugar**
1 can, 20 oz *(567 g)* **crushed**
 pineapple, undrained
2 envelopes **unflavored gelatin**
½ cup *(118 ml)* **cold water**

1 cup *(237 ml)* **sharp cheddar**
 cheese, grated
1 cup *(237 ml)* **pecans, chopped**
3 Tb *(45 ml)* **mayonnaise**

Bring sugar and pineapple to a boil. Meanwhile, melt gelatin in cold water; stir this into pineapple mixture until gelatin is completely dissolved. Set aside until cool. Add cheese, nuts and mayonnaise. Pour into mold to congeal.

Congealed Vegetable Salad

Easy and flavorful

Must do ahead

Serves: 8-10
Preparing: 30 min

2 pkgs **gelatin**
1 pt *(474 ml)* **mayonnaise**
2 **cucumbers, diced**
2 **tomatoes, diced**

2 **green peppers, diced**
2 **stalks celery, diced**
1 **medium onion, diced**
salt as desired

Dissolve gelatin in ¼ cup (59 ml) water, add ¼ cup (59 ml) hot water and mayonnaise. Mix well and add vegetables. Let congeal. Cut in squares or spoon out on a bed of lettuce. Put in a 2 quart (1.9 l) pyrex dish.

Thousand Island Ring Salad

Cool luncheon salad

Must do ahead

Yield: 5 cups (1.18 l)
Preparing: 25 min

2 Tb *(30 ml)* **gelatin**
½ cup *(118 ml)* **cold water**
1 cup *(237 ml)* **chili sauce**
1½ cup *(355 ml)* **mayonnaise**

6 **hard boiled eggs, diced**
1 cup *(237 ml)* **celery, diced**
2 **pimentos, chopped**
1 tsp *(5 ml)* **sugar**
½ cup *(118 ml)* **catsup**

Soften gelatin in cold water. Place over hot water and stir until dissolved. Combine remaining ingredients and blend with gelatin. Mold in a ring or individual molds. Fill ring with chicken salad, shrimp salad, etc.

Cranberry Salad

Must do ahead

Serves: 12-15
Preparing: 35 min

2 oranges
2½ cups (592 ml) fresh cranberries
3 pkgs, 3 oz (85 g) orange
  flavored gelatin
3 cups (710 ml) boiling water
2 Tb (30 ml) freshly squeezed
  lemon juice

1 cup (237 ml) sugar
pinch salt
1½ cups (355 ml) celery, chopped
  fine
1 cup (237 ml) pineapple,
  crushed, drained
½ cup (118 ml) pecans, chopped

Peel oranges; put peeling and cranberries through food grinder or processor. Remove white membrane from oranges and section them, breaking each section into 3 or 4 pieces. Dissolve gelatin in boiling water; add lemon juice, sugar, and salt. Stir until dissolved. Add orange pieces, the ground mixture, celery, pineapple, and nuts. Pour into molds and chill until set. This salad should be made at least 2 days before serving.

Spicy Peach Salad

Simple, refreshing and especially good with poultry

Must do ahead

Serves: 8-10
Preparing: 10 min

1 can, 20 oz (567 g) sliced
  peaches, drained and reserve
  syrup
2 pkgs, 3 oz (85 g) peach gelatin
½ cup (118 ml) sugar

½ tsp (2.5 ml) cinnamon
¼ tsp (1.25 ml) cloves
2 cups (474 ml) boiling water
1½ cups (355 ml) peach syrup
4 Tb (60 ml) vinegar

Drain peaches, reserving syrup and adding water to make 1½ cups (355 ml). Dissolve gelatin, sugar and spices in boiling water. Stir in syrup and vinegar. Chill in 6 cup (1.42 l) mold until gelatin begins to thicken. Add peaches.

Fabulous Aspic

Serves: 4-6
Preparing: 10 min
Chilling: 2-3 hrs

2 Tb *(30 ml)* **unflavored gelatin**
1 cup *(237 ml)* **boiling water**
1 bottle, 14 oz *(397 g)* **Del Monte**
  catsup

3 Tb *(45 ml)* **lemon juice**
2 tsp *(10 ml)* **brown sugar**
1 tsp *(5 ml)* **Worcestershire sauce**
¾ tsp *(3.7 ml)* **salt**

Soften gelatin in ⅓ cup (79 ml) cold water; dissolve in boiling water. Add remaining ingredients and 1¼ cups (296 ml) cold water. Cool till syrupy and pour into 1-quart (946 ml) mold or individual molds. Refrigerate until firm.

Compliments of
Del Monte Corporation

Aspic Supreme Salad

This always brings raves

Must do ahead

Serves: 8
Preparing: 30 min
Cooking: 8 min

4 cups *(946 ml)* **V-8 juice**
⅛ cup *(30 ml)* **onion, chopped**
¼ cup *(59 ml)* **brown sugar**
¼ cup *(59 ml)* **celery leaves**
  chopped
1 tsp *(5 ml)* **salt**

2 small bay leaves
4 whole cloves
2 Tb *(30 ml)* **unflavored gelatin**
¼ cup *(59 ml)* **cold water**
3 Tb *(45 ml)* **lemon juice**

Simmer above ingredients for 5 minutes; then strain. Dissolve gelatin in cold water and add lemon juice. Combine with V-8 juice mixture. Chill until partially set; then add stuffed artichokes, cheese side down.

STUFFED ARTICHOKES:

3 oz *(85 g)* **cream cheese**
mayonnaise
bleu cheese

Worcestershire sauce
lemon juice
1 can, 14 oz *(397 ml)* **artichoke**
  hearts, drained

Soften cream cheese and mix with mayonnaise, bleu cheese, Worcestershire and lemon juice to taste. Spoon in artichoke hearts and place in gelatin mixture. Chill, remove from mold and serve.

281

Frozen Fruit Salad I

Great to double or triple recipe and keep on hand.

Must do ahead

Serves: 12
Preparing: 15 min

2 cups *(474 ml)* **sour cream**
¾ cup *(177 ml)* **sugar**
1 tsp *(5 ml)* **lemon rind,**
  grated
2 Tb *(30 ml)* **fresh lemon juice**
⅛ tsp *(.6 ml)* **salt**
2½ cups *(592 ml)* **crushed**
  pineapple, well-drained

2½ cups *(5.2 ml)* **fruit cocktail,**
  well-drained
½ cup *(118 ml)* **pecans, chopped**
3 Tb *(45 ml)* **maraschino cherries,**
  chopped and drained
2 medium size **bananas, diced**

Mix all ingredients and freeze in molds.

1) Freeze in cylinder shaped seafood containers. (Can buy at fish market). Then slice the number of servings you need. Peel off cardboard around outer edge. Replace top on rest of container and it keeps until you need salad again.

OR

2) Freeze in muffin liners in muffin tins. Then remove salads, still in liners, and store in plastic bag. Liner can be removed before serving if desired.

Frozen Fruit Salad II

Must do ahead

Serves: 4
Preparing: 10 min

1 pkg, 8 oz *(227 g)* **cream cheese**
½ cup *(118 ml)* **mayonnaise**

1 can, 16 oz *(454 g)* **fruit**
  cocktail, drained
1 cup *(237 ml)* **small**
  marshmallows

Soften cream cheese and mix with mayonnaise until well blended. Add drained fruit cocktail and marshmallows. Put in metal ice tray and freeze. Take out about 8-10 minutes before serving.

VEGETABLE SALADS

Orange-Avocado Toss

Can partially do ahead   Serves: 8

1 medium head lettuce, torn
  in bite size pieces
1 small cucumber, thinly sliced
2 Tb *(30 ml)* green onions, sliced

1 avocado, seeded, peeled and
  sliced
1 can, 11 oz *(312 g)* mandarin
  oranges, drained

DRESSING:

¼ cup *(59 ml)* orange juice
½ cup *(118 ml)* salad oil
2 Tb *(30 ml)* sugar

2 Tb *(30 ml)* red wine vinegar
1 Tb *(15 ml)* lemon juice
¼ tsp *(1.25 ml)* salt

In large salad bowl, combine lettuce, cucumber, avocado, mandarin
oranges and green onions. In a screw top jar combine dressing
ingredients. Cover tightly and shake well. Just before serving pour
over salad. Toss lightly.

Lettuce Salad With Sesame Seeds
Delightful change for tossed salad

Can partially do ahead   Serves: 12
                                                Preparing: 10 min

½ cup *(118 ml)* sesame seeds
1 Tb *(15 ml)* butter
¼ cup *(59 ml)* Parmesan cheese
1 cup *(237 ml)* sour cream
½ cup *(118 ml)* mayonnaise
1 Tb *(15 ml)* tarragon vinegar
1 Tb *(15 ml)* sugar

1 tsp *(5 ml)* salt and pepper
1 clove garlic
¼ cup *(59 ml)* green pepper,
  chopped
¼ cup *(59 ml)* cucumber, diced
2 Tb *(30 ml)* onion, minced
2 heads lettuce

Sauté sesame seeds in butter. Take off heat. Let cool slightly and add
Parmesan cheese. Put in dish and set aside. Mix sour cream, mayonnaise, vinegar, sugar, salt, pepper, onion, and garlic. Tear lettuce in
bite-size pieces. Add green pepper and cucumber. Toss salad with
sesame seeds and add sour cream mixture. Use large salad bowl.

Maine Chance Salad

Served at the Greenhouse

Serves: 4-6
Preparing: 10 min

½ cup *(118 ml)* **carrot, cut in
very thin strips**
½ cup *(118 ml)* **turnips, cut in
very thin strips**
½ cup *(118 ml)* **green beans, cut
in very thin strips**
½ cup *(118 ml)* **baby peas**

½ cup *(118 ml)* **cauliflower,
broken into tiny flowerets**
¼ cup *(59 ml)* **Maine Chance
Dressing**
lettuce
truffle, optional
pimento
beet

Cook the first 5 vegetables in separate saucepans in very little water until just tender, about 1 minute. Cool and drain. Toss vegetables with dressing. Place on lettuce leaves; garnish with diced truffle, pimento and strips of beet.

MAINE CHANCE SALAD DRESSING: Yields: 1 pt (474 ml)

½ cup *(118 ml)* **Wesson oil**
½ cup *(118 ml)* **salad oil**
½ cup *(118 ml)* **tarragon vinegar**
1 tsp *(5 ml)* **Vege Sal
(Gourmet Section)**
1 tsp *(5 ml)* **Accent**
1 tsp *(5 ml)* **dry mustard**

1 tsp *(5 ml)* **horseradish**
3 **egg yolks**
1 **bunch watercress, chopped**
1 **bunch parsley, chopped**
6 **shallots, chopped**

Put all ingredients in blender to make a smooth, creamy dressing. Add 1 large tablespoon (15 ml) of ice water to dressing if it is too thick. Store in a screw-top jar in refrigerator. Shake before serving.

Pompeian Caesar Salad

Serve immediately

Serves: 4
Preparing: 10 min

3 Tb *(45 ml)* **olive oil**
3 Tb *(45 ml)* **Worcestershire
sauce**
juice of 1 lemon
**Parmesan OR Romano
cheese, grated**

2 **eggs, coddled, sliced**
**salt, pepper, garlic to
taste**
croutons
1 **large head Romaine lettuce,
broken up**

Combine first six ingredients; toss with lettuce and croutons.

Avocado And Hearts Of Palm Salad
With Herbed Dressing
Excellent with fish

Can partially do ahead

Serves: 6-8
Yield: ⅔ cup (158 ml)
Preparing: 35 min

1 large ripe avocado, peeled
and sliced
1 can, 14 oz (397 g) hearts of
palm, chilled, drained and
sliced (in natural juices)

1 head romaine lettuce, torn
in bite-size pieces

Toss well with Herb Dressing.

HERBED DRESSING:

½ cup (118 ml) olive oil
3 Tb (45 ml) wine vinegar
⅛ tsp (.6 ml) powdered thyme
⅛ tsp (.6 ml) powdered marjoram

¼ tsp (1.25 ml) dried basil leaves
1 Tb (15 ml) onion, chopped
1 Tb (15 ml) water
½ tsp (2.5 ml) salt
1 Tb (15 ml) parsley, chopped

Combine all ingredients in a blender and blend for a few seconds. It makes about ⅔ cup (158 ml).

South Sea Salad
The topping is a must with this salad

Can do ahead

Serves: 4-6
Preparing: 20 min

TOPPING:

½ cup (118 ml) mayonnaise
½ cup (118 ml) sour cream
¼ cup (59 ml) dill pickle juice
½ avocado, peeled, seeded
and mashed

1 Tb (15 ml) parsley
2 tsp (10 ml) chives
1 tsp (5 ml) dried dillweed

Mix all ingredients well and refrigerate.

SALAD:

1 bunch leaf lettuce
1 can, 11 oz (312 g) mandarin
oranges, chilled and drained
1 cup (237 ml) fresh mushrooms,
sliced

1 small onion sliced in rings
1 green pepper, sliced
½ avocado, sliced

Mix and serve with the above dressing.

Asparagus Salad

Can do ahead

Serves: 4
Preparing: 15 min

12 stalks asparagus
lettuce
1 cup *(237 ml)* celery, diced

½ cup *(118 ml)* stuffed olives,
chopped
½ cup *(118 ml)* nut meats

Place asparagus stalks on lettuce. Combine remaining ingredients. Sprinkle on top of asparagus. Top with favorite dressing.

Mother's Potato Salad
Excellent basic potato salad

Must do ahead

Yield: 1 gal (3.79 l)
Serves: 12-16
Preparing: 1 hr
Chilling: 24 hrs

6 lbs *(2.7 kg)* medium potatoes
1 pkg celery
6 hard-boiled eggs, chopped
2 onions, chopped
1 green pepper, chopped
2 small jars pimento, chopped

1 cup *(237 ml)* mayonnaise
2 Tb *(30 ml)* salt
½ tsp *(2.5 ml)* black pepper
¼ tsp *(1.25 ml)* cayenne pepper
1½ tsp *(7.5 ml)* celery seed
1 tsp *(5 ml)* dill weed (optional)

Cook potatoes in unsalted water and cut in chunks. Combine remaining ingredients and mix with potatoes. Prepare the day before to allow salt to blend and flavors to mingle.

German Potato Salad

Can do ahead

Serves: 4-6
Preparing: 30 min

½ lb *(227 g)* bacon, cut in
  small pieces
1 onion, diced
¼ cup *(59 ml)* vinegar
2 Tb *(30 ml)* water
3 Tb *(45 ml)* sugar

1 tsp *(5 ml)* salt
¼ tsp *(1.25 ml)* pepper
4 cups *(946 ml)* cooked, diced
  potatoes
1 Tb *(15 ml)* parsley, minced

Fry bacon in pan, remove bacon and most of fat. Brown onions; add vinegar, water, sugar, salt and pepper. Heat to boiling point, add parsley and potatoes. Heat thoroughly and serve.

Greek Salad

Colorful and tasty

Can do ahead

Serves: 6
Preparing: 15 min

4 cups *(946 ml)* **Boston lettuce, broken up**
2 cups *(474 ml)* **cooked potatoes, sliced**
2 cups *(474 ml)* **cherry tomatoes, sliced**
1 cup *(237 ml)* **radishes, sliced**
¼ cup *(59 ml)* **scallions, sliced**
¼ cup *(59 ml)* **parsley, coarsely chopped**
1 can, 2 oz *(57 g)* **flat anchovy filets**

½ cup *(118 ml)* **feta cheese, crumbled**
1 cup *(237 ml)* **pitted ripe olives OR Greek olives, halved**
¼ cup *(59 ml)* **peanut oil**
2 Tb *(30 ml)* **white vinegar**
½ tsp *(2.5 ml)* **oregano leaves, crushed**
½ tsp *(2.5 ml)* **salt**
¼ tsp *(1.25 ml)* **pepper**

Arrange lettuce over bottom of large salad bowl. Place layers of potatoes, tomatoes, radishes, scallions, parsley, anchovies and feta cheese in center of lettuce. Arrange olives around edge. Combine peanut oil, vinegar, oregano, salt and pepper in a small jar. Cover and shake vigorously until thoroughly mixed. Just before serving, pour over salad and toss lightly.

Slaw

Easily made for any size crowd

Must do ahead

Serves: 10
Preparing: 30 min

1 large head cabbage
1 large green pepper, chopped fine
1 medium onion, chopped fine
1 cup *(237 ml)* sugar

1 cup *(237 ml)* vinegar
¾ cup *(177 ml)* salad oil
1 tsp *(5 ml)* dry mustard
1 tsp *(5 ml)* salt
1 tsp *(5 ml)* celery seed

Shred cabbage fine. Chop onion and pepper fine. Put in bowl in layers, sprinkling with sugar over each layer. Bring vinegar, oil, mustard, salt and celery seed to boil; cool. Pour over cabbage mixture but do not stir at all. Refrigerate 24 hours. Remove from refrigerator and stir. Place in tight container or jar after stirring and refrigerate until ready to use. Will keep in refrigerator for several weeks.

Variation:
Omit dry mustard, salt and celery seed. Substitute 2 Tb (30 ml) mustard seed.

Fruit Slaw

A different exotic slaw

Can do ahead

Serves: 10
Preparing: 35 min

1 small head cabbage, shredded
1 medium apple, chopped
1 cup *(237 ml)* grapes, halved
and seeded
1 can, 11 oz *(312 g)* mandarin
oranges, drained
¼ cup *(59 ml)* raisins

1 cup *(237 ml)* cream-style
cottage cheese
¼ cup *(59 ml)* milk
3 Tb *(45 ml)* lemon juice
2 Tb *(30 ml)* salad oil
2 Tb *(30 ml)* honey

Combine first 5 ingredients in a mixing bowl. In a blender, combine remaining ingredients and blend just until smooth. Add dressing to cabbage mixture and toss to coat.

Green Tomato Salad

red onions
seedless oranges

raw green tomatoes

Try to get all of the above in uniform size. Slice as thin as possible and arrange alternately on a plate over-lapping each other. Pour dressing over all.

DRESSING:

⅓ cup *(79 ml)* olive oil
1 Tb *(15 ml)* lemon juice
1 Tb *(15 ml)* vinegar

½ tsp *(2.5 ml)* salt
ground pepper to taste
½ tsp *(2.5 ml)* parsley, minced

Mix well and chill until ready to serve.

Wonder Salad

Must do ahead

Serves: 10-12
Preparing: 10 min
Chilling: 2 hrs

1 can, 1 lb *(454 g)* French-
style green beans
1 can, 1 lb *(454 g)* small English
peas
1 can, 1 lb *(454 g)* fancy Chinese
vegetables (without meat)
1 can, 8½ oz *(240 g)* water
chestnuts, thinly sliced

1½ cups *(355 ml)* celery,
thinly sliced
1 cup *(237 ml)* sugar
¾ cup *(177 ml)* cider vinegar
1 tsp *(5 ml)* salt
pepper to taste
3 medium onions, thinly
sliced

Drain canned vegetables. Mix all ingredients in large bowl. Cover and refrigerate several hours before serving. Will keep for several weeks.

Fresh Mushroom Salad

Serve immediately

Serves: 6-8
Preparing: 25 min
Chilling: 1 hr

1 lb *(454 g)* **large mushrooms**
6 Tb *(90 ml)* **lemon juice**
1 Tb *(15 ml)* **chives, snipped**
1 Tb *(15 ml)* **parsley, chopped**
1 tsp *(5 ml)* **dried tarragon leaves**
½ cup *(118 ml)* **Italian dressing**

¼ cup *(59 ml)* **pimento, finely chopped**
½ tsp *(2.5 ml)* **salt**
⅛ tsp *(.6 ml)* **pepper**
1½ tsp *(7.5 ml)* **sugar**
2 tsp *(10 ml)* **prepared mustard**
1 small bunch **watercress**

Wash and dry mushrooms. Thinly slice mushrooms into large bowl. Sprinkle with lemon juice, chives, parsley, and tarragon; stir gently. Refrigerate, covered, 1 hour. Meanwhile, in bowl, combine salad dressing, pimento, salt, pepper, sugar, and mustard; stir to mix well. Refrigerate, covered — about 1 hour. To serve: Toss mushrooms with dressing. Arrange on bed of watercress on large platter.

Pepper's Cold Macaroni Cheese Salad With Dillweed

A different macaroni salad

Can do ahead

Serves: 8-10
Preparing: 30 min
Cooking: 10 min

1 pkg, 8 oz *(227 g)* **elbow OR shell macaroni**
1 Tb *(15 ml)* **butter OR margarine**
1 Tb *(15 ml)* **Parmesan cheese**
1 cup *(237 ml)* **celery, sliced diagonally**
1 cup *(237 ml)* **sharp cheese, grated**

⅓ cup *(79 ml)* **sweet-pickle salad cubes, drained**
⅓ -½ cup *(79-118 ml)* **mayonnaise**
1 green onion, diced
salt and pepper to taste
seasoned salt to taste
¼ tsp *(1.25 ml)* **dry mustard**
sprinkle generously with dillweed

Cook macaroni according to package directions; drain. Turn, while still hot, into a bowl that contains butter and Parmesan cheese; toss to coat. Add celery, cheese, salad cubes, mayonnaise to moisten, and salt, pepper and seasoned salt and mustard. Mix well and chill. Turn out on salad greens and, if desired, garnish with asparagus tips and cocktail tomatoes.

VARIATIONS: If desired, 2 cups (474 ml) of slivered ham may be added to salad OR ¼ cup (59 ml) of real bacon crumbles that come in a can.

Egg Ring Mold With Shrimp Salad

Must do ahead

Serves: 8
Preparing: 45 min

2 Tb *(30 ml)* **gelatin**
½ cup *(118 ml)* **cold water**
1 cup *(237 ml)* **boiling water**
¾ tsp *(3.7 ml)* **salt**

1 Tb *(15 ml)* **catsup**
3 Tb *(45 ml)* **lemon juice**
2 cups *(474 ml)* **mayonnaise**
12 hard boiled eggs

Sprinkle gelatin over cold water to soften. Add boiling water. Stir until dissolved. Chop eggs and add all to gelatin. Congeal in ring mold and serve shrimp salad in center.

SHRIMP SALAD:

2 cups *(474 ml)* **shrimp**
2 cups *(474 ml)* **celery, diced**
3 tsp *(15 ml)* **lemon juice**

1 cup *(237 ml)* **mayonnaise**
salt and pepper

Combine and chill.

MEAT, POULTRY/ SEAFOODS SALADS

Julie's Ham Salad

Pretty to look at — refreshing to eat

Serves: 8
Preparing: 30 min

1 medium head lettuce
2 cups *(474 ml)* **cooked OR canned ham, julienned**
2 large pink grapefruit, pared, sectioned and drained
2 large oranges, pared, sectioned and drained

2½ cups *(592 ml)* **pineapple chunks, drained**
1 cup *(237 ml)* **pitted ripe olives, sliced**
1 cup *(237 ml)* **celery, sliced**
1 avocado, sliced
orange juice

Tear lettuce into bite size pieces into serving bowl. Add ham, fruit, olives and celery. Brush avocado slices with orange juice to prevent darkening. Drizzle with honey dressing.

Corned Beef Salad

Must do ahead

Serves: 6 to 8
Preparing: 15 min

1 pkg, 3 oz *(85 g)* lemon jello
¾ cup *(177 ml)* hot water
1 cup *(237 ml)* milk, warmed
1 can Libby's corned beef

1 cup *(237 ml)* celery, chopped
1 Tb *(15 ml)* onion, minced
½ tsp *(2.5 ml)* vinegar
stuffed olives, sliced

Dissolve jello in hot water. Thoroughly mix milk with corned beef and add to jello. Add remaining ingredients and put into flat pan to make about 1½-2 inches thick when sliced. Serve on lettuce with mustard and mayonnaise. Garnish with slices of hard boiled egg, if desired.

Seafood Salad

Can do ahead

Serves: 6
Preparing 15 min

2 lbs *(908 g)* crabmeat
1 can, 8 oz *(227 g)* chunk
  pineapple
1 can, 4 oz *(113 g)* mushrooms,
  sliced

1 cup *(237 ml)* mayonnaise
juice of half lemon
2 Tb *(30 ml)* horseradish
3 Tb *(45 ml)* sugar

Cube crabmeat, add drained pineapple and mushrooms. Add remaining ingredients.

Crab And Avocado Salad
The crab provides an element of elegance

Can do ahead

Serves: 4
Preparing: 15 min

½ cup *(118 ml)* mayonnaise
½ cup *(118 ml)* celery, thinly
  sliced
2 tsp *(10 ml)* lemon juice
dash of Tabasco sauce

⅛ tsp *(.6 ml)* Worcestershire
  sauce
2 ripe avocados, halved
salt and pepper
1½ cups *(355 ml)* crab OR
  lobster meat, chilled

Combine first 5 ingredients. Sprinkle avocados with lemon and salt. Add crab meat to mixture and toss. Place in avocado halves and place on crisp greens. Top with favorite dressing.

Chicken Salad
Very easy and tasty!

Can do ahead

Yield: 1 qt (946 ml)
Preparing: 30 min
Cooking: 1 hr

1 whole chicken (OR 3 whole
  chicken breasts OR 6 halves)
salt
pepper
lemon pepper marinade
celery, several stalks

½ pt *(237 ml)* **Miracle Whip
  salad dressing**
1 heaping Tb *(15 ml)* **Hellman's
  mayonnaise**
1 firm apple, diced (optional)

Boil chicken. Season with salt, pepper and lemon pepper marinade. Cook with lid on for about 1 hour. When tender take out, remove skin, and cut up. Cut celery very fine. Mix in salad dressing and mayonnaise. Add more salt, pepper and several dashes of red pepper.

Variation:
Can add chopped pecans, if desired, and add when adding the apple.

Exotic Luncheon Salad With Chicken
Unusual elegant salad

Must do ahead

Serves: 6-8
Preparing: 30 min
Cooking: 30 min
Chilling: 4 hrs

2½-3 lbs *(1.1-1.3 kg)* **cooked
  chicken, cut in chunks**
1 can, 8 oz *(227 g)* **water
  chestnuts, sliced**
1 lb *(454 g)* **seedless grapes**
2 cups *(474 g)* **celery, chopped**
2-3 cups *(474-710 ml)* **slivered
  almonds, toasted (save ½ cup
  (118 ml) for garnish)**

2-3 cups *(474-710 ml)* **mayonnaise**
1 Tb *(15 ml)* **curry powder**
1 Tb *(15 ml)* **soy sauce**
2 Tb *(30 ml)* **lemon juice**
lettuce, Boston OR Bibb
1 can, 20 oz *(567 g)* **pineapple
  chunks**

Combine first five ingredients. Combine mayonnaise, curry powder, soy sauce and lemon juice; toss with chicken and chill several hours. Spoon onto bed of lettuce or individual plates. Sprinkle with pineapple and rest of almonds.

Desserts

Desperts

Peach Bavarian With Raspberry Sauce

Must do ahead

Serves: 6-8
Preparing: 30 min
Chilling: 3-4 hrs

2 eggs, separated
1 pkg, 3 oz *(85 g)* peach jello
⅛ tsp *(.6 ml)* salt
1 cup *(237 ml)* boiling water
¼ tsp *(1.25 ml)* vanilla
¼ tsp *(1.25 ml)* almond extract

2 Tb *(30 ml)* sugar
1 cup *(237 ml)* peaches, drained
and diced (fresh, canned OR
frozen)
1 cup *(237 ml)* heavy cream,
whipped

Beat egg yolks and add jello and salt. Pour in water and stir until dissolved. Add vanilla and almond extract. Beat egg whites and gradually add sugar. Fold gelatin into egg white mixture. Fold in peaches and whipped cream. Pour into 6-cup (1.42 l) mold and chill until set. Serve with raspberry sauce (p. 317).

Fruit Cottage Pudding

Can do ahead

Serves: 9
Preparing: 15 min
Cooking: 45-50 min

2 cups *(474 ml)* sifted flour
1 Tb *(15 ml)* baking powder
¼ tsp *(1.25 ml)* salt
½ cup *(118 ml)* sugar
½ cup *(118 ml)* butter
¾ cup *(177 ml)* milk

1 egg
2 cups *(474 ml)* fresh, frozen OR
canned fruit (cherries,
blueberries, peaches,
raspberries, cranberries, etc.)

In large mixing bowl, combine flour, baking powder, salt and sugar. Mix well. Cut in butter to make coarse crumb mixture. Add milk and egg; beat until creamy. Stir in fruit. Turn into a greased 9 inch (22.86 cm) square baking pan. Bake at 350° (177° C) for 45-50 minutes. Serve warm with whipped cream, ice cream or cinnamon cream below.

CINNAMON CREAM

1 cup *(237 ml)* light cream
1 Tb *(15 ml)* sugar

½ tsp *(2.5 ml)* ground cinnamon
¼ tsp *(1.25 ml)* ground nutmeg

Mix all ingredients together.

Bread Pudding With Brandy Sauce

Can do ahead

Serves: 8
Preparing: 30 min
Cooking: 10 min
Baking: 1-1½ hrs

PUDDING:

10 slices day old bread
4 cups *(946 ml)* **scalded milk**
1 cup *(237 ml)* **heavy cream**
4 eggs
1 cup *(237 ml)* **sugar**

1 tsp *(5 ml)* **vanilla**
1 tsp *(5 ml)* **cinnamon**
½ tsp *(2.5 ml)* **nutmeg**
¼ cup *(59 ml)* **butter, melted**
½ cup *(118 ml)* **seedless raisins**

Break bread into pieces and combine with milk and cream. Beat eggs and add sugar; pour into bread mixture. Add rest of ingredients. Pour into 3-quart (2.84 l) baking dish; set in pan of warm water. Bake at 350° (177° C) 1-1½ hours.

BRANDY SAUCE:

3 egg yolks
1 cup *(118 ml)* **sugar**
1 tsp *(5 ml)* **vanilla**
1½ cups *(355 ml)* **milk**

1 Tb *(15 ml)* **cornstarch**
¼ cup *(59 ml)* **water**
1½ oz *(45 ml)* **brandy OR bourbon**

In saucepan, slightly beat yolks; add sugar, vanilla and milk. Blend cornstarch into water; stir into hot mixture. Continue cooking until thick. Remove from heat and stir in brandy. Serve over pudding when cool.

Frozen Delight Mousse

Must do ahead

Serves: 6-8
Preparing: 20 min
Freezing: 3-4 hrs

3 eggs, separated
½ cup *(118 ml)* **sugar**
¼ cup *(59 ml)* **sherry**
1 pt *(474 ml)* **whipping cream**

12 lady fingers
2 Tb *(30 ml)* **pecans, chopped**
2 Tb *(30 ml)* **candied cherries**

Beat egg yolks until very light and add sugar. Beat well. Add sherry and fold in well-beaten egg whites. Add cream after whipping it. Line bowl with halves of lady fingers. Add nuts and cherries to the cream mixture and pour into bowl. Freeze for 3 to 4 hours before serving.

Coffee Pumpkin Flan

Must do ahead

1½ cups *(355 ml)* sugar
1 cup *(237 ml)* canned pumpkin
1 tsp *(5 ml)* ginger
¾ tsp *(3.7 ml)* cinnamon
⅛ tsp *(.6 ml)* cloves
⅛ tsp *(.6 ml)* nutmeg
1 Tb *(15 ml)* molasses

1 Tb *(15 ml)* butter, melted
4 eggs
3 egg yolks
1 can, 13 oz *(369 g)* evaporated milk
1 cup *(237 ml)* strong coffee

Caramelize 1 cup (237 ml) of sugar. Pour syrup evenly into 12 four ounce (118 ml) ramekins. Tip back and forth to coat sides. Cool. Combine the pumpkin, ginger, cinnamon, cloves, nutmeg, molasses, and butter. Mix well and set aside. Beat the eggs and egg yolks together. Add the remaining ½ cup (118 ml) sugar, the evaporated milk, and the coffee. Beat well until blended. Pour coffee mixture slowly into pumpkin mixture. Mix well with a wire whisk. Pour mixture into carmel-coated ramekins. Place ramekins in a pan of hot water with the water level equal to the top of the pumpkin mixture. Bake at 350° (177° C) for 1¼ hours or until inserted knife comes out clean. Chill. Serve garnished with whipped cream flavored with Kahlua.

Butterscotch Crunch Squares

Must do ahead
Can freeze

Serves: 12-16
Preparing: 15 min

1 cup *(237 ml)* flour
¼ cup *(59 ml)* quick cooking oats
¼ cup *(59 ml)* brown sugar
½ cup *(118 ml)* margarine, softened

½ cup *(118 ml)* pecans, chopped
1 jar, 12 oz *(340 g)* butterscotch OR caramel ice cream topping
1 quart *(946 ml)* chocolate ice cream

Combine flour, oats and brown sugar. Cut in margarine until mixture resembles coarse crumbs. Stir in nuts. Pat mixture into a 9 x 13 x 2 inch (22.86 x 33.02 x 5.08 cm) baking pan. Bake at 375° (191° C) for 15 minutes. Remove from oven and stir, while still warm, to crumble. Cool. Spread half the crumbs in a 9 x 9 inch (22.86 x 22.86 cm) baking pan. Drizzle half the ice cream topping over crumbs in pan. Spoon ice cream on top of this and pat down. Drizzle with remaining topping and sprinkle with remaining crumbs. Freeze. Hint: Set out when you sit down to eat and it will be soft enough to serve by dessert time.

Spicy Peach Squares

Serves: 12
Preparing: 20 min
Baking: 35 min

½ cup *(118 ml)* **butter OR margarine, softened**
½ cup *(118 ml)* **granulated sugar**
2 **eggs**
½ cup *(118 ml)* **flour**
2 tsp *(10 ml)* **baking powder**
½ tsp *(2.5 ml)* **salt**
¼ tsp *(1.25 ml)* **ground allspice**
2 tsp *(10 ml)* **ground cinnamon**

⅛ tsp *(.6 ml)* **ground cloves**
¼ cup *(59 ml)* **milk**
1 can, 16 oz *(454 g)* **sliced peaches (drained and chopped)**
½ cup *(118 ml)* **walnuts OR pecans, chopped**
54 **vanilla wafers (finely rolled, about 2 cups *(474 ml)*)**
confectioner's sugar

Beat butter and sugar until creamy. Add eggs, one at a time, beating well after each. Sift together the next 6 ingredients; stir in vanilla wafer crumbs. Stir with milk into butter mixture until well blended. Stir in peaches and nuts. Spread in well-greased and floured 9 x 13 x 2 inch (22.86 x 33.02 x 5.08 cm) pan. Bake in preheated 350° (177° C) oven about 35 minutes. Sprinkle with confectioner's sugar. Serve at room temperature or warm, topped with ice cream if desired.

Strawberry-Rhubarb Betty

Serves: 6-8
Preparing: 20 min
Baking: 45 min

¼ cup *(59 ml)* **margarine**
8 **slices bread, cubed**
1 pt *(474 ml)* **fresh strawberries, sliced OR 1 pkg frozen, thawed**

4-5 **stalks fresh rhubarb OR 1 pkg frozen, thawed**
¼ cup *(59 ml)* **sugar**

In a frying pan, melt margarine and lightly brown bread cubes. Mix strawberries and rhubarb and sprinkle with sugar. Place half of the berry-rhubarb mixture in a 2-quart (1.8 l) casserole and sprinkle with half of the bread cubes. Repeat with remaining ingredients. Bake at 325° (163° C) for 45 minutes.

Fruit Cobbler

Can do ahead
Can freeze

Serves: 6
Preparing: 20 min
Baking: 40 min

4 cups *(946 ml)* **berries,**
  sweetened to taste
1 tsp *(5 ml)* **lemon juice**
1 scant cup *(237 ml)* **flour**
1 scant cup *(237 ml)* **sugar**
1 tsp *(5 ml)* **baking powder**

⅛ tsp *(.6 ml)* **salt**
1 **egg, beaten**
½ tsp *(2.5 ml)* **almond extract**
6 Tb *(90 ml)* **butter, melted**
¼ cup *(59 ml)* **sugar**

Sprinkle lemon juice over berries in 2 quart (1.8 l) casserole. Mix dry ingredients with a fork; add egg and extract. Sprinkle over berries with fingers. Pour butter over topping and sprinkle with additional sugar. Bake at 350° (177° C) until golden brown, about 40 minutes.

VARIATIONS:

Peach Cobbler: Use 1 quart (946 ml) peaches mixed with ½ cup (118 ml) each brown sugar and white sugar. Add 1 Tb (15 ml) tapioca and dash of nutmeg to fruit.

Apple Cobbler: Use 1 quart (946 ml) apples mixed with ½ cup (118 ml) each brown sugar and white sugar. Add 1 tsp (5 ml) cinnamon to topping and a dash of apple pie spice to fruit.

Cherry Cobbler: Add 1 Tb (15 ml) tapioca to cherries.

Heavenly Peach

Must do ahead

Serves: 12
Preparing: 40 min
Chilling: overnight

2 cups *(474 ml)* **fresh peaches —**
  add ⅔ cup *(158 ml)* **sugar and let**
  sit for 2 hours. May use canned
  fruit but omit sugar.
1 round **angel food cake**
1 9 oz *(255 g)* **Cool Whip**

1 4½ oz *(127 g)* **Cool Whip**
1 pkg, 3¾ oz *(106 g)* **instant vanilla**
  pudding, mixed according to
  package directions
1 pkg, 6 oz *(170 g)* **frozen coconut**

In a 9 x 13 inch (22.86 x 33.02 cm) pan crumble cake, add fruit, sprinkle half the coconut over this. Mix pudding; add large Cool Whip. Pour over peaches and coconut. Shake pan for pudding to sink through fruit. Spread over small Cool Whip and add rest of coconut. Let sit overnight in refrigerator.

Cheese And Date Tarts

Must do ahead

Yield: 2 doz
Preparing: 25 min
Chilling: overnight
Baking: 15 min

CHEESE PASTRY

½ **cup** *(118 ml)* **margarine**
¼ **lb** *(113 g)* **sharp cheese, grated**

1 **cup** *(237 ml)* **flour**

Cream together and store in refrigerator overnight.

DATE PASTE

1 pkg, 8 oz *(227 g)* **dates, chopped**
½ **cup** *(118 ml)* **light brown sugar**

¼ **cup** *(59 ml)* **orange juice**

Cook over low heat until dates are soft and mixture becomes a thick paste.

Roll pastry out very thin and cut into rounds. Put 1 teaspoon (5 ml) of date paste on each round, fold over and press edges with a fork. Bake at 350° (177° C) for 15 minutes.

Individual Cheese Cakes

Must do ahead
Can freeze

Serves: 30
Preparing: 15 min
Baking: 30 min

3 pkg, 8 oz *(227 g)* **cream cheese, softened**
1 **cup** *(237 ml)* **sugar**

5 **eggs**
1½ **tsp** *(7.5 ml)* **vanilla**

Mix the above ingredients well, adding eggs one at a time. Fill individual aluminum no bake cups with 2 full tablespoons (30 ml) of the mixture (about ½-⅔ full). Bake at 300° (149° C) for 20-25 minutes.

1 **pt** *(474 ml)* **sour cream**
½ **cup** *(118 ml)* **sugar**

1 **tsp** *(5 ml)* **vanilla**

Combine these ingredients and put a spoonful on top of each cake. Bake at 300° (149° C) for 5-8 minutes. Cool and then refrigerate. Top with fruit pie filling if desired.

Dessert Crêpes

Strawberry: Put 2 Tb (30 ml) sliced strawberries in the center of each crêpe. Sprinkle with granulated sugar and roll up placing seam side down in a baking dish. Bake 10 minutes at 350° (177° C). Sprinkle with powdered sugar and top with whipped cream.

Apple: Slice apples and cook in butter, covered, until tender. Put apples on crêpes, roll and put in baking dish. Sprinkle with powdered sugar and run under the broiler to lightly glaze. Top with whipped cream.

325° at 50

Chocolate Cheesecake
Men love it!

Must do ahead
Can freeze

Serves: 12-15
Preparing: 20-25 min
Baking: 1 hr 10 min

CRUST

1 box, 8½ oz *(241 g)* **Nabisco thin chocolate wafers**

¼ tsp *(1.25 ml)* **cinnamon**
½ cup *(118 ml)* **butter, melted**

Put wafers in blender and grind. Mix with other ingredients and chill in a 10 inch (25.40 cm) spring-form pan.

FILLING

4 pkgs, 8 oz *(227 g)* **cream cheese**
4 **eggs**
2 cups *(474 ml)* **sugar**
1 Tb *(15 ml)* **cocoa**

1 Tb *(15 ml)* **vanilla**
1 pkg, 12 oz *(340 g)* **semisweet chocolate morsels, melted**
2 cups *(474 ml)* **sour cream**

In mixer, mix cream cheese until fluffy. Add one egg at a time alternating with sugar. Add cocoa and vanilla. Mix well and fold in melted chocolate. Stir in sour cream and pour into chilled crust. Bake 1 hour 10 minutes at 350° (177° C). Cool, then refrigerate.

HINTS

The longer it sits, the better it is; usually make about five or more days ahead.
It has a hard crust.
Do not fill the pan too full as it rises. Extra can be put in individual soufflé dishes — save a little chocolate wafer mixture for the bottom. Bake 20 to 25 minutes.
Top or garnish with curls of chocolate.

Rum Cheesecake

Must do ahead
Can freeze

Serves: 6-8
Preparing: 25 min
Baking: 45 min
Cooling: 30 min

2 cups *(474 ml)* **graham crackers, crushed**
½ cup *(118 ml)* **butter**
4 pkgs, 8 oz *(227 g)* **cream cheese**
dash **salt**
1 tsp *(5 ml)* **vanilla**

4 **eggs**
1 cup *(237 ml)* **sugar**
½ cup *(118 ml)* **light rum**
2 cups *(474 ml)* **sour cream**
1 tsp *(5 ml)* **vanilla**
½ cup *(118 ml)* **sugar**

Mix graham crackers and butter together and press into 9 inch (22.86 cm) pie plate. Beat together cream cheese, salt, 1 tsp (5 ml) vanilla, eggs, 1 cup (237 ml) sugar and rum until smooth. Pour into crust. Bake at 375° (191° C) for 40 minutes. Let cool 30 minutes. Mix together sour cream, 1 tsp (5 ml) vanilla and ½ cup (118 ml) sugar and pour over cake. Bake at 450° (232° C) for 5 minutes. Refrigerate several days before serving to enhance the flavor.

Strawberry Squares

Must do ahead
Freeze

Serves: 12-15
Preparing: 40 min
Baking: 20 min
Freezing: 6 hrs

1 cup *(237 ml)* **flour**
¼ cup *(59 ml)* **brown sugar**

½ cup *(118 ml)* **nuts, chopped**
½ cup *(118 ml)* **margarine**

Mix ingredients and spread evenly in shallow pan. Bake at 350° (177° C) for 20 minutes stirring occasionally. Sprinkle ⅔ of the crumbs in a 13 x 9 x 2 inch (33.02 x 22.86 x 5.08 cm) pan. Reserve the remainder for topping.

FILLING

2 **egg whites**
⅔ cup *(158 ml)* **sugar**
1 pkg, 10 oz *(284 g)* **frozen strawberries (partially thawed)**

2 tsp *(10 ml)* **lemon juice**
1 cup *(237 ml)* **cream**

Whip cream. With clean beaters and in another bowl, combine egg whites, sugar, berries and lemon juice. Beat at high speed to stiff peaks — about 10 minutes. Fold in cream. Place on top of crumbs and top with remaining crumbs. Freeze at least 6 hours.

Pineapple Mint Supreme

Must do ahead
Can freeze

Serves: 16
Preparing: 45 min
Chilling: 4 hrs

CRUST

1 cup *(237 ml)* flour
½ cup *(118 ml)* walnuts, chopped

¼ cup *(59 ml)* brown sugar
½ cup *(118 ml)* butter

Combine flour, nuts and sugar. Cut in butter until fine. Press into greased 9 x 13 inch (22.86 x 33.02 cm) pan. Bake at 400° (204° C) 12 minutes. Cool.

FILLING

1 can, 1 lb 4 oz *(567 g)* crushed pineapple
1 pkg, 8 oz *(227 g)* cream cheese
1 pkg, 3 oz *(85 g)* lime jello

1 cup *(237 ml)* sugar
1 cup *(237 ml)* whipping cream
⅛ tsp *(.6 ml)* peppermint extract

Drain pineapple into saucepan. Bring juice just to boiling point. Dissolve jello in juice. Cool. Cream cream cheese with sugar. Blend in jello mixture. Stir in pineapple. Chill until thick but not set. Chill whipping cream and extract until very cold, then beat until thick. Fold into pineapple-cheese mixture. Spoon over baked crust and refrigerate. Make glaze and spoon over filling. Spread carefully. Chill at least four hours.

GLAZE

½ cup *(118 ml)* chocolate chips
⅓ cup *(79 ml)* evaporated milk

1 Tb *(15 ml)* butter
¼ tsp *(1.25 ml)* peppermint extract

Melt chocolate in milk. Add butter and extract.

Pumpkin Shells

Can do ahead

Yield: 2½ cups (592 ml)
Preparing: 15 min

1 pkg, 1½ oz *(42 g)* Dream Whip
½ cup *(118 ml)* milk
½ tsp *(2.5 ml)* vanilla
1 pkg, 3¾ oz *(106 g)* instant vanilla pudding

⅔ cup *(158 ml)* milk
1 can, 1 lb *(454 g)* canned pumpkin (not pie filling)
¾-1 tsp *(3.7-5 ml)* pumpkin pie spice

Mix Dream Whip, ½ cup (118 ml) milk and vanilla. Mix vanilla pudding, ⅔ cup (158 ml) milk. Combine the two and add canned pumpkin and spice. Mix well and fill small shells.

Ambrosia

Must do ahead

Serves: 6-8
Preparing: 30 min

6 navel oranges, peeled and
sliced, membranes and seeds
removed

shredded coconut
sugar
sherry (optional)

Put a double layer of oranges in the bottom of a glass bowl. Sprinkle lightly with sugar, then cover with coconut. Repeat until all fruit is used, ending with a layer of coconut. Sprinkle with sherry. Chill until very cold.

OR

10 navel oranges
2 cups *(474 ml)* fresh coconut,
finely grated

1 cup *(237 ml)* powdered sugar
1½ cups *(355 ml)* pecans,
chopped

Blitz Torte

Can do ahead

Serves: 12-16
Preparing: 20 min
Baking: 25-30 min

½ cup *(118 ml)* butter
½ cup *(118 ml)* sugar
4 egg yolks, beaten
1 cup *(237 ml)* flour
1 tsp *(5 ml)* baking powder
4 Tb *(60 ml)* milk
1 tsp *(5 ml)* vanilla

4 egg whites
1 cup *(237 ml)* sugar
1 tsp *(5 ml)* vanilla
pinch salt
strawberries
whipped cream

Cream butter and sugar. Add egg yolks and beat well. Combine flour and baking powder and add alternately with milk and vanilla. Grease 2 cake pans and line with wax paper and grease again. Add cake mixture to pans. Beat egg whites, sugar, vanilla, and salt until stiff. Cover cakes completely and bake at 350° (177° C) for 25-30 minutes. Cut into pie wedges and top with strawberries and whipped cream.

French Strawberry Dessert

Can do ahead

Serves: 6
Preparing: 15 min
Cooking: 4 min

¾ cup *(177 ml)* **sugar**
½ cup *(118 ml)* **whipping cream**
¼ cup *(59 ml)* **light corn syrup**
2 Tb *(30 ml)* **margarine**

½ cup *(118 ml)* **Heath bars,
chopped (2 large bars)**
2 pts *(946 ml)* **fresh strawberries**
8 oz *(227 g)* **sour cream**

Combine sugar, cream, corn syrup and margarine in saucepan. Bring to a boil one minute. Remove from heat; stir in chopped candy. Cool; stirring occasionally. Serve fresh strawberries topped with toffee sauce and sour cream. Can also serve sauce over ice cream or angel food cake slices.

Julie's Bridge Meringue Torte

Must do ahead

Serves: 16
Preparing: 45 min
Chilling: 8 hrs or
overnight

MERINGUE

6 egg whites
2 tsp *(10 ml)* **vanilla**
½ tsp *(2.5 ml)* **cream of tartar**

dash salt
2 cups *(474 ml)* **sugar**

Have egg whites at room temperature. Add vanilla, cream of tartar, and dash of salt; beat to soft peaks. Gradually add sugar, beating to very stiff peaks. Cover 2 cookie sheets with pastry paper (ungreased paper). Draw a 9 inch (22.86 cm) circle on each and spread meringue evenly within circles. Bake in very slow oven 275° (135° C) for 1 hour. Turn off heat; let dry in oven with door closed at least 2 hours or overnight.

TOPPING AND FILLING

6 ¾ oz *(21 g)* **chocolate-coated
English Toffee Bars, chilled and
crushed**

dash salt
2 cups *(474 ml)* **whipping cream,
whipped**

Fold crushed candy and dash of salt into whipped cream. Spread one-third of the whipped cream between layers. Frost top and sides with remainder. Chill 8 hours or overnight. Garnish with additional crushed candy.

Chocolate Ice Box Dessert

Must do ahead

Serves: 8
Preparing: 30 min

18 lady fingers
18 macaroons
6 eggs
1 cup *(237 ml)* **butter**

4 oz *(113 g)* **chocolate**
1 cup *(237 ml)* **sugar OR 2 cups**
(474 ml) **powdered sugar**

Melt chocolate. Cream butter and beat into chocolate. Add pinch of salt. Beat sugar into egg yolks. Stir into first mixture. Whip egg whites and fold into mixture. Pour into bowl lined with lady fingers. Crunch macaroons and sprinkle on top. Store in refrigerator and serve with whipped cream.

Delicious Yuletide Chocolate Dessert

Must do ahead

Serves: 9
Preparing: 45 min
Chilling: 24 hrs

2 cups *(474 ml)* **fine vanilla wafer**
crumbs
⅓ cup *(79 ml)* **melted butter**
½ cup *(118 ml)* **butter**
1½ cups *(355 ml)* **powdered sugar**
2 eggs
¼ cup *(59 ml)* **sugar**

2 Tb *(30 ml)* **cocoa**
1 cup *(237 ml)* **heavy cream**
1 cup *(237 ml)* **chopped walnuts**
OR pecans
2 fully ripe bananas, mashed
¼ cup *(59 ml)* **sliced maraschino**
cherries

Combine crumbs and melted butter, reserving 2 tablespoons (30 ml) for topping; press remainder into bottom of 8 x 8 inch (20.32 x 20.32 cm) or 9 x 9 inch (22.86 x 22.86 cm) pan. Cream butter and powdered sugar. Add eggs, one at a time, beating well after each; spread over crumbs. Combine sugar, cocoa and cream; whip until thick. Fold in nuts and fruits. Pile atop mixture in pan. Sprinkle with reserved crumbs. Chill 24 hours.

Baked Egg Custard

Serves: 6
Preparing: 15 min
Baking: 45 min

½ cup *(118 ml)* sugar
2 eggs
2 cups *(474 ml)* scalded milk

½ tsp *(2.5 ml)* salt
½ tsp *(2.5 ml)* vanilla
nutmeg

Preheat oven to 325° (163° C). Beat eggs, sugar and salt. Stir in scalded milk and add vanilla. Fill custard dishes and place in a pan with 1 inch (2.54 cm) of water. Bake for about 45 minutes. Sprinkle tops with nutmeg when serving.

Boiled Custard

Can do ahead

Serves: 8-10
Preparing: 20 min

1 qt *(946 ml)* milk
5 eggs
1 cup *(237 ml)* sugar

2 tsp *(10 ml)* vanilla
¼ tsp *(1.25 ml)* salt

Put 3 cups (710 ml) milk in double boiler. Let cook until a skim is on top. Stir constantly. Then add very gradually the rest of the milk into which the eggs and sugar have been added and slightly beaten. Stir constantly until it drops a little thick from the spoon. Strain and add vanilla. Serve plain or over ice cream.

VARIATION: 2 Tb (30 ml) of sherry can be substituted for the vanilla.

Frozen Grand Marnier Soufflé

Must do ahead
Freeze

Serves: 8
Preparing: 15 min
Freezing: 3½-4 hrs

6 egg yolks
¾ cup *(177 ml)* sugar
2 cups *(474 ml)* whipping cream

1½ oz *(45 ml)* Grand Marnier
¾ cup *(177 ml)* whipped cream for decoration

Beat egg yolks until very thick, adding sugar gradually. Beat cream and fold into yolk mixture, adding Grand Marnier last. Serve in small soufflé dishes. Freeze and top with whipped cream just before serving.

Creme De Menthe Mousse

Can do ahead
Can freeze

Serves: 8
Preparing: 20 min
Freezing: 8 hrs or
overnight

16 marshmallows
1 pt *(474 ml)* **whipping cream,**
  whipped

⅔ cup *(158 ml)* **green creme de**
  menthe
strawberries

Put marshmallows and creme de menthe in top of double boiler or in a bowl in microwave oven. Stir until marshmallows are melted. Cool thoroughly and fold into heavy whipped cream. Freeze. Unmold and serve with strawberries or whipped cream. Fills a 1-quart (946 ml) mold.

Variation: Substitute other liqueurs.

Rhubarb Mousse

Must do ahead

Serves: 4-6
Preparing: 25-30 min
Chilling: 2-3 hrs

1 bunch rhubarb, trimmed and
  cubed
½ cup *(118 ml)* **water**
1 stick cinnamon
¾ cup *(177 ml)* **sugar OR ½ cup**
  (118 ml) **of honey**

2 Tb *(30 ml)* **gelatin**
½ tsp *(2.5 ml)* **salt**
¼ cup *(59 ml)* **cold water**
2 egg whites, beaten stiff with a
  pinch of salt

Cook rhubarb in the half cup (118 ml) of water with cinnamon stick, covered, until soft. Soak gelatin in the ¼ cup (59 ml) cold water. Allow to stand 5 minutes. When soft, stir into hot rhubarb mixture and stir over low heat until gelatin dissolves. Remove cinnamon stick, add sugar or honey and salt. Pour into refrigerator dish and cool until half jelled. Remove from refrigerator and whip with egg beater or whisk until frothy. Carefully fold in stiff egg whites. Pour into serving dishes and chill.

Fresh Grape Dessert
This makes a nice light dessert

Must do ahead

Serves: 6
Preparing: 15 min
Chilling: 10 min

2 lbs *(908 g)* **seedless grapes**
¼ cup *(59 ml)* **brandy**
½ cup *(118 ml)* **sour cream**

½ cup *(118 ml)* **heavy cream**
2 Tb *(30 ml)* **confectioner's sugar**
dark brown sugar

Remove stems from grapes. Place in a shallow serving dish. Sprinkle with the brandy; turn the grapes to coat evenly. Whip the cream and combine it with the sour cream and confectioner's sugar. Blend. Place this in the freezing compartment for about 10 minutes to chill. Serve grapes in individual dessert bowls. Top with cream mixture and sprinkle over a small amount of dark brown sugar.

Crème Brûlée

Must do ahead

Serves: 4-6
Cooking: 30 min
Baking: 5 min

1 pt *(474 ml)* **heavy cream**
3 Tb *(45 ml)* **sugar**
4 egg yolks, well beaten
1 tsp *(5 ml)* **vanilla extract**

brown sugar
½ cup *(118 ml)* **whipping cream**
(optional)

In double boiler, heat cream to just under boiling point. Beat egg yolks until light and blend well with sugar and vanilla. Add to cream and stir constantly until thick. Pour into individual custard cups. Let cool thoroughly and then spread brown sugar over top and put in broiler just long enough to melt sugar. Cool. Set in refrigerator until ready to serve. Serve as is or top with whipped cream if desired.

Strawberries A La Chantilly
Light, springtime dessert

Must do ahead

Serves: 6
Preparing: 25 min
Chilling: 3 hrs

1½-2 pt *(711-948 ml)* **fresh whole strawberries, hulled**
1 cup *(237 ml)* **heavy cream**

¼ cup *(59 ml)* **sweet chocolate, grated**
1 Tb *(15 ml)* **confectioner's sugar**
1 Tb *(15 ml)* **light rum**

Whip cream until foamy and just slightly thickened. Fold in chocolate, confectioner's sugar, and rum. Chill. At serving time arrange berries in serving dishes and pass the sauce.

Orange Ice
A good, light dessert

Must do ahead
Freeze

Serves: 6-8
Preparing: 2 hrs

2 cups *(474 ml)* **sugar**
4 cups *(946 ml)* **water**
2 cups *(474 ml)* **fresh orange juice**

juice of 2 lemons
grated rind of 2 lemons
grated rind of 2 oranges

Boil together sugar and water for 2 to 3 minutes. Combine juice and grated rind with sugar and water mixture and let it cool. When cool, strain and freeze. Stir occasionally while freezing. This prevents it from freezing into a hard sheet.

Brandied Ice
A great dessert drink in the summer

Can do ahead
Can freeze

Serves: 4
Preparing: 5-10 min

1 pt *(474 ml)* **vanilla ice cream**

1 oz *(30 ml)* **banana liqueur**

Put ice cream and liqueur in blender long enough to blend. Serve in champagne glasses. May double or triple recipe.

Variation: Use any fruit liqueur such as Grand Marnier, Tia Maria, or Cointreau.

Bananas Flambé

Serves: 4-6
Preparing: 10 min
Cooking: 15 min

5 Tb *(75 ml)* sugar
8 bananas, sliced lengthwise OR
coin size
8 small rolls of butter

juice of 1 orange
1 jigger of Grand Marnier
1 jigger of Tavraud cognac
cocktail cherries (optional)

Melt sugar in a saucepan until it is light brown (caramelized). Then add the butter, orange juice and Grand Marnier. Let simmer for 8 to 10 minutes. Now comes the moment everyone is waiting for: pour the Tavraud cognac over the bananas and set it ablaze. This is best done by slightly withdrawing and tilting the pan so that its rim approaches the flame. To serve, put the ice cream on the plates, or pretty glass bowls, add bananas to sauce and pour sauce over ice cream.

A Grand Finale

Can do ahead

Serves: 8
Preparing: 15 min

1 qt *(946 ml)* **vanilla ice cream**
1 cup *(237 ml)* **mince meat**

¼ cup *(59 ml)* **brandy, divided**
½ cup *(118 ml)* **nuts, chopped**

Spoon ice cream into 8 dessert dishes. Store in freezer until serving time. Combine mince meat, 2 tablespoons brandy and nuts in saucepan. Heat until hot — **do not boil.** Warm remaining brandy. Set ablaze and pour over mince meat. Serve over ice cream while flaming.

Myrtie Moon's Cranberry Crunch

Can do ahead

Serves: 9
Preparing: 10 min
Baking: 45 min

1 cup *(237 ml)* **uncooked oatmeal**
½ cup *(118 ml)* **dark brown sugar**
½ cup *(118 ml)* **flour**

¼ cup *(59 ml)* **butter**
1 can, 16 oz *(454 g)* **whole
cranberry sauce**

Mix oatmeal, brown sugar, and flour; cut in butter until crumbly. Pack half of the mixture in an 8 x 8 inch (20.32 x 20.32 cm) greased baking dish. Cover with cranberry sauce. Top with balance of crumb mixture. Bake 45 minutes at 350° (177° C). Serve warm topped with ice cream or Dream Whip.

Blueberry-Peach Crisp

Can do ahead

Serves: 8
Preparing: 20-25 min
Baking: 35 min

FILLING:

1 pt *(474 ml)* **fresh blueberries,
washed and hulled**
2 cups *(474 ml)* **fresh peaches,
peeled and sliced**
1 Tb *(15 ml)* **lemon juice**

½ cup *(118 ml)* **sugar**
¼ cup *(59 ml)* **unsifted flour**
½ tsp *(2.5 ml)* **cinnamon**
¼ tsp *(1.25 ml)* **ground cloves**

Combine the fruit and lemon juice and add remaining ingredients. Put in a greased 8 x 8 x 2 inch (20.32 x 20.32 x 5.08 cm) pan. Sprinkle with topping, and bake at 375° (191° C) for 35 minutes.

TOPPING:

¾ cup *(177 ml)* **flour, sifted**
⅓ cup *(79 ml)* **raw rolled oats**

⅓ cup *(79 ml)* **butter, melted**
½ cup *(118 ml)* **light brown sugar,
firmly packed**

In bowl, combine flour, oats and brown sugar. Stir in the butter to make a crumbly mixture.

California Tarts

Can do ahead
Can freeze

Yield: 10-12
Preparing: 20 min
Baking: 25 min

CRUST:

1 pkg, 8 oz *(227 g)* **cream cheese**
½ cup *(118 ml)* **butter**

1 cup *(237 ml)* **flour, sifted**

Work cream cheese, butter and flour together. Shape into small muffin tins.

FILLING:

1 cup *(237 ml)* **raisins**
1 cup *(237 ml)* **nuts**
1 cup *(237 ml)* **sugar**

2 eggs, beaten separately
½ cup *(118 ml)* **butter, melted**
1 tsp *(5 ml)* **vanilla**

Put into crust. Bake at 350° (177° C) about 25 minutes.

Vanilla Ice Cream

Yield: 1½ gal (5.68 l)

2½ cups *(592 ml)* **sugar**
6 eggs, beaten
1 can, 14 oz *(397 g)* **condensed milk**

2 cans, 13 oz *(384 g)* **evaporated milk**
2 qts *(1.89 l)* **milk**
1 Tb *(15 ml)* **vanilla**

Combine and mix all ingredients. Pour into a 2 gallon (7.58 l) freezer. Freeze according to directions.

Ice Cream Custard

Must do ahead
Must freeze

Yield: 1 gal (3.79 l) freezer
Preparing: 40 min
Cooking: 10 min

2 qts *(1.89 l)* **whole milk**
6 eggs, well beaten
2 cups *(474 ml)* **sugar**

2 Tb *(30 ml)* **flour**
1 tsp *(15 ml)* **vanilla**

Heat milk, but do not boil. Pour over beaten eggs. Add sugar mixed with flour. Cook in double boiler or over **very** low heat, stirring with wide spatula until it is coated a little. Cool, and add vanilla. Freeze this for vanilla or add peaches, (already sweetened), strawberries or bananas, etc.

Note: Omit vanilla if adding fruit. I also like lemon juice with the peaches or strawberries. I add as much fruit as I can and not fill the freezer too full.

Ice Cream Dessert

Must do ahead
Must freeze

Serves: 8-10
Preparing: 30 min
Marinating: 3 hrs
Freezing: 2 hrs

¼ **cup** *(59 ml)* **rum**
1 cup *(237 ml)* **candied fruit, chopped**
1 tsp *(5 ml)* **vanilla extract**
1 qt *(946 ml)* **vanilla ice cream, softened**

2 Tb *(30 ml)* **powdered sugar**
1 cup *(237 ml)* **heavy cream, whipped OR Cool Whip**
toasted, flaked coconut

Combine rum and fruit; let stand several hours, stirring occasionally. Add vanilla and fruit to ice cream. Put in 1½ quart (1.42 l) mold or bowl. Cover with foil and freeze. To serve, unmold on chilled plate. Sprinkle with powdered sugar. Frost with whipped cream. Top with coconut. Slice to serve.

Homemade Peppermint Ice Cream

Must do ahead

Yield: 3 qts (2.84 l)
Preparing: 45 min
Cooking: 25 min
Chilling: 60-90 min
Freezing: 3 hrs

2 qts *(1.89 l)* milk
16 ozs *(454 g)* peppermint candy, crushed (use stick if you can find it)
2 Tb *(30 ml)* flour

½ cup *(118 ml)* sugar
½ tsp *(2.5 ml)* salt
2 eggs, beaten
1 pt *(474 ml)* whipping cream

Heat milk and peppermint candy slowly until candy dissolves and milk is scalded. Mix the dry ingredients. Add the beaten eggs to dry ingredients. Add the hot milk to the egg mixture slowly to warm the egg mixture. Put the milk-egg mixture back on low to medium heat and cook slowly until thickened. Cool. When ready to churn, whip the whipping cream until slightly thickened but not stiff. Mix in with custard and churn in hand or electric ice cream freezer.

Coffee Ice Cream

Yield: 1 gal (3.79 l)

2 Tb *(30 ml)* instant coffee
1½ cups *(355 ml)* boiling water
2 cans, 14 oz *(397 g)* condensed milk

3 cups *(710 ml)* half and half
3 cups *(710 ml)* milk
1 Tb *(15 ml)* vanilla

Dissolve coffee in boiling water. Add remaining ingredients, mixing well. Freeze according to freezer directions.

Raspberry Ice Cream

Must do ahead
Must freeze

Yield: 1 gal (3.79 l)
Preparing: 15 min
Freezing: 3 hrs

2 cups *(474 ml)* sugar
juice of 1½ lemons
1 cup *(237 ml)* sour cream
1 qt *(946 ml)* half-and-half

milk
2 pkgs, 10 oz *(284 g)* frozen raspberries, thawed and mashed

Mix sugar, lemon juice and sour cream. Combine raspberries and half-and-half. Combine the two mixtures and put in an ice cream freezer. Add milk to fill a 1-gallon (3.79 l) freezer can two-thirds full. Freeze until firm according to instructions.

Fruit Sherbet

Must do ahead

Serves: 10-12
Preparing: 15 min
Freezing: 3 hrs

2 cups *(474 ml)* orange juice
½ cup *(118 ml)* lemon juice
2 cups *(474 ml)* sugar
1 can, 8 oz *(227 g)* pineapple,
  crushed

2 bananas, mashed
1 jar, 4 oz *(113 g)* maraschino
  cherries, chopped
1 cup *(237 ml)* milk
1 cup *(237 ml)* heavy cream

Mix all ingredients; freeze. Take out, beat until mushy; then refreeze. May substitute another cup (237 ml) milk for cream.

Ice Cream Sandwiches

Yield: 20

1 egg white
2 Tb *(30 ml)* sugar
1 cup *(237 ml)* whipping cream
¼ cup *(59 ml)* sugar
1 Tb *(15 ml)* powdered instant
  coffee

1 tsp *(5 ml)* vanilla
¼ cup *(59 ml)* toasted almonds,
  chopped
40 chocolate wafers

Beat egg whites until soft peaks form. Gradually add the 2 Tb (30 ml) sugar, beating to form stiff peaks. Combine cream, remaining sugar, coffee and vanilla and beat to form soft peaks. Fold in egg whites and nuts. Spread about 2 Tb (30 ml) of the mixture on each wafer, topping with another wafer. Place on a cookie sheet and freeze. Serve as soon as frozen or wrap individually and keep in the freezer.

Pineapple Ice Cream

Must do ahead

Yield: 1 gal (3.79 l)
Preparing: 15 min

2 qts *(1.89 l)* milk
4-5 eggs, beaten
1½ cups *(355 ml)* sugar
1 can, 20 oz *(457 g)* crushed
  pineapple

1 jar, 6 oz *(170 g)* maraschino
  cherries
1 can, 13 oz *(384 ml)* evaporated
  milk

Mix together and place in freezer. Freeze according to freezer directions.

D
E
S
S
E
R
T
S

DESSERT SAUCES

Topping For Ice Cream
Can be served hot or cold

Can do ahead

Yield: 1 pt (474 ml)
Preparing: 15 min
Cooking: 10 min

1 cup *(237 ml)* **brown sugar**
1 cup *(237 ml)* **white sugar**
1 scant cup *(237 ml)* **water**
1 cup *(237 ml)* **strawberry preserves**
1 orange, sectioned

1 lemon rind, grated
1 orange rind, grated
juice of 1 lemon
½ cup *(118 ml)* **bourbon**
1 cup *(237 ml)* **nuts, chopped**

Boil the first three ingredients until the mixture spins a thread. Add the remaining ingredients to the hot mixture. Will keep indefinitely in the refrigerator.

Fudge Sauce And Frosting

Can do ahead

Yield: 3 cups (710 ml)
Preparing: 5 min
Cooking: 10 min

5 squares unsweetened chocolate
½ cup *(118 ml)* **margarine**
3 cups *(710 ml)* **confectioner's sugar**

1 can, 14½ oz *(411 g)* **evaporated milk**
1¼ tsp *(6.25 ml)* **vanilla**

Melt chocolate and margarine; remove from heat. Mix in sugar, alternately with milk. Bring to a boil over medium heat, stirring constantly. Cook and stir about 8 minutes, or until thickened and creamy. Remove from heat; stir in vanilla. Serve warm. Will keep in refrigerator for months.

FROSTING

Cook 2 cups (474 ml) of fudge sauce and 2 cups (474 ml) confectioner's sugar and blend. Will frost a two-layer cake.

Nesselrode Sauce

Must do ahead

Serves: 8
Preparing: 30 min
Ripening: 2 weeks

¾ cup *(177 ml)* **maraschino cherries, chopped**
⅓ cup *(79 ml)* **orange peel, chopped**
1½ cups *(355 ml)* **orange marmalade**

½ cup *(118 ml)* **candied ginger, chopped**
2 Tb *(30 ml)* **maraschino cherry juice**
1 cup *(237 ml)* **fresh cooked chestnuts, chopped**
½ cup *(118 ml)* **rum**

Combine cherries and orange peel and mix well. Add remaining ingredients. Place in jars and ripen for two weeks in refrigerator. Delicious over ice cream or puddings. Also a nice gift to give for Christmas.

Kentucky Delight

Must do ahead
Can freeze

Yield: 1 qt (946 ml)
Preparing: 1 hr 15 min
Chilling: 2 hrs

½ cup *(118 ml)* **bourbon**
½ lb *(227 g)* **miniature marshmallows**

2 doz **macaroons, crumbled**
1 pt *(474 ml)* **heavy cream, whipped**

Soak bourbon and marshmallows for 1 hour. Whip cream and add macaroons. Add the two mixtures in a large crock. Chill. Use over angel food cake or ice cream, or freeze and serve as a frozen dessert.

Raspberry Sauce

Can do ahead

Serves: 6-8
Preparing: 15 min

1 pkg, 16 oz *(454 g)* **frozen red raspberries OR strawberries**
1 tsp *(5 ml)* **cornstarch**
1 Tb *(15 ml)* **water**

¼ cup *(59 ml)* **sugar**
½ cup *(118 ml)* **red currant jelly**
¼ cup *(59 ml)* **cherry Cointreau**
1 Tb *(15 ml)* **flour**

Thaw berries, heat and strain through a sieve. Mix cornstarch and water and add to strained berries in a saucepan. Cook and stir for 5 minutes. Add sugar and jelly and heat to dissolve fully. Add flour and Cointreau. Serve over fresh sliced peaches, canteloupe, ice cream or cake.

Marinated Fruit Dessert Sauce

Must do ahead

Serves: 6
Preparing: 5 min
Chilling: 4 hrs

1 can, 11 oz *(312 g)* mandarin
oranges
1 can, 1 lb 4 oz *(567 g)* pineapple
chunks

¼ cup *(59 ml)* white creme de
menthe
fresh mint, crushed (optional)

Combine above ingredients, place in jar, and marinate at least 4 hours in refrigerator. Turn jar upside down occasionally so that all fruit comes in contact with liqueur. Serve over lemon or orange sherbet.

Pineapple Sauce

Can do ahead

Yield: approx 2 cups
(474 ml)
Preparing: 10 min
Cooking: 5 min

⅓ cup *(79 ml)* brown sugar,
packed
1 Tb *(15 ml)* cornstarch

1 cup *(237 ml)* pineapple juice
2 Tb *(30 ml)* butter
1 Tb *(15 ml)* lemon juice

In a saucepan, mix brown sugar and cornstarch. Stir in pineapple juice. Bring to a boil, then boil for 1 minute over medium heat, stirring constantly. Remove from heat, add butter and lemon juice. Serve warm. Good over pound cake or upside-down cake with Cool Whip or whipped cream.

Whiskey Sauce For Cake
Nice to give as a Christmas present to friends

Can do ahead

Yield: 2 cups (474 ml)
Preparing: 15 min

1 cup *(237 ml)* butter
2 cups *(474 ml)* sugar
1 egg, beaten

½ cup *(118 ml)* whipping cream
bourbon

Cream butter and sugar with an electric mixer. Add egg and cream. Cook in double boiler. Add bourbon to taste. Serve on fruit cake or pound cake. Will keep indefinitely in refrigerator. Reheat in double boiler.

Pies

Pies and Pastry

Tips For Pies

Use a pastry cloth and stockinet covered rolling pin when rolling pie crust. You will use less flour, fewer strokes and have a tender, more flaky pie crust.

Shiny metal pans do not bake bottom crusts as well as top crust. Use aluminum pans with a dull finish or heat proof glass pie plates. When baking fruit pies, place a sheet of aluminum foil directly under pie plate on bottom of oven to catch the drippings from the pie.

To keep the bottom crust of a pie from getting soggy, brush surface with well beaten white of an egg.

To prevent juices in berry pies from running over, stick a few pieces of large macaroni through top of crust.

Chill pie dough 10 minutes in refrigerator to reduce the amount of flour needed on the board when rolling out. Excess flour results in a tough product.

Roll out pie dough between 2 sheets of waxed paper; peel one layer off, turn dough upside down in pie shell and carefully peel off the other sheet. **Never fail** method of a good pie crust.

Handle pie dough very little after adding water to dough. Excess handling results in tough crust that is not flaky.

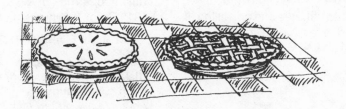

Never Fail Pie Crust

Can do ahead
Can freeze

Yield: 2 double-
crust pies
Preparing: 10 min

4 cups *(946 ml)* **flour**
1¾ cups *(414 ml)* **shortening**
1 Tb *(15 ml)* **sugar**
3 tsp *(15 ml)* **salt**

1 Tb *(15 ml)* **vinegar**
1 egg
½ cup *(118 ml)* **water**

Cut shortening into flour. Add other ingredients and mix to form soft ball. Roll and make 2 double crusts.

One Crust Pie Shell

Yield: 1 crust
Preparing: 15 min

1 cup *(237 ml)* **all-purpose flour**
½ tsp *(2.5 ml)* **salt**

⅓ cup *(79 ml)* **shortening**
3 Tb *(45 ml)* **cold water**

Sift flour and salt together. Cut in shortening with pastry blender until it is the size of small peas. Sprinkle water over mixture while tossing lightly with a fork until particles stick together. Form into a smooth ball. Wrap in waxed paper and chill. Lightly roll pastry into a circle one inch (2.54 cm) larger than pie plate. Lift loosely into pie plate, pat out the air, fold edges under and crimp. Prick the entire crust thoroughly before baking. Bake at 450° (232° C) about 12 minutes or until golden brown. Cool and fill.

Make-A-Choice Pie Crusts

Yield: one 9-inch crust — add filling desired

GRAHAM CRACKER CRUST

1½ cups *(355 ml)* **fine crumbs —
18 crackers**
¼ cup *(59 ml)* **sugar**
dash of cinnamon (optional)
½ cup *(118 ml)* **butter OR
margarine, softened**

Mix well; press into pie plate. Chill 45 minutes and add filling. If you desire a baked crust, bake at 375° (191° C) for 8 minutes. Cool.

CHOCOLATE OR VANILLA WAFER CRUST

1¼ cups *(296 ml)* **wafer crumbs —
38 wafers**
⅓ cup *(79 ml)* **butter OR
margarine, melted**

Mix well, press into pie plate and chill. If desired, bake at 375° (191° C) for 8 minutes; cool.

ZWIEBACK CRUST

1⅓ cups *(316 ml)* **Zwieback
crumbs**
¼ cup *(59 ml)* **sugar**
⅓ cup *(79 ml)* **butter OR
margarine, melted**

Mix well, press into pie plate and chill. If desired, bake at 375° (191° C) for 8 minutes; cool.

CEREAL FLAKE CRUST

1 cup *(237 ml)* **corn flakes, wheat
flakes or rice cereal, crushed**
¼ cup *(59 ml)* **sugar**
⅓ cup *(79 ml)* **butter, melted**

Mix until crumbly. Press into pie plate and chill. If desired, bake at 375° (191° C) for 8 minutes; cool.

GINGERSNAP CRUST

1½ cups *(355 ml)* **fine crumbs —
24 snaps**
¼ cup *(59 ml)* **butter, softened**

Mix well; press into pie plate and bake at 375° (191° C) for 8 minutes. Cool.

Chocolate Meringue Pie

Old-fashioned chocolate pie

Can do ahead

Serves: 6-8
Preparing: 10 min
Cooking: 10-15 min
Baking: 10 min

2 cups *(474 ml)* **milk**
4 egg yolks
3 Tb *(45 ml)* flour
1 cup *(237 ml)* sugar
2 squares bitter chocolate

1 tsp *(5 ml)* vanilla
1 9'' *(22.86 cm)* deep dish pie
crust, baked
4 egg whites
4 Tb *(60 ml)* sugar

Combine milk and egg yolks in top of double boiler. Combine flour and sugar and add. Add remaining ingredients and cook, stirring frequently until mixture is thick. Pour into baked crust. To make meringue, beat egg whites until soft peaks form. Gradually add sugar until stiff peaks form. Spread over pie filling being sure that all edges are sealed. Bake at 400° (204° C) for 10 minutes or until golden brown.

Brownie Pecan Pie

Can do ahead
Can freeze

Serves: 6-8
Preparing: 20 min
Cooking: 2 min
Baking: 50 min

½ cup *(118 ml)* **Post Grape Nuts**
½ cup *(118 ml)* warm water
⅔ cup *(158 ml)* sugar
⅛ tsp *(.6 ml)* salt
1 cup *(237 ml)* light corn syrup
1 pkg, 4 oz *(113 g)* Baker's
German sweet chocolate

3 Tb *(45 ml)* butter OR margarine
3 eggs, slightly beaten
1 tsp *(5 ml)* vanilla
½ cup *(118 ml)* pecans
1 unbaked pie shell

Combine cereal and water. Let stand until water is absorbed. Heat sugar, salt, and syrup to boil over high heat, stirring to dissolve sugar. Boil 2 minutes. Remove from heat. Add chocolate and butter, stir until blended. Slowly pour over eggs, stirring constantly. Add cereal mixture, vanilla and nuts. Mix well. Pour into unbaked pie shell. Bake at 375° (191° C) about 50 minutes or until filling puffs and begins to crack around edges. Cool. Serve with whipped cream.

German Chocolate Angel Pie

Must do ahead

Serves: 6-8
Preparing: 15 min
Baking: 50-55 min
Chilling: 2 hrs

SHELL

2 egg whites
⅛ tsp *(.6 ml)* salt
⅛ tsp *(.6 ml)* cream of tartar
½ cup *(118 ml)* sugar

⅛ tsp *(.6 ml)* vanilla
½ cup *(118 ml)* finely chopped
nuts

Beat egg whites with salt and cream of tartar until foamy. Add sugar, 2 Tb (30 ml) at a time, beating well after each addition; continue beating until stiff peaks form. Fold in vanilla and nuts. Spoon into lightly greased 8 inch (20.32 cm) pie pan to form nest-like shell, building side up to ½ inch (1.27 cm) above edge of pan. Bake at 300° (149° C) 50-55 minutes. Cool.

CHOCOLATE CREAM FILLING:

1 bar, 4 oz *(113 g)* Baker's German
sweet chocolate
3 Tb *(45 ml)* water

1 tsp *(5 ml)* vanilla
1 cup *(237 ml)* heavy cream,
whipped

Stir chocolate in water over low heat until melted; cool until thick. Add vanilla. Fold whipped cream into chocolate mixture. Pile into cooled shell. Chill 2 hours.

Variation: 5 oz (142 g) Hershey chocolate bar for German chocolate.

Variation: Double amounts of egg whites, sugar, cream of tartar and vanilla for deeper meringue crust. Use larger pie pan.

Pecan-Chocolate Chip Pie

Can do ahead
Can freeze

Serves: 12-16
Preparing: 15 min
Baking: 40 min

½ cup *(118 ml)* butter
1 cup *(237 ml)* sugar
1 cup *(237 ml)* white syrup
4 eggs

1 tsp *(5 ml)* vanilla
6 oz *(170 g)* chocolate chips
1 cup *(237 ml)* pecans, chopped
2 9″ *(22.86 cm)* pie shells

Melt butter. Mix sugar, syrup, eggs in bowl. Add butter, vanilla, chocolate chips, and pecans. Mix well. Pour into 2 pie shells. Bake 40 minutes at 350° (177° C).

Chocolate Ice Box Pie

Must do ahead

Serves: 6-8
Preparing: 30 min
Chilling: overnight

½ lb *(227 g)* **vanilla wafers,
crushed fine**
1 cup *(237 ml)* **powdered sugar**
½ cup *(118 ml)* **butter, room
temperature**

3 eggs, separated
2 squares chocolate, melted
1 cup *(237 ml)* **walnuts, chopped**
1 tsp vanilla
whipped cream

Place a little more than half of the vanilla wafers in the bottom of an 8 inch (20.32 cm) pie pan or square pan. Blend sugar and butter. Add egg yolks, one at a time. Beat constantly. Add melted chocolate and walnuts. Beat egg whites until stiff; fold in with vanilla. Spread this mixture over the crumbs. Top with whipped cream, with sugar and vanilla to taste. Sprinkle remaining crumbs over the cream. Place in refrigerator overnight.

Mocha Nut Pie

Must do ahead

Serves: 8
Preparing: 45 min
Baking: 50 min
Chilling: 3 hrs

⅓ cup *(79 ml)* **egg whites**
¼ tsp *(1.25 ml)* **cream of tartar**
¼ cup *(118 ml)* **sugar**
¼ cup *(59 ml)* **pecans, chopped**
1 tsp *(5 ml)* **vanilla**

1 cup *(237 ml)* **semi-sweet
chocolate**
3 oz *(90 ml)* **very strong coffee**
1 cup *(237 ml)* **heavy cream,
whipped**

Beat egg whites and cream of tartar until foamy. Gradually add sugar and pecans. Pour into buttered pie pan and bake at 275° (135° C) for 50 minutes. Melt chocolate and add coffee and vanilla. Fold in cream. Mash cooled shell down with fingers and then pour mixture into shell. Chill.

Frozen Cream Cheese Pie

Must do ahead
Must freeze

Yield: 2 pies
Preparing: 30 min

3 pkg, 3 oz *(85 g)* **cream cheese**
1 cup *(237 ml)* **sugar**
3 eggs, separated
1 cup *(237 ml)* **whipping cream**

1 tsp *(5 ml)* **vanilla**
pinch of salt
graham cracker crumbs

Cream cheese with sugar. Beat egg yolks and add to cream cheese and sugar. Whip cream and fold into mixture along with vanilla and salt. Beat egg whites until stiff and fold into mixture.

Line pie tins with crumbs and pour mixture over them. Sprinkle top with reserved crumbs and freeze.

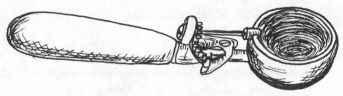

Quick Ice Cream Pie
An easy do ahead dessert

Must do ahead
Must freeze

Yield: 1 pie
Preparing: 15 min

1 9″ (22.86) graham cracker crust
1 qt (946 ml) vanilla ice cream
5 egg whites, beaten stiff

1 jar, 7 oz (1.98 g) marshmallow cream

Partially melt ice cream and put into crust, heaping in the middle. Put in freezer. Beat egg whites with electric mixer until very stiff. Add marshmallow cream and beat until well blended. Heap onto pie so that it looks like a mountain. Freeze. Run under broiler just before serving and serve with hot chocolate sauce or prepared hot fudge sauce.

CHOCOLATE SAUCE

1 square, 1 oz (28 g) unsweetened chocolate
¼ cup (59 ml) butter

1 cup (237 ml) sugar
1 can, 5.33 oz (158 ml) evaporated milk

Melt chocolate and butter over low heat. Add sugar and milk. Bring to a boil stirring constantly. Stores weeks in refrigerator. Reheat when ready to serve. Yield: 1 cup.

Strawberry Pie

Can do ahead

Serves: 6-8
Preparing: 30 min

1 9″ (22.86 cm) pie shell, baked
2 Tb (30 ml) confectioner's sugar
2 Tb (30 ml) strawberry gelatin
1 cup and 1 Tb (252 ml) hot water
1 cup (237 ml) sugar
2 Tb (30 ml) cornstarch

1 tsp (5 ml) vanilla
red food coloring
2 cups (474 ml) fresh strawberries, whole
whipped cream

Sprinkle pie shell with confectioner's sugar. Dissolve gelatin in 1 Tb (15 ml) hot water. Cook sugar and cornstarch in 1 cup (237 ml) hot water until thick. Add gelatin and vanilla to cooked syrup. Add couple of drops of red food coloring. Cool. When thickened some, fold in strawberries and pour into shell. Top with whipped cream.

Frozen Mile-High Strawberry Pie

Can do ahead
Must freeze

Serves: 8
Preparing: 20 min
Freezing: 4 hrs

1 pkg, 10 oz *(284 g)* frozen
  strawberries
1 cup *(237 ml)* sugar
2 egg whites
1 Tb *(15 ml)* lemon juice
⅛ tsp *(.6 ml)* salt

½ pt *(237 ml)* whipping cream,
  whipped
1 tsp *(5 ml)* vanilla
1 deep pie shell, baked and
  cooled

Beat the first 5 ingredients with an electric beater until very thick and it holds a peak. Fold in whipped cream and vanilla and put into pie shell, piling high. Freeze, then cover with plastic wrap. Take out of freezer a few minutes before serving.

Layered Lemon Pie

Must do ahead
Must freeze

Serves: 8
Preparing: 35 min
Cooking: 15 min
Chilling: 30 min
Freezing: 4-6 hrs

CRUST

20 chocolate wafers   ¼ cup *(59 ml)* **butter, melted**

Crumble chocolate wafers or pulverize in blender. Mix with butter and pat into pie shell. Bake 8 minutes at 350° (177° C).

FILLING

¼ cup *(59 ml)* butter, melted
⅓ cup *(79 ml)* lemon juice
¾ cup *(177 ml)* sugar

dash salt
3 eggs, slightly beaten
1 pt *(474 ml)* vanilla ice cream

Melt butter, stir in lemon juice, sugar, and salt. Stir to dissolve. Pour half into 3 slightly beaten eggs. Return eggs to rest of butter mixture and cook over medium heat until thick. Chill. Divide ice cream in half. Put half into cookie crust. Pour half lemon mixture over. Freeze. Repeat layers. Freeze. Garnish with cookie crumbs or chocolate curls. Let stand 10 minutes at room temperature before serving.

Apple Pie With Nut Topping

Can do ahead

Can freeze

Serves: 6-8

Preparing: 20 min

Baking: 45-60 min

3 cups *(710 ml)* **cooking apples,**
   chopped
1 9″ *(22.86 cm)* **pie shell, unbaked**
¾ cup *(177 ml)* **sugar**
1 tsp *(5 ml)* **Angostura bitters**

½ cup *(118 ml)* **brown sugar**
½ cup *(118 ml)* **nuts, chopped**
¾ cup *(177 ml)* **flour**
¼ cup *(59 ml)* **margarine, melted**

Put apples in pie shell; sprinkle with sugar and bitters. Mix brown sugar, nuts, flour and margarine; spread over apples. Bake at 350° (177° C) about 45 minutes or until apples are tender.

Cream Cheese Pie

Must do ahead

Serves: 6-8

Preparing: 30 min

Chilling: 2 hrs

1 pkg, 8 oz *(227 g)* **cream cheese,**
   softened
1 can, 14 oz *(397 g)* **Eagle Brand**
   condensed milk

⅓ cup *(79 ml)* **bottled OR fresh**
   lemon juice
¼ tsp *(1.25 ml)* **vanilla**
1 graham cracker crust

Combine all ingredients and pour into crust. Chill 2 hours.

Peacharoon Freezer Pie

A summer pie

Must do ahead

Must freeze

Serves: 6-8

Preparing: 20 min

4 cups *(946 ml)* **fresh peaches,**
   peeled and sliced
1 cup *(237 ml)* **sugar**
¼ tsp *(1.25 ml)* **almond extract**

1½ cups *(355 ml)* **macaroon**
   crumbs, approx 30 cookies
1 cup *(237 ml)* **whipping cream**

Peel and pit peaches, cut into chunks and mash fine with a potato masher. Stir in sugar and almond extract; mix well. Refrigerate while preparing crust. Place cookies between waxed paper and crush with rolling pin or use food processor. Line bottom and sides of 9 inch (22.86 cm) pan, saving ¼ for topping. Whip cream until stiff. Fold in peaches and pour into pan. Cover with foil and freeze. Remove from freezer 20 minutes before serving.

Blueberry Or Cranberry Pie

Can do ahead

Serves: 6-8
Preparing: 15 min
Baking: 35-40 min

FILLING

2 cups *(474 ml)* **raw blueberries
OR cranberries**

½ cup *(118 ml)* **sugar**
½ cup *(118 ml)* **nuts, chopped**

Grease 10 inch (25.4 cm) pie plate. Wash and drain berries and place on bottom of pan. Sprinkle sugar and nuts over berries.

BATTER

1 cup *(237 ml)* **sugar**
¾ cup *(177 ml)* **margarine, melted**
1 cup *(237 ml)* **flour**

2 eggs, beaten
1 tsp *(5 ml)* **almond OR vanilla
extract**

Mix sugar and margarine and add rest of ingredients. Pour over berries. Bake at 325° (163° C) for 35-40 minutes. Serve with whipped cream or ice cream.

Raspberry Bavarian Cream Pie

Must do ahead

Yield: 2 pies
Preparing: 20 min
Chilling: 2-3 hrs

1 qt *(946 ml)* **fresh raspberries,
hulled**
1¼ cups *(296 ml)* **sugar**
2 tsp *(10 ml)* **gelatin**
3 Tb *(45 ml)* **water**

3 Tb *(45 ml)* **boiling water**
1 Tb *(15 ml)* **lemon juice**
2 cups *(474 ml)* **heavy cream,
whipped**
2 pie crusts, baked

Combine raspberries and sugar; let stand at room temperature 30 minutes. Soak gelatin in cold water; dissolve it with boiling water. Stir this mixture into berries along with lemon juice. Cool the gelatin mixture. When it is about to set, fold in lightly the whipped cream. Pour into pie shells and chill. Serve when the mixture has set. Can add 3 drops red food coloring to raspberry mixture, if desired.

Angel Pie

Must do ahead

Serves: 6-8
Preparing: 30 min
Baking: 1 hr
Chilling: 3-4 hrs

MERINGUE

4 egg whites, reserve yolks for
   filling
½ tsp *(2.5 ml)* baking powder
⅛ tsp *(.6 ml)* salt

1 cup *(237 ml)* sugar, sifted
1 tsp *(5 ml)* vanilla
1 tsp *(5 ml)* vinegar
1 tsp *(5 ml)* water

Beat egg whites, baking powder and salt until very stiff. Combine vanilla, vinegar and water. Add sugar alternately with vanilla mixture. Beat constantly for several minutes. Heap meringue lightly into an oven-proof 9-inch (22.86 cm) plate spreading like a pie or tart with heavy edges. Bake at 275° (135° C) for 1 hour or more. Let cool in oven with door open.

FILLING

4 egg yolks, beaten
½ cup *(118 ml)* sugar
juice and rind of 1 lemon
1 Tb *(15 ml)* flour

½ cup *(118 ml)* water
1 cup *(237 ml)* heavy cream
½ tsp *(2.5 ml)* vanilla

Combine yolks, sugar, lemon, flour and water in double boiler. Stir and cook until filling is thick. Cool. When pie and filling are cool, whip cream. Fold in vanilla. Place a layer of cream in pie shell, then filling, then another layer of cream. Chill several hours.

Banana Split Pie
The best ever!

Can do ahead

Serves: 12
Preparing: 20 min
Chilling: 2 hrs

2 cups *(474 ml)* graham crackers, crushed
½ cup *(118 ml)* margarine, softened
3 cups *(710 ml)* confectioner's sugar
1 pkg, 8 oz *(227 g)* cream cheese, softened

1 egg
6 bananas, sliced lengthwise
1 can, 20 oz *(567 g)* crushed pineapple
1 box non-dairy whipped topping, whipped
½ cup *(118 ml)* pecans, finely chopped

Combine graham cracker crumbs and margarine and form a crust in a 9 x 13 inch (22.86 x 33.02 cm) pan. Mix sugar, cream cheese and egg and spread over crust. Add bananas, pineapple and topping in layers. Sprinkle with nuts and refrigerate.

Cheesecake Pie

Must do ahead

Serves: 6-8
Preparing: 20 min
Baking: 40 min

GRAHAM CRACKER CRUST

1 cup *(237 ml)* crumbs
¼ cup *(59 ml)* margarine, melted

2 Tb *(30 ml)* sugar

Mix above ingredients and press in 9 inch (22.86 cm) pie pan or purchase a prepared graham cracker crust.

FILLING

1 pkg, 8 oz *(227 g)* cream cheese
1 pkg, 3 oz *(85 g)* cream cheese
½ cup *(118 ml)* sugar
2 eggs
1 Tb *(15 ml)* lemon juice

¼ tsp *(1.25 ml)* salt
1 tsp *(5 ml)* vanilla
1½ pts *(711 ml)* sour cream
½ tsp *(2.5 ml)* vanilla
2 Tb *(30 ml)* sugar

Soften cream cheese in large bowl. Add sugar, eggs, lemon juice, salt and vanilla and mix with mixer until fairly smooth. Pour into crust. Bake 325° (163° C) for 30 minutes or until fairly set. Take out of oven and add sour cream, vanilla and sugar that have been mixed. Cook 10 minutes more. Cool.

Date Pie

Can do ahead

14 saltine squares
12 dates, cut fine
½ cup *(118 ml)* pecans, chopped
1 cup *(237 ml)* sugar

½ tsp *(2.5 ml)* salt
1 tsp *(5 ml)* almond extract
3 egg whites, beaten well
whipped cream

Roll saltines into fine crumbs. Add other ingredients except egg whites and mix well. Fold in egg whites and pour into greased 9 inch (22.86 cm) pie plate. Bake at 300° (149° C) for 45 minutes. Serve with whipped cream.

Praline Cheese Pie

Can do ahead
Can freeze

Yield: 2 pies
Preparing: 12 min
Baking: 45 min

3 pkgs, 8 oz *(227 g)* cream cheese
1¼ cups *(296 ml)* light brown
  sugar
2 Tb *(30 ml)* flour

3 eggs
1½ tsp *(7.5 ml)* vanilla
½ cup *(118 ml)* pecans, chopped
2 graham cracker pie shells

Cream cream cheese; add sugar; blend well. Add flour, eggs, vanilla, and pecans. Pour into graham cracker crust. Bake at 350° (177° C) for 45 minutes.

Coconut Buttermilk Pie

Can do ahead

Serves: 12-16
Preparing: 15 min
Baking: 1 hr

½ cup *(118 ml)* butter, melted
2 cups *(474 ml)* sugar
4 eggs, separated
1 cup *(237 ml)* buttermilk
1 tsp *(5 ml)* vanilla

1 tsp *(5 ml)* flour
1 cup *(237 ml)* Baker's Angel Flake
  coconut
2 pie shells, unbaked

Mix butter, sugar, and egg yolks. Add buttermilk, flour, and vanilla. Beat egg whites until stiff and add to mixture. Add coconut last. Pour into unbaked pie shells and bake one hour at 300° (149° C).

Sherry Pie

Must do ahead

Serves: 6-8
Preparing: 25 min
Chilling: 8-10 hrs
Baking: 15 min

¼ lb *(113 g)* **margarine**
1 cup *(237 ml)* **flour**
¼ cup *(59 ml)* **brown sugar**
½ cup *(118 ml)* **pecans, chopped**

½ lb *(227 g)* **marshmallows**
½ cup *(118 ml)* **sherry**
½ pt *(237 ml)* **cream, whipped**

Prepare crust by mixing margarine with flour and brown sugar. Blend well and add pecans. Cook in a 9 inch (22.86 cm) pie plate at 375° (191° C) 15 minutes. Stir occasionally. Press into shape while hot. Reserve 3 Tb (45 ml) for topping. Cool.

For the filling, melt the marshmallows and sherry in top of double boiler. Cool. Fold in whipped cream. Pour into shell. Sprinkle crumbs on top. Refrigerate overnight for flavors to blend.

Chiffon Pumpkin Pie
Great after a heavy holiday meal!

Must do ahead

Serves: 6
Preparing: 45 min
Chilling: overnight

1 pkg **Knox gelatin**
¼ cup *(59 ml)* **cold water**
3 **egg yolks**
½ cup *(118 ml)* **sugar**
1¼ cups *(296 ml)* **cooked pumpkin**
½ cup *(118 ml)* **milk**
½ tsp *(2.5 ml)* **salt**

½ tsp *(2.5 ml)* **ginger**
½ tsp *(2.5 ml)* **cinnamon**
½ tsp *(2.5 ml)* **nutmeg**
½ cup *(118 ml)* **sugar**
3 **egg whites**
1 **baked pie crust**
whipped cream

Dissolve gelatin in cold water. Beat yolks and ½ cup (118 ml) sugar until creamy. In a double boiler, combine pumpkin, milk, salt, ginger, cinnamon, and nutmeg and cook until thick. Fold in yolk mixture. While still hot, add gelatin and mix thoroughly. Add last ½ cup (118 ml) sugar. Cool in cold water. Beat egg whites and fold into cooled mixture. Pour into baked 9 or 10 inch (22.86 or 25.4 cm) pie crust. Refrigerate overnight. Top with whipped cream.

Chess Pie

Can do ahead

Yield: 2 pies
Preparing: 5 min
Baking: 30 min

4 eggs, lightly beaten
2 cups *(474 ml)* sugar
¼ cup *(59 ml)* butter OR margarine
3 Tb *(45 ml)* whole cream OR milk

½ tsp *(2.5 ml)* salt
1 tsp *(5 ml)* vanilla
2 9'' *(22.86 cm)* pie crusts,
    unbaked

Combine all ingredients. Pour into shells. Bake at 375° (191° C) 30 minutes or until knife comes out clean — do not overcook.

Lemon Chess Pie

Can do ahead
Can freeze

Serves: 12-16
Preparing: 5 min
Baking: 40 min

3 cups *(710 ml)* sugar
3 Tb *(45 ml)* corn meal
2 Tb *(30 ml)* flour
6 eggs, unbeaten
6 Tb *(90 ml)* butter, melted

6 Tb *(90 ml)* milk
6 tsp *(30 ml)* lemon rind, grated
6 Tb *(90 ml)* lemon juice
2 9'' *(22.86 cm)* pie crusts

Mix sugar, corn meal and flour. Add remaining ingredients and mix well. Pour into pie shells. Bake at 325° (163° C) for 40 minutes.

Aunt Willie's Raisin Pecan Pie

Can do ahead

Serves: 6-8
Preparing: 20 min
Baking: 1 hr

½ cup *(118 ml)* raisins
½ cup *(118 ml)* water
¾ cup *(177 ml)* sugar
½ cup *(118 ml)* margarine
2 eggs

½ tsp *(2.5 ml)* cinnamon
½ tsp *(2.5 ml)* nutmeg
½ cup *(118 ml)* pecans, chopped
1 tsp *(5 ml)* vinegar

Have all ingredients at room temperature. Bring raisins to a boil in water; strain and let cool to room temperature. Mix all ingredients in order given and put in pie shell. Bake at 300° (149° C) for 1 hour.

Heath Bar Pie

Can do ahead

Serves: 24
Preparing: 20 min
Baking: 1¼ hrs

8 egg whites
1 tsp *(5 ml)* **cream of tartar**
2 cups *(474 ml)* **sugar**
pinch of salt

½ tsp *(2.5 ml)* **vanilla**
8-9 large Heath bars, crumbled
2 cartons, 9 oz *(255 g)* **Cool Whip**

Beat egg whites until foamy; add cream of tartar and beat until fluffy. Add sugar gradually and beat until stiff. Fold in salt and vanilla. Pour into 2 pans 13 x 9 x 2 inch (33.02 x 22.86 x 5.08 cm) or 2 square and 1 round pan. Bake at 250° (121° C) 45 minutes or until crusty and tannish color. Sprinkle Heath bars on top, then cover with Cool Whip. Chill overnight.

Variation: Use fresh fruit on top instead of Heath bars, or a layer of custard over meringue and top with fruit and whipped cream.

Coffee Ice Cream-Oreo Pie

Can do ahead
Must freeze

Serves: 8-10
Preparing: 35 min
Baking: 8 min

18 Oreo cookies, crushed
½ cup *(118 ml)* **margarine**
2 pts *(946 ml)* **coffee ice cream,**
  softened
3 squares unsweetened chocolate
¼ cup *(59 ml)* **margarine**
⅔ cup *(158 ml)* **sugar**

pinch of salt
⅔ cup *(158 ml)* **evaporated milk**
1 tsp *(5 ml)* **vanilla**
1 cup *(237 ml)* **whipping cream**
3 Tb *(45 ml)* **powdered sugar**
¾ cup *(177 ml)* **almonds, toasted**

Make a 10 inch (25.4 cm) pie crust with the first 2 ingredients. Bake at 350° (177° C) for 8 minutes. Cool. Spread ice cream on crust and freeze 1-2 hours. Make a fudge sauce by melting chocolate and margarine. Stir in sugar and salt, then add milk. Cook in double boiler for 4 minutes. Add vanilla. Cool. Pour this chocolate sauce over ice cream, top with whipped cream sweetened with powdered sugar, and garnish with almonds. Freeze.

Cookie Sundae Pie

Must do ahead

Serves: 6-8
Preparing: 30 min
Chilling: 45 min
Baking: 10-12 min

½ cup *(118 ml)* butter, soft
¼ cup *(59 ml)* confectioner's
  sugar, sifted
½ tsp *(2.5 ml)* vanilla
1 cup *(237 ml)* flour, sifted

⅛ tsp *(.6 ml)* salt
peach ice cream
3-4 peaches, sliced very thin
heavy cream, whipped

Cream butter, sugar and vanilla. Sift flour and salt together and add to creamed mixture. Chill 45 minutes. Pat dough into 9 inch (22.86 cm) pie pan and bake at 400° (204° C) 10-12 minutes; cool. Fill with peach ice cream, peaches, and whipped cream. Other flavors of fruit and ice cream can be substituted.

Hershey Bar Pie

Must do ahead

Serves: 8+
Preparing: 5 min
Cooking: 1-2 min
Chilling: 2 hrs

½ lb *(227 g)* Hershey bar with
  almonds

1 carton, 9 oz *(255 g)* Cool Whip
1 graham cracker crust

Melt Hershey bar in double boiler. Fold in Cool Whip and blend well. Pour into pie crust and chill.

Variation: Use a plain ½ lb (227 g) Hershey or crunch up 6 or 8 Heath bars.

German Chocolate Pie

Can do ahead

Yield: 3 pies
Preparing: 15 min
Baking: 35-40 min

3 cups *(710 ml)* sugar
6 Tb *(90 ml)* cocoa
pinch of salt
4 eggs
2 cups *(474 ml)* cookie coconut
1 cup *(237 ml)* nuts, chopped

1 tsp *(5 ml)* vanilla
1 can, 13 oz *(384 g)* evaporated
  milk
½ cup *(118 ml)* butter, melted
3 ready-to-bake pie crusts

Mix first 3 ingredients; add eggs and blend well. Stir in milk and vanilla; add butter, coconut and nuts. Pour into crusts and bake at 350° (177° C) about 35 to 40 minutes.

Cakes and Frostings

Cakes and Frostings

Tips For Cakes

Better results are obtained when butter, cream cheese and eggs are at room temperature.

Test for doneness: The cake is done when it springs back when lightly touched in center. It will pull away slightly from edge of the pan.

To remove cake layers: Cool cakes on a wire rack away from drafts about 10 minutes. Loosen the edges with a knife or small metal spatula. Place wire rack on top of cake. Invert cake pan on rack. Tap bottom of pan and remove.

Measure butter the easy way:
4 sticks equal 1 pound equal 2 cups
2 sticks equal ½ pound equal 1 cup
1 stick equals ¼ pound equal ½ cup or 8 tablespoons.

Place a lace doily over the top of an unfrosted cake. Sprinkle powdered sugar over the doily; then remove the doily gently so as not to disturb the lace design on the cake.

When slicing cake, dip knife into water before slicing each slice.

Dust a little flour or cornstarch on cake before icing; this way the icing won't run off.

After pouring cake batter into pans, bang pans on drainboard to prevent air holes (tunnels) in cake when done. Angel food cakes are an exception.

Coat raisins, dates, etc. with some flour before adding to a batter to prevent their settling to the bottom.

Grease and line the bottom of cake pans with waxed paper when making chocolate cakes to assure their always coming out and not falling apart.

Use cake flour for all cakes. It produces larger, more velvety and more even grain cakes than all-purpose flour.

If using all-purpose flour instead of cake flour, reduce the amount by 2 Tb (30 ml) per cup of flour.

To get buttermilk, mix 1 cup (237 ml) milk plus 1 Tb (15 ml) lemon juice or vinegar; let sit 5 minutes.

Jamaican Pound Cake

Excellent — so moist and good

Can do ahead

Yield: 1 loaf cake
Preparing: 10 min
Baking: 75 min

1 large ripe banana
2 eggs
¼ cup *(59 ml)* dark Jamaican Rum
1 pkg, 17 oz *(482 g)* pound cake
mix

½ cup *(118 ml)* sour cream
⅛ tsp *(.6 ml)* nutmeg
3 Tb *(45 ml)* sliced almonds

Mash banana; blend with eggs and rum. Beat into pound cake mix until smooth. Beat in sour cream and nutmeg. Butter a 9 x 5 3 inch (22.86 x 12.70 x 7.62 cm) loaf pan and sprinkle with almonds. Pour cake batter into pan. Bake in a pre-heated oven 325° (163° C) for 70 to 75 minutes. Place on wire rack to cool 10 minutes before removing from pan. Cool thoroughly before cutting. Can be reheated many times.

Apricot-Brandy Pound Cake

Can do ahead
Can freeze

Serves: 15-20
Preparing: 35 min
Baking: 1 hr 10 min

3 cups *(710 ml)* sugar
1 cup *(237 ml)* butter OR
margarine
6 eggs, separated
½ tsp *(2.5 ml)* rum flavoring
½ tsp *(2.5 ml)* lemon flavoring
¼ tsp *(1.25 ml)* almond flavoring
1 tsp *(5 ml)* orange flavoring
1 tsp *(5 ml)* vanilla flavoring

1 tsp *(5 ml)* butter flavoring
3 cups *(710 ml)* flour
½ tsp *(2.5 ml)* soda
½ tsp *(2.5 ml)* baking powder
½ tsp *(2.5 ml)* salt
1 cup *(237 ml)* sour cream
½ cup *(118 ml)* apricot brandy OR
apricot liqueur

Cream butter and sugar. Add egg yolks one at a time and beat well. Add flavorings. Add dry ingredients alternately with sour cream and brandy. Fold in stiffly beaten egg whites. Bake in greased tube pan or 4 one-pound (454 g) coffee cans filled half way each. Bake 1 hour 10 minutes at 300°-325° (149°-163° C). Delicious topped with whipped cream flavored with sugar and rum flavoring.

Butter'N Nut Pound Cake

Can do ahead

Yield: 1 Bundt cake
Preparing: 20 min
Baking: 1½ hrs

**C
A
K
E
S**

2½ cups *(592 ml)* **sugar**
1 cup *(237 ml)* **shortening**
½ cup *(118 ml)* **margarine**
5 **eggs**
1 cup *(237 ml)* **milk**

3 cups *(710 ml)* **flour, sifted**
½ tsp *(2.5 ml)* **baking powder**
1 Tb *(15 ml)* **vanilla, butter and nut
combination flavoring**

Cream sugar, shortening and margarine well. Add eggs, one at a time. Add milk and flour alternately. Add baking powder and flavoring. Grease and flour Bundt pan. Bake at 300° (149° C) 1½ hours. Cool 10 minutes and remove from pan.

ICING

1 pkg, 8 oz *(227 g)* **cream cheese**
½ cup *(118 ml)* **margarine**
1 box, 1 lb *(454 g)* **powdered sugar**
1 Tb *(15 ml)* **vanilla, butter and nut
combination flavoring**

1 cup *(237 ml)* **pecans, chopped
(optional)**

Cream margarine and cream cheese. Add other ingredients. Pecans can be put into icing, used as garnish, or not at all. Cream well. This is enough icing for 2 cakes. Let cake cool completely before icing.

Ice Cream Cone Cakes
Good for school parties

Can do ahead

Serves: 14
Preparing: 25 min
Baking: 30 min

one 2 layer cake mix
14 flat bottom cones
white frosting
food coloring

shortening
aluminum foil in strips 9″ x
9½″ *(22.86 x 24.13 cm)* **one strip
per cone**

Fold foil strips in half widthwise. Grease inside of foil collar. Form collars by wrapping foil tightly around cone pressing gently along sides. Use scotch tape to secure. Strips should extend 2 inches (5.08 cm) above cones. Pour batter to top of cone. Place in muffin tins. Bake at 350° (177° C) for 30 minutes. Cool on wire racks. Remove foil. Tint icing different colors and frost.

Chocolate Pecan Sour Cream Cake

Can do ahead

Yield: 1 sheet cake
Preparing: 20 min
Baking: 35-45 min

½ cup *(118 ml)* margarine
2 cups *(474 ml)* brown sugar
2 large eggs
3 Tb *(45 ml)* cocoa
⅔ cups *(158 ml)* water
2¼ cups *(533 ml)* cake flour, sifted
OR 2 cups *(474 ml)* plain flour,
sifted

1 tsp *(5 ml)* soda
1 tsp *(5 ml)* salt
⅔ cup *(158 ml)* sour
cream
1½ tsp *(7.5 ml)* vanilla
1 cup *(237 ml)* pecans, chopped

Preheat oven to 350° (177° C). Cream margarine and brown sugar together until fluffy. Beat in eggs. Blend cocoa and water and stir in. Sift together flour, soda and salt. Stir in alternately with sour cream and vanilla. Add pecans, stir. Bake in greased and floured 13 x 9 x 2 inch (22.86 x 33.02 x 5.08 cm) pan for 35-45 minutes. Does not do well in layer pans. When cool, frost with sour cream chocolate frosting. It helps cut the sweetness of the cake.

CHOCOLATE SOUR CREAM
FROSTING

1 pkg, 6 oz *(170 g)* semi-sweet
chocolate pieces

¾ cup *(177 ml)* sour cream
dash of salt

Melt chocolate pieces over hot water. Remove from heat and stir in sour cream and salt. Beat until creamy and spread on cake. This is too creamy to use on layer cakes.

Rosie's Chocolate Chip Cake

Can do ahead
Can freeze

Serves: 20
Preparing: 10 min
Baking: 1 hr

1 pkg yellow cake mix
½ cup *(118 ml)* oil
1 pkg, 3¾ oz *(106 g)* instant
chocolate pudding
1 ctn, 8 oz *(227 g)* sour cream

4 eggs
¼ cup *(59 ml)* rum OR brandy
1 tsp *(5 ml)* vanilla
1 pkg, 6 oz *(170 g)* chocolate chips
1 cup *(237 ml)* chopped pecans

Mix first seven ingredients; beat 3-4 minutes. Add chocolate chips and pecans and blend well. Pour into well-greased Bundt or tube pan and bake at 350° (177° C) 1 hour.

Raisin Chocolate Dutch Cake

Can do ahead

Serves: 15-18
Preparing: 20 min
Baking: 50 min

1½ cups *(355 ml)* raisins, chopped
½ cup *(118 ml)* walnuts, chopped
2 sq, 1 oz *(28 g)*
 unsweetened chocolate
1 tsp *(5 ml)* instant coffee
½ cup *(118 ml)* soft butter
1¾ cups *(414 ml)* brown sugar
2 tsp *(10 ml)* vanilla

2 eggs, well beaten
2 cups *(474 ml)* sifted flour
1¼ tsp *(6.25 ml)* salt
1 tsp *(5 ml)* soda
1 tsp *(5 ml)* cinnamon
½ cup *(118 ml)* sour cream
powdered sugar
1 cup *(237 ml)* boiling water

Chop chocolate and place in bowl with coffee. Add boiling water and let stand until melted. Stir. Beat butter with half of brown sugar until light. Beat in remaining brown sugar and vanilla until fluffy. Add eggs. Stir in raisins, nuts and chocolate. Sift dry ingredients and add alternately with sour cream. Stir only until blended. Turn into greased and floured 2 quart (1.8 l) pan (or tube pan). Bake at 325° (163° C) for 50 minutes. Cool and sprinkle with powdered sugar.

Moist Fudge Sheet Cake

Can do ahead
Can freeze

Serves: 12-15
Preparing: 20 min
Baking: 20 min

2 cups *(474 ml)* sugar
2 cups *(474 ml)* flour
½ cup *(118 ml)* butter
½ cup *(118 ml)* Crisco
4 Tb *(60 ml)* cocoa

1 cup *(237 ml)* water
½ cup *(118 ml)* buttermilk
2 eggs
1 tsp *(5 ml)* soda
1 tsp *(5 ml)* vanilla

Sift together sugar and flour in large bowl. Put butter, Crisco, cocoa, and water in pan. Bring to a rapid boil. Pour over sugar and flour and mix well. Add buttermilk, eggs, soda, and vanilla. Mix well and pour into a greased 15½ x 10½ inch (39.37 x 26.67 cm) pan. Bake at 400° (204° C) for 20 minutes.

FROSTING

½ cup *(118 ml)* butter
1 Tb *(15 ml)* cocoa
6 Tb *(90 ml)* sweet milk

1 box powdered sugar
1 tsp *(5 ml)* vanilla
1 cup *(237 ml)* pecans

Combine butter, cocoa, and sweet milk in pan and bring to a boil. Remove from heat and add powdered sugar, vanilla and pecans. Spread on hot cake.

Chocolate Pound Cake

Can do ahead

Serves: 16
Preparing: 25-30 min
Baking: 1 hr 15 min

1 cup *(237 ml)* butter
1 cup *(237 ml)* shortening
3 cups *(710 ml)* sugar
5 eggs
2½ cups *(592 ml)* cake flour

½ cup *(118 ml)* cocoa
½ tsp *(2.5 ml)* baking powder
1 tsp *(5 ml)* vanilla
1 cup *(237 ml)* milk

Cream butter and shortening. Add sugar and mix well. Add eggs and half of dry ingredients; then add milk; add remainder of dry ingredients and vanilla. Beat well. Pour into tube pan. Bake at 350° (177° C) for 1 hour and 15 minutes. Allow cake to cool for about 1 hour before removing from pan. Will keep 1 to 1½ weeks wrapped in refrigerator.

FROSTING (optional)

1 box confectioner's sugar
½ cup *(118 ml)* Hershey's cocoa,
   leveled
2½ Tb *(37.5 ml)* margarine,
   softened

½ cup *(118 ml)* Carnation milk,
   warm
1 tsp *(5 ml))* vanilla
1 Tb *(15 ml)* shortening,
   heaping

Cream margarine, shortening, and vanilla together. Add confectioner's sugar and cocoa; add warm Carnation milk until creamy and smooth. Swirl icing onto cooled cake.

Waldorf Chocolate Cake

Can do ahead

Serves: 12
Preparing: 15-20 min
Baking: 35 min

½ cup *(118 ml)* butter
2 cups *(474 ml)* sugar
4 sqs bitter chocolate, melted
2 eggs, beaten
2 cups *(474 ml)* cake flour

1 tsp *(5 ml)* salt
2 tsp *(10 ml)* baking powder
2 tsp *(10 ml)* vanilla
1½ cups *(355 ml)* milk
1 cup *(237 ml)* pecans, chopped

Cream butter and sugar until fluffy. Add melted chocolate and beaten eggs, mixing well. Sift together flour, salt and baking powder and add to batter alternately with milk and vanilla. Fold in pecans last. Bake in 2 9-inch (22.86 cm) pans at 375° (191° C) for 35 minutes. Frost with Rector's Mocha Cream Icing (p. 355).

Fudge Pudding Cake

Can do ahead

Serves: 6
Preparing: 30 min
Baking: 50 min

1 cup *(237 ml)* flour
2 tsp *(10 ml)* baking powder
1 tsp *(5 ml)* salt
⅔ cup *(158 ml)* sugar
2 Tb *(30 ml)* cocoa

½ cup *(118 ml)* milk
1 tsp *(5 ml)* vanilla
2 Tb *(30 ml)* butter, melted
1½ cups *(118 ml)* walnuts,
  chopped

Combine first 5 dry ingredients. Add milk, vanilla and butter and beat until smooth. Stir in the walnuts and spread the batter in a buttered 6 cup (1.42 l) casserole. Over the batter sprinkle a mixture of:

1 cup *(237 ml)* brown sugar

¼ cup *(59 ml)* cocoa

Over this pour 1½ cups (355 ml) boiling water. Bake in a 350° (177° C) oven for 50 minutes. Do not attempt to turn out this cake. The bottom is full of fudge sauce. Serve warm with ice cream or whipped cream.

Java Angel Cake

Very good and pretty dessert
Nice for summer dessert or after a heavy meal

Must do ahead

Serves: 16
Preparing: 45 min

1 pkg Angel Food cake mix
1 Tb *(15 ml)* instant coffee

1 tsp *(5 ml)* vanilla

Prepare cake according to directions, dissolving coffee in the water. Add vanilla.

ICING

2 pkg Dream Whip, prepared
6 Tb *(90 ml)* sugar
4-5 tsp *(20-25 ml)* coffee OR 4½
  tsp *(23 ml)* Tia Maria Liqueur

½ cup *(118 ml)* instant cocoa
1½ tsp *(7.5 ml)* vanilla

Combine, spread on cake and chill. Make topping while cake is baking. Keep in refrigerator till ready to ice cake.

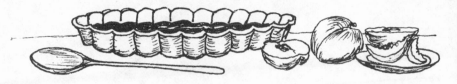

Fruited Cake Flan

Can do ahead

Serves: 8-10
Preparing: 20 min
Baking: 8-10 min

3 eggs, room temperature
⅛ tsp *(.6 ml)* **salt**
⅔ cup *(158 ml)* **sugar**
½ tsp *(2.5 ml)* **vanilla**
⅔ cup *(158 ml)* **sifted cake flour**
3 Tb *(45 ml)* **butter, melted and clarified (pour off clear liquid to use)**
1 cup *(237 ml)* **red currant jelly OR apricot preserves, depending on fruit**

2 Tb *(30 ml)* **Cognac**
¼ cup *(59 ml)* **crushed macaroons OR chopped nuts**
2 cups *(474 ml)* **fresh fruit (peaches, nectarines, apricots, plums, cherries, blueberries, strawberries OR raspberries)**
whipped cream, optional

Preheat oven to 400° (204° C). Place the eggs, salt and sugar in a large mixer bowl and warm gently over hot water or keep in a warm place until room temperature. Stir occasionally to keep from drying. Add vanilla to egg mixture and beat until very pale in color and very thick (a long time). Fold in the cake flour and then the butter. Pour batter into two 10 inch (25.4 cm) cake flan tins (greased and floured). Bake 8 to 10 minutes or until done. Loosen around edges and turn onto rack to cool. The underside of the cake provides the space for the filling. Melt the jelly or preserves in a small pan. Add cognac; strain through a fine sieve. Cool slightly. Brush bottom of cake with glaze, sprinkle nuts or macaroons. Arrange fruit, spoon over remaining glaze. Cool. Serve with whipped cream.

Rum Cakes

Must do ahead
Can freeze

Serves: 8-12
Preparing: 20 min

1 Angel Food cake (bought)
6 Tb *(90 ml)* **butter**
1 lb *(454 g)* **confectioner's sugar**

rum
chopped pecans

Cut cake into bite-size pieces. (Be sure to lightly scrape crumbs from cake before icing.) Mix butter, sugar and enough rum to make icing of spreadable consistency. Ice cake pieces and roll in pecans. Refrigerate until ready to use.

Dr. Bird Cake

A very moist cake

Can do ahead

Serves: 12-16
Preparing: 20-30 min
Baking: 1 hr 10 min

3 cups *(710 ml)* instant flour
1 tsp *(5 ml)* baking soda
1 tsp *(5 ml)* cinnamon
2 cups *(474 ml)* sugar
1 tsp *(5 ml)* salt
1½ cups *(355 ml)* cooking oil

1 can, 8 oz *(227 g)* crushed
   pineapple, undrained
1½ tsp *(7.5 ml)* vanilla
3 eggs, beaten
2 cups *(474 ml)* bananas, diced

Mix dry ingredients. Add remaining ingredients, stirring by hand. Mix by hand till blended. Do not beat. Bake in greased and floured tube pan for 1 hour and 10 minutes at 350° (177° C). Cool in pan. Can use a butter or sugar icing on cake if desired.

Out Of This World Cake

Can do ahead

Serves: 14-16
Preparing: 30 min
Baking: 40 min

1 cup *(237 ml)* margarine
2 cups *(474 ml)* sugar
4 eggs
1 lb *(454 g)* graham cracker
   crumbs

1 cup *(237 ml)* nuts, chopped
1 cup *(237 ml)* coconut
1 Tb *(15 ml)* baking powder
1 cup *(237 ml)* sweet milk

Cream margarine and sugar, add eggs and beat. Add cracker crumbs, nuts and coconut. Add baking powder and milk. Bake in three 9-inch (22.86 cm) cake pans (buttered and floured) at 350° (177° C) for 40 minutes.

ICING

½ cup *(118 ml)* margarine
1 box, 1 lb *(454 g)* confectioner's
   sugar
1 pkg, 8 oz *(227 g)* cream cheese

1 Tb *(15 ml)* pineapple juice
1 can, 8¼ oz *(234 g)* crushed
   pineapple, drained

Cream margarine and cream cheese until smooth. Add sugar and pineapple juice. Beat until creamy. Top each layer with frosting and pineapple.

347

Sweet Potato Surprise Cake

Can do ahead

Yield: 3 layer cake
Preparing: 45 min
Baking: 25-30 min

1½ cups *(355 ml)* cooking oil
2 cups *(474 ml)* sugar
4 eggs, separated
4 Tb *(60 ml)* hot water
2½ cups *(592 ml)* cake flour, sifted
3 tsp *(15 ml)* baking powder
¼ tsp *(1.25 ml)* salt

1 tsp *(5 ml)* ground cinnamon
1 tsp *(5 ml)* ground nutmeg
1½ cups *(355 ml)* raw sweet
   potatoes, grated
1 cup *(237 ml)* pecans, chopped
1 tsp *(5 ml)* vanilla

Combine oil and sugar; beat until smooth. Add egg yolks and beat well. Add hot water, then the dry ingredients which have been sifted together. Stir in potatoes, nuts, and vanilla; beat well. Beat egg whites until stiff; fold into mixture. Bake in 3 greased 8-inch (20.32 cm) layer cake pans at 350° (177° C) for 25-30 minutes. Cool and frost.

FROSTING

1 can, 13 oz *(385 ml)* evaporated
   milk
1 cup *(237 ml)* sugar
1 tsp *(5 ml)* vanilla

½ cup *(118 ml)* margarine
3 egg yolks
1⅓ cups *(316 ml)* flaked coconut

Combine in saucepan all ingredients except coconut. Cook over medium heat about 12 minutes, stirring constantly, until mixture thickens. Remove from heat and add coconut. Beat until cool and of spreading consistency.

English Trifle

Can do ahead

Serves: 10-12
Preparing: 24 min
Cooking: 15 min
Baking: 30 min

½ cup *(118 ml)* hot milk
2 Tb *(30 ml)* margarine
2 eggs
1 cup *(237 ml)* sugar

1 cup *(237 ml)* flour
⅛ tsp *(.6 ml)* salt
1 tsp *(5 ml)* baking powder
1 tsp *(5 ml)* vanilla

Heat milk and margarine together until quite warm. Set aside; then beat eggs until thick. Slowly add sugar and beat for 3 minutes. Sift together flour, salt, and baking powder and add to egg mixture. Work quickly and add hot milk and margarine. Add vanilla and pour into 8 inch (20.32 cm) or 9 inch (22.86 cm) cake pan that has been greased and floured. Bake at 350° (177° C) for 30 minutes.

continued

BOILED CUSTARD

4 eggs
4 cups *(946 ml)* milk

⅔ cup *(158 ml)* sugar
1 tsp *(5 ml)* vanilla

Beat eggs in top of double boiler. Add milk and stir until mixture coats the spoon. Add sugar and cook a few minutes more. Add vanilla and cool.

1 cup *(237 ml)* sherry (or more if desired)
½ cup *(118 ml)* almonds, sliced and toasted
10-12 maraschino cherries, halved

½ pt *(237 ml)* whipping cream, whipped
1 tsp *(5 ml)* sugar
1 tsp *(5 ml)* vanilla

Using a large bowl, break cake into pieces and pour sherry over it. Let it sit a few minutes and then pour boiled custard over cake. Add cherries and almonds. Whip cream and sweeten with sugar; then add vanilla. Cover the entire top with the whipped cream. Cover with Saran Wrap and refrigerate until ready to serve. This is pretty in a cut glass bowl and is a lovely Christmas dessert. It improves with age.

Neiman Marcus Cherry Nut Cake

Wonderful for a Thanksgiving or Christmas dessert

Can do ahead

Serves: 16-18
Preparing: 20-25 min
Baking: 1¾ hrs

2 cups *(474 ml)* butter
2 cups *(474 ml)* sugar
6 egg yolks, well beaten
3 cups *(710 ml)* cake flour
¾ lb *(340 g)* candied cherries

¼ lb *(113 g)* candied pineapple, coarsely chopped
5 cups *(1.18 l)* nuts, broken into pieces
2 Tb *(30 ml)* lemon extract
6 egg whites

Cream butter and gradually work in sugar until mixture is smooth and light. Beat in egg yolks. Sift cake flour and toss with fruit and nuts using hands until well coated with flour. Stir flour mixture into creamed mixture and add lemon extract. Beat egg whites until stiff but not dry and fold into batter thoroughly but gently. Pour the batter into a well-oiled and floured 10 inch (25.4 cm) tube pan and bake at 300° (149° C) for 1¾ hours or until done. Cool on wire rack for 10 minutes, remove from pan and cool completely before slicing.

Orange Delectable Cake

Must do ahead

Serves: 12
Preparing: 25 min
Chilling: 8 hrs
or overnight

1 envelope gelatin
1 tsp *(5 ml)* **orange rind**
¾ cup *(177 ml)* **orange juice**
3 eggs, separated
¼ cup *(59 ml)* **flour**
1 cup *(237 ml)* **sugar**

½ tsp *(2.5 ml)* **salt**
2 cups *(474 ml)* **milk**
3 Tb *(45 ml)* **sugar**
1 lb *(454 g)* **angel food cake**
½ pt *(237 ml)* **whipping cream OR**
  1 ctn, 9 oz *(255 g)* **Cool Whip**

Soak gelatin and orange rind in orange juice. Make custard out of egg yolks, flour, sugar, salt and milk. When custard thickens a little, take off heat and add orange juice and gelatin. Cool custard. Beat egg whites and sugar and fold into first mixture. Break angel food cake into bits. Line bottom of tube cake pan, large loaf pan, or 13 x 9 inch (33.02 x 22.86 cm) casserole dish with half of cake, then half of custard. Repeat layers. Chill 8 hours or overnight. When ready to serve, put cake onto cake plate and ice with whipping cream or Cool Whip. Sprinkle with coconut.

Orange Chiffon Deluxe Cake

Must do ahead

Serves: 12
Preparing: 25 min
Baking: 25 min
Chilling: overnight

1 large orange chiffon OR pound
  cake (mix is fine)
1 cup *(237 ml)* **soft margarine**
1 cup *(237 ml)* **sugar**
4 eggs
1 scant tsp *(5 ml)* **vanilla**

1 can, 8 oz *(227 g)* **crushed**
  pineapple
1 can, 3½ oz *(99 g)* **Angel Flake**
  coconut
½ cup *(118 ml)* **nuts, chopped**

Bake cake and cut into three layers. Blend margarine with sugar. Add eggs, one at a time beating 5 minutes after each addition. Add vanilla. Fold in pineapple, coconut and nuts. Put this between layers and on sides of cake. Refrigerate overnight. Cut with sharp knife to keep from tearing.

Italian Cream Cake

Serves: 16
Preparing: 45 min
Baking: 25 min

½ cup *(118 ml)* butter
½ cup *(118 ml)* vegetable
shortening
2 cups *(474 ml)* sugar
5 egg yolks
2 cups *(474 ml)* flour, sifted

1 tsp *(5 ml)* soda
1 cup *(237 ml)* buttermilk
1 tsp *(5 ml)* vanilla
1 can, 3½ oz *(99 g)* coconut
1 cup nuts, chopped
5 egg whites, beaten

Cream margarine, shortening and sugar well. Add egg yolks one at a time. Combine flour and soda. Add flour and soda to creamed mixture alternately with buttermilk. Stir in vanilla. Add coconut and nuts. Fold in egg whites. Pour in three 8 or 9 inch (20.32 or 22.86 cm) greased and floured cake pans. Bake at 350° (177° C) for 25 minutes or until cake is done. Frost with Cream Cheese Frosting.

CREAM CHEESE FROSTING

1 pkg, 8 oz *(227 g)* cream cheese
¼ cup *(59 ml)* butter OR margarine
1 lb *(454 g)* powdered sugar

1 tsp *(5 ml)* vanilla
pecans, chopped, OR coconut

Beat cream cheese and butter until smooth and fluffy. Add powdered sugar and vanilla until consistency is right for spreading. Spread on cool cake and sprinkle top with pecans or coconut.

Hermit Cake

Can do ahead

Yield: 1 tube cake
Preparing: 15-20 min
Baking: 2½-3 hrs

2 cups *(474 ml)* margarine
1¼ lb *(567 g)* brown sugar
6 eggs
6 cups *(1.42 l)* flour
2 tsp *(10 ml)* baking powder
1 tsp *(5 ml)* cinnamon

3 pkgs, 8 oz *(227 g)* dates,
chopped
½ lb *(227 g)* English walnuts,
chopped
2 tsp *(10 ml)* vanilla
1 tsp *(5 ml)* lemon juice

Cream margarine; add sugar gradually. Add eggs one at a time. Mix thoroughly. Gradually add 5 cups (1.18 l) flour, baking powder and cinnamon. Mix dates with reserved cup of flour and add to mixture. Then add nuts, vanilla and lemon juice. Bake in a tube pan lined with waxed paper for 2½ to 3 hours at 275° (135° C). This will keep a long time.

Easter Ice Box Cake

Must do ahead
Do not freeze

Serves: 24
Preparing: 15 min per day
Cooking: 3 min
Chilling: 3 days

3 pkgs, 3 oz *(85 g)* **jello (1 lemon, 1 lime, 1 strawberry OR raspberry)**
1½ cups *(355 ml)* **sugar**
3 cups *(710 ml)* **boiling water**
3 lemons, juice and rind

3 cans, 13 oz *(385 ml)* **evaporated milk, chilled**
2 dozen lady fingers
½ pt *(237 ml)* **whipping cream**
1 Tb *(15 ml)* **sugar**

Dissolve ½ cup (118 ml) sugar, 1 pkg jello and juice and rind of 1 lemon in 1 cup (237 ml) boiling water. Whip 1 can chilled milk and mix well. Arrange lady finger halves around large spring-form pan or two small pans. Pour jello mixture into pan. Refrigerate. The next day, prepare the next flavor of jello the same way. The third day, the third flavor. Whip the heavy cream with 1 Tb (15 ml) sugar to go over it. This is a very light, tasty dessert, and is very pretty in the spring with the three pastel colors.

Jam Cake

Must do ahead

Serves: 12-14
Preparing: 30 min
Baking: 30-60 min

1½ cups *(355 ml)* **sugar**
½ cup *(118 ml)* **Crisco**
3 eggs
1 tsp *(5 ml)* **allspice**
2 tsp *(10 ml)* **cinnamon**
1 tsp *(5 ml)* **ground cloves**
1 tsp *(5 ml)* **nutmeg**
1½ tsp *(7.5 ml)* **cocoa**
½ tsp *(2.5 ml)* **salt**
2½ cups *(592 ml)* **self-rising flour**

1¼ tsp *(6.25 ml)* **soda**
1½ cups *(355 ml)* **buttermilk**
1 tsp *(5 ml)* **vanilla**
1 cup *(237 ml)* **blackberry OR raspberry jam**
½ cup *(118 ml)* **cherry preserves**
½ cup *(118 ml)* **applesauce**
1 cup *(237 ml)* **raisins**
1 cup *(237 ml)* **pecans, chopped**

Cream sugar and Crisco. Add eggs, one at a time. Mix well. Measure spices and salt and add to the flour; set aside. Put soda in the buttermilk and add alternately with the flour mixture to the egg mixture, mixing well. Add vanilla. Slowly add the preserves, applesauce, raisins and nuts. Blend well. Pour into 3 greased 9-inch (22.86 cm) layer pans or a Bundt pan. Bake at 350° (177° C) for 30 minutes if using layer pans, and at least 1 hour if using a Bundt pan. Frost with icing for Jam Cake (p. 354).

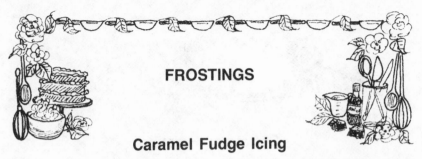

FROSTINGS

Caramel Fudge Icing

Do after cake has cooled

Yield: Covers a 2 layer cake
Preparing: 10 min
Cooking: 30 min

2 cups *(474 ml)* **brown sugar**
1 cup *(237 ml)* **granulated sugar**
1 cup *(237 ml)* **sour cream**

1 Tb *(15 ml)* **butter**
1 tsp *(5 ml)* **vanilla**

Combine sugars and sour cream. Cook, stirring constantly, to 238° (114° C) or until a small amount forms a soft ball when dropped into cold water. Add butter and vanilla and cool to lukewarm without stirring. Beat until thick enough to spread. If it becomes too thick while spreading, beat in a few drops of hot water.

Butter Frosting
Good stand-by-frosting with variations

Make after cake has cooled

Yield: Covers a 2 layer cake
Preparing: 20 min

½ cup *(118 ml)* **butter**
3 cups *(710 ml)* **confectioner's sugar, sifted**

4 Tb *(60 ml)* **cream or evaporated milk**
1 tsp *(5 ml)* **vanilla**

Cream butter; add remaining ingredients and cream until well-blended and fluffy.

LEMON

Add ½ tsp (2.5 ml) grated lemon rind and use lemon juice instead of vanilla and ½ of the cream.

MOCHA

Add 3 Tb (45 ml) cocoa and use cold strong coffee instead of cream.

ORANGE

Add 1 Tb (15 ml) grated orange rind and use orange juice instead of cream.

PINEAPPLE

Use ⅓ cup (79 ml) crushed pineapple with juice instead of cream.

Christmas Frosting
An unusual combination

Yield: frosts one 9″
(22.86 cm) square cake

6 egg yolks
1 cup *(237 ml)* **sugar**
¼ cup *(59 ml)* **margarine**
¼ tsp *(1.25 ml)* **salt**
¼ cup *(59 ml)* **brandy OR fruit juice**

½ cup *(118 ml)* **pecans, chopped**
½ cup *(118 ml)* **fresh coconut,**
grated
½ cup *(118 ml)* **raisins**
Maraschino cherries for garnish

Mix together sugar, melted margarine, salt and egg yolks. Stir in brandy slowly, stirring constantly. Cook over medium heat, stirring constantly until thick. Add pecans, coconut, raisins. Garnish with maraschino cherries if desired. Good with old-fashioned applesauce cake.

Icing For Jam Cake

1 tsp *(5 ml)* **vanilla**
1 box light brown sugar
½ cup *(118 ml)* **margarine**

½ cup *(118 ml)* **heavy cream**
½ tsp *(2.5 ml)* **salt**
½ box confectioner's sugar, sifted

Bring the first 5 ingredients to a boil and count rapidly to 100. Remove from heat and blend in confectioner's sugar. Spread on cool cake. You might have to double recipe if making 3 layers.

Coconut Cream Frosting
Must refrigerate

Can do ahead

Yield: Covers 2 layer cake
Preparing: 20 min

1 cup *(237 ml)* **heavy cream**
½ tsp *(2.5 ml)* **vanilla**
3 Tb *(45 ml)* **confectioner's sugar,**
sifted

1 cup *(237 ml)* **grated coconut,**
fresh

Whip cream until stiff. Add vanilla and fold in sugar. Spread between layers and over top of cake. Sprinkle with coconut.

Peppermint Frosting
Different

Make after cake has cooled

Yield: Covers a 2-layer cake
Preparing: 10 min
Cooking: 15 min

¼ cup *(59 ml)* **peppermint stick candy, crushed**
½ cup *(118 ml)* **milk**

1 lb *(454 g)* **confectioner's sugar, sifted**

Heat candy and milk over hot water until candy is melted. Add enough sugar to make frosting thick enough to spread.

Rector's Mocha Butter Cream Icing

⅓ cup *(79 ml)* **butter**
1 box **powdered sugar**
4 Tb *(60 ml)* **strong coffee**
few grains salt

¼ tsp *(1.25 ml)* **vanilla**
1 sq **chocolate, melted**
cream

Cream butter first and gradually work in sugar. Add coffee, vanilla and salt. Beat in melted chocolate and smooth to proper consistency with cream.

Never-Fail Seven Minute Frosting

2 **egg whites**
1 cup *(237 ml)* **sugar**
1 tsp *(5 ml)* **vinegar**

4 Tb *(60 ml)* **water**
1 tsp *(5 ml)* **vanilla**

Put in double boiler; beat with electric mixer over range. Beat until it fluffs or stands in a peak. Add vanilla. Frost cake and garnish with German chocolate curls.

Banana Frosting

Make after cake has cooled

Yield: Covers a 2-layer cake
Preparing: 20 min

½ cup *(118 ml)* **banana, mashed**
½ tsp *(2.5 ml)* **lemon juice**
¼ cup *(59 ml)* **butter**

1 lb *(454 g)* **confectioner's sugar, sifted**

Mix banana and lemon juice together. Cream butter with 1 cup (237 ml) sugar, then add banana and enough sugar to make spreadable.

Cooked Chocolate Icing

Can do ahead

Yield: Covers 2-layer cake
Preparing: 15 min
Cooking: 5 min

1½ **cups** *(355 ml)* **sugar**
½ **cup** *(118 ml)* **milk**
1 **Tb** *(15 ml)* **corn syrup**
2 **squares chocolate**

2 **Tb** *(30 ml)* **vegetable shortening**
2 **Tb** *(30 ml)* **butter**
1 **tsp** *(5 ml)* **vanilla**

Put all ingredients in a saucepan; let come to a boil and boil for one minute. Remove from heat and stir for a few minutes. Double for a 3-layer cake.

Chocolate Whipped Cream Frosting
Quick — Easy — Cool Dessert

Must do ahead

Preparing: 10 min
Chilling: 2-3 hrs

1 **cup** *(237 ml)* **whipping cream**
6 **Tb** *(90 ml)* **sugar**

5 **Tb** *(75 ml)* **cocoa**
pinch salt

Combine the four ingredients in a bowl; chill 2-3 hours, then whip until stiff. Spread on angel food cake.

Boiled Frosting

Yield: Covers 2-layer cake
Preparing: 10 min
Cooking: 5 min

2 **cups** *(474 ml)* **sugar**
¼ **cup** *(59 ml)* **white corn syrup**
6 **Tb** *(90 ml)* **water**

2 **egg whites**
1 **tsp** *(5 ml)* **vanilla**

Cook syrup, sugar and water until soft ball forms — 240° (115° C). Turn off heat and let stand over warm burner while quickly beating egg whites. Pour syrup slowly over beaten egg whites, beating with a spoon. Add vanilla and beat until almost cold. Can add melted chocolate while beating.

Cookies and Candies

Cookies and Candies

Tips For Cookies

When making rich butter cookies, mix dry ingredients thoroughly with creamed mixture, or dough will be crumbly.

Baking sheets with little or no sides will let your cookies bake evenly and quickly. The sheets should be shiny, and clear the sides of the oven at least two inches (5.08 cm) for best circulation of heat and even baking.

Cool baking sheets before placing unbaked cookies on them, or the heat will melt the shortening in the dough, thereby causing cookies to spread too much during baking.

If crisp cookies soften in storage, place them in a 300° (149° C) oven about five minutes.

Keep soft cookies soft by placing a slice of bread in the container.

Coat raisins, dates, etc. with some flour before adding to a batter to prevent them from settling to the bottom.

Chill dough 10 minutes in refrigerator to reduce the amount of flour needed on the board when rolling out. Excess flour results in a tough product.

Save time chopping raisins and marshmallows by using scissors.

Tiger Cookies

Can do ahead

Yield: 10 doz
Preparing: 10 min
Cooking: 12-15 min per sheet

¾ cup *(177 ml)* **maple syrup**
¾ cup *(177 ml)* **dark brown sugar**
4 eggs
¾ cup *(177 ml)* oil
1 tsp *(5 ml)* vanilla

1 cup *(237 ml)* **powdered skim milk, unprepared**
2¾ cups *(650 ml)* **quick rolled oats**
1 cup *(237 ml)* **wheat germ**
1 cup *(237 ml)* **chopped walnuts**
1 cup *(237 ml)* **raisins**

Cream first five ingredients. Add next five ingredients. Mix and drop by teaspoonfuls on cookie sheets. Bake at 350° (177° C) 12-15 minutes. These keep well in refrigerator.

Welsh Cookies

Can do ahead
Can freeze

Yield: 9-11 doz
Preparing: 8 min
Baking: 10-12 min

4 cups *(946 ml)* flour
2 cups *(474 ml)* sugar
1 Tb *(15 ml)* baking powder
1 tsp *(5 ml)* nutmeg
1 tsp *(5 ml)* salt

1 cup *(237 ml)* Crisco
2 cups *(474 ml)* currants
3 eggs
milk

Break eggs into a 1 cup (237 ml) measurer and fill to the top with milk. Combine with other ingredients and roll thin. Cut with drinking glass or cookie cutter. Bake on griddle like pancakes until lightly browned or in oven at 350° (177° C). Store in tins. This recipe may be halved.

Pom-Poms

Yield: 3 doz
Preparing: 10-15 min
Baking: 18 min

1 cup *(237 ml)* flour
½ tsp *(2.5 ml)* baking powder
½ cup *(118 ml)* oil
3 Tb *(45 ml)* cherry jello
1 pkg, 3¾ oz *(106 g)* vanilla
 instant pudding mix

2 eggs, separated
3 Tb *(45 ml)* milk
½ tsp *(2.5 ml)* almond flavoring
¾ cup *(177 ml)* nuts, chopped
1 pkg, 7 oz *(198 g)* flaked coconut
1 tsp *(5 ml)* water

Combine all ingredients except nuts, coconut, egg whites and water. Blend well with mixer. Add nuts and ⅓ cup (158 ml) coconut. Shape into balls the size of a large marble. Beat egg whites with water. Roll each ball in egg whites, then in remaining coconut. Place on cookie sheet and flatten slightly. Bake at 350° (177° C) for 15 to 18 minutes.

Peanut Butter Bars

Can do ahead
Can freeze

Yield: 32 bars
Preparing: 10 min

1 cup *(237 ml)* peanut butter
 (crunchy is best)
1 cup *(237 ml)* melted margarine
1½ cups *(355 ml)* cornflake OR
 graham cracker crumbs

1 tsp *(5 ml)* vanilla
¾ lb *(340 g)* confectioner's sugar

Combine all ingredients and pat in a greased 1½ quart (1.42 l) oblong pyrex dish. Chill and cut in bars.

Oatmeal Carmelitas
Very Rich

Must do ahead

Yield: 24 bars
Preparing: 30-40 min
Baking: 30 min
Chilling: 1-2 hrs

1 cup *(237 ml)* **flour**
1 cup *(237 ml)* **quick-cooking rolled oats**
¾ cup *(177 ml)* **brown sugar, firmly packed**
½ tsp *(2.5 ml)* **soda**
¼ tsp *(1.25 ml)* **salt**

¾ cup *(177 ml)* **butter, melted**
1 pkg, 6 oz *(170 g)* **semi-sweet chocolate bits**
½ cup *(118 ml)* **pecans, chopped**
¾ cup *(177 ml)* **caramel ice cream topping OR butterscotch**
3 Tb *(45 ml)* **flour**

Preheat oven to 350° (177° C). Combine flour, oats, sugar, soda, salt, butter. Blend well at low speed to form crumbs. Press half of crumbs into bottom of 11 x 7 inch (27.94 x 17.78 cm) pan. Bake at 350° (177° C) for 10 minutes. Remove from oven. Sprinkle with chocolate pieces and pecans. Blend caramel topping and flour, pour over chocolate and pecans to cover. Sprinkle with remaining crumb mixture. Bake 15 to 20 minutes or until golden brown. Chill 1 to 2 hours. Cut into bars.

Sharon's Butterscotch Oaties

Can do ahead
Can freeze

Yield: 5-6 doz
Preparing: 20 min
Baking: 10 min

1 pkg, 6 oz *(170 g)* **butterscotch morsels**
¾ cup *(177 ml)* **butter**
2 Tb *(30 ml)* **boiling water**
1 tsp *(5 ml)* **baking soda**

2 cups *(474 ml)* **rolled oats**
1 cup *(237 ml)* **flour, sifted**
¾ cup *(177 ml)* **sugar**
dash salt

Preheat oven to 350° (177° C). Combine morsels and butter. Melt in top of double boiler. Remove from heat. Mix boiling water with baking soda and add to butterscotch mixture. Gradually blend in remaining ingredients. Drop by slightly rounded teaspoonfuls. Bake at 350° (177° C) about 10 minutes. Remove from sheet while still warm to avoid breaking.

Lemon Tea "Cakes"

Yield: 4 doz
Preparing: 30 min
Baking: 12-14 min

1½ tsp *(7.5 ml)* **vinegar**
½ cup *(118 ml)* **milk**
½ cup *(118 ml)* **butter OR**
  margarine
¾ cup *(177 ml)* **sugar**
1 **egg**

1 tsp *(5 ml)* **lemon peel, shredded**
1¾ cups *(414 ml)* **all-purpose**
  flour, sifted
1 tsp *(5 ml)* **baking powder**
¼ tsp *(1.25 ml)* **soda**
¼ tsp *(1.25 ml)* **salt**

Stir vinegar into milk. Cream butter and ¾ cup sugar till fluffy. Add egg and peel; beat well. Sift together dry ingredients; add to creamed mixture alternately with the milk, beating smooth after each addition. Drop from teaspoon, 2 inches apart, on ungreased cookie sheet. Bake in moderate oven 350° (177° C) 12 to 14 minutes or till done. Remove at once from pan and immediately brush tops with lemon glaze; cool.

LEMON GLAZE

Mix ¾ cup *(177 ml)* **sugar and**   ¼ cup *(59 ml)* **lemon juice**

Molasses Cookies

Can do ahead
Can freeze

Yield: 4 doz
Preparing: 15 min
Chilling: 15 min
Baking: 8-10 min per sheet

¾ cup *(177 ml)* **shortening**
1 cup *(237 ml)* **sugar**
¼ cup *(59 ml)* **molasses**
1 **egg, beaten**
2 cups *(474 ml)* **flour**

2 tsp *(10 ml)* **baking soda**
½ tsp *(2.5 ml)* **salt**
½ tsp *(2.5 ml)* **cloves**
1 tsp *(5 ml)* **cinnamon**
½ tsp *(2.5 ml)* **ginger**

Melt shortening in saucepan and cool. Add sugar, molasses and egg and beat well. Sift dry ingredients together and add to first mixture; chill. Form into small balls, roll in granulated sugar, place on greased cookie sheets and bake at 350° (177° C) for 8-10 minutes.

Lemon Squares

Can do ahead

CRUST

1 cup *(237 ml)* **butter OR margarine**

½ cup *(118 ml)* **powdered sugar**
2 cups *(474 ml)* **flour**

Cream butter and sugar; add flour. Press into 9 x 13 inch (22.86 x 33.02 cm) pan. Bake at 350° (177° C) 20 minutes.

TOPPING

2 cups *(474 ml)* **sugar**
4 Tb *(60 ml)* **flour**
½ tsp *(2.5 ml)* **baking powder**
4 eggs, slightly beaten

6 Tb *(90 ml)* **fresh lemon juice**
½ tsp *(2.5 ml)* **lemon rind**
powdered sugar

Sift sugar, flour and baking powder. Add eggs, lemon juice and rind. Pour over baked crust; bake at 350° (177° C) 25 minutes or until lightly browned. Sprinkle with powdered sugar. Cut into squares.

Crescent Cookies

Can do ahead
Can freeze

1 cup *(237 ml)* **butter**
½ cup *(118 ml)* **powdered sugar**
1 Tb *(15 ml)* **water**
2 cups *(474 ml)* **flour**

2 tsp *(10 ml)* **vanilla**
1 cup *(237 ml)* **slivered almonds**
powdered sugar

Cream butter; add all but nuts and mix thoroughly; stir in nuts. Roll mixture in hand and form u-shapes for each cookie. Place on ungreased cookie sheet. Bake at 300° (149° C) for 15 minutes or until light brown. While still warm, but not hot, roll each cookie in powdered sugar.

VARIATION: For Swedish Christmas Cookies, omit water and substitute pecans for almonds; roll in walnut-size ball, mash down and top with green or red cherries. Bake as above and roll in sugar.

Prunies

Yield: 3 doz
Preparing: 10 min
Baking: 15-18 min

2 cups *(474 ml)* flour
1 tsp *(5 ml)* salt
½ tsp *(2.5 ml)* soda
½ cup *(118 ml)* sugar
½ cup *(118 ml)* brown sugar,
    firmly packed

¾ cup *(177 ml)* shortening
1 egg
1 tsp *(5 ml)* vanilla
1 cup *(237 ml)* cooked prunes,
    drained and chopped
grated coconut

Combine all ingredients except prunes and coconut. Blend well; add prunes. Drop by teaspoonfuls onto greased cookie sheets; sprinkle coconut on top. Bake at 350° (177° C) for 15 to 18 minutes. Cool on wire rack.

Coconut Balls
A snap to make and delicious

Can do ahead
Can freeze

Yield: 4 doz
Preparing: 1 hr
Cooking: 10 min

½ cup *(118 ml)* butter, melted
2 cups *(474 ml)* sugar
1 pkg, 8 oz *(227 g)* chopped dates
1 egg

1 tsp *(5 ml)* vanilla
2 cups *(474 ml)* rice crispies
1 cup *(237 ml)* pecans, chopped
1 can, 7 oz *(198 g)* coconut

Add sugar to melted butter and stir until mixture comes to a boil. Stir in dates. Add a little of the hot mixture to egg, then stir into mixture and let cook 10 minutes on low heat, stirring constantly. Let cool. Add vanilla, rice crispies and pecans. Roll into small balls and roll balls in coconut.

Kefflings
Norwegian Almond Cookies
Serve with sherbet at end of heavy meal

Can do ahead

Yield: depends on shape
Preparing: 30 min
Baking: Depends on shape

C
O
O
K
I
E
S

1 OR 2 vanilla beans, dry if
  possible
1 lb *(454 g)* almonds, unblanched
1¾ cups *(414 ml)* butter

¾ cup *(177 ml)* sugar
1 tsp *(5 ml)* vanilla
4 cups *(946 ml)* flour
powdered sugar

Put nuts and vanilla beans through food chopper until well ground. Cream butter and sugar and add vanilla. Combine all ingredients, mixing thoroughly and shape as desired (crescents, etc). Bake at 360-370° (182-188° C) until delicately browned. When cool, roll in powdered sugar.

Ischler Tortchen

Preparing: 1 hr
Chilling: 1 hr
Baking: 10-15 min

1¼ cups *(296 ml)* unsalted butter
⅔ cup *(158 ml)* sugar
2 cups *(474 ml)* sifted all purpose
  flour

1¾ cups *(414 ml)* almonds,
  ground in blender
⅛ tsp *(.6 ml)* cinnamon
red raspberry jam
confectioner's sugar

Cream butter and sugar well. Beat in flour ½ cup (118 ml) at a time. Add almonds and cinnamon and beat until mixture becomes slightly stiff. Shape into ball and wrap in wax paper and refrigerate for 1 hour. Preheat oven to 325° (163° C).

Roll dough on lightly floured board and roll to ⅛ inch (.32 cm) thick. Use a cookie cutter and cut as many circles as possible. Re-ball dough and roll out again and cut more circles. Repeat until all dough is cut. Cut center out of half of the circles with a ¼ inch (.64 cm) cookie cutter (or center of a doughnut cutter). Place on ungreased cookie sheet and bake in center of oven for 10-15 minutes or until brown.

Remove with a spatula and cool. Spread whole circles with jam and top with circles with holes. Put a little jam in center hole. Sprinkle with confectioner's sugar and serve.

Butter Cookie Crispies

Can do ahead
Can freeze

Yield: 60
Preparing: 1 hr
Baking: 10-12 min

½ cup *(118 ml)* **butter**
¾ cup *(177 ml)* **sugar**
1 **egg**
1 tsp *(5 ml)* **vanilla**

1½ cups *(355 ml)* **flour, sifted**
¼ tsp *(1.25 ml)* **baking powder**
½ tsp *(2.5 ml)* **salt**

Melt butter in 2-quart (1.9 l) pan. Remove from heat and cool slightly. Add sugar, egg, and vanilla and beat until smooth. Sift flour with baking powder and salt over mixture and blend thoroughly. Place pan with dough in refrigerator 30 minutes. Divide chilled dough in half and shape each half into roll, 1½ inches in diameter. Wrap in wax paper and freeze. Slice ¼ inch thick and place on greased cookie sheet. Decorate with sprinkles, raisins, nuts, etc. if desired. Bake 10 to 12 minutes at 350° (177° C).

Ice Box Cookies
This recipe will be requested often!

Can do ahead

Yield: 4-6 doz
Preparing: 30 min
Chilling: 2 hrs

graham crackers
1 cup *(237 ml)* **butter OR**
  margarine
1 cup *(237 ml)* **sugar**
1 **egg**

½ cup *(118 ml)* **milk**
1 cup *(237 ml)* **nuts**
1 cup *(237 ml)* **coconut**
1 cup *(237 ml)* **graham cracker**
  crumbs

Line a 9 x 13 inch (22.86 x 33.02 cm) pan with graham crackers. Melt butter. Beat egg, milk and sugar together. Mix with butter. Bring to a boil. Remove from heat and add nuts, coconut, and cracker crumbs. Pour over layer of graham crackers. Top with graham crackers and ice with the following:

6 Tb *(90 ml)* **butter**
2 cups *(474 ml)* **confectioner's**
  sugar

1 Tb *(15 ml)* **milk**
1 tsp *(5 ml)* **vanilla**

Combine and beat until smooth. Ice cookies. Chill about 2 hours. Cut into bars.

Coffee Thins

Can do ahead
Can freeze

Yield: 6 doz
Preparing: 10 min
Chilling: approx 1 hr
Baking: 10 min per pan

2 cups *(474 ml)* **flour**
3 Tb *(45 ml)* **instant coffee**
½ tsp *(2.5 ml)* **baking soda**
½ tsp *(2.5 ml)* **baking powder**
½ tsp *(2.5 ml)* **salt**
⅓cup *(79 ml)* **shortening**

⅓ cup *(79 ml)* **butter**
¾ cup *(177 ml)* **brown sugar**
⅓ cup *(79 ml)* **sugar**
1 egg, beaten
1 Tb *(15 ml)* **rum extract**
pecan halves

Sift first five ingredients. Cream shortening, butter and sugars. Add egg and rum extract; beat thoroughly. Stir in dry ingredients. Shape in rolls 2-inches (5.08 cm) in diameter. Wrap in wax paper and chill until firm. Slice thin and put pecans on top. Bake at 400° (204° C) 8-10 minutes.

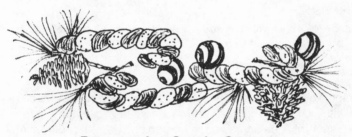

Peppermint Candy Canes
A delightful treat for children

Can do ahead
Can freeze

Yield: 2 doz
Preparing: 30 min
Baking: 9 min per tray

1 cup *(237 ml)* **Crisco**
1 cup *(237 ml)* **sifted
  confectioner's sugar**
1½ tsp *(7.5 ml)* **almond flavoring**
1 tsp *(5 ml)* **vanilla**
1 egg

2½ cups *(592 ml)* **sifted flour**
1 tsp *(5 ml)* **salt**
½ tsp *(2.5 ml)* **red food coloring**
½ cup *(118 ml)* **candy canes,
  crushed**
½ cup *(118 ml)* **sugar**

Mix together Crisco, confectioner's sugar, almond flavoring, vanilla and egg. Blend flour and salt and mix with above. Divide dough in half. Add red food coloring to half. Roll 1 teaspoon (5 ml) of white dough and 1 teaspoon (5 ml) of red dough into 4-inch (10.16 cm) strips and twist together. Place on cookie sheet and curve cane handle. Bake 9 minutes at 375° (191° C). Sprinkle warm cookies with crushed candy canes mixed with sugar.

Peppermint Rounds

Good to do in heart shapes for Valentines

Can do ahead
Can freeze

Yield: 4 doz
Preparing: 20 min
Baking: 8 min

1 cup *(237 ml)* butter OR
  margarine, softened
½ cup *(118 ml)* sugar
1 egg, beaten
1 tsp *(5 ml)* vanilla

2½ cups *(592 ml)* flour, sifted
½ tsp *(2.5 ml)* salt
1 cup *(237 ml)* rolled oats
⅓ cup *(79 ml)* peppermint candy,
  crushed

Preheat oven to 350° (177° C). Cream butter; add sugar gradually. Blend in egg and vanilla. Sift flour and salt and add to creamed mixture gradually. Stir in oats and candy; chill. Roll out to ⅛ inch (.32 cm) thickness on board lightly dusted with confectioner's sugar and cut with floured cutter. Place on greased, foil-covered cookie sheets. Bake 8 to 10 minutes, then cool.

FROSTING

4 cups *(946 ml)* powdered sugar
4-8 Tb *(60-120 ml)* light cream
dash of salt

1 tsp *(5 ml)* peppermint extract
red food coloring

Sift sugar and mix with enough cream to make spreadable. Add salt and extract. Take out a small portion and color with red food coloring and thin with water. When cookies have cooled, frost with white frosting. Make several lines across each frosted cookie with red frosting before the white frosting sets. Draw a toothpick lightly back and forth across lines to give a swirled look.

Eleanor's Herdesand
(German Sand Cookie)

Can do ahead

Yield: approx 60
Preparing: 20 min
Baking: 15-20 min

1¼ cups *(296 ml)* butter, melted
  and lightly browned
1¼ cups *(296 ml)* sugar

3 cups *(710 ml)* flour, sifted before
  measuring
2 tsp *(10 ml)* baking powder

Mix all ingredients thoroughly. Cool slightly. Form into small balls (size of walnut). Bake at 350° (177° C) for 15 to 20 minutes, or until slightly brown.

Apricot Chews

½ cup *(118 ml)* **dried apricots,**
finely chopped
½ cup *(118 ml)* **raisins**
⅓ cup *(79 ml)* **water**
1 cup *(237 ml)* **flour**
1 tsp *(5 ml)* **baking powder**
¼ tsp *(1.25 ml)* **soda**

1 cup *(237 ml)* **sugar**
2 **eggs**
1 Tb *(15 ml)* **lemon juice**
½ cup *(118 ml)* **crushed pineapple,**
drained
½ cup *(118 ml)* **nuts, chopped**
powdered sugar OR frosting

Cook apricots and raisins in water over low heat until water is absorbed. Cool slightly and add remaining ingredients except powdered sugar or frosting. Blend well and spread in a greased 9 inch (22.86 cm) square pan. Bake at 350° (177° C) for 35 to 40 minutes. Cut into bars while warm and sprinkle with powdered sugar or spread with frosting.

FROSTING

1 cup *(237 ml)* **powdered sugar**
1 Tb *(15 ml)* **butter, softened**

¼ cup *(59 ml)* **apricot preserves**

Blend well and mix until smooth. Spread on bars.

Dream Bars
Quick, easy and melt in your mouth

Can do ahead
Can freeze

CRUMB LAYER

½ cup *(118 ml)* **butter**
½ cup *(118 ml)* **brown sugar**

1 cup *(237 ml)* **flour**

Combine butter, sugar, and flour until the texture of coarse meal. Pat into a buttered 9 x 9 inch (22.86 x 22.86 cm) pan. Bake approximately 10 minutes at 350° (177° C) or until slightly browned.

BAR MIXTURE

1 cup *(237 ml)* **brown sugar**
1 tsp *(5 ml)* **vanilla**
½ tsp *(2.5 ml)* **baking powder**
1 cup *(237 ml)* **coconut**

2 Tb *(30 ml)* **flour**
2 **eggs**
¼ tsp *(1.25 ml)* **salt**
½-1 cup *(118 ml-237 ml)* **nuts,**
chopped

Mix all ingredients together. Pour over baked crumb layer. Bake again at 350° (177° C) for 20 to 25 minutes or until brown. Cool. Cut into bars.

Dark Secrets

Super Rich

Can do ahead
Can freeze

Yield: 12-16 small bars
Preparing: 10 min
Baking: 20 min

1 cup *(237 ml)* sugar
2 Tb *(30 ml)* butter, melted
3 eggs, unbeaten
1 cup *(237 ml)* pecans, chopped
1 cup *(237 ml)* dates, chopped

1 can, 3½ oz *(99 g)* coconut
5 Tb *(75 ml)* flour
1 tsp *(5 ml)* baking powder
1 pkg, 6 oz *(170 g)* chocolate chips

Combine all ingredients. Spread in a 9 x 9 inch (22.86 x 22.86 cm) pan and bake at 350° (177° C) for approximately 20 minutes. If an 8 x 8 inch (20.32 x 20.32 cm) pan is used, bake for 30 minutes.

Chocolate Date Bars

Different and good

Can do ahead

Yield: 24 bars
Preparing: 20 min
Baking: 25 min

1 pkg, 8 oz *(227 g)* chopped dates
¾ cup *(177 ml)* brown sugar
½ cup *(118 ml)* water
½ cup *(118 ml)* butter
1 pkg, 6 oz *(170 g)* chocolate chips
2 eggs, unbeaten
1¼ cups *(296 ml)* flour, sifted

¾ tsp *(3.7 ml)* soda
½ tsp *(2.5 ml)* salt
⅓ cup *(79 ml)* orange juice
¼ cup *(59 ml)* milk
1 cup *(237 ml)* nuts, coarsely
   chopped

By hand, mix dates, sugar, water, and butter in a large saucepan. Cook 5 minutes over low heat stirring until dates are soft. Remove from heat. Stir in chocolate. Beat in eggs. Sift flour, soda, salt and add to date mixture alternately with orange juice, then milk. Stir in nuts. Turn into well-greased 10 x 15 inch (25.4 x 38.10 cm) pan. Bake at 350° (177° C) for 25 minutes or until done. Cool 5 minutes and glaze. If desired, batter can be divided between a 9 inch (22.86 cm) pan and an 8 inch (20.32) square pan.

ORANGE GLAZE

2 Tb *(30 ml)* soft butter
1¼ cups *(296 ml)* powdered
   sugar
dash salt

2 Tb *(30 ml)* lemon juice
2 Tb *(30 ml)* orange juice
2 tsp *(10 ml)* orange rind

With an electric mixer, combine butter, sugar, salt, lemon juice and orange juice. Stir in orange rind. Mix well and spread over bars.

Devil's Food Drop Cookies

Yield: 4½ doz
Preparing: 45 min
Baking: 10 min

½ cup *(118 ml)* butter OR margarine
1 cup *(237 ml)* brown sugar
1 egg
1 tsp *(5 ml)* vanilla
2 squares, 1 oz *(28 g)*
unsweetened chocolate, melted
and cooled

2 cups *(474 ml)* all-purpose flour,
sifted
½ tsp *(2.5 ml)* soda
¼ tsp *(1.25 ml)* salt
¾ cup *(177 ml)* dairy sour cream
½ cup *(118 ml)* walnuts OR pecans,
chopped

Cream butter and sugar till fluffy; beat in egg and vanilla. Stir in chocolate. Sift together dry ingredients; add to chocolate mixture alternately with sour cream. Mix well; stir in nuts. Drop from teaspoon, 2 inches apart on greased cookie sheet. Bake in 350° (177° C) oven for 10 minutes or until done. Remove from sheet, cool. Frost with Mocha Frosting.

MOCHA FROSTING

Cream ¼ cup (59 ml) soft butter or margarine, 2 Tb (30 ml) cocoa, 2 tsp (10 ml) instant coffee, dash salt; slowly cream in 1 cup (237 ml) confectioner's sugar. Add 2 cups (474 ml) confectioner's sugar, 3 Tbs milk (45 ml), 1½ tsp (7.5 ml) vanilla; beat smooth.

Fudge Brownies

Yield: 16
Preparing: 10 min
Baking: 30 min

½ cup *(118 ml)* sifted flour
⅛ tsp *(.6 ml)* baking powder
⅛ tsp *(.6 ml)* salt
½ cup *(118 ml)* butter OR
margarine, softened
1 cup *(237 ml)* sugar

2 eggs
2 squares unsweetened
chocolate, melted
½ tsp *(2.5 ml)* vanilla
1 cup *(237 ml)* nuts, chopped

Preheat oven to 325° (163° C). Sift flour, baking powder and salt together. In another bowl, beat at medium speed the butter, sugar and eggs until light and fluffy. Beat in chocolate and vanilla. At low speed, blend in flour mixture; fold in nuts. Spread in a greased 8 inch (20.32 cm) square pan. Bake 30 minutes. Cool for 10 minutes then cut into squares. Allow to cool in the pan completely before removing.

CANDIES

Candy Temperature Chart

Stage	Standard Degrees F	Metric Degrees C	Consistency
Thread	230-234	110-112	spins a thread when dropped from spoon
Soft Ball	234-240	112-115	forms a soft ball when dropped in cold water
Firm Ball	244-248	118-120	forms a firm ball when dropped in cold water
Hard Ball	250-265	121-130	forms a ball hard enough to hold its shape when dropped in cold water
Soft Crack	270-290	132-143	separates into threads in cold water
Hard Crack	300-310	149-154	separates into threads that are hard and brittle in cold water
Clear Liquid	320	160	sugar liquifies
Brown Liquid	338	170	liquid becomes brown

Blanching Almonds

Place shelled almonds in saucepan, cover with cold water and bring to a boil. Remove from the heat, drain and run cold water over them. Drain again and remove the outer skin.

To Stuff Prunes or Figs

Steam for 15 minutes until soft and plump. Remove pits from prunes and cut slits in the sides of the figs. Stuff with the filling of your choice.

Stuffing Dates

Remove stones and stuff with fondant, nut meats, marshmallows, coconut, seedless raisins or preserved ginger and cherries chopped together. After stuffing, close dates and brush with beaten egg white. Roll in colored sugar, colored coconut or chopped nuts.

How to Color Coconut

Sprinkle shredded coconut on waxed paper, add food coloring and rub together until the color is even. Dry and store in jars.

When Dipping Chocolates:

Dip only one piece at a time, using a two-tined kitchen fork.

Make sure that the room temperature is rather cool.

Keep dipped chocolates out of steam and cold air.

When chocolate has set, store in boxes lined with waxed paper.

Never expose them to the air for any length of time.

If chocolate thickens before you are finished dipping, put more water in the bottom part of the double boiler.

Decorator Icing for Candy

2 cups *(474 ml)* **confectioner's sugar**
2 egg whites
2 tsp *(10 ml)* **lemon juice**

Sift sugar into bowl. Add egg whites and lemon juice. Stir until well mixed then beat with a wooden spoon about 15 minutes. Icing should be creamy but not too stiff to drop from a spoon. If too thick, add more egg white; if too thin, add more sugar. Tint if desired. Use small bag and tube for decorating candy. Allow icing to set before serving.

Orange Walnuts

Can do ahead

Yield: 18-24 pieces
Preparing: 30 min
Cooking: 5 min

1 cup *(237 ml)* **sugar**
⅓ cup *(79 ml)* **orange juice, concentrated**
1 tsp *(5 ml)* **lemon extract**

2 Tb *(30 ml)* **butter OR margarine**
2½ cups *(592 ml)* **walnut halves OR pecans, toasted before using**

Combine sugar and orange juice and cook until mixture forms a soft ball in cold water — about 234° (112° C). Add extract and butter. Beat well until creamy then add walnuts. Pour onto waxed paper. Cut or break into pieces.

Easter Eggs

2 cups *(474 ml)* **confectioner's sugar**
1 egg white

water
2 tsp *(10 ml)* **vanilla**
unsweetened chocolate, melted

Sift sugar into bowl. Beat egg white with equal amount of cold water; add to the sugar. Add vanilla and stir until mixture is creamy. Stir until it is too stiff to stir. Using hands, mold into a large egg or several smaller ones. Dip in chocolate and allow to set.

Miss Mattie Lou's Fudge

Super rich, super yummy

Can do ahead
Can freeze

Yield: 24-30 sq
Preparing: 10 min
Cooking: 8-9 min

1 cup *(237 ml)* **butter, melted**
5 cups *(1.18 l)* **sugar**
1 can, 14 oz *(397 g)* **condensed milk**
3 pkgs, 6 oz *(170 g)* **semi-sweet chocolate chips**

1 jar, 7 oz *(198 g)* **Marshmallow Creme**
1 tsp *(5 ml)* **vanilla**
1 cup *(237 ml)* **nuts, chopped**

Mix butter, sugar and milk in a saucepan. Bring to a hard boil and cook for 8-9 minutes. Remove from heat and stir in chocolate bits. Stir in Marshmallow Whip, vanilla and nuts until well mixed. Pour into buttered 9 x 13 inch (22.86 x 33.02 cm) pan. Cool and set.

Note: This can be cooked in electric frypan — fun with children.

Rum Fudge

A good Christmas candy

Can do ahead
Can freeze

Yield: 24-36 pieces
Preparing: 20 min
Cooking: 20 min

2 cups *(474 ml)* **light brown sugar**
1 cup *(237 ml)* **white sugar**
½ cup *(118 ml)* **butter**
1 cup *(237 ml)* **evaporated milk**
2 pkgs, 6 oz *(170 g)* **butterscotch bits**
1 jar, 7 oz *(198 g)* **Marshmallow Creme**

½ cup *(118 ml)* **white raisins soaked in rum overnight (3-4 hrs will do)**
1 tsp *(5 ml)* **rum flavoring**
½ tsp *(2.5 ml)* **vanilla**
1 cup *(237 ml)* **pecans, chopped**

Put sugars, butter, milk in pan and cook to soft ball 238° (115° C) on candy thermometer). Cook on medium heat. Stir constantly or it will stick and scorch. Remove from heat and stir in butterscotch bits. Stir until mixture is even in color. Add Marshmallow Creme. Drain raisins and add. Then add flavoring and nuts. Pour into buttered pan 9 x 13 x 2 (22.86 x 32.02 x 5.08) and let set for several hours or overnight. Keeps a long time in a tin container.

Hints: Put Marshmallow Creme jar in hot water on stove and warm when starting recipe as it will be easier to remove from jar. Have all ingredients ready before starting to make as it sets up quickly.

English Toffee

Can do ahead

Yield: 50 pieces
Preparing: 30 min
Cooking: 2-3 hours

1 cup *(237 ml)* **white sugar**
½ cup *(118 ml)* **dark brown sugar**
1 cup *(237 ml)* **white Karo syrup**
1¼ cups *(296 ml)* **canned milk**

3 oz *(85 g)* **butter**
1 cup *(237 ml)* **pecans, chopped**
½ tsp *(2.5 ml)* **vanilla**

Mix white sugar, brown sugar, Karo syrup and milk. Cook slowly for 2-3 hours, stirring often. When a firm ball is formed in cold water or a candy thermometer reaches 244° - 250° (118 - 121° C); add butter, pecans and vanilla. Stir and pour into a buttered 9 x 13 inch (22.86 x 33.02 cm) dish. Cool. Cut and wrap individually in wax paper.

Candied Citrus Fruit

Can do ahead

Yield: 1½ lbs (680 g)
Preparing: 1½ hrs
Cooking: 1 hr
Total Time: 5 hrs

grapefruit, lemon, orange peels
2 cups *(474 ml)* **sugar per drained pint** *(474 ml)*
1½ cups *(355 ml)* **water per drained pint** *(474 ml)*

⅛ tsp *(.6 ml)* **salt per drained pint** *(474 ml)*
1 envelope **gelatin**
sugar

Peel and cut into strips or petals, grapefruit, lemon, or orange peels. Cover peelings with water and boil 15-20 minutes 3 different times. Measure peeling and for each pint (474 ml) of drained peel, add 2 cups (474 ml) sugar, 1½ cups (355 ml) water, and ⅛ tsp (.6 ml) salt. Cook until syrup is quite heavy (almost an hour). **Do not let caramelize!** Remove from heat and add one envelope gelatin. Let cool, drain and roll in sugar.

Pralines

Yield: 18 3'' (7.62 cm)
Preparing: 20 min

3 cups *(710 ml)* **light brown sugar, packed**
¼ cup *(59 ml)* **butter**

1 cup *(237 ml)* **heavy cream**
1½ cups *(355 ml)* **pecans, chopped**

Mix sugar, butter and cream in a heavy pan. Cook to soft ball stage, 236° (114° C). Remove from heat. Beat until almost cold. Add nuts. Drop by spoonfuls on a marble slab or wax paper.

C
A
N
D
I
E
S

Martha Washington's

Can do ahead
Can freeze

Yield: 4 doz
Preparing: 1½ hrs

1 box, 1 lb *(454 g)* **confectioner's sugar**
½ cup *(118 ml)* **butter, softened**
2 tsp *(10 ml)* **vanilla**
1 Tb *(15 ml)* **cream OR milk**

toasted whole pecans
50 small maraschino cherries
6 oz *(170 g)* **unsweetened chocolate**
⅓ block paraffin wax

To make the fondant, combine sugar, butter, vanilla and cream or milk in a bowl. Work it well with your hands until smooth. Meanwhile, melt the chocolate and paraffin in a double boiler and pour into a small deep cup. Cut cherries in half and drain on paper towels. Shape the fondant into a ball around a cherry half. Let it sit a few minutes. Then dip it into the chocolate with a toothpick. Place it on waxed paper to harden and top with a toasted half pecan.

VARIATION: Add a bit of green food coloring to the fondant. Split a date almost in half and shape the fondant into it. Roll the stuffed date in granulated sugar and top with a whole toasted pecan.

Millionaire Candy
Tastes like "turtles"

Can do ahead

Yield: 4 doz
Preparing: 5 min
Cooking: 45-50 min
Chilling: 30 min
Dipping: 30 min

1 cup *(237 ml)* **white sugar**
1 cup *(237 ml)* **brown sugar**
1 cup *(237 ml)* **dark Karo syrup**
1 cup *(237 ml)* **margarine**
2 cups *(474 ml)* **evaporated milk**

1 Tb *(15 ml)* **vanilla**
1 lb *(454 g)* **pecan halves**
1 bar, 9¾ oz *(277 g)* **Hershey candy**
½ block paraffin

Mix sugars, Karo syrup, margarine, and 1 cup (237 ml) of the milk. Let it come to a hard boil, stirring constantly. Gradually stir in the rest of the milk. Do not let it stop boiling. Cook until it reaches the soft ball stage on a candy thermometer 234°-240° (112° C-115°) slowly stirring, take off the heat. Beat until thick and creamy. Add vanilla and nuts. Pour into well-buttered pans very thin. Let set in refrigerator 20-30 minutes. Cut in squares. Melt Hershey bar and paraffin together and dip squares in this. Cool on wax paper.

Almond Crunch

Yield: 1¼ lbs (567 g)

1 cup *(237 ml)* **butter**
1 cup *(237 ml)* **sugar**
4 oz *(113 g)* **chocolate, melted**

½ cup *(118 ml)* **blanched almonds,
lightly toasted and finely
chopped**

Mix butter and sugar and heat slowly, stirring constantly, until sugar dissolves. Cook to hard-crack stage, stirring occasionally. Be careful not to burn. Add ¼ cup (59 ml) nuts and pour into a buttered 8 x 8 inch (20.32 cm) pan. When cold, spread half of the chocolate over candy and sprinkle with 2 tablespoons (30 ml) nuts. When firm, invert crunch and cover with remaining chocolate and nuts. When this side is firm, break into small pieces.

Peanut Brittle

Must do ahead

Yield: 2 lbs (908 g)
Preparing: 25 min
Cooking: 10 min
Cooling: 60 min

3 cups *(710 ml)* **white sugar**
1 cup *(237 ml)* **white Karo syrup**
⅛ tsp *(.6 ml)* **salt**

1 inch *(2.54 cm)* **slice of paraffin**
4 cups *(946 ml)* **raw peanuts**
3 tsp *(15 ml)* **baking soda**

Mix first 4 ingredients in a deep, heavy saucepan. Stir until sugar dissolves. Add peanuts and cook until nuts are parched (they pop and the liquid turns beige). Remove from heat and add baking soda (it will bubble up). Pour into buttered pans and smooth down; cool. Break into pieces.

Pecans

Can do ahead

Yield: 3½ cups *(828 ml)*
Preparing: 15 min
Baking: 30 min

3½ cups *(828 ml)* **pecans**
2 egg whites
¼ tsp *(1.25 ml)* **salt**

1 cup *(237 ml)* **sugar**
½ cup *(118 ml)* **butter, melted**

Brown pecans in open pan in oven at 325° (163° C) (just a minute til brown). Take out and cool. Beat egg whites, salt and sugar until stiff peaks form. Add pecans to egg whites. In meantime, melt butter in large cake pan, 9 x 13 inch (22.86 x 33.02 cm). Spread pecan mixture over melted butter. Bake 325° (163° C) for 30 minutes. Stir every 10 minutes until butter is absorbed.

Pecan Rolls

Can do ahead
Can freeze

Yield: 4 rolls
Preparing: 25 min
Cooling: 20 min

1 pkg, 12 oz *(340 g)* **butterscotch fudge mix**
1 pkg, 8 oz *(227 g)* **vanilla caramels**

¼ cup *(59 ml)* **milk**
1½ cups *(355 ml)* **pecans, chopped**

Prepare fudge mix according to package directions; cool. Roll into 4 rolls, each about 1 inch (2.54 cm) in diameter. Melt caramels with milk; spread rolls with caramel mixture and roll in pecans. Chill. Cut into half inch (1.27 cm) slices.

Almond Delight

Can do ahead
Can freeze

Yield: 20-24 pieces
Preparing: 10-15 min
Chilling: 2 hrs

1 pkg, 6 oz *(170 g)* **semi-sweet chocolate chips**
2 oz *(57 g)* **bitter chocolate OR ⅓ cup** *(79 ml)* **semi-sweet chocolate chips**

1 oz *(30 ml)* **butter, melted**
1 cup *(237 ml)* **sliced almonds**
3 oz *(85 g)* **candied orange peel OR cherries**

Melt together chocolates. In frying pan, toast almonds in butter until golden brown; add to chocolate. Add fruit and mix thoroughly. Put wax paper on cake racks. Drop candy by teaspoons onto paper. Refrigerate, uncovered, until hard. This will keep in tight container in freezer or refrigerator. You can substitute crystallized ginger for candied fruit.

 # Lollypops

1 cup *(237 ml)* **sugar**
⅓ cup *(79 ml)* **light corn syrup**
⅔ cup *(158 ml)* **water**

6 to 8 drops peppermint oil
food coloring

Mix first 3 ingredients and cook over low heat stirring until sugar dissolves and mixture boils. Boil, without stirring, until hard-crack stage is reached. With a damp cloth, wash away any crystals on the sides of the pan. Slow down cooking at the end so as not to discolor. Remove from heat; add remaining ingredients and stir only to blend in. Drop quickly from a spoon onto a flat, greased surface. Press wooden skewer into edge of each lollypop. When firm, but still warm, loosen from surface to prevent cracking.

Basic Fondant

2 cups *(474 ml)* **sugar**
1½ cups *(355 ml)* **boiling water**

⅛ tsp *(.6 ml)* **cream of tartar OR 2 Tb** *(30 ml)* **light corn syrup**

Butter the sides of a heavy saucepan. Add above ingredients and stir over medium heat until sugar dissolves and it comes to a boil. Cook to soft-ball stage. Remove from heat and allow to stand about 2-3 minutes to remove air bubbles. Pour on a large platter or marble slab immediately. Allow to cool to lukewarm. Then scrape fondant towards the center and work until stiff and creamy. Knead to remove lumps. Wrap and put in a covered container for 24 hours. Tint and flavor if desired. Use to stuff dates, prunes or figs and then roll in confectioner's sugar.

Mints

Yield: 5 doz

I.

4 cups *(946 ml)* **confectioner's sugar**
⅔ cup *(158 ml)* **Eagle Brand milk**
¼ tsp *(1.25 ml)* **peppermint**
food coloring

II.

4 cups *(946 ml)* **confectioner's sugar, sifted**
1 cup *(237 ml)* **butter, softened**
10-14 drops oil of peppermint
food coloring

Using either of the recipes above; mix well and knead until smooth. Roll into small balls and press flat with a fork or other type press. Chill. Store in airtight container.

After Dinner Mints

Make one recipe of basic fondant. Melt fondant in double boiler, color and flavor:

Color Mint Desired	Flavoring To Use
white	use vanilla or peppermint
pink	use wintergreen
green	use spearmint, lime or almond
red	use cinnamon or clove

After fondant is melted, colored and flavored, drop from the tip of a spoon on waxed paper to desired size. When firm, loosen and transfer to a clean cloth to set.

"Taffy Pull" Sugar Candy

Must do ahead

Yield: 1 lb (454 g)
Preparing: 20 min
Cooling: 40 min
Cooking: 10 min

2 cups *(474 ml)* sugar
1 cup *(237 ml)* water
1 Tb *(15 ml)* vinegar

1 tsp *(5 ml)* vanilla
margarine for greasing pan and
hands

Mix together and cook to hard ball stage, 265°-270° (130°-132° C). **Do not stir.** Pour in well-greased platter until cool enough to work with. Lightly grease hands and pull taffy until white. Twist and cut into bite size pieces. Set aside to harden on wax paper.

Chocolate Taffy

1 cup *(237 ml)* brown sugar
⅓ cup *(79 ml)* corn syrup
⅔ cup *(158 ml)* water
1 cup *(237 ml)* molasses

¼ tsp *(1.25 ml)* salt
2 Tb *(30 ml)* butter
4 oz *(113 g)* chocolate, melted
1 Tb *(15 ml)* vanilla

Mix first 6 ingredients and cook slowly, stirring constantly, until it begins to boil. Cook to soft-crack stage. Pour into buttered pan and pour chocolate over it. As edges cool, fold toward the center. Add vanilla and fold until cool enough to pull. Pull until mixture is cold and cut into pieces.

Bourbon Balls

Can do ahead

Yield: approx 100 ¾" balls
Preparing: 60 min
Cooking time: 5 min

¼ cup *(59 ml)* butter
1 1-lb *(454 g)* box powdered sugar
⅓ cup *(79 ml)* bourbon
1 Tb *(15 ml)* butter

2 Tb *(30 ml)* paraffin (optional)
1 box semi-sweet chocolate
1 square bitter chocolate

Cream butter, sugar and bourbon. Form into balls and drop onto cookie sheet. Allow to harden. Melt butter, paraffin, and chocolate in double boiler but do not allow mixture to boil. Allow this to cool somewhat before dipping balls with fingers.

Pickles, Relishes and Jellies

Pickles, Relishes and Jellies

Pickle and Preserving Pointers

NEVER use copper, brass or iron utensils in canning. Glass or pottery is preferred.

Slaked lime, also called calcium hydroxide, is available at drugstores.

Sterilize regular canning jars in boiling water for 10 minutes. Pack pickles in jars, fill to overflowing with hot brine and cover immediately with tops unless the recipe gives special directions.

Vegetables and fruits should be slightly underripe so that the finished pickle will be crisp.

Salt should be pure, not table salt, which causes the liquid to be cloudy.

Spices should be fresh. To keep pickles from darkening, use whole spices.

Store in a dark, cool place to prevent discoloration. To enhance the flavor, allow the pickles to "set" about 6 weeks before using.

Canned Marinated Mushrooms

Must do ahead

Serves: 4 half pts (946 ml)
Preparing: 30-35 min

1 lb *(454 g)* **fresh whole**
mushrooms
2 medium onions, thinly sliced
1½ cups *(355 ml)* red wine vinegar
1½ cups *(355 ml)* water

½ cup *(118 ml)* brown sugar,
firmly packed
4 tsp *(20 ml)* pickling salt
1 tsp *(5 ml)* dried tarragon

Wash mushrooms and trim stems. Combine remaining ingredients in saucepan and bring to a boil. Add mushrooms and simmer uncovered for 5 minutes. Remove mushrooms and onions with slotted spoon and pack into sterilized hot jars leaving ½ inch (1.27 cm) headspace. Cover with boiling water, level with headspace in jars. Process in water bath for 5 minutes.

Sweet Garlic Pickles
Easy and delicious!

Must do ahead

Preparing: 15-20 min
Actual time: 3 days

1 gal *(3.79 l)* sour pickles
1 bag, 5 lb *(2.3 kg)* sugar

1 small box mixed pickling spices
3 little garlic bulbs

Pour juice off of the sour pickles. Slice or cut in desired shape or size. Add sugar, spice and garlic. Mix and let stand for 3 days, stirring once a day. This needs to be done in a large crock with a lid. When ready, remove three garlic bulbs before putting in jars. Best when served chilled.

Mom's Bread And Butter Pickles

Must do ahead

Yield: 7 qts (6.6 l)
Preparing: 4-5 hrs

2 gal *(7.56 l)* cucumbers
14 small onions
4 large green peppers
¾ cup *(177 ml)* salt
10 cups *(2.37 l)* sugar

1 tsp *(5 ml)* tumeric
1 tsp *(5 ml)* ground cloves
¼ cup *(59 ml)* mustard seed
2½ qts *(2.36 l)* vinegar

Slice vegetables and sprinkle salt over all. Let stand 3 hours. Drain. Heat sugar, tumeric, ground cloves, mustard seed and vinegar thoroughly (do not boil). Add to vegetables. Pack in jars and seal. These are best if kept in jars three weeks before opening.

Squash Pickles

Must do ahead

Yield: 8 pts (3.79 l)
Soaking: 12-18 hrs
Preparing: 40-45 min

10-12 large yellow squash
3 large onions
1 gal (3.79 l) water
1 cup (237 ml) salt
5 cups (1.18 l) vinegar
2 cups (474 ml) sugar

1 cup (237 ml) water
½ cup (118 ml) brown sugar
5 Tb (75 ml) whole mustard seed
2 Tb (30 ml) celery seed
1 tsp (5 ml) turmeric

Thinly slice squash and onion and soak in the gallon (3.79 l) of water with the salt for 12 to 18 hours. Drain for 1 hour. Combine remaining ingredients and boil 5 minutes; add squash and onion and simmer 30 minutes. Bring to a boil and put in hot sterilized jars.

Vegetable Relish
Ideal for hot dogs

Must do ahead

Yield: 8 pts (3.79 l)
Standing: overnight
Preparing: 15-20 min

12 medium onions
1 medium cabbage
10 green tomatoes
12 green peppers
6 sweet red peppers
½ cup (118 ml) salt

6 cups (1.42 l) sugar
2 Tb (30 ml) mustard seed
1 Tb (15 ml) celery seed
1½ tsp (7.5 ml) tumeric
4 cups (946 ml) cider vinegar
2 cups (474 ml) water

Grind all vegetables and sprinkle with salt; let stand overnight. Rinse and drain. Combine remaining ingredients and pour over vegetables. Heat to boiling; simmer 3 minutes. Seal in hot, sterilized jars. Leave ¼ inch (.64 cm) headspace.

Mustard Pickle

Yield: 6-8 pts (2.84-3.79 l)

1 qt (946 ml) cucumbers, chopped
1 qt (946 ml) green tomatoes, chopped
1 head cabbage, chopped
4 bell peppers, chopped
1 cup (237 ml) salt

1 gal (3.79 l) water
6 Tb (90 ml) mustard
1 Tb (15 ml) tumeric
1 cup (237 ml) flour
2 qts (1.89 l) vinegar

Make a brine of salt and water. Add first 4 ingredients and let stand for 24 hours. Drain. Mix last 4 ingredients and add, cooking for 3 minutes. Seal in jars.

Tomato Apple Chutney

Must do ahead

Yield: 12 half pts (3.04 l)
Preparing: 1½ hrs
Cooking: 2 hrs 45 min

10 large ripe tomatoes (about 5 lbs (2.3 kg))
6 large tart apples (about 3 lbs (1.4 kg))
2 cups (474 ml) onions, chopped
15 oz (425 g) seedless raisins
2 cloves garlic, minced
1 lb (454 g) dark brown sugar

1 Tb (15 ml) salt
2 tsp (10 ml) dried red peppers, crushed
1 Tb (15 ml) ground cinnamon
1 tsp (5 ml) ground allspice
½ tsp (2.5 ml) ground ginger
½ tsp (2.5 ml) ground cloves
2 cups (474 ml) cider vinegar

Place tomatoes in scalding water, peel and dice (10 cups (2.36 l)). Pare, core and dice apples (6 cups (1.42 l)). Combine all ingredients. Simmer covered for 10 minutes. Uncover and simmer 30 minutes, stirring often. Simmer and cook down until mixture is thick — approximately 2 hours. Ladle into 12 hot sterilized half pint jars to within one inch of rim. Seal as manufacturer directs: process with hot water 10 minutes.

Cucumber Or Green Tomato Pickles

7 lbs (3.2 kg) cucumbers OR green tomatoes
2 gal (7.58 l) water
3 cups (710 ml) lime
5 lbs (2.3 kg) sugar

3 pts (1.42 l) vinegar
2 Tb (30 ml) pickling spice
1 tsp (5 ml) white mustard seed
pinch of salt

Slice cucumbers or green tomatoes and cover with a solution of water and lime for 24 hours. Rinse; then soak in cold water for 4 hours. Make a syrup of sugar and vinegar. (May need to make more to adequately cover the pickles.) Pour this syrup over cucumbers and let stand overnight. Bring syrup to a boil in a large pot containing the pickles. Add pickling spice and white mustard seed, tied in a cheese cloth bag; add a pinch of salt. Let boil for 1 hour. Seal in jars. Turn upside down to cool.

PICKLES RELISHES JELLIES

Pickled Okra

Must do ahead

Yield: 1 pt (474 ml) jar
Preparing: 10 min

Place in each hot sterilized jar:

uncut okra
1 clove of garlic
wedge of onion
several pepper corns

½ tsp *(2.5 ml)* **mustard seeds**
1 tsp *(5 ml)* **sugar**
1 tsp *(5 ml)* **salt**

Pour hot vinegar over all, and seal. Ready to eat in a week and better cold.

Jelly, Jam And Preserve Pointers

Have ready a kettle large enough to hold four times the volume of the juice and sugar.

Fruit for jelly should be slightly underripe.

Prepare the fruit in small amounts to keep its fresh flavor. Do not pare any fruit except pineapple, because fruit skin is rich in pectin.

Short periods of cooking (10-20 minutes) yield extractions of better jellying power than does long boiling.

Most fruit extractions yield better jellies with ¾ cup (177 ml) of sugar per cup (237 ml) of extraction. If the sugar is added before the juice is boiled, the jelly strength is not decreased.

Seal by covering with a thin layer of paraffin. Tilt the glass so that the paraffin touches the edge all around. The jelly should be completely covered, but the layer of paraffin no thicker than ⅛ inch (.32 cm). A thick layer will pull away from the edge.

Store in a cool, dark place.

Pear Honey
Great on toast or English muffins

Yield: 4-5 pts (1.89-237 l)

3 lbs *(1.4 kg)* **ripe pears, chopped**
1 cup *(237 ml)* **pineapple, diced**

1 lime, juice and grated rind
5 cups *(1.18 l)* **sugar**

Combine ingredients and bring to a boil; cook slowly for 20-25 minutes, stirring often. Pack in hot jars and seal.

Peach Raspberry Jam

Must do ahead

Yield: 9 jars, 8 oz (236 ml)
Preparing: 1 hr

2¾ cups *(651 ml)* **ripe peaches, peeled, pitted, crushed finely**
1 pkg, 10 oz *(284 g)* **frozen red raspberries, thawed**

¼ cup *(59 ml)* **lemon juice (2 lemons)**
6 cups *(1.42 l)* **sugar**
½ bottle **Certo fruit pectin**

Add enough peaches to raspberries to make 4 cups (946 ml). Combine fruit and lemon juice in very large pot; add sugar and mix. Bring to full, rolling boil and boil hard for one minute, stirring constantly. Remove from heat and immediately add pectin. Skim off foam with metal spoon and continue stirring and skimming 5 minutes to cool slightly and prevent fruit from floating. Fill sterilized 8 oz (236 ml) jars, seal and label.

Sweet Red Pepper Jelly

Yield: 4-5 glasses
Standing: 3-4 hrs
Cooking: 15 min

1 doz **sweet red peppers**
1 pt *(474 ml)* **vinegar**

1½ lbs *(680 g)* **sugar**
1 Tb *(15 ml)* **salt**

Chop peppers fine and sprinkle with salt. Let stand 3 or 4 hours; rinse well. Cover with sugar and vinegar. Boil slowly until thick, stirring often. Put in jelly glasses and seal.

Hot Pepper Jelly

Can do ahead

Yield: 6 half pts (1.42 l)
Preparing: 1 hr

1 cup *(237 ml)* **bell peppers, ground**
¼ cup *(59 ml)* **hot, red chili OR jalapeno peppers, ground**

6½ cups *(1.54 l)* **sugar**
1½ cups *(355 ml)* **cider vinegar**
1 bottle **Certo**

Clean the peppers. Wear rubber gloves when working with hot peppers. Discard all seed except some from the hot peppers. Grind or chop very fine. Mix all ingredients except the Certo. Boil mixture about 5 minutes; remove from heat and let stand for 20 minutes. Strain. Heat again to a hard rolling boil, stirring constantly, for 2 minutes. Remove from heat and add 6-8 drops of red or green food coloring and the Certo. Stir well, put in jars and seal.

Burgundy Wine Jelly

Must do ahead

Yield: 6 half pts (1.42 l)
Preparing: 30 min

3 cups *(710 ml)* **burgundy wine**   **4 cups** *(946 ml)* **sugar**
1 box Sure Jell

Bring wine and Sure Jell to a hard boil. Add sugar all at once and stir while mixture returns to a hard boil. Boil for one minute, stirring constantly. Remove from heat. Pour into sterilized half-pint jars and seal immediately.

Variations: To get different shades of jelly, use the following chart:

Wine	Color
Sherry or Muscatel	golden
Port or Cherry	ruby
Concord grape	purple

Strawberry Fig Jam

Must do ahead

Yield: 6-8 half pts
(1.42-1.89 l)
Preparing: 60-90 min

7 cups *(1.65 l)* **peeled figs**   **½ cup** *(118 ml)* **water**
6 cups *(1.42 l)* **sugar**   **pinch of salt**
4 pkgs, 3 oz *(85 g)* **strawberry jello**

Dissolve jello in water. Combine all ingredients in saucepan and cook over low heat for 45 to 60 minutes. Stir occasionally. Pack in sterilized jars. Will keep for months.

Cranberry Sauce

Must do ahead

Yield: 3½ cups (828 ml)
Preparing: 20 min

2 cups *(474 ml)* **sugar**   **4 cups** *(946 ml)* **cranberries**
½ cup *(118 ml)* **water**   **½-1 orange, chopped fine**
3 cloves   **½ cup** *(118 ml)* **Cognac**
1 stick cinnamon

Mix sugar and water and bring to a boil. Continue boiling for about 3 minutes. Add cloves, cinnamon stick, cranberries and orange rind and pulp. Cook over low heat until cranberries pop; stir often. Remove from heat and add Cognac. Chill.

Greater Greensboro Open

The Greater Greensboro Open

The Greater Greensboro Open

Since its beginning on March 26, 1938, the Greater Greensboro Open Golf Tournament has built a rich heritage which forms a part of this area's life. From its start, the tournament has been sponsored by the Greensboro Jaycees, and it has become synonymous with that group's success.

The tournament began as an ambitious fund raising and public relations project and has since undergone much change until today the GGO is the largest project of its kind in the Jaycee world.

The first GGO was played using two clubs: Starmount Country Club had the first two rounds, and a thirty-six hole wrap-up was played at Sedgefield Country Club on Sunday. Sam Snead won the first GGO with a 272 score.

In later years, the GGO moved between Starmount and Sedgefield Country Clubs, but in 1961 the tournament began a sixteen year stay at Sedgefield. It seemed the GGO had found a permanent home until 1977, when the tournament moved to Forest Oaks Country Club.

Many well-known professional golfers have participated in and won the GGO. Hogan, Finsterwald, Casper, Sanders, Trevino, Littler and Weiskopf are just a few of the winners of the Greensboro PGA tournament. Sam Snead holds the record for the most wins at the GGO, a total of eight victories.

The historical trends of the nation have played an important role in the evolution of the tournament. The late thirties and early forties were hard economic times when the nation was coming out of the depression. The late forties and fifties saw the GGO develop larger purses and become more complex. In the sixties, the Greensboro tournament grew in prize money and sophistication.

During the 1978 GGO, for instance, the total prize money was $240,000. This was quite an increase from the $5,000 purse of 1938. The money is good but the GGO means more than just plain money to the touring professionals. The GGO is a tournament the professionals remember because the GGO remembers the professionals. It has been said that no other tournament does as much for the touring pro, his wife and family, as the GGO. Every attempt is made to familiarize Greensboro's golfing guests in the meaning of true "Southern Hospitality."

On the following pages are some favorite recipes of golf professionals who have participated in the GGO. The Junior League of Greensboro extends a special word of thanks to the wives of the touring professionals who were most kind in responding to our request for recipes.

Sugared Bacon Strips

Can do ahead   Baking: 25-30 min

½-1 lb *(227-454 g)* **bacon, room**   **1 cup** *(237 ml)* **brown sugar**
temperature

Roll, pat or shake raw bacon in brown sugar and place on any flat pan with sides. Bake in a slow oven 275-300° (135-149° C) for about 25-30 minutes until dark brown. Turn over once with tongs. When bacon appears well done, remove with tongs and drain on brown paper thoroughly. Grocery bags are excellent for this. As it cools, it will get hard and can then be broken into smaller pieces or served whole. This tedious chore can be done earlier in the day and stored in aluminum foil, then reheated to serve.

Mrs. Arnold Palmer

Spanish Soup

Can do ahead   Serves: 5
Preparing: 30 min
Soaking: 1 hr
Cooking: 2 hrs

2-3 qts *(1.89-2.84 l)* **water**
1 cup *(237 ml)* **Great Northern**
white beans
½ lb *(227 g)* **lean smoked ham or**
prosciutto, cut in ½" *(1.27 cm)*
cubes
2 oz *(57 g)* **salt pork, in 1 piece**
½ cup *(118 ml)* **finely chopped**
onions
2 tsp *(10 ml)* **salt**

2 6" *(15.24 cm)* **pieces of**
pepperoni sausage OR ⅓ lb
(152 g) **of other seasoned**
smoked sausage
½ lb *(227 g)* **turnip greens,**
washed, trimmed and coarsely
shredded, OR 1 pkg frozen
chopped turnip greens
2 potatoes, peeled and diced

In a 3-qt (2.84 l) or larger saucepan, bring water to boil over high heat. Drop in beans and boil for 2 minutes. Remove pan from heat and soak for 1 hour. Drain beans over a sieve set over a bowl and return them to pan. Measure drained liquid and add enough fresh water to make 2 qts (1.89 l). Pour water into pan, add ham, salt pork, onions and salt; bring to boil over high heat. Reduce heat to low and simmer, partially covered, for 1½ hours. When this has cooked, add sausages, turnip greens and potatoes and continue to cook, partially covered for 30 minutes, or until tender. With slotted spoon, remove sausages and salt pork and slice into ½" (1.27 cm) pieces. Return them to soup and taste for seasoning.

Note: You may substitute chopped collard greens for turnip greens and then also add 2-3 turnips, peeled and diced.

Mrs. Raymond Floyd

Zucchini Bread

Must do ahead

Yield: 2-3 loaves
Preparing: 15 min
Baking: 45-55 min

4 eggs
1½ cups *(355 ml)* **sugar**
1 cup *(237 ml)* **oil**
3½ cups *(828 ml)* **flour**
1½ tsp *(7.5 ml)* **soda**
1½ tsp *(7.5 ml)* **salt**

1 tsp *(5 ml)* **cinnamon**
¾ tsp *(3.7 ml)* **baking powder**
2 cups *(474 ml)* **zucchini, grated**
1 cup *(237 ml)* **nuts, chopped**
1 tsp *(5 ml)* **vanilla**
1 cup *(237 ml)* **raisins (optional)**

Blend eggs, sugar and oil together well. Add remaining ingredients and stir until well mixed. Fill loaf pan half full and bake at 350° (177° C) for 45-55 minutes.

Mrs. Arnold Palmer

Cheese Bread

Can do ahead

Serves: 6-8
Preparing: 15 min
Baking: 20 min

1 loaf French bread, cut off crusts
on top and sides, thin sliced
1 cup *(237 ml)* **butter OR**
margarine, room temperature

1½ tsp *(7.5 ml)* **prepared mustard**
1 Tb *(15 ml)* **poppy seed**
⅓ cup *(79 ml)* **onion, chopped**
Olde English cheese

Make a paste with all ingredients except bread and cheese. Mix well and spread inside the sliced loaf and over top and sides. Cut across Olde English cheese, cut into triangles and place flat edge down between the slices of bread. Place loaf in foil, exposing the top. Bake at 400° (204° C) for 20 minutes. Do not cover top.

Mrs. Jerry McGee

Guacamole

Can do ahead

Serves: 5-6
Preparing: 10 min

5 large avocados, peeled and
chopped (reserve 1 sliced
avocado for top)
2 eggs, hard boiled and chopped
1 medium size tomato, chopped

1 medium size onion, chopped
1 tsp *(5 ml)* **Season-All**
½ tsp *(2.5 ml)* **garlic salt**
2 Tb *(30 ml)* **lemon juice**
1 head lettuce

Combine all ingredients except reserve avocado. Toss lightly, being careful not to bruise avocados. Serve on bed of lettuce. Garnish with reserved avocado slices.

Mrs. Lee Elder

7-Up Salad

Must do ahead

Serves: 12
Preparing: 20 min
Chilling: 2-3 hours
Cooking: 5 min

2 pkgs, 3 oz *(85 g)* lemon jello
2 cups *(474 ml)* boiling water
1¾ cups *(414 ml)* 7-Up
1 can, 20 oz *(567 g)* crushed
   pineapple, drained

1 cup *(237 ml)* miniature
   marshmallows
2 bananas, cut in small pieces

Dissolve jello in boiling water. When cool, add 7-Up. When it begins to harden, add pineapple, marshmallows and bananas. Chill until firm.

TOPPING:

1 Tb *(15 ml)* butter
1 Tb *(15 ml)* flour
¼ cup *(59 ml)* sugar

1 egg, slightly beaten
½ cup *(118 ml)* pineapple juice
½ cup *(118 ml)* whipping cream

Make sauce with flour, sugar, egg, pineapple juice and butter. Cook until thick; cool. Add whipped cream and spread over jello. Sprinkle with nuts or cheese if desired. Keep refrigerated until served.

Mrs. Peter E. Jacobsen

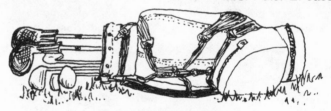

Jalapeno Pudding

Can do ahead
Can freeze

Serves: 8
Preparing: 10 min
Baking: 50-60 min

3 Tb *(45 ml)* butter
1 cup *(237 ml)* yellow corn meal
1 cup *(237 ml)* cream-style corn
3 tsp *(15 ml)* baking powder
1 tsp *(5 ml)* salt
1 small can jalapeno peppers
   (I found that 1 pepper and 1 Tb
   (15 ml) is enough)

⅔ cup *(158 ml)* vegetable oil
2 eggs
1 cup *(237 ml)* cheddar cheese,
   grated
8 oz *(227 g)* sour cream
1 medium onion, chopped
3 medium garlic cloves, crushed

Melt butter in iron skillet. Mix rest of ingredients and pour into pan. Bake at 350° (177° C) for 50-60 minutes.

Mrs. Charles Coody

Baked Stuffed Flank Steak

Can partially do ahead

Serves: 6
Preparing: 30 min
Cooking: 25 min
Baking: 45-60 min

1¾-2 lb *(794-908 g)* **flank steak,
wiped off and scored on both
sides**
1 clove **garlic, crushed**
2 Tb *(30 ml)* **soy sauce**
½ tsp *(2.5 ml)* **pepper**
2 Tb *(30 ml)* **margarine OR butter,
room temperature**

RICE STUFFING

½ cup *(118 ml)* **onion, chopped**
1 clove **garlic, crushed**
¼ cup *(59 ml)* **butter OR margarine**
1½ cups *(355 ml)* **cooked rice**
½ cup *(118 ml)* **parsley, chopped**

½ cup *(118 ml)* **beef broth,
condensed**
½ cup *(118 ml)* **water**
1 Tb *(15 ml)* **crystallized ginger,
chopped OR** ¾ tsp *(3.7 ml)*
powdered ginger

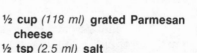

½ cup *(118 ml)* **grated Parmesan
cheese**
½ tsp *(2.5 ml)* **salt**
½ tsp *(2.5 ml)* **pepper**

Rub meat with garlic, soy sauce and pepper on both sides; lay flat and spread with 1 Tb (15 ml) butter. For stuffing, sauté onions and garlic in butter until golden; stir in rice, parsley, cheese, salt and pepper. Preheat oven to 350° (177° C). Place stuffing on flat steak and roll into a log. Butter outside with remaining 1 Tb (15 ml) butter; place in roasting pan. Dilute broth with water and pour over steak. Sprinkle with ginger. Roast 45-60 minutes, basting often. Serve on platter with a bowl of juice.

Mrs. Tommy Jacobs

Pork Roast Hawaiian

Can do ahead

Serves: 10
Preparing: 15 min
Baking: 2½ hrs

1 can, 15¼ oz *(432 g)* **pineapple
slices**
6 lb center **pork loin roast (have
butcher loosen back bone)**
¼ cup *(59 ml)* **honey**

1 can, ⅓ cup *(79 ml)* **Kikkoman
soy sauce**
¼ tsp *(1.25 ml)* **garlic powder**
¼ tsp *(1.25 ml)* **ginger powder**

Drain pineapple slices and blend syrup with rest of ingredients. Roast in 325° (163° C) oven for 2-2½ hours. Brush pork with marinade every 10 minutes and last half hour of cooking. Remove roast to serving platter and cut into 10 portions. Heat remaining marinade and serve with pork. Serve with rice and fruit salad.

Mrs. Chi Chi Rodriguez

Oven Roasted Lamb Shank Dinner

Can do ahead

Serves: 4
Preparing: 15 min
Cooking: 3 min
Baking: 3½ hrs

4 large lamb shanks
2 cloves of garlic, cut in half
1 tsp *(5 ml)* **rosemary**
½ tsp *(2.5 ml)* **oregano**
½ tsp *(2.5 ml)* **dill**

1 large onion, sliced thin
1 can, 8 oz *(227 g)* **tomato sauce**
¼ cup *(59 ml)* **brown sugar**
1 cup *(237 ml)* **dry white wine**
hot buttered rice OR noodles

Place lamb and garlic in a roaster or heavy baking pan. Combine rosemary, oregano, dill, onion, tomato sauce, brown sugar and wine. Pour this over lamb. Cover roaster or pan tightly and cook at 300° (149° C) 3 hours; uncover pan and cook for 30 minutes more to brown meat. Pour sauce from pan into saucepan and cook over medium heat 3 minutes or until it reduces itself to half its original volume. Pour back over tender shanks and serve at once over rice or noodles.

Mrs. Gene Littler

Capon Stuffed With Ground Veal

Can partially do ahead

Serves: 8-10
Preparing: 20 min
Cooking: 5 min
Baking: 1½ hrs

1, 5-lb *(2.3 kg)* **whole dressed**
capon
1 lb *(454 g)* **lean veal, finely**
ground
2 eggs
1 medium onion, chopped
1 tsp *(5 ml)* **garlic, chopped**
2 tsp *(10 ml)* **Italian seasoning**
¼ tsp *(1.25 ml)* **ground white**
pepper

¼ lb *(113 g)* **salted butter**
1½ lb *(680 g)* **sausage meat,**
ground
1½ cup *(355 ml)* **dry bread**
crumbs, seasoned OR plain
½ cup *(118 ml)* **white wine**
1 medium green pepper, chopped
¼ tsp *(1.25 ml)* **celery salt OR**
fresh celery, chopped

Wipe inside of capon with paper towel. Set aside. Mix veal, eggs, and wine. Set aside. Melt butter in pan and add bread crumbs. Cook until golden brown. In a large bowl, combine the browned bread crumbs with sausage meat, onions, garlic and pepper. (Usually mix by hand.) Add rest of seasonings and gently, but thoroughly, add the veal mixture. Stuff capon completely with this mixture. Bake at 350° (177° C) for 1½ hours or until tender.

Mrs. Lee Elder

Fried Chicken
Jerry's and Sooji's favorite recipe

Can do ahead

Preparing: 5 min
Cooking: 20-25 min

Chicken pieces (allow ¼-½ bird
 per person)
salt and pepper, to taste
flour

egg, slightly beaten
1 tsp *(5 ml)* water OR milk
cooking fat

Before cooking wipe pieces of chicken dry as possible; season with salt and pepper and roll in flour. Or, dip in slightly beaten egg diluted with water or milk and then roll in flour. Place chicken in a thick frying pan containing ½ inch or more of hot fat. Put thickest pieces of chicken in the pan first. Leave enough space for fat to come up around each piece; do not crowd. Cover pan and cook at moderate heat. Turn when brown. The thickest pieces of a 3 pound chicken (dressed weight) usually require from 20-25 minutes to cook.

Mrs. Jerry Pate

Spaghetti Or Chili
A family favorite

Can do ahead
Can freeze

Yield: 2½ cups (2.37 l)
Preparing: 20 min
Cooking: 2 hrs

1 medium onion, sliced
2 Tb *(30 ml)* margarine
½ cup *(118 ml)* green pepper,
 chopped
2½ lbs *(1.3 kg)* ground sirloin OR
 round, browned
2 tsp *(10 ml)* salt
½ tsp *(2.5 ml)* black pepper,
 freshly ground
1 tsp *(5 ml)* chili powder
1 tsp *(5 ml)* sweet basil
1 tsp *(5 ml)* oregano
1 tsp *(5 ml)* Beau Monde

1 tsp *(5 ml)* spaghetti powder
1 tsp *(5 ml)* sugar
½ pkg prepared chili OR spaghetti
 mix
1 can, 1 lb *(454 g)* stewed
 tomatoes
1 can, 12 oz *(340 g)* tomato paste
1 can, 15 oz *(426 g)* tomato sauce
1 cup *(237 ml)* water
½ lb *(227 g)* fresh mushrooms,
 washed and sliced OR 2 cans, 4
 oz *(113 g)* sliced mushrooms,
 drained

Combine all ingredients, except mushrooms; simmer 2 hours. Add mushrooms after cooking 1½ hours. When serving as spaghetti, use very few noodles and serve with Parmesan cheese. For chili, add beans and more chili powder.

Mrs. Hale Irwin

Kroppkaker

A delicious Scandinavian ham and potato dish

Can do ahead

Yield: 12
Preparing: 30 min
Cooking: 20 min

6 medium potatoes, boiled,
  cooled, mashed
2 eggs
2 egg yolks
1 cup *(237 ml)* flour

1½ lb *(680 g)* salt pork, diced
3 cups *(710 ml)* cooked ham, diced
2 medium onions, chopped
½ cup *(118 ml)* flour
butter, melted

Combine potatoes, eggs, egg yolks and flour. Fry pork, ham and onions. Shape potato mixture into 12 balls. With thumb, make an indentation into potato ball. Fill with 2 tsp (10 ml) of ham mixture. Close opening. Roll in flour. Drop in boiling water, a few at a time. When they rise, remove with a slotted spoon. Serve with leftover mixture and lots of melted butter.

Mrs. Bob Lunn

Chicken Crêpes

Can do ahead
Can freeze

Yield: about 30 crêpes
Preparing: 60 min
Resting: 2 hrs
Cooking: 60 min

CRÊPES

1 cup *(237 ml)* cold water
1 cup *(237 ml)* cold milk
4 eggs

½ tsp *(2.5 ml)* salt
4 Tb *(60 ml)* butter, melted
2 cups *(474 ml)* sifted flour

Place ingredients in blender; cover and blend at top speed for 1 minute. Scrape sides of blender with a spatula and blend for another few seconds. Let rest in refrigerator for 2 hours, or overnight.

To cook crêpes, oil the botton of a crêpe pan and wipe off excess with a dry paper towel. Pour a small portion of batter, about ¼ cup (59 ml), in a pie plate and add more as needed. Dip the bottom of the crêpe pan in the batter, lift 2 inches (5.08 cm) and hold a few seconds to drain excess batter. Then place pan upside down on burner. Start with medium heat at first and experiment for right temperature and time length. The crêpe, when done should be pale in the middle and golden around the edges. When the crêpe is done, set the bottom of the pan on a pie plate and the crêpe should peel right off as you lift it again. Stack the crêpes in this matter, setting the pan on top of the stack as you cook. They won't stick if they are done.

continued

CHICKEN FILLING:

Can do ahead
Can freeze

Yield: 20-30 min
Preparing: 45 min
Cooking: 10 min
Baking: 20-30 min

3 Tb *(45 ml)* onion, minced
6 Tb *(90 ml)* butter
6 Tb *(90 ml)* flour
1½ cups *(355 ml)* milk
1½ cups *(355 ml)* chicken stock
4½ Tb *(67.5 ml)* white wine
salt and pepper, to taste
2 Tb *(30 ml)* onion, minced

1 Tb *(15 ml)* butter
2 cups *(474 ml)* chicken, chopped
¾ cup *(177 ml)* sliced mushrooms
½-1 tsp *(2.5-5 ml)* curry powder
¾ cup *(177 ml)* pimento, chopped
   (optional)
2 egg yolks, beaten
4½ Tb *(67.5 ml)* light cream

Sauté 3 Tb (45 ml) onion in 6 Tb (90 ml) butter, stir in flour, then add milk, chicken stock, wine, salt and pepper; cook, stirring until thickened. Cover with wax paper and lid; set aside. In skillet, sauté 2 Tb (30 ml) onion in 1 Tb (15 ml) butter; add chicken, mushrooms, curry powder, pimento, egg yolks, and light cream. Add enough of first sauce to chicken to make a creamy but not thin filling for crêpes. Place 2 Tb (30 ml) filling on each crêpe, roll up and tuck ends under. Place in lightly buttered baking dish. Cover with remaining sauce and bake at 350° (177° C) until sauce bubbles, about 20 minutes.

If freezing, freeze sauce separately and assemble just before baking.

Mrs. Rik Massengale

Oven Braised Doves
A favorite recipe of Julius Boros

Can do ahead

Preparing: 15 min
Cooking: 5 min
Baking: 1¼-1½ hrs

doves
seasoned flour
vegetable oil
celery, chopped
onion, chopped
parsley, chopped

1 can, 3 oz *(85 g)* sliced
   mushrooms, plus liquid
   (mushroom soup OR fresh
   mushrooms is good)
2-3 chicken bouillon cubes
2 cups *(474 ml)* water
½ cup *(118 ml)* white wine

Coat birds with flour and brown in oil. Place in Dutch oven or casserole. Sprinkle with celery, onion, and parsley. Add mushrooms plus liquid. Dissolve bouillon cubes in water and pour over dove. Cover and cook at 325° (163° C) 1¼-1½ hours. Pour wine over the doves during the last 15 minutes of baking.

Mrs. Julius Boros

Scalloped Potatoes And Carrots

A favorite family recipe

Can partially do ahead

Serves: 6
Preparing: 20 min
Cooking: 35 min
Baking: 1 hr

3 Tb *(45 ml)* butter
6-7 carrots, peeled and sliced ⅛″
  (.32 cm) thick
6-7 green onion bulbs, minced
salt

1 cup *(237 ml)* water
4-5 white potatoes, peeled and
  sliced ⅛″ *(.32 cm)* thick
several twists of white pepper mill
2 cups *(474 ml)* heavy cream

Combine 2 Tb (30 ml) of the butter with the carrots, onions, salt and water in a heavy saucepan. Bring to a boil, reduce heat to simmer and cook 20-30 minutes, or until the carrots are tender and all the liquid has evaporated. Take the remaining butter and grease the bottom and sides of a 2-qt (1.89 l) baking dish that can be used for serving. Starting with the potatoes, make layers of potatoes and carrots, finishing with potatoes. Sprinkle each layer with salt and pepper. Add the cream. Bake at 325° (163° C) for about 1 hour or until potatoes are tender when pierced with a sharp knife and the top is lightly browned.

Mrs. Al Geiberger

Shrimp And Artichoke Casserole

Can partially do ahead

Serves: 6
Preparing: 25 min
Cooking: 8-10 min
Baking: 30 min

6½ Tb *(97.5 ml)* butter
¼ lb *(113 g)* fresh mushrooms,
  sliced
4½ Tb *(67.5 ml)* flour
¾ cup *(117 ml)* milk
¾ cup *(117 ml)* cream
salt and pepper to taste
1 pkg frozen Artichoke hearts,
  drained

1½ lbs *(680 g)* fresh OR frozen
  shrimp, cooked
¼ cup *(59 ml)* sherry wine
1 Tb *(15 ml)* Worcestershire sauce
¼ cup *(59 ml)* Parmesan cheese,
  grated
paprika
rice

Preheat oven to 375° (191° C). Melt butter and sauté mushrooms for 2 minutes. Stir in flour and blend. Gradually add milk and cream stirring constantly with wisk. When thickened, add salt and pepper. Arrange artichokes on bottom of baking dish and place shrimp over them. Add sherry and Worcestershire to mushroom sauce and pour over dish. Sprinkle with cheese and paprika. Bake 30 minutes. Serve over rice.

Mrs. Joe Inman, Jr.

Broccoli Cheese Dish

Can do ahead
Can freeze

Serves: 6
Preparing: 10 min
Baking: 45 min

2 pkgs, 10 oz *(284 g)* frozen
  chopped broccoli, cooked and
  drained
1 can, 10¾ oz *(305 g)* mushroom
  soup
2 eggs, well beaten

1 cup *(237 ml)* mayonnaise
1 cup *(237 ml)* cheddar cheese,
  grated
2 Tb *(30 ml)* dried onions
salt and pepper

Mix all ingredients together and put in any dish with a cover or lid.
Bake at 350° (177° C) for 45 minutes.

Mrs. Skip Guss

Whole Raw Spinach Salad

Can partially do ahead

Serves: 4
Preparing: 25 min
Cooking: 5 min

1 lb *(454 g)* whole raw spinach,
  cleaned and torn into desired
  size
6 strips bacon, chopped
4 Tb *(60 ml)* salad oil

1½ Tb *(22.5 ml)* wine vinegar
4 oz *(113 g)* sugar
salt and pepper to taste
juice from 1 lemon
½ red bermuda onion, chopped

Cook bacon; save drippings. Mix oil, vinegar, sugar, salt and pepper,
and lemon juice. Toss the spinach with the dressing and onion. Just
before serving pour bacon and hot drippings over spinach. Mix
thoroughly and serve immediately.

Mrs. Lanny Wadkins

Pumpkin Ice Cream

Freezes
Must do ahead

Serves: 12-18
Preparing: 15 min
Chilling: 8-10 hours

½ gal *(1.89 ')* vanilla ice cream,
  softened
1 can, 16 oz *(454 g)* pumpkin
2 cups *(474 ml)* sugar

cinnamon and nutmeg, to taste,
  as in pie, or other spices
gingersnaps
Cool Whip (optional)

Line an oblong pyrex dish (or plastic container) with gingersnaps.
Line bottom and sides. Mix ice cream, pumpkin, sugar and spices with
mixer until thoroughly mixed. Pour this mixture into container and
freeze. Cut into squares and serve. Pecans can be used for a different
flavor. Cool Whip may be used as a decorative topping.

Mrs. Leonard Thompson

Banana Pudding

Can do ahead

Serves: 4
Preparing: 20 min
Cooking: 30 min

¾ **cup** *(177 ml)* **sugar**
5 **Tb** *(75 ml)* **cornstarch**
¼ **tsp** *(1.25 ml)* **salt**
2 **cups** *(474 ml)* **milk**
2 **egg yolks, beaten**

1 **tsp** *(5 ml)* **vanilla**
1 **small box, 9 oz** *(255 g)* **vanilla wafers**
2 **medium bananas, sliced**

Mix the dry ingredients. Heat milk in double boiler and stir in dry ingredients. Cook slowly for about 30 minutes, stirring frequently. Stir in egg yolks and cook until the yolks thicken the mixture. Add vanilla. Using half the box of vanilla wafers, one banana and half the pudding, layer into an oven-proof dish (making two layers with each half). This pudding can be topped with a meringue made from the left-over egg whites and browned in the oven, or just plain.

Mrs. Charles Coody

Oatmeal Cake

Larry's favorite cake recipe

Can do ahead
Can freeze

Serves: 12-18
Preparing: 20 min
Standing: 20 min
Baking: 35 min
Broiling: 5 min

1 **cup** *(237 ml)* **quick cook oats**
½ **cup** *(118 ml)* **margarine**
1¼ **cups** *(296 ml)* **boiling water**
1 **cup** *(237 ml)* **white sugar**
1 **cup** *(237 ml)* **brown sugar**
2 **eggs**
1⅓ **cups** *(316 ml)* **cake flour**
½ **tsp** *(2.5 ml)* **salt**
1 **tsp** *(5 ml)* **baking soda**
½ **tsp** *(2.5 ml)* **nutmeg**

1 **tsp** *(5 ml)* **cinnamon**
1 **cup** *(237 ml)* **raisins (optional)**
6 **Tb** *(90 ml)* **margarine, room temperature**
½ **cup** *(118 ml)* **cream OR canned milk**
½ **cup** *(118 ml)* **sugar**
½ **tsp** *(2.5 ml)* **vanilla**
1 **cup** *(237 ml)* **chopped nuts**
1 **cup** *(237 ml)* **Angel Flake coconut**

Combine the oats, margarine and boiling water. Let stand 20 minutes. Add white and brown sugars and eggs; mix well. Sift together and add cake flour, salt, soda, nutmeg and cinnamon. Stir in raisins. Bake in 9 x 13 inch (22.8 x 33.02 cm) greased pan at 350° (177° C) 35 minutes. For topping, mix together margarine and milk or cream in the sugar and vanilla. Add nuts and coconut. As soon as the cake is done spread on top. Put under broiler about 5 minutes or until topping is brown. Be careful as top burns easily.

Mrs. Larry Ziegler

Moist Coconut Cake

Can do ahead
Can freeze

Serves: 24
Preparing: 20 min
Baking: 30-35 min

½ lb *(227 g)* **butter, room
temperature**
3 cups *(710 ml)* **cake flour**
2 cups *(474 ml)* **sugar**

1 cup *(237 ml)* **coconut milk**
3½ tsp *(17.5 ml)* **baking powder**
4 eggs, separated
2 tsp *(10 ml)* **vanilla**

Cream butter and sugar until fluffy. Sift flour and baking powder together. Add egg yolks and vanilla to batter mixture and blend well. Add dry ingredients alternately with coconut milk. Beat egg whites until stiff. Add to batter and fold gently. Pour into oblong pyrex cake pan. Bake for 30-35 minutes at 325° (163° C).

Mrs. Chi Chi Rodriguez

French Cherry Pie

Must do ahead

Serves: 8
Preparing: 20 min
Baking: 10 min
Chilling: 1 hr

PIE CRUST:

1 cup *(237 ml)* **butter OR
margarine**
1 cup *(237 ml)* **graham cracker
crumbs**

1 cup *(237 ml)* **pecans OR walnuts,
chopped**
½ cup *(118 ml)* **confectioner's
sugar**

Melt butter in sauce pan; add other ingredients. Mix together then press into an oblong glass pan. Press mixture just on the bottom of pan, not the sides. Bake at 325° (163° C) for 10 minutes, then cool.

FILLING:

1 pkg **Dream Whip, made
according to pkg directions**
1 pkg, 8 oz *(227 g)* **cream cheese**

1 cup *(237 ml)* **confectioner's sugar**
2 cans, 16 oz *(454 g)* **cherry pie
filling**

Mix first 3 ingredients with electric mixer until thick and creamy and pour into cooled cracker crumb bottom. Place in refrigerator for about one hour. After filling has cooled, top with cherry pie filling. Refrigerate until ready to serve.

Mrs. Skip Guss

Million Dollar Pie

Must do ahead

Serves: 12-16
Preparing: 10 min
Chilling: 4-6 hrs

2 pkgs, 8 oz *(227 g)* **cream cheese, softened**
3 cups *(710 ml)* **heavy cream, not whipped**

1½ tsp *(7.5 ml)* **vanilla**
1½ cups *(355 ml)* **powdered sugar**
2 **graham cracker pie crusts**

Cream the cream cheese and heavy cream at low speed in mixer until smooth. Add vanilla and sugar and whip. Pour into pie crusts. Chill.

Topping variations:

1. Lightly toasted almond shavings or finely chopped walnuts
2. Finely crushed graham crackers
3. Blueberry or strawberry pie topping
4. Whipped cream with various flavorings (almond, lemon, orange, etc.)

Mrs. Billy Casper

99 Cookies

Can do ahead
Can freeze

Yield: 99
Preparing: 15 min
Baking: 10-15 min per cookie sheet

1¾ cup *(414 ml)* **brown sugar**
1 cup *(237 ml)* **butter, room temperature**
1 cup *(237 ml)* **oil**
3½ cup *(828 ml)* **flour**
1 tsp *(5 ml)* **baking soda**
1 tsp *(5 ml)* **cream of tartar**
½ tsp *(2.5 ml)* **salt**

1 **egg**
1 tsp *(5 ml)* **vanilla**
1 cup *(237 ml)* **coconut**
1½ cups *(355 ml)* **rice crispies**
1 cup *(237 ml)* **oatmeal**
2 cups *(474 ml)* **granola**
1 cup *(237 ml)* **chocolate chips**
½ cup *(118 ml)* **nuts, chopped**

Mix ingredients in order given. Drop by teaspoonfuls on ungreased cookie sheet and bake at 350° (177° C) 10-15 minutes.

Mrs. Al Geiberger

Menu

Chicken Crêpes
Fresh Asparagus
Strawberries n' Cream Salad
Rolls
Assorted Butter Cookies and Cakes

Menu

Barbeque Brisket
Fresh Black-Eyed Peas
Fried Okra
Cantaloupe, Tomatoes, and Red Onions
Jalapeno Pudding
Banana Pudding

Gifts from the Kitchen

Gifts From The Kitchen

Parfait glass, punch cup, lucite recipe file or apothecary jar filled with your favorite candies.

Long French bread basket or mushroom basket filled with jams or marmalades.

Child a bright beach pail or toy dump truck filled with goodies — nice gift for a child in the hospital.

Jar of relish in a shiny paper tote bag tied with bright ribbon.

Picnic hamper filled with a variety of spiced fruits and relishes.

Loaf of bread on a bread board or in a bread box or baking pan wrapped with cellophane with a yarn or plaid ribbon.

Mustard pot filled with your favorite mustard or sauce together with a little spoon or small spreader.

Special container overflowing with your favorite cookies and include the recipe — a sand pail would be good for children.

Sourdough starter and attach the recipe.

Favorite friend a picnic basket filled with a variety of breads.

Chocolate or fudge sauce in a glass crock with a cork top tied with brown and white checked ribbon.

Old-fashioned Mason jar filled with your favorite homemade soup.

Homemade barbeque sauce in your leftover salad dressing bottles; glue a small piece of burlap on the top surface of the lid and tie with yarn or twine.

Gingerbread or applesauce cake along with a jar of your favorite lemon topping.

Dessert in a pretty glass or ceramic bowl, a copper mold or a soufflé dish.

Bunch of homemade cookies in a large mixing bowl, a useful gift in itself.

Straw pocketbook or basket filled with foil-wrapped candies — delightful for little girls.

Wooden spoon or some cookie cutters when giving cookies.

Wire whisk with a dessert or a basting brush with a sauce.

Box of fine imported biscuits with a homemade cheese spread.

Large, beautiful melon with a special dessert sauce.

Jar of coffee beans with a coffee cake.

L'egg stocking container filled with homemade silly putty from our "Keep the Kids Busy" section.

Pasta sauce in a pretty glass jar wrapped in a fresh piece of gingham cloth tied with yarn and an appropriate card.

Copy of OUT OF OUR LEAGUE plus a dish that you prepared from the cookbook.

Set of different kinds of mustard.

Dozen meringues to be served with ice cream and/or fresh berries — put in a clear glass container.

Basket filled with all kinds of salamis, sausages, cheeses and crackers.

Crock pitcher filled with homemade eggnog.

Small wicker waste basket filled with a large plastic bag of cooked popcorn.

Jar of boiled custard to a sick friend — excellent for those on a liquid or bland diet.

Plum Pudding — the traditional Christmas dessert — elegant accompanied by a jar of Hard Sauce or Whiskey Sauce.

Pottery crock packed with your favorite cheese spread or herb butter; cover with saran wrap, secure with rubber band and tie with twine.

Add Your Own Ideas...

A Few Gift Ideas To Help You Fill All Of Those Cute Containers...

M & M Cookies

1 cup *(237 ml)* **shortening**
1 cup *(237 ml)* **brown sugar, firmly packed**
½ cup *(118 ml)* **sugar**
2 eggs, beaten
2 tsp *(10 ml)* **vanilla**
2¼ cups *(533 ml)* **flour, sifted**
1 tsp *(5 ml)* **baking soda**
1 tsp *(5 ml)* **salt**
1½ cups *(355 ml)* **M & M's**

Cream shortening, sugars, eggs, and vanilla. Sift together flour, soda and salt. Add dry ingredients gradually to creamed mixture. Mix well. Stir in ½ cup (118 ml) M & M's. Reserve remaining M & M's for decorating. Drop by teaspoons on ungreased cookie sheet. Decorate tops with rest of M & M's. Bake at 375° (191° C) in top third of oven for 5-10 minutes.

Lemon Cookies

1 pkg lemon cake mix
2 cups *(474 ml)* **Cool Whip**
½ cup *(118 ml)* **confectioner's sugar**

Preheat oven to 350° (177° C). Mix the first two items. Drop by teaspoonfuls into confectioner's sugar. Roll until coated. Place 1½ inches (3.81 cm) apart on cookie sheet. Bake 10-15 minutes. Remove from pan and cool. Do not taste them while hot or warm. They really taste better the next day. You could possibly try this with a chocolate cake mix.

Hickory-Flavored Cheese Spread

1 pkg, 8 oz *(227 g)* **cream cheese, softened**
1 cup *(237 ml)* **sharp cheddar cheese, finely shredded**
½ tsp *(2.5 ml)* **hickory salt**
⅓ cup *(79 ml)* **blanched almonds, toasted and finely chopped**

Combine all ingredients until well blended. Add almonds and mix well. Pack into small crocks and refrigerate. Serve at room temperature. Makes 1½ cups (355 ml).

Peanut Butter-Cereal Snack

½ cup *(118 ml)* **sugar**
½ cup *(118 ml)* **white syrup**
½ cup *(118 ml)* **peanut butter**
1 cup *(237 ml)* **Spanish peanuts**
3 cups *(710 ml)* **Special-K cereal**

Bring sugar, syrup, and peanut butter to boil. Pour over cereal and peanuts. Mix until all cereal is coated. Pour and press into 7 x 11 inch (17.78 x 27.94 cm) pan that is lightly greased. Let cool, then cut into squares.

Homemade Mustard

½ cup *(118 ml)* **sifted flour**
¼ cup *(59 ml)* **sugar**
⅛ tsp *(.6 ml)* **salt**
½ cup *(118 ml)* **dry mustard**
¾ cup *(177 ml)* **cider vinegar**

Mix dry ingredients. Add vinegar and blend until smooth. Let stand several days to season. Keep in refrigerator. Yield: 2 cups (474 ml).

Kahlúa

1½ cups *(355 ml)* instant coffee
3 cups *(710 ml)* boiling water
6 cups *(1.42 l)* sugar
1 vanilla bean
1 fifth *(768 ml)* vodka

Dissolve coffee in water; add sugar and vanilla bean. Cool, then add vodka. Pour into a gallon (3.79 l) jug, seal and let stand 30 days to ripen before using. Yield: ½ gal (1.89 l).

Creme de Menthe

5 lbs *(2.3 kg)* sugar
3 qts *(2.84 l)* water
2 oz *(59 ml)* essence of peppermint
1 qt *(946 ml)* grain alcohol — 190 proof
green food coloring

Mix sugar and water together and boil until mixture clears and is slightly syrupy — about 20 minutes. Put the pot you cook it in in a pot of cold water. When cold, add peppermint and alcohol and green food coloring. Bottle and let stand 1 month to ripen. Makes 1 gallon + (3.79 l).

Herb Butter

½ lb *(227 g)* butter, softened
1 Tb *(15 ml)* fresh chives, chopped
1 Tb *(15 ml)* fresh parsley, chopped
½ tsp *(2.5 ml)* dry marjoram
½ tsp *(2.5 ml)* dry basil
1 tsp *(5 ml)* lemon juice

Mix all ingredients thoroughly. Keep in refrigerator.

Herb Butter II

Snip fresh chives, chervil, tarragon and marjoram into a mortar. Grind with dry bread crumbs and a drop of brandy. Blend with butter; chill. Good to serve on steaks and broiled fish.

Bloody Mary Mix

9 lbs *(4.1 kg)* tomatoes
¼ cup *(59 ml)* lemon juice
2 tsp *(10 ml)* salt
1 tsp *(5 ml)* onion powder
1 Tb *(15 ml)* celery salt
2 Tb *(30 ml)* Worcestershire
½ tsp *(2.5 ml)* Tabasco
¼ tsp *(1.25 ml)* pepper
dash cayenne pepper

Remove stems and cores from tomatoes; cut up and cook slowly, covered, until soft — about 12-15 minutes. Stir often so the tomatoes do not stick. Press tomatoes through a food mill to get 12 cups (2.84 l) of juice. Mix juice with remaining ingredients, bring to a boil and boil for 2 minutes. Pour mixture into hot canning jars leaving ½ inch (1.27 cm) headspace. Process in hot water bath 10 to 15 minutes. Yields: 3 quarts (2.84 l).

Homemade Mayonnaise

1 egg, separated
salt to taste
juice of 1 fresh lemon
2 cups *(474 ml)* Wesson oil
1 small onion, chopped fine

Before you start, chill well all of the ingredients along with your bowls, beaters, and other utensils. This can be made in a blender or by using a rotary beater. Beat the egg yolk with ¼ tsp (1.25 ml) salt and about 1 tsp (5 ml) of the lemon juice. Beating constantly, drip oil in drop by drop to begin, then as it thickens, add remaining lemon juice and the egg white. Add salt to taste and paprika for a little color. Fold in onion last and chill. Makes 1 pint (474 ml).

Miscellaneous Tips

Soufflé will remain light and fluffy if ¼ tsp (1.25 ml) cream of tartar is added to egg whites during mixing.

When separating an egg, if yolk gets into white, remove with a piece of shell.

Rinse raisins thoroughly in hot water and drain before adding to breads and cakes. This will make them plump and juicy and they will not withdraw moisture from batter.

To measure molasses, grease cup in which it is to be measured.

Put lemons in hot water for several minutes before squeezing and they will yield more juice.

When making meringue, use 1 egg white to ¼ cup (59 ml) sugar.

A large lump of charcoal placed in an open jar in your refrigerator will greatly reduce ice box odors.

When poaching eggs, add some vinegar to the water to keep the whites from spreading.

Melt cheese over low heat; high heat will make it stringy.

A little butter on the lip of a cream pitcher will eliminate the usual drip when pouring.

For crushed garlic, put between layers of waxed paper and hit it with a hammer — nothing to clean.

If you place oranges in a hot oven before you peel them, no white fiber will be left on the orange.

When using oven glass baking pans, always lower the temperature by 25° (-4° C).

Cut dates up fine with scissors after measuring.

To make nut meats come out whole, soak whole nuts in salted water overnight before cracking.

To scald milk without scorching, rinse pan in hot water before using.

Light or excessive heat causes deterioration in vanilla. Always keep bottle in the box in which it comes.

After removing a roast from the oven, let it rest at least 15 minutes for easier carving.

Pouring a strong solution of salt and hot water down the sink will help eliminate odors and remove grease from drains.

Use baking soda on a damp cloth to shine up your kitchen appliances.

Stains or discolorations on aluminum utensils can be removed by boiling a solution of 2-3 tablespoons (30-45 ml) cream of tartar, lemon juice, or vinegar to each quart (946 ml) water in the utensil for 5 to 10 minutes.

Keep the Kids Busy

Keep The Kids Busy

The following pages contain "fun things" to make for your children on a rainy day or when their friends are visiting.

You will be their "good cooker," because you made something special just for them at home which can mean so much more than buying it at the store. After the last recipe there are various party suggestions for children of all ages. These suggestions may be useful as they are or give you additional ideas to make your child's party a big success.

Papier Maché

newspapers, magazines OR paper
   towels
¼ cup *(59 ml)* wheat paste, library
   paste OR flour

1 cup *(237 ml)* water
waxed paper

Tear paper into tiny pieces until you have 4 cups (946 ml). Soak in warm water overnight; squeeze dry. Make a smooth paste by mixing paste with water. Pour some of the paste over the paper and work it with your hands. Add paste a little at a time until papier maché feels like clay. Let core of papier maché article be a styrofoam ball or shape, a cardboard tube, a box, a balloon or wire or pipecleaners. Apply papier maché to core, shaping into desired form. Dry on waxed paper for several days at room temperature. If painting, cover with gesso first; then paint with tempra and cover with shellac.

Picture Transferring

sheet of waxed paper
colored newspaper OR comic
   book page

spoon OR wooden ice cream stick
plain sheet of paper

Place waxed paper on the top of the comic page. Rub the entire surface with the spoon or piece of wood. Lift the waxed paper; lay it face down on the plain paper and rub again. The original picture will have been picked up by the waxed paper and then deposited on a new sheet.

Bubbles

1 cup *(237 ml)* lemon Joy
1 tsp *(5 ml)* glycerin (get at a drug
   store)

1 cup *(237 ml)* white Karo syrup
5 cups *(1.18 l)* water

Mix all ingredients well. Can be used right away, but better if allowed to sit overnight. Try blowing bubbles through a funnel, a soda straw, or an old thread spool.

Modeling Clay

1 cup *(237 ml)* **cornstarch**
2 cups *(474 ml)* **baking soda**

1¼ cups *(296 ml)* **cold water**
food coloring

Add food coloring to water and mix well with other ingredients in a saucepan. Cook over medium heat about 3-4 minutes, stirring constantly until mixture thickens to the consistency of mashed potatoes. Cover with a damp cloth to cool. Knead until smooth. Objects may be left to dry overnight and then painted. Store unused clay in an airtight container.

Silly Putty

¼ cup *(59 ml)* **white glue (Elmer's)**   **2 Tb** *(30 ml)* **Sta-flo liquid starch**

Mix glue and starch together well. Allow to dry a bit until it is workable. Store in an airtight container. If you use Elmer's school glue instead of regular white, it does not bounce or pick up pictures but is still lots of gooey fun for children. Use on a smooth surface.

Paste

½ cup *(118 ml)* **flour**
2 cups *(474 ml)* **cold water**

oil of peppermint OR wintergreen

Mix together flour and cold water to make a creamy mixture. Boil over slow heat for 5 minutes, stirring constantly; cool. Add cold water to thin if necessary. Add a few drops of oil of peppermint to make a pleasant smell and prevent spoiling. Store covered in refrigerator.

Stained Glass Crayons

You will need broken crayon pieces

Remove any paper from the crayons and place the crayon pieces in a well-greased muffin pan (or line with aluminum foil) and put in a 400° (204° C) oven for a few minutes until melted. Remove from oven and cool completely before removing from pan. Mixed crayon colors give a stained glass effect and are great fun to color with.

Soap Paint

1 cup *(237 ml)* **powdered**
   detergent

4 Tb *(60 ml)* **liquid starch**

Beat detergent and starch with rotary beater until peaks form. Tempra coloring can be added. Apply with hands, brushes or sticks.

Finger Paint

½ cup *(118 ml)* **Argo starch**
1 qt *(946 ml)* **boiling water**
½ cup *(118 ml)* **Ivory flakes**

¼ cup *(59 ml)* **talcum powder**
poster paint OR food coloring

Soften starch in a small amount of cold water. Over medium-low heat, add boiling water stirring constantly until mixture bubbles up. Remove from heat, let cool somewhat and add Ivory flakes and powder. Stir until well mixed. Divide the portions and add different colorings. Use glazed shelf paper to paint. Wet on both sides with a sponge. Turn glazed side up and smooth out bubbles before spreading on paint.

Variations:
1. Beat warm water into Lux or Ivory flakes until the consistency desired; add paint or food coloring.
2. Add a drop of food coloring to aerosol shaving soap and "paint" on a cookie sheet.
3. Mix up instant pudding with water or milk and paint on cookie sheet.

Play Dough

2 cups *(474 ml)* **flour**
1 cup *(237 ml)* **salt**
4 tsp *(20 ml)* **cream of tartar**

2 cups *(474 ml)* **water**
2 Tb *(30 ml)* **vegetable oil**
food coloring

Mix dry ingredients in a large saucepan; add oil and water until smooth. Cook over medium heat, stirring until mixture leaves the side of the pan. Turn out on waxed paper and knead in food coloring. Keep in an airtight container. This recipe can be doubled.

Crystal Garden

4 Tb *(60 ml)* **salt**
4 Tb *(60 ml)* **water**
1 Tb *(15 ml)* **ammonia**

charcoal
colored inks

Mix together salt, water and ammonia. Pour this mixture over several small pieces of charcoal in a small bowl. Put several drops of different colored inks on various parts of it; leave undisturbed for several days and crystals will cover it in an interesting formation, growing and spreading every day. It will be white where no ink is used.

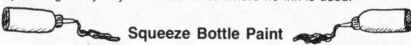

Squeeze Bottle Paint

1 Tb *(15 ml)* **powdered tempra paint**

1 cup *(237 ml)* **liquid starch**

Mix starch and paint together. Fill squeeze bottle half full. Have fun!

Party Suggestions

Save yourself a lot of time –
In paper-lined foil baking cups, place scoops of ice cream.
Place filled baking cups in muffin tins; cover with Saran
wrap and freeze until ready to serve.

A Hobo Hike party. Boys and girls love this active kind of party. Ask each guest to come as patched and tattered as he can. Post a sign on front door stating: "Tramps, back door, please!" Present to each child a stick with a gay bandana, filled with part of lunch, tied on the end. As soon as the hikers and you or Dad set off, take remaining necessities to the spot you have chosen and have a fire blazing and the food ready when the hikers arrive.

For an **Art In The Yard** preschool party, use large cardboard boxes from moving companies or furniture boxes. Put rocks or bricks in the boxes so they won't tip over. Then tape large sheets of paper around all four sides of boxes and let children paint their own creations. Give painting smocks as favors.

Start out an **Easter Bunny Party** by sending egg-shaped invitations cut out of construction paper and trimmed with bits of rick-rack, yarn and glitter. Ask guests to wear a favorite Easter bonnet or hat and award prizes for the prettiest, funniest and most original. Let the children frost and decorate their own cupcakes with tinted coconut and jelly beans.

A **Boxed Lunch Party** for toddlers is easily accomplished by spreading out bath towels to sit on in the yard and giving each child a school box (cardboard activity type) with meal in it. Moms and Dads can have their own party while little ones have pigs in a blanket, happy face cheese toasts, dry cereal, carrot and celery sticks and peanut butter sandwich squares. Children may take their boxes home as favors.

Little girls love to act grown up. A **Dainty Dolly** party gives them a chance to dress up like their moms. When serving, bring out the good china and crystal. For favors and prizes, give items that make a little girl feel glamorous — necklaces, bracelets, barettes, hankies, ribbons, etc.

Plan a **Come To The Fair Party.** Set up booths. A card table, plus tall poles attached to two front legs, makes a frame. Decorate each with crepe paper of a different color. Set up refreshment booth by the kitchen door for ice cream and soda, have children turn in tickets, which they received at the beginning of the party.

Have a NEIGHBORHOOD PARADE PARTY. Ask children to bring their bike, wagon or scooter and decorate with balloons, horns, whistles and crepe paper as soon as they arrive. Let your youngster lead the parade; serve refreshments when you return.

An EMERGENCY PARTY can include having someone come to teach a mini-version of first aid. Give triangular bandages as favors and let them learn to tie slings. Arrange with the rescue squad to show the inside of an emergency vehicle.

To have a KITE PARTY, give each child a kite kit; let him assemble it then go to a nearby field to fly kites. Serve lunches packed in paper bags.

Children eight years old and older love to go on a SCAVENGER HUNT. Prepare list and check with neighbors to be called on before the party. Divide kids into groups of 3 or 4 and give each team a different area of houses to call on. Set a time for them to return. The team with the most items wins. Have appropriate prizes.

Check to see if local drama department or teenagers have a PUPPET SHOW they will present.

Have a SUNDAE PARTY. Let each child make his own sundae from an assortment of different toppings.

OTHER PARTY THEMES

Monster Party	Space	Zoo
Costume Party	Robots	Sports
Circus	Magic	Mexican Fiesta
Cooking	Dolls	Cartoon Characters

PARTY EXCURSIONS

Ice Skating	City Park	Pizza Parlor
Roller Skating	Zoo	Ball Game
Putt-Putt golf	Circus	Train Ride
Amusement Park	Boat Ride	Bus Ride
Ice Cream Parlor	Movie	Fire Station

INDEX

423

425

427

THE JUNIOR LEAGUE OF GREENSBORO
113 South Elm Street
Greensboro, N. C. 27401

Send me _____ copies of *OUT OF OUR LEAGUE* at
$7.95 per copy plus $1.50 for postage and handling for
each book. North Carolina residents please add 32¢
sales tax per book.

NAME _____

STREET _____

CITY _____

STATE_____ ZIP _____

Make checks payable to *OUT OF OUR LEAGUE.* Proceeds from the sale of this cookbook will go
to support the many worthwhile projects sponsored by The Junior League.

THE JUNIOR LEAGUE OF GREENSBORO
113 South Elm Street
Greensboro, N. C. 27401

Send me _____ copies of *OUT OF OUR LEAGUE* at
$7.95 per copy plus $1.50 for postage and handling for
each book. North Carolina residents please add 32¢
sales tax per book.

NAME _____

STREET _____

CITY _____

STATE_____ ZIP _____

Make checks payable to *OUT OF OUR LEAGUE.* Proceeds from the sale of this cookbook will go
to support the many worthwhile projects sponsored by The Junior League.

THE JUNIOR LEAGUE OF GREENSBORO
113 South Elm Street
Greensboro, N. C. 27401

Send me _____ copies of *OUT OF OUR LEAGUE* at
$7.95 per copy plus $1.50 for postage and handling for
each book. North Carolina residents please add 32¢
sales tax per book.

NAME _____

STREET _____

CITY _____

STATE_____ ZIP _____

Make checks payable to *OUT OF OUR LEAGUE.* Proceeds from the sale of this cookbook will go
to support the many worthwhile projects sponsored by The Junior League.